Communication, Media, and American Society

Communication, Media, and American Society

A Critical Introduction

Daniel W. Rossides

ROWMAN & LITTLEFIELD PUBLISHERS, INC.
Lanham • Boulder • New York • Oxford

ROWMAN & LITTLEFIELD PUBLISHERS, INC.

Published in the United States of America
by Rowman & Littlefield Publishers, Inc.
A Member of the Rowman & Littlefield Publishing Group
4720 Boston Way, Lanham, Maryland 20706
www.rowmanlittlefield.com

12 Hid's Copse Road, Cumnor Hill, Oxford OX2 9JJ, England

British Library Cataloguing in Publication Information Available

Library of Congress Cataloging-in-Publication Data

Rossides, Daniel W., 1925–
  Communication, media, and American society : a critical introduction / Daniel W.
Rossides.
    p. cm.
  Includes bibliographical references and index.
  ISBN 0-7425-1939-2 (alk. paper)—ISBN 0-7425-1940-6 (pbk. : alk. paper)
    1. Communication—Social aspects. 2. Mass media—Social aspects. 3.
Communication—Social aspects—United States. 4. Mass media—Social
aspects—United States. 5. United States—Social conditions. 6. United
States—Politics and government. I. Title.
HM1206 .R67 2003
302′.0973—dc21   2002001783

Printed in the United States of America

♾ ™ The paper used in this publication meets the minimum requirements of American
National Standard for Information Sciences—Permanence of Paper for Printed Library
Materials, ANSI/NISO Z39.48–1992.

Contents

Preface

This book analyzes the relation between communication and social structure in the West, with an emphasis on the United States and corporate world-market capitalism. It is intended for the general reader; sociology of communication courses; introductory courses in communication, business, journalism, popular culture, or the professions; and science-technology-society programs. All forms of communication are discussed, though the central role of the computer in today's service economy is highlighted.

A major theme of the book explores the relation of fast, inexpensive communication to the globalization of the world's economies, polities, and voluntary organizations. The book pays special attention to the impact of computerization on the professions, giving extra attention to the communication difficulties faced by professionals—especially policy and negotiation professionals—who must work in or deal with cultures other than their own. In general, the book provides a comprehensive analysis of the near-miraculous harnessing of electricity to seemingly any purpose. More specifically, it provides an empirically grounded analysis of all aspects (as they appear in context) of the emerging integrated, interactive communication system centered on the Internet—making every effort, however, to avoid Internet hype and ideology.

Chapter by chapter, changes in communication capabilities are related to changes in wealth and income distribution, the structure of economic organizations, work, the professions, politics-law-government, urbanization and residential patterns, journalism, policy groups, foundations, think tanks, popular culture, gender, and intersocietal communication. The book's main theme is that communication is an integral part of all systems of social power. To understand communication is to understand how institutions work to serve some better than others. Communication capabilities and practices are windows into how society works—that is to say, how priests, palace scribes, imperial civil servants, explorers, merchants, fur traders, media owners, business executives, government officials, political consultants and fundraisers, professions of all kinds (including journalists, textbook authors, advertising executives, teachers, and so on) do their work.

To understand communication and social power requires going beyond the printing press, radio, television, and the computer to bring into relief such things as oral and written language, roads, the horse, the ocean-spanning ship, the railroad, postal services, buildings, monuments, and urban spaces. It requires going beyond the mythologies that have substituted for reality from the ancient past to the present day. To establish the theme of communication as social power, the three chapters of part I show how distinctive clusters of communication capabilities are related to distinctive structures of social power and their respective mythologies.

Since World War II, research into communication has multiplied enormously and yielded valuable results. One theme in this research, however, is troubling—too many communications specialists stress the complexity of communication and its multiplicity of causes. The world of communication, we are told, is too complex to yield generalizations or to establish causation—there are too many factors and too much change. This conclusion conforms to a basic perspective in American public life—that it is impossible to draw generalizations about causation to be used in managing society, because causes are lodged in diverse and dynamic individuals, technologies, groups, and professionals. In the final analysis, in this view, the social world is knowable, even if studied empirically, only in linear terms—that is, in the future, after the fact. One consequence of this perspective is to denigrate politics and to deny that society needs explicit management. Aside from ethical exhortations and incremental reform, social outcomes, we are told, must be left to the impersonal rationality of existing economic, political, and educational markets. Since impersonal, rational markets do not exist anywhere (nor are they likely ever to exist), what this means is that decisions about the development of human and material resources will continue to be made by a power structure that lacks both competence and legitimacy.

Along with the general movement away from value-neutral and objective social science in other fields, a more critical, interpretive, political outlook on communication and communication technology emerged from the 1970s on. It is worth noting that America's bland, nonpolitical, ahistorical scientific culture is so powerful that many of the creative currents counter to mainstream communication research have had to come from abroad (the same is true in many other disciplines).

The sociopolitical view that informs this book (balanced by other perspectives to avoid dogmatism) explores a wide variety of questions. How does communication take place between owners and employees (especially in complex organizations), between professionals and clients, between governing elites and masses (in politics, policy groups and foundations, journalism, entertainment, and schools), and between men and women? What difficulties appear when organizations operate in countries other than their own and when multinational organizations have coworkers of different nationalities? What cultural barriers clog and misdirect communication between members of different cultures? But the most important question of all is: What is the record of both private and public communication organizations and of America's knowledge professions in making American society more adaptive, equitable, and democratic? The preponderance of evidence says that they not only do not promote a democratic citizenry and polity but actively retard them. The stalled movement toward a just, adaptive, and democratic society is analyzed from a number of angles throughout the book but perhaps most strikingly by outlining the way in which the upper classes (business and political leaders, professionals, journalists, mass media content providers, advertisers, policy analysts, clergy, and social scientists) have created and maintained a fictitious picture of the history and nature of American society.

The sociopolitical perspective assumes that the study of social power does not end there but that knowledge about it should be brought to bear on managing the fortunes of American society. America's commitment to market solutions has failed to solve social problems, and in recent decades it has failed to lift living standards. At present America is experiencing the greatest concentration of wealth and inequality of income in its history, and these imbalances have become our biggest barriers to progress. The book's focus, therefore, is not on academic knowledge but on political knowledge, or knowledge for action and policy making. Society is a haphazardly created historical entity, and knowledge should promote a more effective and comprehensive negotiation among citizens about the kind of society they want to live in.

I

KIND OF SOCIETY AND KIND OF COMMUNICATION

1

Communication and Types of Power Structure in the Premodern World

THE CONCEPT OF COMMUNICATION

Communication is an all-purpose word signifying an effort (not always successful) to establish a shared meaning through symbolic interaction. Human communication occurs largely through language and conveys the meaning (beliefs and values) that given cultures attach to everything. Human communication makes human society (a durable division of labor) possible. As we shall see shortly, communication made the human being itself possible.

Human communication takes place through many media. Speech utilizes sound waves to convey meaning. Gestures, facial expressions, pictures, artifacts (clothing, buildings, and so on), smoke-fire-flag signals, and of course writing, convey meaning in physical form and through light waves (sight). Messages can be carried either on foot (runner, courier); or by humans (using animals, canoes, or other transport); or be sent by carrier pigeon. From the eighteenth century on, Westerners gradually developed the use of electricity to send messages. An electrical current through a wire can be altered to form intelligible patterns and thus convey messages through a code (for example, the Morse code). A way was later found to alter electricity to carry the sounds of a human voice and then convert it back to sound (the telephone). Radio waves (part of the world of electricity) were discovered at the end of the nineteenth century, and the human voice was conveyed through them. At the same time, pictures were put on film and projected to audiences. By the end of the 1920s, the ability to convey sound and picture simultaneously had resulted in the

3

motion picture, much as we know it today. The 1920s also saw the beginning of television, the ability to project sound and pictures through the air.

Harnessing the power of electricity to serve human purposes reached its high point to date in the computer. The computer emerged at the same time as television. Thought of at first largely as a calculator and a way to store information, the computer was destined to become a powerful and unique communication device. Computers are based on electrical flows, and computer communication began by wire, as one computer communicated with another. More recently, the computer has been freed from its dependence on wire, as has the telephone. Today, all electronic means of communication are interconnectable. It is now possible to send messages, visual, oral, and written, from humans to humans (next door or across the globe) via wire, then through space, back to wire, and onto telephone, television screen, or printer. This development in communication technology has profound implications for contemporary society, and understanding it is a major theme of this book.

The concept of communication can fruitfully include the movement of people and goods. Visitors, ambassadors, invaders, tourists, missionaries, traders, and so on all convey messages by their presence and by what they bring and do. Trade in fur, silk, spices, textiles, fruit, hardware, books, film, and so on represent an exchange of values and thus have meaning. The movement of people and goods can take place through varied means of transport: by foot, riding on animals, using animal power to move vehicles, using wind and water to move vessels, and burning fuel of various kinds to generate power that is harnessed to move trains, vehicles, vessels, airplanes, missiles, and spacecraft.

Communication must also be analyzed as a social or power relation, since its use is invariably an attempt to influence behavior.[1] Many definitions of communication refer to it as something that occurs between individuals. It is much more useful to think of it as something that takes place between social actors (individuals and groups) with different amounts of power. Accordingly, communication can be a one-sided form of interaction (a father's or husband's command, lord versus serf, males dominating conversation, or corporations and political parties persuading or deceiving consumers and voters). It can be two sided (friends conversing) or many sided (a legislative debate, family conversation). It can be intimate, face-to-face interaction; impersonal face-to-face interaction (a committee); or impersonal one-way action (a radio or television broadcast, a lecture). It can be pseudo-personal, as in call-in radio shows or letters to advice columnists. It can be deliberative, as in genuine policy discussion, or pseudo-deliberative, as in a television talk show or a political campaign speech or debate.

To understand communication as a structure of power, one must analyze how humans are shaped to suit power relations as well as how technology supports them. Humans have to be socialized to understand not merely language in the abstract but the myths that are buried in language and that make it possible for individuals and audiences to decipher messages (whether they are aware that they are doing so or not). Here we also encounter a unique aspect of the human condition—the capacity of an individual to communicate with itself through interior dialogue. This ability, to be a reflexive self, is not always developed in the human personality, and we will be at pains later to analyze how well the United States is doing in this respect. In any case, whether humans are communicating with others or with themselves, they everywhere use culturally prescribed beliefs and sentiments. The social circumstances under which humans become creative—that is, say new things—will also concern us greatly.

The various types of communication technology and the uses they are put to are best analyzed initially in terms of macrostructures of power (types of society). It will become apparent that the various forms of communication technology and the forms and levels of social relations (social power) that they help shape cannot be separated. The invention of writing and the occupation of scribe became integral parts of the agrarian power structure. The intense oral deliberation required by the Greek city-state seems to have been decisive for the unique creation of rationalism and democracy (see later in this chapter). Teaching both the masses and elites to read and write via a nonpolitical, academic curriculum is an indispensable part of the capitalist power structure.

It is well to note early that communication technology can mean very different things. Some use it as a way to celebrate human intelligence, the triumph of human mental power. Others focus on communication technology as property—no matter what its origins, it serves those who own it.

The term *power* does not refer to something that is necessarily bad. There are good and bad power relations, legitimate and illegitimate power relations. Parents who raise children to be autonomous, productive citizens are exercising power to benefit others. Political candidates and officials who clearly enunciate what they stand for and behave accordingly are in a legitimate power relation, one that benefits both ends of the relationship. Illegitimate power can be seen when mutual benefit is promised and expected but is not forthcoming.

COMMUNICATION AND HUMAN EVOLUTION

Biology and Culture as Concurrent Evolutionary Processes

Communication played an important role in the biopsychological evolution of human beings. Though there are gaps in the record, the fact of human evolution out of the family of great apes is established beyond doubt. But while it is no longer necessary to argue the fact of human evolution, care must be taken to avoid the notion that humans emerged as finished, superior beings and then went on to create human behavior and culture. Our prehuman ancestors used tools for three to four million years *before* they evolved into full humans over the last five hundred thousand years. Further, the use of tools (and other cultural behaviors) played a large part in *causing* prehumans to evolve into humans. Thus sociocultural behavior grew *concurrently* with human biopsychological evolution, and both processes must be viewed collectively, as a single process of reciprocal cause and effect.[2]

The exact path taken by prehumans as they evolved is not known. One plausible theory runs as follows. Unlike monkeys, who walk on the palms of their arms (front legs), apes knuckle-walk. In the forest the ape can move quickly and safely on all fours from tree clump to tree clump, thus achieving a wider range of movement, a better food supply, and greater safety than does the monkey. As a knuckle-walker, the ape can carry food in its "hands" and even use one "arm" to carry its young. The ape has also been observed to wield sticks and throw stones. Human evolution is essentially the story of the transformation of these front legs into arms. It took millions of years for the knuckle-walking primate to develop into a tool-using animal. The utilization of stones and sticks to augment bodily skills and strengths provided these apelike creatures with an incentive to stand upright. In turn, standing upright made it easier for them to use and make tools (for example, giving stones edges by chipping them), in a reciprocal cause-effect relation.

The time span of evolution is difficult to grasp. Primates go back approximately seventy million years. Biopsychological evolution is essentially the story of random mutations in genes (genes direct cell development). Under selective pressure over millions of years, the ape-becoming-human developed an inventory of genes that enabled it to survive and increase its adaptability. The selective pressures that produced upright posture took millions of years; the achievement of bipedalism is a key stage of evolution. Further developments also took millions of years, but the tempo of development, though still slow, was speeded—bipedalism freed the front legs from the single, unspecialized function of locomotion, allowing the multipurpose human hand to develop. The extensive use of the hands meant tool making and use in a food-gathering, hunting environment. Hands and eyesight developed in tandem. Above all, the intense use of the hands in conjunction with the other senses generated an enormous flow of traffic in the nervous system, thus accelerating brain development.

Biopsychological evolution was speeded by changes in climate and the natural environment. As the world grew drier some fifteen million years ago, the earth's forests shrank, and some apes moved into the dry savannas and bush country of southern and eastern Africa. The new environment increased the pressure to stand upright (to see over tall grass, for example) and to fashion tools (to become more efficient hunters in a harsher environment). The steady and more complex use of hands and eyes further exercised the brain, which continued to grow and specialize. By at least fifty thousand years ago, human beings with brains the size of those of contemporary humans lived in many parts of the world. Between fifty thousand years ago and the Agricultural Revolution (approximately ten thousand years ago), human beings (biopsychologically the same as contemporary human beings) lived and flourished as highly skilled hunters and food gatherers.

Any number of items can be cited as important causes in the evolution of *Homo sapiens:* for example, bipedalism, tools, fire, climatic changes, and language. Any single cause makes the most sense, however, if it is framed as a multicausal process. Even language, however important in the biological evolution of apes into humans, must be seen as part of a larger, multicultural causal process.

The Preeminent Importance of Language

The origins and development of language can only be surmised. Prehumans, like a wide range of animals, undoubtedly communicated at the beginning with bodily movements and rudimentary sounds. As their capability to cope with more features in their environment grew, pressure also grew to store the information they had about the habits of animals, the location of plants and water, and so on. Thus their memory capacity grew. As environmental complexity grew, there was incentive to work in groups, which required communication about strategy and tactics. The advent of fire effectively enlarged the duration of the day and gave the developing human more time to exchange information and plan the next day's hunt—and so on.

At a certain point, the human brain went far beyond the brain of even the most communicative of the primates. The brain of *Homo sapiens* is a complex switchboard connecting sensory input with muscular locomotion. It is also a vast storage center of past experience. Language use requires a larynx capable of making a large range of sounds to which meanings are attached. It means a memory bank that can recall these meanings—that is, a brain that over millions of years became an enormously skillful and efficient processor of sounds. It means an almost infinite ability to create meanings, not merely with vocabulary but also, and especially, by syntax or the positioning of sounds. Above all, perhaps, human language allows us to reconstruct a world that we once experienced but is no longer present. It also allows us to construct worlds that we have never experienced (heaven, hell, golden ages in the past or future). Using language, humans can construct both fanciful myths and scientific models describing how nature and society work.

The ability to be a language user is a social phenomenon. We acquire language use from the socialization process (rather easily, as is also the case with eating, walking, sexuality, and various emotions, making it appear that all these are somehow innate or instinctual). In acquiring a language, we also acquire the meanings attached to the world through language from the existing creators and carriers of that world, the people we interact with. The human brain is a remarkable entity, but its most important attribute is its shapelessness—that is, its lack of content. In a real sense, the brain is like a computer without software, an inert capacity waiting to be programmed. Like a computer, it can be programmed to perform many functions.

The analysis of language is important in understanding both communication and social structure. Communication differs if linguistic use is oral or written. Language varies by society, and competence in its use varies by social level. Actually, the unequal mastery of language is not merely characteristic of social classes[3] but one of the most insightful ways of characterizing power relations in all societies.

In any case, communication in the prehuman era meant brain growth as well as brain use and group action. The latter enhanced communication, which led to more brain growth, more group action, and the ability to identify and share more information about the outer world. Over the space of millions of years, *Homo sapiens* emerged not as self-activated being but as a sociocultural interactor—more simply, as essentially a *social* animal.

COMMUNICATION AND THE EXCHANGE OF CULTURALLY DEFINED MEANINGS

The exchange of meaning can be one sided or a mutual give and take. In either case, actors can relate to each other because they share expectations and can take certain things about each other for granted. To interact, therefore, actors must share a language; they must understand or have some notion of the identities of the actors they are interacting with, and vice versa; and they must have an understanding of at least some goals and the means for achieving them. In short, interaction is by social actors whose personalities are organized in terms of cultural values and norms. Whether scientists stress the overall macrostructure's impact on behavior or focus on behavior at the micro level, they recognize that in one way or another human behavior is essentially geared to the transmission of culturally established meanings.

Actors exchange meaning through a wide variety of symbols, the most important of which is language. Even the simplest words can express rich meanings for people who share a culture. Simple colors and well-known animals signify a large range of moral meanings. In our culture, but not in others, yellow is a code word for cowardice, a red is a communist, white symbolizes purity, and black is the color of mourning. Doves and hawks are code words for political and social groups that stress peaceful and forceful policies respectively. The reader can supply the moral symbolism of the lion, jackal, snake, and other animals.

Actors exchange meanings also in ways other than spoken and written language. Physical objects such as flags, limousines, paintings, sculpture, buildings, clothing, and gifts all convey meaning. Humans also convey meaning through physical movements: the use of eyes, facial expressions, touch, bodily gestures and movements, even spatial location.[4] The amazing range and skillfulness of human interaction can be illustrated by a simple example; regardless of differences in education, religion, sex, or skin color, almost all Americans know what a shrug of the shoulder means. That example can be multiplied to yield literally thousands of nonlanguage symbols: the wink, the frown, the caress, the clenched fist, the thumb up, the thumb down, the thumb on the nose, the salute, the restaurant seat near the kitchen, the seat on the fifty-yard line, and so on. As Hall argues, even where we stand when talking to someone is not a casual choice. Americans give each other space when conversing, while Latin Americans stand close to each other; in each case the relation is patterned and has meaning—Americans respecting each other's privacy, Latin Americans expressing a sense of emotional closeness through physical closeness.

CLOTHING: A RICH AND VARIED COMMUNICATION

Clothing keeps us warm and promotes modesty but also tells us who everybody is and what behavior is expected. Clothing symbolizes social status and is an easily recognizable aid to social interaction. Clothing separates the high from the low. For example, Chinese upper-class males once wore silk robes and had long fingernails, both symbols of their exemption from work. The American upper class also dresses differently from those below it. The terms "three-piece suit" and "blue collar" identify contrasting worlds of work.

Clothing sends signals of all kinds. It advertises a woman's sexual availability or nonavailability. In the Muslim world, the veil symbolizes the inferior worth of women. In the secular West, at least in the past, a woman's clothing often announced the worth of her husband. Clothing often tells the days of the week, the time of day and the type of activity one is engaged in (work, marriage, sports, job interview, worship). Fights also occur between parents and teenage children over what clothes the latter should wear—the youngster eager to gain autonomy and conform to the standards of his or her age group, while the parents are determined to project a proper family image in terms recognized by other adults.

Clothing also carries explicit written messages indicating where actors have been and what causes they believe in. Clothing often comes stamped with a manufacturer's name. Clothing can send false messages: a confidence person dresses like a banker, a burglar dresses like a plumber to gain access to an apartment. The upwardly mobile can dress beyond their class. The investigative reporter, the spy, and a participant observer all dress to fit into worlds they want to gain knowledge about.

Social actors become highly skilled at decoding the meaning of clothing, but some status relations are too important to be left to chance—hence the *uniform*. When boarding an airplane, the flight attendant must be instantly recognizable. It would not do to strike up a conversation with a waiter at a cocktail party. There must be no doubt as to who does what at a hospital, church, or prison, or on a battlefield.

The uniform helps to organize precise and complex behavior because it recalls (and reinforces) shared meanings about status obligations and rights. It helps to order status priorities and establish the boundaries of groups. It ensures uniformity of behavior and makes it easier to see deviation from status obligations. It announces to citizens, customers, and clients that someone has the skills and authority to go with a particular status.[5]

COMMUNICATION AND SIMPLE SOCIETY

Humans interacted with sounds, gestures, and artifacts that had meaning for them for millions of years before they even became human. Meaning can be attached to any sound, and thus all languages are arbitrary. Meanings successfully interchanged become the means by which individuals can be welded into groups and be organized according to a division of labor that vastly augments the power of isolated individuals. It means specialization and inequality in the family as well as cooperation in hunting parties.

Reliance on oral communication is characteristic of simple society. Simple societies range from hunting-and-gathering peoples to people that earn their living through some combination of hunting, gathering, fishing, herding, plundering, trading, or subsistence (nonmarket) farming. For many thousands of years, our human predecessors lived off the natural environment as foragers; they collected wild plants, scavenged, hunted, and fished. A gathering-hunting-fishing economy produces little surplus, and the members of a foraging society are relatively equal (except where big-game hunting appears). Simple society has a simple division of labor based largely on ascriptive status (cultural definitions of kinship, sex, and age). Behavior is anchored in the family, which is the basis of social organization.

Simple societies are highly adapted to their environment. Women and men both work hard at economic tasks, though men monopolize the occupation of big-game hunter (something that leads to a monopoly of military status in more complex societies and contributes to the generalized superiority of males over women in such societies). Those who are especially skilled at the hunt are accorded a measure of extra prestige, but it is not possible for families to accumulate enough property to make them superior to other families over time. Though there are positions of leadership, these cannot be turned into hereditary statuses and passed on to children. Hunting and gathering societies also lack states, and they are peaceful rather than warlike. Also notable is the absence of slavery.

The symbolic culture of simple society has the following distinguishing features:

1. Norms governing all behavior are explicit and predictable.
2. There is considerable empirical knowledge about the workings of nature.
3. Magic and exotic mythology exist side by side with empirical knowledge derived from and validated by experience.
4. The symbolic world is not centered on the assumption that the world is unitary or governed by universal laws. The members of simple societies live in a polytheistic world in which magical and empirical causation are practiced and experienced as meaningful and noncontradictory.
5. The simple division of labor generates considerable homogeneity and communication among all is easy and reliable.

COMMUNICATION AND ADVANCED
HORTICULTURAL AND AGRARIAN SOCIETIES

The Agricultural Revolution

The movement toward advanced horticultural and agrarian societies is the story of the momentous shift in human life that occurred when humans began to derive their food from domesticated plants. The movement to farming, essentially a way to harness the power of the sun, soon led to a large number of technological developments, both physical and social. The movement to advanced *horticulture* (a gardening, family-based form of farming coordinated by a state derived from hereditary nobles) soon led in a number of places to *agrarian society* (the cultivation of large plots of land by serf, slave, or tenant labor). The first agrarian societies emerged out of advanced horticultural societies in the Middle East approximately five thousand years ago.[6] An (advanced) agrarian society is unique in that it can produce food, tools, and other things, including belief and value systems, on a scale far exceeding even an advanced horticultural society. New technology, especially iron metallurgy and the plow, along with other productive techniques, such as irrigation and the harnessing of animal energy, combined with such economically central sociocultural inventions as slave and serf labor, family-tenant labor, administrative structures, standing armies, forms of taxation (including forced labor), money, writing, quantitative skills, religion, and legal codes, resulted in a unique type and level of social existence.

The Advent of Writing and Social Bookkeeping

The advent of writing (our earliest records are from Sumer and date back approximately five thousand years) signifies both a momentous advance in communication technology and the emergence of advanced horticultural and agrarian societies. These societies were marked by an increase in inequality in all sectors, including an inequality of communicative power. Only a handful learned how to read and write, helping to establish a hierarchy of hereditary families and to create an official reality reflecting the new structure of power. That reality was communicated to each generation of the masses orally through the family and, in the case of the elite,[7] through both the family and formal education. The official reality was also communicated and reinforced through public buildings, rituals, celebrations, and punishments.[8]

The advent of writing meant that knowledge could be accumulated, allowing each generation to start where the last one left off—certainly a momentous change in the nature of society. But above all, it meant that a governing class could socialize its members easily, become a cohesive force, and advance only knowledge that did not threaten its power. The advent of writing, therefore, also marks a significant increase in the ability of agrarian elites to manage, augment, and maintain their highly diverse and unequal societies. Writing became a narrowly kept monopoly; those who could write were the privileged keepers of sacred beliefs and values, all of which were centered on hereditary inequality. Writing enabled kings and nobles to coordinate their activities and maintain the official reality. It also allowed them to keep track of their property, including their subjects.

A pronounced feature of complex agrarian society is the keeping of detailed records about births, deaths, the movement of the stars, economic activities of all kinds, laws, taxes, diplomatic activities—everything. The bookkeeping (or empirical) bent of these societies is connected, of course, to the needs of power. In this sense, it holds interest for those who want to understand modern social science as well as communication. Then, as now, data gathering was used to inform policy makers and maintain the existing structure of society. For example, a careful record was kept of seasonal changes and was used to explain good and bad crops in a super-

natural context. Obviously, a careful record of economic facts in feudal-authoritarian systems prompts questions about fact gathering in the modern world. To what
extent has the support of science and the practice of empirical research (aided by
communication technology) in the modern world been a support for a particular
structure of power? This question will concern us greatly in future chapters.

The question about data gathering and bookkeeping raises the related question
of the use of mathematics in the establishment and maintenance of social power.
Mathematics is a supremely efficient mode of communication, one that evokes easily
understood meanings among those who understand it. Consensus is so easy in a
mathematical framework that it fosters the idea of objectivity and political neutrality. All this will concern us again later as we explore the emergence and maintenance
of social power in the modern world.

Writing was limited by the technological necessity of writing by hand until the
early modern period, when cheap paper replaced parchment and machine printing
emerged. Writing with a stylus on wet clay was more primitive than pen and papy-
rus, but both were in keeping with the state of technology of early civilizations and
played the same role in the system of power—keeping the means of knowledge and
communication in the hands of those who also controlled the other means of power.
Today, despite the new communication technology of modern society (printing
press, telephone, radio, television, and computer) and political democracy, the structure of power may not be as dissimilar from the past as many believe. Just as fact
gathering in feudal-authoritarian systems prompts questions about fact gathering in
the modern world, so too the monopoly over the means of communication in those
systems prompts questions about economic concentration in the communication
media today.

ESTABLISHING AND MAINTAINING
A POLITICAL ECONOMY

Communication and the Limits of Power

The above description of agrarian (or feudal-authoritarian) society is not entirely
accurate—actually, it is how rulers saw themselves and how many scholars, until
recently, have looked upon such societies. Michael Mann argues that the idea of a
large-scale unitary society in the premodern world does not square with the historical record. Instead, the ancient world had four kinds of social power (ideological,
economic, military, and political) that did not coalesce into unitary societal forms;
rather, they remained in various uncoordinated forms. Each form of power could
have temporary primacy, but blending all forms into a stable unitary system was not
really possible.[9]

Three different preindustrial systems of power can be discerned: feudal-authoritarian systems or "empires" (for example, Sumer, Babylon, Egypt, China, India) and
the hybrid systems represented by Rome and by Athens (see later sections in this

chapter). "Empires" were all limited in their ability to construct and maintain centralized state societies, argues Mann, by the communication technology available to them. Essentially, they existed by military power, and the reach of such power was limited. Overland travel was difficult, and deploying soldiers by foot was even more difficult. Most empires existed only in the sense that they needed incessant military campaigns to assert effective control.

Sometimes the sources of power came together. The communication technology of the premodern world facilitated trade, and that required military protection; in turn, military protection facilitated trade. As a result, an important mutual support developed between these two forms of power. Trade also required political support—standardized money, weights, measures, contracts, and property rights. Also, the "state" and "church" provided standardized language and standardized belief systems (as best they could).

The problem of power first appeared in complex horticultural and agrarian societies. Here, power was largely a struggle among landlords, or rather between a ruling landlord and other landlords (though there were also occasional stirrings from below). Various devices emerged to maintain stable power relations. The ruler kept absolute power by scattering land holdings to dilute the power of rival landlords. The ruler assigned civil servants away from the locality of their origins. The ruler employed foreigners and eunuchs as civil servants and palace guards.

The unprecedented diversity generated by locality, occupation, and economic interest within agrarian society, as well as continuing threats from the outside, posed serious problems for the powerful. One response was the resort to umbrella symbols or universalisms in hopes of overcoming particularism—thus the creative outburst of religiously framed ideals and vague abstractions in many different premodern complex societies at roughly the same time. The extensive use of universalisms by elites to define and manage modern societies was no accident. Communication between superiors and inferiors that explores causation and value realization on a careful empirical basis might well become a relation of equals and might democratize power. Reliance on universalisms effectively anchors the social structure in nature, human nature, and supernature, making alterations in power impossible. At the same time, universalistic thinking provides the powerful with ample opportunity to pretend they know how to reach ideals and room to explain why they are not being reached.

Abstractions cannot do the job of directing life in the concrete; rulers saw to it that there were rules and regulations for all aspects of behavior. Codes of law were drawn up, and there were proverbs and precepts for all occasions. Those who violated the moral code (which really meant the entire normative system) were punished. Those who transgressed against the established order were condemned personally—that is, the blame was put on rotten apples, leaving the feudal barrel unscrutinized.

All meanings were embedded in myth. There may once have been a golden age, its members were told, but that lay in the past, and reasons were given to explain why there had been a decline. There may be a better future, but that could come about only through moral regeneration or through another outsider (a prophet, messiah, a returning god, and so on).[10] All these devices for deflecting attention from the structures of power were needed because of the gross unworkability of these systems. Agrarian society had economic growth but brought no increase in the standard of living (if anything a decline), because most of the social surplus was consumed by luxury, by monuments and rituals to awe the masses, and by war. The major contradiction in complex agrarian society was requiring the masses to work hard for few rewards when it was transparent that rewards were grossly incommensurate with output.[11]

The premodern world could not create fully unified systems of power, because, for one important thing, their primitive communication capabilities severely limited their military, economic, political, and ideological effectiveness. The same may not be true of modern society; the communication capabilities currently available to powerful groups in today's world could conceivably be wedded and combined with other sources of power to render modern society immune to change or even reform, a matter that will certainly concern us later.

Communication and the Success of the Roman Empire

Communication technology can develop to a point where, in combination with other causes, it can help form a new social structure. The terms currently used to describe communication technology, *integrated* and *interactive,* also apply to the past. The combined effects of communication technology are especially apparent in the case of ancient Rome. The source of Rome's power and its success in creating the first relatively integrated and durable empire was its military. The effectiveness of Roman military power was due to (among other things) a unique structure of communication technology. The Roman soldier was both a fighter and construction worker. Most of the equipment that he carried was for building—roads, canals, supply depots, and fortifications. The result was an army that moved on its own, living off conquered lands and extending its lines of communication as it went. This allowed it to wed effectively military with economic power to yield a "military Keynesianism." Rome's military conquests facilitated trade, but trade in a multiethnic empire required common meanings if "uncommon" peoples were to communicate; thus the Romans (actually the Roman elite) worked to establish a common language and a legal system usable by all, especially standardizing such meanings as "property" and "contract." They also worked to establish stable currency values and a universal system of weights and measures, communication devices vitally important for trade.[12]

Rome's success in building a multiethnic "military-market" economy also provided its elite with the means to become a cohesive governing class. Those who would understand communication technology must go beyond such things as roads, writing, common language, coinage, and standardized weights and measures; what these mean, especially in combination, is the ability to establish and maintain a created reality. Like any society, Rome created one reality and blocked others when it created its economy, polity (politics, government, military, law), literature, and (Stoic) worldview. Also, of course, it created the human personalities needed to make this world a behavioral reality. In short, Rome was an integrated communication structure; Roman landlords, senators, soldiers, civil servants, merchants, laborers, and slaves were at once both the carriers of meaning and the instruments of communication.

COMMUNICATION AND THE INVENTION OF RATIONALISM IN ANCIENT GREECE

Understanding why the ancient Greeks created a rational universe, and the role of communication in that achievement, is vitally important to understanding the relation between communication and society down to the present day. One need only recognize that reason and rational thought about society did not emerge in the many other human societies of pre- and early history to gain an important insight into the nature of reason and into the unique kinds of thinking and communication characteristic of stages of Western development. Thinking about nature and thinking about society are not natural (normal, inherent, innate, intrinsic) to human beings as human beings. The fortunes of human thought are very much dependent on the social environment and on the forms of communication it makes possible and requires. The theme of the following analysis is that the West's rational worldview emerged from a distinctive sociological and natural environment that generated a unique set of sociopolitical relations and a unique communicative process—a high-density, egalitarian politics conducted through oral discourse and aided by a unique alphabet.

Novelty and Diversity: The Unique Greek Experience

Ancient Greece as a historical entity developed and declined over a thousand years (roughly 1300 to 300 B.C.). Its story is first of all the result of a distinctive natural environment. Greece lies upon inhospitable land having easy access to the sea. Indeed, Greece should be thought of geographically as both sea and land. Its land is mountainous, with no large, level areas; its soil is thin; and water is scarce. All in all, Greece was not fertile ground for the emergence of large-scale agriculture and large centralized kingdoms.

Early Greece was a set of small aristocratic societies ruled by warrior kings. From 1300 down to 700 B.C., the Greek population was divided into a small stratum of aristocrats and an undifferentiated multitude. From 700 on, the power of kings and aristocracy declined, and a large peasant class of small landowners appeared. There also emerged the *polis,* that unique density of interaction (communication) that was at once a city, society, and a state. By 500 B.C., the population of Athens had diversified enormously. In addition to nonworking, aristocratic landowners and a substantial number of small peasants and herdsmen, the urban core had numerous small producers, shopkeepers, traders, and artisans, as well as wage laborers. Thanks to democratic reforms, all were citizens regardless of their economic status (in the context of the Greek city-state, and unlike modern society, citizens had substantial political power). In addition, there were slaves and *metics* (foreigners resident in Athens) who were not citizens but who engaged in all the occupations that citizens engaged in.

Greece's austere natural environment promoted specialized farming—for example, olive orchards—rather than economic self-sufficiency. The surplus of olive oil in turn spurred the manufacture of pottery (as containers for oil), trade in oil, and thus a simple market economy. The nonself-sufficiency of the Greek economy made it necessary for Greeks to buy and sell; they eventually engaged in extensive market relations, a unique communicative experience. The net outcome of this unique experience was a market mentality (the ability to calculate the worth of one thing in terms of another), a momentous first step toward a rational worldview. The small-scale Greek economy, based on a tradition of small, freeholding farmers, also produced a relative equality among Greek families and made necessary a strong self-reliance (similar, say, to the individualism required by the settlement of the United States). The Greek stress on autonomy and equality (like the American emphasis on self-reliance) is important also because the idea of reasoning had to be located in individuals rather than a hereditary upper strata.

The emergence of city-states throughout Greece reflected the need to trade in order to be self-sufficient. The Greeks understood the conflict between dependence on others and their tradition of self-sufficiency, and that conflict helped to stimulate their unique political mentality. A political mentality—how does one think about and reconcile the interests of the many?—is central to the emergence of rationalism. The existence of numerous city-states in frequent contact, all inhabited by Greeks but with different customs and political systems, certainly stimulated thought about the nature of society. The Greeks also traveled widely outside of Greece and were aware that other kinds of societies existed besides the city-state. The need to make sense of all this was another stimulus leading to new forms of communication skills and technology.

The Alphabet as Rational Communication Technology: The Unique Greek System of Writing

The powerful communication technology of writing appeared earlier than Greek society. But the Greeks developed a writing system that had enormous implications for the development of how humans thought about themselves and their universe. Derived from that of the Phoenicians (some time between 1200 and 700 B.C.), the Greek alphabet was a small and arbitrary code of signs from which one could construct an endless supply of words, each of which was itself an arbitrary sign.[13] Writing before the Greek alphabet had involved either the pictorial system of Egypt and China (each thing in the world had to have its own sign) or the syllabic system (an attempt to represent linguistic sounds through syllables), examples of which are the

Phoenician, Persian, Hebrew, Arabic, and Japanese writing systems. Both systems, says Havelock, failed to meet the three requirements of an efficient and creative writing system:

1. The visible signs must trigger the reader's memory of all sounds that are distinctive in the language;
2. The triggering must be precise, calling forth one and only one *phoneme* (the smallest unit of sound) and requiring no guesswork or choice on the part of the reader; and
3. The visible signs must be few in number to avoid overburdening the memory by requiring the mastery of a large list before recognition or reading can begin. The brain is biologically encoded to respond to acoustical signals, the spoken language; it has not been encoded to manage a corresponding variety of visible signs.

The Greek alphabet satisfied all three requirements, resulting in a profoundly important communication technology. What that meant was that the full complexity of human experience could be put in written form. Earlier writing had tended to be focused around repetitive themes, easily recognized persons and legends, and easily remembered parables and proverbs. The reason was that earlier writing systems had been separated from how human oral-based thinking takes place, had been difficult to read, had allowed too many choices, and had contained too many ambiguities. In contrast, says Havelock, in Greek literature from Homer on "one encounters a larger dimension of human experience, so much more diverse, personal, critical, subtle, humorous, passionate, ironic, and reflective."

The Greek alphabet, says Havelock, had enormous consequences:

1. There was no longer a need to rely on memory and the rhythm needed to make memory reliable. As a result, considerable mental energies were released.
2. Efficient writing made it possible to record "novel statements." Under the inefficient writing systems, novelty was discouraged by the need to stay within the already cumbersome system. The "novel statements" of the West, both in natural and social sciences as well as the humanities, are largely due to the Greek alphabet and the ability of first Rome and then Western European countries to develop native equivalents of the Greek writing system.
3. The Greek alphabet was also used to learn; indeed, with it children can learn to read aloud simultaneously with learning the sounds of their oral vocabulary.

The emergence of this efficient technology of writing went beyond the consequences cited in Havelock. For one thing, the ease with which it could be learned complemented Greece's democratic tradition of oral discourse, unlike other writing systems, which had become monopolies of special professions in the service of oligarchy or monarchy. But another consequence was perhaps the most important. The creation of efficient writing united sound and sight, ears and eyes, thus creating the possibility of a unified human consciousness—that is, the possibility of an integrated mind. Since all this took place in a world of relative equality among economic actors (male citizens who were small farmers, traders, shopkeepers, craftsmen, laborers, sailors), it was also possible to identify the integrated mind (reason) as a possession of all humans.

Writing had an added subdimension. The ability to represent thoughts efficiently in writing—that is, to store them, revise them, sequence them, round them out, and reflect on them—meant that a writer could come to feel that the human mind, not outside forces, was the creator of reality. Further, the writer could see "mind" not as shapeless consciousness but as reason—not mind as the source of controversy and class struggle, but mind as the source and seeker of the objective (permanent, unified) reality beyond the diversity and impermanence of experience. It seems plausible to argue, therefore, not that the Greek alphabet created Western rationalism (the lawfulness of the world corresponds to the disciplined human mind) but that it was a necessary element in that momentous invention.

The impact of communication technology and communication forms on society are not always easy to separate from the impacts of other technologies or causes. The movement of ancient Greeks out of their traditional world was caused by the novel experiences (communications) that grew out of trade, travel, class politics, and warfare. Staying in a customary world of single answers was not possible once the Greeks came into routine contact with dissimilar Greek city-states and with foreign cultures. Since no overarching feudal-authoritarian system of power could establish itself on the inhospitable geography of Greece (meaning, to repeat, that power was uniquely dispersed and relatively equal), the Greeks eventually began to make rival claims about the comparable worth of goods and services in the emerging division of social labor. To cope with social conflict, the Greeks both relied on and more fully developed two unusual forms of communication—oral public discourse and efficient writing as ways to settle social disputes and policy issues—both important components in their invention of democracy.

NOTES

1. The term *power* refers to institutional or socioeconomic norms and values that give some unequal power to defend or enhance their interests not only against others but by shaping the interests, beliefs, and behavior of others.

2. For a compact account of how the human organism developed concurrently with tools, fire, and socioeconomic life, see S. L. Washburn, "Tools and Human Evolution," *Scientific American,* September 1960. For a highly readable single account of human evolution, see S. L. Washburn and Ruth Moore, *Ape into Man* (Boston: Little, Brown, 1974).

3. For the classic studies, see Basil Bernstein, *Class Codes and Control,* vol. 1: *Theoretical Studies toward a Sociology of Language* (London: Routledge and Kegan Paul, 1971); William Labov, *Sociolinguistic Patterns* (Philadelphia: University of Pennsylvania Press, 1972); and J. J. Gumperz, *Discourse Strategies* (Cambridge: Cambridge University Press, 1982).

4. For explorations in nonverbal interaction, see Edward T. Hall, *The Silent Language*

(Garden City, N.Y.: Doubleday, 1959), and *The Hidden Dimension* (Garden City, N.Y.: Doubleday, 1966); Paul Ekman et al., *Emotion in the Human Face* (New York: Pergamon, 1972); Desmond Morris, *Manwatching: A Field Guide to Behavior* (New York: Abrams, 1977); Michael Argyle, "The Human Gaze: Silent Language of the Eyes," in *Readings in Sociology*, ed. Philip Whitten (New York: Harper and Row, 1979), 59–66; Nancy M. Henley, *Body Politics: Power, Sex, and Nonverbal Communication* (New York: Touchstone, 1986), with special attention to "Tactual Politics: Touch," 94–123; and the delightful comparative analysis of Roger E. Axtell, *Gestures: The Do's and Taboos of Body Language around the World* (New York: Wiley, 1991).

5. Nathan Joseph and Nichols Alex, "The Uniform: A Sociological Perspective," *American Journal of Sociology* 77 (January 1972), 719–30.

6. This is not to imply that advanced horticultural societies always became agrarian systems. Africa and South America have had many advanced horticultural societies that never went beyond that state. It is noteworthy that the Aztecs established a far-flung empire using an extensive communication system based on roads despite the fact that they lacked writing, metallurgy, and the wheel.

7. The term *elite* is used throughout this book to refer to historically and institutionally created individuals and power groups that emanate from distinctive economies or historically unique situations and that can make decisions, especially about the use of economic resources, affecting the life of both their own and other societies. Some use the term to refer to individuals supposedly possessing qualities that propel them to leadership.

8. Social science is indebted to Harold A. Innis, *The Bias of Communication* (Toronto: University of Toronto Press, 1951), and Carl J. Couch, *Information Technologies and Social Orders,* ed. and intro. by David R. Maines and Shing-Ling Chen (New York: Aldine de Gruyter, 1996) for their pioneering research into the role of communication in a wide variety of societies. Though not unmindful of the economic and technological basis of social formations, both scholars tended to favor ideational explanations.

9. Michael Mann, *The Sources of Social Power: A History of Power from the Beginning to* A.D. 1760 (New York: Cambridge University Press, 1986), vol. 1.

10. Heroes who come out of nowhere to save the community or solve a community problem are common in American popular culture (see chapter 8) and, of course, in our populist politics (see chapter 5).

11. The same contradiction is present in modern society, though disguised by a rising standard of living for many from 1850 through the 1960s. As we see, the stagnation in living standards and the widespread violation of expectations since the 1960s in the United States has many implications for contemporary politics. Our focus, of course, will be to analyze the role of modern communication technology in containing and deflecting contradictions in the American system of power and politics.

12. Mann, *The Sources of Social Power,* vol. 1, chap. 9.

13. The following is based on Eric A. Havelock, *Origins of Western Literacy* (Toronto: Ontario Institute for Studies in Education, 1976).

2

✠

Communication and the Rise of Capitalism, 1100–1800

THE FEUDAL BACKGROUND

The Local and Personal as Real

D aily interaction in feudal Europe from the fall of Rome in the fifth century A.D. until approximately the twelfth century took place on subsistence-oriented manors and in terms of strict hierarchical personal relations—a lord and his immediate family, lord and overseers, and overseers and serfs-tenants. Each manor had a relation with the clergy, with other manors, and with an overlord or king (who was considered merely the first among equals).

The transition to the modern world took place slowly, in the sense that it took centuries (say, from 1100 to 1800), but also rapidly, in the sense that such a time period is as nothing compared to the tens of thousands of years after the emergence of *Homo sapiens* when little new took place. The movement toward capitalism and modernity is apparent in the "renaissance" of the twelfth century. The doing of history requires an empathic re-creation of times and places different from our own. It is easy to bias such re-creations by applying present-day ideas and values to the past. One such bias is to talk of "high" and "low" technology. Strictly speaking, no such distinction exists, if by it one means that our present technology has more profound or better social consequences than that of the past, or that technology can be understood as part of a progressive, linear social pattern. The ability to use the full power of the horse that emerged in the high Middle Ages, for example, is not less important socioeconomically, or for understanding the history of communication, than the utilization of steam power in the eighteenth century or of electricity in the nineteenth.

The Stirrup and Western Feudalism

Analyzing the role of horse power in fostering communication and economic development is instructive, because it not only places technology in a historical context but shows how cultural variables interact.[1] The horse in human culture was first used as food, but its military potential was soon discovered, and history was profoundly affected thereby.

For thousands of years, the cereal-growing civilizations of the Middle East, China, and India were preyed upon by the horse warriors of the Asian steppes. The role of the horse in Europe's history, however, begins with the Arab conquest of Spain and invasion of what is now France in the eighth century A.D. Stretched thin, the Arabs were defeated by Charles Martel at Tours. Impressed by the Arab's military use of the horse but wedded to the idea of heavily armed soldiers, Martel blended the two. To effect this wedding, he introduced an innovation (source unknown, but probably China) in horse warfare that had profound implications—the stirrup. Before the stirrup, the horseman had to rely on the strength of his arm to wield a sword or throw a spear. The stirrup blended man and horse, allowing the full power of the horse to be focused at the end of the lance, and of course, making the horseman much more secure in all his exertions. The result was the heavily armed mounted knight, who could be countered only by a similar military instrument.

The economic and political consequences of relying on the mounted knight as the ultimate tool of military power were profound. The horse requires extensive pasturage and a considerable amount of auxiliary labor. Martel, to develop his military, distributed large plots of land (many seized from the church) to those who promised military service. Unlike China and India, which had dense populations and limited land, Europe could develop a horse-based military, something that required a special use of economic resources and that led to the special form that Western feudalism took.

The Horse Collar and Capitalism

The heavy reliance on horses for warfare set the stage for another revolutionary economic innovation. The horse is a more powerful and faster animal than the ox, but its energy cannot be harnessed without the horse collar. The horse had been used for thousands of years, but why it took until the tenth or eleventh century to harness its energy for work is not clear. The fact that those who used the horse for warfare did not do the manual work of their societies is probably the reason. But the heavy, wet soil of Europe, the need for a heavier plow, and a plentiful supply of powerful military horses eventuated in the invention of the horse collar (or harness), a technology that had a profound impact on Europe's economic development and communication capability.

The collar, or harness, seems simple by today's standards, but not when put in historical context. Until the tenth or eleventh century, horses had been used mostly for hunting, warfare, transportation, and ceremony. If a horse is forced to pull a heavy load without an adequate harness, its windpipe will be choked. If, however, a collar was fitted over the horse's shoulders, energy was released at a rate and in levels of significance comparable to the steam engine of the eighteenth century (keeping the historical contexts clearly in mind). Harnessing the full power of horses unleashed an important chain of causation. The horse could now pull the heavy plow required by northern Europe's soil, replacing both oxen and human muscle. The net result was greater food productivity. The countryside could now support urban dwellers (who worked in factories making leather harnesses and metal plows). But the chain of causation went much farther. A harnessed horse would slip under heavy burdens and in icy conditions, and its hooves would deteriorate in moist soil; horses were therefore fitted with shoes to increase traction and protect their feet. Variations on the harness allowed teams of horses to be put in tandem. Harnessed teams of animals could pull heavier loads which meant a shift to four-wheeled and stronger wagons. The mining and metalworking industries were stimulated by the new demand for metal to make plows, horseshoes, axles, and wheels.

The horse harness did not by itself cause capitalism. But in it one can see not merely a powerful cause but a new society. The horse harness meant that society was no longer tied to less efficient oxen and human muscle power (associated with serfdom), the economic bases of simple feudalism. The more productive horse-based agriculture undermined serf labor as landlords shifted to what they thought was a more profitable arrangement, rent-paying tenancy. Also undermined was *noblesse oblige,* the feudal idea that all must adhere to status identifications and be responsible personally for the discharge of social obligations. The new technology of the harness also meant the growth of specialized businesses and occupations.

The deeper meaning of the new technology was that it undermined subsistence farming by producing food surpluses that had to be sold—thus inaugurating that momentous shift to capitalist or market-oriented agriculture. Even more fundamental was a more specialized division of labor in which the buyers and sellers of diverse products were forced to reduce the valuation of their products and services to a common denominator—money—thus giving impetus to a full-fledged exchange, or market, economy. Seen from another angle, the new technology meant individualism and the growth of private property; for example, individuals, aided by the power of animals, could now run farms on their own. The harness also meant that society needed a more efficient and flexible form of labor than serfdom—hence "possessive individualism," the idea that individuals owned themselves and were free to use or sell their labor.[2] Just as the horse-drawn plow changed the relation of humans to nature from one of mutual dependence to one of exploitation, so too were labor relations changed from mutual dependence to market relations. The new technology cleared the way for the self-propelled, self-controlled Protestant-bourgeois personality. At first, particular humans were required to develop "selves" distinct from birth and static custom in order to participate in the new economy; a fully developed capitalist economy would eventually require that every person must have such a self.

COMMUNICATION, THE HORSE, AND
OTHER ECONOMIC DEVELOPMENTS

The Horse and Social Organization

Why the emphasis on the horse in a book on communication? A horse is a way to send messages, yes—but horses pulling plows? The focus on the horse serves several purposes. The horse was an important means of cultural diffusion—that is, cultures exchanging novel ideas and artifacts. The Arabs' use of the horse as a military weapon influenced Charles Martel and helped create Europe's distinctive feudalism. The workhorse that resulted from the horse collar reflects the interdependent, additive nature of technology, on the one hand, and the relation between technology and society, on the other. The special needs of northern European agriculture required a heavy plow, leading to the horse collar, leading to new forms of land cultivation and new settlement patterns. The heavy plow meant the end of crisscrossing small plots of land with "scratch" plows and the need to plow long strips of land with teams of animals. The substitution of the faster horse for oxen meant humans could live farther away from their work and thus that a denser form of town interaction could develop. Peasants had to engage in extensive planning to organize the use of land, plows, and animals. Food surpluses led to pressures for stronger wagons and better roads to transport the food, leading to a significant reduction in the cost of overland travel. In a deeper sense, the harnessing of horsepower meant the end of subsistence farming, the end of a way of life in which humans lived in close dependence on the cycles and whims of nature. Henceforth humans would aspire to the mastery of nature. It meant the end of personal, hierarchical feudal relations and the emergence of labor markets. It meant the full emergence of that powerful communication medium, money, because arithmetic was the only way that humans could calculate the worth of diverse resources, goods, services, and labor. In their new sense of mastery over nature via the horse and a host of auxiliary devices, humans were really constructing a new hierarchy of power (capitalism), one based on any and all forms of property, not just land.

Printing, Assorted Technologies, and Economic Growth

The economic expansion of Europe from the twelfth century on was many sided, fitful, and without design or intent. Many other technologies came into play—the crank, gunpowder, printing press, and telescope, among others. Communication by water continued to be more important than overland travel—indeed, improvements in oceangoing travel augmented communication among diverse cultures and expanded European trade. The ability to print fairly accurate maps made it impossible for any nation to think of itself as lord of Europe or as a monopolist of trade.[3]

Economic growth also accelerated the use of writing, and here again technological developments enlarged literacy as part of the new power relations that were emerging. Social bookkeeping became increasingly important to keep track of landhold-ings, rents, profits, taxes, and inheritances, the latter requiring knowledge of marriages, births, and deaths. The development of such communication devices as the letter of credit, investment contracts (known as *commenda*), and, of course, dou-ble-entry bookkeeping were also important to economic growth.

The printing press and the development of cheap paper as a substitute for expen-sive parchment drastically changed how Europeans communicated. The introduc-tion of printing from 1450 on had many short and long-term consequences. The immediate consequence was to introduce classical (Roman and Greek) learning to Europe and thus upset the monopoly of Christian learning. In fairly short order, it also undercut the linguistic unity of Christendom represented by Latin; books began to be printed in the various languages of Europe, helping to consolidate an organiza-tion of society on ethnic grounds. The printing of books also made it possible for individuals to rely on the Bible, rather than a clergy, for salvation and thus helped the Protestant revolt to succeed, further splitting Western Christendom.[4]

As Eisenstein stresses, printing also furthered the development of modern science. Printing made it possible to standardize texts and to compare them side by side. Printing made it possible for scholars across Western Europe to communicate more easily and to be "on the same page." It made it possible to shed the old and establish the new on a cumulative basis. It produced cross-fertilization among many different occupations, both old and new. It brought confidence in the human capacity to obtain knowledge about all aspects of nature. Even as printing "made the word of God more multiform, it made His handiwork more uniform."

Eisenstein also points out that printing was used differently in China and Korea and argues that institutional context must be kept in mind when evaluating techno-logical innovations. Its special impact on Western society would not have occurred if the press had been "monopolized by priests and rulers and withheld from free-wheeling urban entrepreneurs."[5]

The growing prominence of printing would have enormous consequences for the future, comparable to the switch from oral to written discourse in ancient Greece. It broke the monopoly of learning by the clergy. It liberated thought from immedi-ate social relations, both intensifying it and allowing it to stray from immediate real-ity. Printing, together with advanced levels of literacy and the political and printing dominance of London, undermined England's secret and privileged world of politi-cal communication during the English Civil War (1640–1660), and led to the unin-tended creation of a public sphere and of public opinion as influential political forces.[6] Printing led to the class nature of knowledge so characteristic of the modern world, in that money was now the means to acquire and convey information and to obtain education. As the basis of education and all the professions, unequal access to book learning became an integral part of the power or class structure of capitalist society.

Communication and European Imperialism

Improvements in oceangoing navigation eventually had repercussions beyond the improvement of coastal trade. From the fifteenth century on, European ships mastered the major oceans of the planet, inaugurating the age of exploration. But exploration was not driven by mere curiosity; it was also prompted by motives of gain and national power, and it resulted in the age of empire imperialism. The economic expansion of Europe was considerably augmented by the new flow of world trade. Enhanced economic activity from foreign trade (the exploitation of colonies) stimulated Europe's domestic economies and provided career opportunities for the surplus (male) children of the upper class, as well as a way to pacify the masses with cheap food and nationalistic values. In both cases, overseas expansion provided European societies with political safety valves. Needless to say, the competition for empire also led to numerous wars, the costs of which retarded economic growth and the fervors of which distorted the meaning of nationalism.

The enormous increase in interaction among the world's societies that began in the fifteenth century has had important consequences in every century since. One consequence that appeared as early as the eighteenth century was to make Europeans aware, especially the French, that being a Westerner was a cultural, historical state of being. New facts are always subject to interpretation, and Europeans responded in various ways to their encounters with other cultures. One was to become racist, a response especially characteristic of the Anglo-American world. But another was to become aware of the cultural basis of all behaviors, an outcome clearly reflected in the enormously influential anthropological relativism of Montesquieu (1689–1755).

COMMUNICATION AND
POLITICAL DEVELOPMENTS

The economic expansion of Europe had profound implications for political relations. Complex economic activities cannot take place without strong political support, and this was provided by the growth of the territorially based state. The earliest kind of state to support the developing capitalist economy was the absolute monarchy. Here one finds the various communication practices and artifacts that aid economic development: the king's currency, law, and highways, all vital adjuncts to effective economic communication among the new and specialized economic actors.

There were other intertwined economic and political developments. Information is vital to businesspersons, political leaders, and government officials. One must keep abreast of doings out of sight and often far away, actions by others that can seriously affect one's fortunes: the rise of new competitors, the creation of new technology or products, political events and legislation that affect the economy, the actions of foreign governments that might affect trade or currency rates, and so on. Thus by the seventeenth century "news" had become a commodity to sell, much like corn or clothing. Some "news" was gathered by government statistical services, but much of it was developed and distributed by profit-making businesses.

By the seventeenth century, governments were engaged in social bookkeeping on a vast scale, much of it done in the same spirit, as a private business. Society under mercantilist assumptions is thought of as a vast corporation—an assumption still with us, though few are aware of it. Governments began to take over the recording of marriages, births, and deaths, among other data, and it is no accident that statistical or probability mathematics had its origins in the seventeenth century. By the eighteenth century, empirical research done or sponsored by governments would flourish throughout Europe to satisfy the new hunger for information.

The Emergence of Public and Private Spheres

The meaning of "public" and "private" varies with historical circumstances.[7] For the ancient Greeks, the public was all that mattered, a civic or political arena where humans (males) could fully develop through interaction with their fellow citizens. In ancient Rome, the concept of the public was stripped of its political dimension and conceived in narrowly legalistic terms. The public realm disappeared altogether during the feudal period, as society dissolved into a hierarchy of private rights and duties.

The rise of capitalism introduced a novel private-public dichotomy. By the seventeenth and eighteenth centuries, the private (civil society) was important, if not all-important, and the public meant a polity that was organized to reflect and support the private realm. The private realm consisted of property owners, especially the new commercial-manufacturing middle class. It also makes sense, following Habermas, to think of this private world as a public sphere, or as the interaction of property owners in public—in coffeehouses, taverns, clubs, salons, theaters, museums, and the like. This is a public in the sociological sense, a group of people who have something in common and who engage in social relations for various purposes— recreation, business, politics. Property owners were especially interested in protecting and enhancing their interests politically; in simplest terms, they sought the best ways to organize the polity on their behalf. By the eighteenth century, the male property owner was also the head (owner) of his family and the owner of the polity, all on behalf of himself as human being (which among other things now meant, in this new capitalist world, someone who owned himself).

Salons, coffeehouses, literary societies, and the like became places for interaction by the middle class, places that could disregard birth status and become accessible to anyone with property and education. They were also places where the taken-for-granted assumptions of feudalism were transformed into issues for discussion. Theaters became public, and music (in concert) became a commodity rather than an accompaniment to feudal occasions (church, court ceremonies)—that is, it was no longer tied to a purpose. Art became "free choice"—that is, subject to the market. The same was true of painting; here as elsewhere, access to valued experience and the right to judge broadened to include all (male) property owners. The architecture of the home reflected the new family life—more individual, solitary, more a home for individuals than for the family as whole, Gone, for example, was the great hall of the feudal manor. The underlying reality of the new family was still patriarchal, however, as was the economy, polity, the church, and other sites of social interaction. By the eighteenth century, the new world of social power, derived from any and all forms of property, was firmly in place, not least because it was disguised by such terms as *human nature, human rights,* the *people,* the *public,* the *private,* the *general,* the *constitutional,* the *rational,* and *progress.*

Communication Density and the Emergence of the Self

The emergence of a private world characterized by high interaction density led to a preoccupation with self. A world of routine interaction produces personalities that find sustenance and validation in others. The world of diverse and novel interaction characteristic of capitalism produces a personality that must calculate consequences of alternatives. A dynamic world of rich stimuli puts a premium on cerebral skills and reflexive abilities. It is not mere coincidence that the science of psychology emerges with John Locke and Benedict Spinoza in the seventeenth century.

The individual as the source of action and thought leads to the characteristic liberal[8] demands for freedom of speech and freedom from arbitrary interference from public authorities. The flowering of capitalism also led to the redefinition of the human being in terms of "possessive individualism"—that is, individuals conceived as proprietors or owners of themselves. The new capitalist self was helped by Protestantism and by the new character traits that emerged to facilitate, indeed make possible, interaction (communication) among strangers—for example, empathy and sincerity.[9]

Forging Consensus: Communication as Deliberation

The European world of the seventeenth and eighteenth centuries was well acquainted with deep social conflict. In consequence, there emerged a widespread feeling that new methods for settling economic, political, and philosophical disputes were needed. This gave added value to the network of coffeehouses, taverns, clubs, academies of science, salons, theaters, and museums, where, as noted, varied forms of discourse could take place outside the constraints of feudal institutions. In addition, an extensive network of correspondence linked not only parts of the new nation-states but groups in various nation-states.[10] These sites were places where the new property groups, along with intellectuals, could meet to converse and inform each other in an informal atmosphere of equality.

Oral discourse among relatively equal citizens had been profoundly important in the development of ancient Greek culture, and one wonders what its role was in the emergence of English, American, and French liberal democracy. One can only speculate, but its role in the emergence of the modern liberal polity (courts of law, political campaigns, legislative debates) cannot have been unimportant. Those who counted, not only in the sense of the commercial counting house but in terms of political power, met in various fora to relax, chat, be entertained, talk business, and debate politics and points of law. Could it have been otherwise? The richness and creativity of the ideas that came out of the Army Debates during the English Civil War were largely due to oral interaction between diverse members of English society thrown together by the contingencies of revolution. Certainly the English House of Commons and House of Lords were sites of intense oral discourse. It is clear that James Madison did not believe that some magical political market (i.e., elections) would integrate the diverse interests ("factions") that made up the American colonies. Rather, Madison stressed the need for deliberation in legislative bodies to forge operational consensus. (Whether communication devices, in or out of politics, are used for that purpose today will concern us greatly in later chapters.)

There emerged a widespread belief among early liberals that the free flow of ideas and explicitly arranged forms of interaction would get to the truth of things and yield the consensus needed for a viable society. That belief is still widespread today, though it was being contradicted even as it emerged.

The Real World of Communication

The image of free exchange among equals, leading to truth and consensus, is a useful fiction, but it should not be confused with historical reality. The public sphere was clearly revealed as one of unequal social relations in the nineteenth century and as one of one-sided interaction (mass relations) in the twentieth century (as corporate capitalism made even property owners radically unequal). Those who spoke of equality and freedom for human beings in the early modern period were really talking about a small group of male property owners and individuals with marketable skills (professionals). The feverish political and pamphleteering activity of that period was directed *by* the propertied *at* the propertied. By the twentieth century, the purveyors of symbols were doing much the same, only now, in addition to influencing the politically active (about 50 percent of the eligible electorate in the United States), they were also providing a huge volume of depoliticizing symbols for the less powerful (academic education, textbooks, objective journalism, professionalism, popular culture).[11]

COMMUNICATION AND DEVELOPMENTS IN THE SYMBOLIC CULTURE OF THE WEST

The medieval view of nature and human nature, which was essentially the same as the Greek view, pictured them as a unitary, teleological order. The emphasis on final cause meant that nature, as well as human beings and society, could best be known in terms of their ends or purposes. Everything and everyone had a purpose established in and through the mind of God, the first and final Cause. Each being, it was thought, had an essence it strove to realize, and its success was the measure of its participation in the mind of God.

The medieval worldview was updated by Thomas Aquinas (1225–1274), who incorporated Aristotelian philosophy into the framework of Catholic Christendom. Despite Thomas's efforts, however, the elaborate symbolic edifice that he constructed through reason began to collapse even in his lifetime. The expanding European economy needed a much different symbolic system—in contemporary terms, a much better way to grapple with the novelty and diversity that were appearing daily.

William of Occam (c. 1290–1349) and the Empirical Outlook

Thomas's union of the particular and the universal, the secular and the spiritual, the sensible and the rational (and all with revelation) was disputed by other scholastics long before the onset of secular science. This is a reference, of course, to the profound controversy between the realists and the nominalists. The realist position, which reached a modified form in Thomas, rested on the assumption that real things are not only the particular things of the senses but also universal essences. It is the mind that gives form to matter by realizing its potential or essence and thereby making it actual. The mind finds ascending levels of actuality until it reaches God, who is pure form and pure actuality. All this was challenged by the nominalists, within the framework of Christianity.

The outstanding figure in the nominalist movement was William of Occam, who systematized and enlarged upon a nominalist position that had emerged somewhat earlier. The aspect of Occam's thought that was decisively important for the success of modern science and for the emergence of new ways of communicating was his insistence that mind and nature be separated. For Occam, the operations of the mind dealt with relations among ideas, while nature contained only individual things and relations among them. The easy identification between mind and nature, which the Greeks had started and the medieval realists had continued, was ended by Occam, who gave each an independent existence. The mind no longer established universals but only subjective abstractions based on the common properties or contrasts of things—abstractions that had no objective reality.

Occam's perspective was no doubt stimulated by the social changes that were upsetting the static agrarian world of medieval Europe. Given a rationalist culture, the mind as reason was finding it difficult to generate the concepts needed to understand the surging novelties and diversities that now characterized European life. What Occam was arguing, of course, was that knowledge comes not from logic but from the direct perception of individual things and relations. The denial that reason can establish the reality of things also means, Occam insisted, that there is no logical proof of religious beliefs, including the belief that God exists. Thus, since religious beliefs cannot stem from sensory perception, they must rest on faith alone. Occam's work not only separated mind from nature but separated religion from both. His definition of nature as a collection of individuals and relations among individuals contained neither the concepts of the mind nor the morals, purposes, or values of religion.[12]

The Rise of Early Modern Science and the World System

Robert Wuthnow has pointed to the way in which the emergence of distinct nation-states during the fifteenth and sixteenth centuries helped the rise of modern science.

Governments did not support science for the practical benefits it might bring, but to acquire legitimacy by associating the nation-state with higher learning and the cosmic forces that learning had uncovered (the Newtonian world scheme of balance).[13] In an age of religious and political conflict, science also served as a way in which the state could claim that it was in tune with a natural normative order that transcended historical diversity and uncertainty.

By the end of the sixteenth century, scientists were communicating easily across Europe and belonging to many scientific academies besides those in their native countries. Scientists also found it easy to move from one country to another as nation-states vied for the legitimacy that they provided. The association of science with the state had many consequences for the nature of science. Science could now claim to be nonpolitical and autonomous, public spirited, and devoted to the pursuit of knowledge for its own sake. But whatever was true of the period that Wuthnow discusses, the history of the relation between the state and science since the early modern period can be stated in more explicit terms. Today, the priorities of not only natural science but all science, including scientific education, are deeply influenced by the state. Today, science is used more openly for the practical benefits it might bring. Further, the state still obtains legitimacy from science, even for its policies outside science.[14]

The Mature Scientific Worldview: The French (and Scottish) Enlightenment

The power over nature that Europeans acquired after 1100 grew exponentially. The nominalist separation of nature from its religious and teleological moorings admirably suited the needs of an expanding economy. The old view of nature gradually gave way before the growth of technology, commerce, experimentation, and the new anti-Aristotelian metaphysics. By the time of Copernicus, but especially with Galileo and Newton, the Scholastic view of nature had undergone a momentous transformation. Nature now existed separately from God and no longer embodied any purpose. Henceforth, nature was simply a vast, machinelike structure of dead, homogeneous matter in law-governed motion. By the end of the seventeenth century, the mechanistic view of nature had largely displaced Aristotelian science and was firmly established in the intellectual community of Europe. Instead of searching for purpose in nature, science now tried to express nature's forces and processes in abstract, quantitative terms.

The current in the seventeenth century that was destined to triumph, however, was John Locke's emphasis on experience as the source of knowledge and his nominalist view of not only logic but language itself. This line of thought was climaxed by the thought of David Hume and Étienne Bonnot de Condillac in the eighteenth century. In a wider sense, the entire Scottish, and even more so the French, Enlightenment signaled the triumph of both capitalism and the empirical method it needed to conduct its affairs.

The development in France of a fairly advanced capitalist economy from the Middle Ages down through the sixteenth and seventeenth centuries, within feudal institutions, produced *anomie* at the societal level. The deep contradiction between France's legitimating feudal norms and values and the advanced state of French commerce, fabrication, technology, communication, and science could not but encourage creative, indeed revolutionary, thinking about society. The Enlightenment's revolution in thought consisted, first, in making Western rationalism empirical; second, in saying that both nature and human nature were rational and that both could and should be studied empirically; third, that the passions were lawful; and fourth, that a humanity existed beyond feudal particularism and that its needs should be served by the new science and the new scientific society.

The role of communication in all this was important though difficult to pinpoint exactly. The enormous expansion of the European economy had generated new kinds of individuals and had thrown them together both inside and among the various nation-states. Communication took place through many means and in many formats: mail, pamphlets, books, newspapers, literary societies, coffeehouses, counting houses, salons, and correspondence societies, both scientific and political. But beyond the role of communication technology and relations lies the role of technology in general, from the horse harness to the telescope, printing press, improved navigational devices, wind and water mills, and so on, in refashioning the European mind. One outcome of the mechanistic world of Isaac Newton was its use in fashioning the early liberal world of the eighteenth century—the social Newtonianism of laissez-faire economics (Adam Smith and David Ricardo) and American constitutionalism (James Madison). Perhaps a deeper outcome of defining reason in terms of its activity and success in subdividing nature and serving human nature was its explicit transformation into method by Hume.

The Redefinition of Gender

The middle-class (male) revolt against feudalism can be framed as an attempt to substitute skill at growing food, making things, and providing mundane services (thus making possible the satisfaction of ordinary human needs) for skills at warfare, leisure pursuits, lavish consumption, and command. One unintentional outcome of this revolt, and one that took centuries, was to reduce the distance between the new ideal human male and the female portion of the human race. The latter had the same ordinary needs and was clearly able to perform, indeed was performing, many of the behaviors valued by the middle class.

The redefinition of gender took a long time; indeed, it came rather in a flood during the eighteenth century. To the Enlightenment belongs the credit for the first large-scale discussion of gender relations. By and large, the bulk of the thinkers in this century, including Voltaire, Montesquieu, Rousseau, and Diderot, continued the conventional view that the sexes were different and unequal. What was new, however, was the widespread, open discussion of the nature of women and the fact that they were given a new role to play in the development of a better society. Women had to be better educated, declared a large number of both male and female authors, largely so that they could turn out better sons and thus improve the public sphere. Though it became a commonplace in the next century, this was quite innovative given the eighteenth-century context. The function assigned to women was so important that while they were not to be given legal or political rights, they would be considered citizens. (It should be noted that advocating legal-political equality for men at this time was considered dangerously subversive.)

Though it may appear sexist today, those in the eighteenth century who emphasized the special role of women in raising children, especially sons, regarded this function as central to the creation of a new and better France. In any case, women in eighteenth-century France responded enthusiastically to what could only be considered an elevation in their status.

The creativity of the Enlightenment, however, did not open the matter of gender relations solely to assign women to an improved but still unequal status. A strong minority tradition, exemplified by Holbach, Helvetius, D'Alembert, Condorcet, and Babeuf, openly declared the sexes as equal in capacity for most political and occupational-professional tasks, arguing that the contemporary inequality was due to a social environment that was warping the personality of both sexes.[15]

COMMUNICATION AND POWER: COMPARING THE PAST AND THE EARLY MODERN PERIOD

The importance of new forms of communication in undermining European feudalism and bringing about capitalism are easy to see in their general outline. Appreciation of developments in communication from 1100 to 1800 can be heightened by comparison with earlier epochs. Identifying similarities in history is always dangerous; nonetheless, it is useful to note that qualitative historical spurts in social development have been associated with communication spurts. Obviously, nothing in the history of human communication matches the importance of upright posture, language, or fire. One could cite fire alone as a cause of a more dense and fruitful interaction (communication), but that would do violence to the multiple and additive nature of causation. The other significant revolution in communication prior to the onset of modernity occurred with the agricultural revolution—that is, with the urbanization to which plant cultivation led. Urban social interaction had many positive advantages for Sumer, Egypt, China, Greece, and Rome. Of these, it will be recalled, the special conditions that produced the Greek city-state also generated the ideal and practice of political discourse as the basis of public power and policy.

The modern period was profoundly influenced by the ideals of the Greek city-state. Despite its new empirical bent, the modern world accepted the Greek ideal that society itself, not just things or limited groupings, could be reformed or even reconstructed.

Communication was a public phenomenon in the prehuman era and continued as such in the hunting-gathering world (if it makes sense to apply such terms to these periods). Communication became both public and private as complex societies

Communication and the Rise of Capitalism

emerged. Power groups communicated with the masses through public announcements and through force, buildings, ceremonies, festivals, rituals, and such public activities as circuses and welfare programs. But power groups in the agrarian period communicated privately among themselves, and their main concern was each other, not the masses. Public communication consisted essentially of telling the masses what their betters had decided.

Was communication different in the early modern period because power slipped from a landed nobility to commercial and manufacturing groups? It is best to be careful and see this period as merely an enlargement and diversification of the powers that were. Certainly the masses were not participants in this new public sphere; highways, currency, law, courts, books, public meeting places, legislatures, places of business, and so on, were all in service to private power groups. In that sense society had not changed; the propertied were still in charge of society. What was new was that the propertied had been much enlarged and diversified. Whether this process has led to (or can lead to) pluralistic power and democracy is a matter that we will take up in the chapters to come.

NOTES

1. The identification of the role of animal power in the social and economic development of the West, especially the new uses of the horse, is the work of Lefebvre des Noëttes, as elaborated by Marc Bloch, both Marxist scholars. The definitive summary of this and other scholarship in this area is by a non-Marxist, Lynn White, Jr., *Medieval Technology and Social Change* (New York: Oxford University Press, 1962), chaps. 1, 2. For an historical account of the horse and its impact on various societies, including a popularization of its role in the economic development of the West, see Matthew J. Kust, *Man and Horse in History* (Alexandria, Va.: Plutarch, 1983).

2. C. B. Macpherson, *The Political Theory of Possessive Individualism: Hobbes to Locke* (London: Oxford University Press, 1962).

3. Chandra Mukerji, "Mass Culture and the Modern World System: The Rise of the Graphic Arts," *Theory and Society* 8 (1979), 245–68.

4. Lucien Febvre and Henri-Jean Martin, *The Coming of the Book: The Impact of Printing, 1450–1800*, trans. David Gerard, ed. Geoffrey Nowell and David Wooton (London: North London Branch [hereafter NLB], 1976, first published 1958).

5. Elizabeth L. Eisenstein, *The Printing Revolution in Early Modern Europe* (New York: Cambridge University Press, 1983).

6. David Zaret, *Origins of Democratic Culture: Printing, Petitions, and the Public Sphere in Early-Modern England* (Princeton, N.J.: Princeton University Press, 2000).

7. The following relies on Jürgen Habermas, *The Structural Transformation of the Public Sphere*, trans. Thomas Burger with the assistance of Frederick Lawrence (Cambridge, Mass.: MIT Press, 1989).

8. The terms *liberal* and *liberalism* refer to the acceptance of private property, private economic motives and actions, profit making through exchange relations (markets), competition and science as keys to economic growth and social progress, and political and legal equality as central social institutions. In the Anglo-American world, liberals believe that individuals

exist prior to society and that the latter should take its form from the actions of self-oriented individuals. As they behave, individuals transform nature into private property and economic growth occurs. The state exists largely as a mediator of disputes among private actors. In contrast, Continental European liberalism (for example, Emile Durkheim and Max Weber) defines individualism and private property, etc. as social phenomena and sees the state as a formative agent in their creation and maintenance.

Thus, both Democrats and Republicans in the United States are liberals (Left and Right liberals); that is, both accept the validity and superiority of capitalist/liberal society while disagreeing on how to run it. Right liberals emphasize reliance on private actors and markets, while Left liberals emphasize the need of the state to help individuals, groups, and markets work better. Regardless of what they say, Right and Left liberals are equally prone to use the state to serve their values, beliefs, and clients. Regardless of what they say, both do and say what they must to get elected, further compromising their principles, given the monstrous diversity of the American economy and electorate. For a fuller discussion of historical, European developments in liberal social thought, see *The Encyclopedia of the Social Sciences* (New York: Macmillan, 1930–1935); or its successor, *The International Encyclopedia of the Social Sciences* (New York: Macmillan and Free Press, 1968); and *The Encyclopedia of Sociology* (New York: Macmillan, 1992).

9. For the emergence of sincerity in modern literature, with only an occasional hint that it had social roots, see Lionel Trilling, *Sincerity and Authenticity* (Cambridge, Mass.: Harvard University Press, 1972), chap 1.

10. The role of the salons and the correspondence networks in politicizing pre-Revolutionary France and the American colonies is well known. Robert Wuthnow has used world-system theory to identify the role played by corresponding scientific societies in the development of European societies. See below, "The Rise of Early Modern Science and the World System."

11. For the various forms of depoliticization, see later chapters.

12. For a concise account of four of the major figures in the controversy between the realists and the nominalists—Saint Augustine, Peter Abelard, Thomas Aquinas, and William of Occam—see H. Carre Meyrick, *Realists and Nominalists* (London: Oxford University Press, 1946).

13. Robert Wuthnow, "The Emergence of Modern Science and World System Theory," *Theory and Society* 8 (1979), 215–43.

14. Chandre Mukerji, *A Fragile Power: Scientists and the State* (Princeton, N.J.: Princeton University Press, 1989).

15. For the above developments, see Jean H. Black, "Women and the Reform of the Nation" and Elizabeth J. Gardner, "The 'Philosophes' and Women: Sensationalism and Sentiment," both in *Women and Society in Eighteenth-Century France,* ed. Eva Jacobs et al. (London: Athlone, 1979), chaps. 1, 2.

3

Communication, Media, and the Emergence of Corporate Capitalism in the United States, 1800–1940

IDENTIFYING THE STAGES OF CAPITALISM

U nderstanding communication in a sociohistorical context requires something more precise than the broad abstraction *capitalism*—namely, a need to distinguish *stages* in its history. The period from 1100 to 1800 was marked by the emergence of capitalist agriculture, manufacturing for exchange, and an intensive commercial capitalism. There was also an overt political dimension to early capitalism, a dimension that is not captured fully by the term *mercantilism*. In the struggle between feudalism and capitalism, control of the state was vital. In England, the struggle for state control, even as early as the fourteenth century, was essentially a struggle among "capitalists" as much as anything else. England's landed nobility, including the monarchy, was essentially engaged in capitalist agriculture; from the earliest days its members thought of their households, regions, and nation in capitalist terms. They were later joined by those engaged in commercial-professional-manufacturing activities; a distinct stage of entrepreneurial or small-scale capitalism was evident by 1800.

The period from 1800 to 1940 in the West (and Japan) saw the emergence of corporate capitalism. Identifying stages of capitalism is an expository device; the stages should not be taken literally. The corporate age covered in this chapter (the nineteenth century), for example, had important sectors of small property owners. Understandably, entrepreneurial ideology flourished in the nineteenth century, partially reflecting and partially hiding the nature of the economy. Nonetheless, the main thrust of the American economy during the nineteenth century was toward economic concentration under the auspices of the corporation, aided and abetted by state and federal governments.[1]

The corporate era can also be depicted as the age of inanimate energy (coal and oil) and the end of the wood-water-wind-animal age of capitalism. This age completed the separation of humans and society from nature, giving priority to the impersonal over the personal. It was an age in which economic growth, profit and success, and research in the abstract became primary values, taken for granted. It was an age in which the metaphysical abstractions of the Enlightenment were modernized to suit mass manufacturing, mass marketing, mass communication, and mass politics.

THE EMERGENCE OF CORPORATE CAPITALISM

American society was a growth machine from its origins, though this was obscured by the fact that most Americans worked the land or tended small-scale enterprises until well into the nineteenth century. The spectacular industrial growth in the nineteenth century, though interpreted in terms of entrepreneurial imagery, was largely the doing of large-scale corporations, aided by government. Significantly, the movement toward large-scale enterprise was under way before the Civil War. Here the preeminent example was the railroad—the dominant, pace-setting technology between 1850 and 1950. The trend toward large organizations meant that compared to America's rural past, individuals would no longer live in a world centered on primary groups—family, friends, work teams. Primary groups remained important, of course, but increasingly life would now be conducted either in or in relation to large, impersonal, formally organized groups. Increasingly, what happened to Americans resulted from the actions of large-scale groups, such as corporations, governments, foundations, charities, political parties, and trade and professional associations. In this fact lay a trend of far-reaching significance: the American people would become a nation of *employees,* as the self-employed, small business, small-farm sectors shrank steadily.

As Roy shows, the emergence and eventual dominance of the corporation was not a natural process stemming from the logic of efficiency. Efficiency theory assumes that economic actors make rational choices in regard to the best utilization of resources, technology, or practices. Over time, the competition among actors sees to it that the most efficient actors and economic forms prevail. In contrast to economics, Roy adopts a sociopolitical stance that emphasizes power, or the ability of some actors, thanks to institutional and state structures, to shape the choices of other actors. The corporate form evolved haphazardly from the colonial era up through the corporate "revolution" of the 1890s. Up to the early nineteenth century, corporations were mostly quasi-government agencies established to perform public functions (schools, urban services, churches, charities, canals, turnpikes, bridges) and financed by government bonds. As such, they enjoyed (where relevant) such privileges as monopoly rights, eminent domain, and liability protection.

Once the corporate form was applied to railroads, it lost its public accountability and ushered in the rise of the large profit-making entity financed by a growing capital-assembling structure (Wall Street). In the 1890s, the corporate form was applied to manufacturing, ushering in an explosion of economic concentration and a further enlargement of the scope of Wall Street financing. In all this, argues Roy, efficiency certainly played a role but the primary role went to an institutional and political system that was characterized by unequal power. Individual economic actors certainly made rational decisions from the choices available to them: to wit, either compete against powerful, well-connected corporate entities, not above resorting to predatory pricing, or sell out at a profit or in some cases to survive.[2]

Large organizations were made possible by a variety of factors including bureaucratic administration (effective command and control structures that were more efficient than previous forms of administration). The emergence of bureaucratic (rational, efficient, accountable) administration was a solution to the problem of how to administer large and complex enterprises, especially in a competitive environment. More efficient administration developed slowly until the nineteenth century, when the problem of size and complexity outpaced administrative forms. The nineteenth century is known today for dramatic achievements in industry, science, and technology. What is not so well known is that it made equally dramatic breakthroughs in administration. In a relatively short time, new administrative forms appeared across the basic institutional sectors of society. In general, developments in business, government, law, and warfare between 1800 and 1940 (that is, broadly, the nineteenth century) produced the essential features of our present-day, taken-for-granted society.

The Corporate Economy

The basic pattern in the early American economy consisted of exporting food and staples (slave-grown cotton, for example) in order to import machinery. At first, business firms were small and oriented toward local markets. But the explosion of industry made possible by new organizational forms (and by communication technology, especially the railroad and the telegraph) soon changed all this. The first new organizational form in business focused on the problem of how to run a railroad. In the 1850s, the first large-scale business organization appeared, the Erie Railroad. Its president, Daniel C. McCallum, had developed a geographically based division of labor. He produced an organizational chart specifying the duties of all division heads and subordinates, thus allowing control from a central point. Further developments in corporate capitalism followed apace, as special administrative problems of various types of businesses arose.[3]

The United States also expanded in another sense—American history makes more complete sense if the United States is seen as an imperialist society. Whether by purchase or force of arms, the United States expanded its territory from the beginnings of the republic. Even the Civil War can be thought of as a way to bring a plantation society into the dynamic world of manufacturing and capitalist commercialization of land, labor, and consumption. By the end of the nineteenth century, the United States was completing its continental expansion at the expense of native peoples and Mexico, and it was fully engaged in an expansion into Latin America and across the Pacific. This was no mere military adventurism but a strategy designed to support American agrarian and manufacturing businesses.[4]

The Corporate Polity (Government, Law, and Politics)

The United States was no exception to the general trend in the West toward centralized states. As the exemplar of laissez-faire and a country suspicious of government, the United States today gives the appearance of having created a federal government only yesterday. This is a gravely mistaken picture. All industrializing societies, the United States included, make extensive use of government to further economic expansion. What is different about the United States is that a large and influential body of thinkers has falsified the nature of government throughout its history. Central government in the United States has always been as strong as needed to defend against foreign enemies, put down rebellions (and, often, stifle legitimate dissent), settle and develop the West, further national and overseas expansion, help distressed groups (such as farmers, manufacturers, and the poor), and perform such public functions as supplying a common currency, water, police protection, and so on. The misunderstanding of the nature of the state has been a serious deficiency of American social thought and contemporary politics.

The development of American politics and law was also quite different than either the elite or popular conception of it. The United States did not hold an election until eight years after winning its war of independence, and when it did, the vote was restricted (and was until the 1850s) to white males who satisfied a property qualification. Long before the extension of the suffrage, the American legal system was shaped to benefit dynamic property-holding groups. Legal historians and philosophers have portrayed American law as an objective, apolitical, and autonomous code of norms. Despite disagreements—say, between Roscoe Pound and Oliver Wendell Holmes—American jurisprudence has argued that the development of American law has been marked by consensus and that its outcomes serve the common good. Even legal analysts who see the law in relation to economic and political developments have tended to adopt a functional and consensus approach in their interpretations. A minority of legal historians has argued, however, that law is better seen from a conflict perspective; M. J. Horwitz,[5] for example, argues that American law was drastically altered during the formative years of the republic, primarily through judicial interpretations. The eighteenth century regarded law as stemming from community customs derived from "natural law." Property meant the absolute right to enjoy something and to be able to prevent others from interfering with that enjoyment. From 1780 to 1860, argues Horwitz, the legal conception of property was made to mean that one had the right to develop and use property *regardless of injury to others.*

Not surprisingly, argues Horwitz, the changed meaning of property was accompanied by a change in the meaning of a contract. In the eighteenth century, a contract had to be fair and could be set aside if it was unfair. By the mid-nineteenth century, however, a contract was enforceable even if its provisions were patently unfair. The law was simply reflecting a fact of economic life. Strong commercial and industrial interests used their competitive advantages to exploit smaller businesses, consumers, and workers, and they legalized their exploitation by putting it in the form of a contract. They protected their economic power also by getting the courts to reduce their responsibility for damages (in keeping with the new dictum that the central meaning of property was the right to develop it), and juries saw their power to make judgments and award damages on the basis of fairness gradually curtailed.

The extension of the suffrage after the 1850s, as well as the emergence of tax-supported, mandatory mass education in the same decade, added the trappings of democracy to an already fully established economic and political-legal system. Between the Civil War and the Great Depression of the 1930s, the U.S. Supreme Court effectively blocked all attempts to regulate business. The entire state and legal system displayed consistent and effectual hostility toward any effort by American workers to organize against the dreadful working conditions and wages of the period; indeed, American business, working through the state (both legally and illegally), largely succeeded in neutralizing the working class.[6] In 1883, the Pendleton Act made access to civil service positions dependent on education (which, of course, could be effectively acquired only by the propertied classes). The extension of high-school education to the masses after 1900, of the vote to women in 1919, and of effective civil rights to minorities in the 1960s came *after* the capitalist economy and polity had established themselves safely beyond interference by voters.

The reform efforts of the late nineteenth century that led to the great regulatory agencies did not contradict the antidemocratic thrust of the American polity. The regulatory agencies were largely put in place to prevent dangerous competition and to secure the interests of the regulated. For its part, the New Deal of the 1930s is best thought of as a reform movement to restore the capitalist economy and its legitimacy. Even the reform of the political machines during the first half of the twentieth century was really a way to prevent the masses from funneling their demands into the chambers of political power. In any case, the imbalances in electoral districts between the 1850s and the reforms begun in the 1960s, by which five thousand rural and small-town voters had the same power as five hundred thousand voters in urban districts, made the idea of popular voting hollow. Today, the gerrymander (or arranging electoral districts to neutralize an opponent's supporters) and the power of private money still undermine the ideals of representative government, and certainly the idea of a social democracy.

The Persistence of Entrepreneurial Imagery

The spectacular growth of corporate state-supported enterprise ran counter to contemporary economic beliefs. Early capitalist theorists—such as John Locke, Thomas

Malthus, Adam Smith, and the Physiocrats—all assumed that the basic economic unit is the individual human being. The individual, they argued, is characterized by concrete and self-evident drives, needs, and skills. Many theorists also assumed that individuals are rational and that the sum of individual actions necessarily leads to a rational economy. Using models from nature, especially Newtonian mechanics, theorists argued that a natural economy works like a machine in perpetual equilibrium. The master idea that eventually emerged was that something called "markets" (transactions among individuals in given areas, using an agreed-upon unit of exchange) would balance out the supply and demand of raw materials, labor, money, goods, and services, thus yielding the most efficient (rational) use of economic resources. The role of other institutions, said early classical economists, is to allow this naturally self-balancing system to work.

Industrialization forced a change in the static Newtonian framework in which liberal thought was embedded. In the United States, the period after the Civil War produced a ferment of ideas, but the outcome was American exceptionalism in new clothing. Previously, American exceptionalism had been rooted in the belief that God had specially favored America. Now, mainstream thinkers, using Darwinian imagery, propounded a philosophy of progress through liberal institutions, especially a private competitive economy. Using Christian ideas and values, often stated explicitly, blended with the values of nationalism and representative government, American thinkers affirmed the exceptional status of America even as they warded off democracy and socialism.[7]

It should now be recognized that the self-interested, rational individual and the self-equilibrating market were cultural fictions, rationalizations that emerged during the early stages of capitalism to help thinkers make sense of, and feel at home in, the novel and uncertain world of an expanding capitalist economy. Further, it is time to discard other aspects of the theory of human nature on which early capitalism was based. Human beings are not driven by instincts of hunger and gain; they are no more driven by self-interest than by altruism, and no more oriented toward work and success than the opposite. The human being that early economists talked about is actually highly socialized, with acquired motives, expectations, interests, and skills. An individual's personality reflects the general socioeconomic level of his or her society. The fiction of the rational individual who pursues self-evident economic values must give way. Humans must *learn* how and what to eat, when and how to work, what to need, and what to value.

The sociocultural perspective has redefined other aspects of the economy as well. Nature is not a ready-made entity waiting to be utilized by ready-made individuals. Familiar aspects of nature such as land, water, animals, and timber do not exist as economic values until they have been culturally defined. Serfdom, slavery, "free" labor, ambition, strikes, greed, profit, slowdowns, property, money, contract, work-to-rule, and absenteeism do not exist in human nature—all must be created and institutionalized by given sociocultural systems. No conception of human nature, therefore, can explain the sharp variations in economic behavior in history, or the spectacular economic growth in the West of the past few centuries. Far from being self-evident and natural, economic behavior is culturally directed and thus open to choice. How and why humans pursue economic values depends on religious and family values, on tax codes, and military expenditures—it is a matter neither of technical economic analysis nor of obeying principles laid down by nature.

The classic image of the economy by liberal economists was a thoroughgoing fiction based on arbitrary assumptions and definitions. The entire notion of an autonomous, self-explanatory entity called an "economy" is an absurdity. The assumptions and definitions of liberal economics are arbitrary; some feminists, for example, have asked us to abandon the idea that unpaid labor in the home (including the raising of children) is not work. The definitions of capital, labor, profit, efficiency, unemployment, and so on, are also not self-evident. To refer to government, politics, taxes, education, etc., as "externalities"—that is, to assume that the economy can be analyzed without taking account of such variables—is unscientific in the extreme. But the absurd idea of a separate natural economy, animated by a released human nature, suited the interests of the powerful, and with the fanciful analysis provided by economists, it prevails to this day.

COMMUNICATION AND INDUSTRIALIZATION

The New Energy Sources

By the eighteenth century, reliance on horses was a burden on the English economy. Feeding them was expensive at a time when high tariffs on imported food kept domestic food prices high for animals as well as humans. Elsewhere the development of better machinery to harness waterpower, and then perfection of the steam engine, made cost comparisons among different energy sources inevitable. By the end of the eighteenth century, the long reliance on water, wind, wood, and animals for energy had come to an end, as was symbolized by the huge piles of coal that began to dot (and mar) the English countryside.

Mass Printing: Newspapers, Books, and Textbooks

Steam was used to run printing presses early in the nineteenth century, and there were significant advances in industrializing the way in which texts were printed. A process to make paper out of wood pulp by machine completed the prerequisites of mass-produced written material. By the mid-nineteenth century, the newspaper as conveyor of information, as political advocate, and as entertainer of audiences beyond small localities had emerged. Linked quickly to the telegraph, the newspaper became a force for nation building. Eventually journalism would become (allegedly) nonpolitical and use a variety of media to convey its messages.

The advent of mass education in the 1850s and of a growing middle-class reading public made a rich market for books, textbooks, and lectures. There was also a huge market for popular culture and for popular religious materials.

The Early Age of Electricity: Telegraph, Telephone, Radio, and Film

The use of electricity for communication quickly outstripped science's understanding of its fundamental nature. Employing an electrical current in one form or another to convey messages represented a quantum jump over conveying messages by signal fires, drums, pigeons, boats, runners, or on horseback. The telegraph led the way (1844), followed by the telephone (1876), the radio (1890s), and film (1900 on). (Television and the computer emerged in the 1920s, but their story takes place after 1950.) Significantly, electricity was destined to link not only all parts of even a huge nation like the United States but all parts and peoples of the globe. The first transatlantic cable was completed in 1866, signaling the beginning of the electronic communication networks that would eventually encompass the globe.

The Railroad: The Need to Think of Technology in a Social Context

The steam engine meant industrial manufacturing but also industrial transportation of both goods, messages (mail, magazines, catalogs), and people both by water and rail (and for a while even by car). The steamboat led the way, because the United States had a large number of navigable and connectable rivers. But the railroad was destined to be the transportation-and-communication technology of corporate capitalism in the early industrial era. The railroad, properly understood, stands for the age of industry, urbanization, and technical advance by design. The railroad served as an inspiration for creativity in group organization (the corporation). The railroad helped create a far-flung, highly specialized economy. The railroad was also a source of huge political corruption and economic exploitation. The railroad changed the way in which armies were organized and wars were fought.

No technology stands alone, however; the railroad needed the telegraph, accurate timekeeping, and standardized time zones, for example. In short, what emerged was a cluster of developments to serve a burgeoning economy by providing efficient transport of things, people, and messages. The railroad was a significant contributor to another aspect of modern (capitalist) culture as well—it had a profound effect on how people related to each other and to the natural environment, by disembedding them from time, place, and social context.

ROUNDING OUT CORPORATE CAPITALISM

Industrialization on a vast continent allowed American property owners to think and act in grand terms. The nineteenth century's main accomplishment was to commercialize all reaches of culture, which meant that it commercialized human beings and nature too.

The Commercialization of Land, Labor, Knowledge, Religion, Time, Place, and Power

The essential thrust of the American economy was to turn nature into a source of private profit. Indeed, the main thrust of American beliefs, values, practices, and technology (at least until the environmental movement of the 1960s) was to exploit nature; this thrust was exemplified by canal building and river travel, the railroad, wagon technology, the U.S. cavalry, Homestead Act, mining, smelting, manufacturing, giveaway programs of federal lands, and the right by law to use private property as one saw fit.

Labor was also commercialized, as the practice of buying the labor time of individuals became the norm. Knowledge was commercialized, in the sense that newspapers, books, private schools, private and public universities, and researchers assembled it and dispersed it for money. The social sciences provided the ideology of laissez-faire and American exceptionalism. Organized religion, as well as popular and civil religion, supported capitalism by claiming that it was sanctioned by God, nature, and human nature.

Communication technology changed the way in which time and space were defined. Both were rationalized and turned into controllable abstractions, helping to create the timeless, placeless world of ahistorical liberalism. The railroad played a key role in severing Americans from the rhythms of nature and from the uniqueness of times and places.[8]

Political power was also commercialized. Universalisms such as liberty, equality, and happiness for all posed a threat to propertied and professional groups. The history of American communication capabilities is essentially the story of how they were used—without most people, including many at the top, realizing it—to prevent democracy. The antidemocratic nature of power took many forms:

Property qualifications for voting up to the 1850s

The need for organizational skills and money to run for political office

The need to pay for political messages by which to influence voters, and lobbyists to influence legislators, government officials, regulators

The use of money from Washington's day to the present to buy, support, or rent the services of legislators, judges, and government officials.

Providing a Common Faith and Natural Leaders: The Myths of Education

The United States has enormous faith in the power of education to generate a meritocracy and improve society. By providing all citizens equal opportunities in education, Americans believe that educational markets, along with the competitive processes of the economy and polity, would reveal a natural hierarchy and a legitimate set of leaders. Equal opportunity in education meant equal exposure to a standard curriculum, something that would help homogenize students into a viable citizenry as well as make for a fair race to the top. Research has contradicted all these beliefs, but to little avail—they have long since hardened into comforting myths.

The first myth about American education is its equality. The fact is that it is far from equal. Unlike most developed capitalist societies, which fund education centrally, the United States relies heavily on state and local governments. The result is wide disparity in educational resources among the fifty states and within each of them.

A second myth about education is its power to shape students and achieve social goals. In contrast, from the 1920s on, study after study confirmed the dominance of social class in all forms of educational achievement.[9]

A third myth, related to the second, is that schooling produces better workers and citizens. There is no evidence that success in primary or secondary schools or the achievement of high test scores is connected to success beyond school. Thanks to a compilation of studies about higher education, we know that there is no evidence that graduates of colleges and universities, etc., in the aggregate, make better workers, managers-professionals, or better citizens.[10] This means that even when education achieves its academic goals (as do our elite high schools and colleges), it fails to meet social goals. One-way communication of apolitical content from teacher (or professor) to student is incapable of achieving stated goals. The main explanation for what happens in school, however, lies outside the classroom, in the hierarchy of social class from whence students come. It goes without saying that education is a depoliticizing, antidemocratic force of the first magnitude. It is not surprising that whenever the upper classes are confronted by deficiencies of the American economy, they call for education as the solution (for more on education, see "Teachers and Professors" in chapter 9).

The Separation of Elite and Mass: Professionalism

The advent of mass education did not mean a democratization of knowledge. The nineteenth century was an era of mass education on the surface, but of class education in reality. It was also the formative era of professionalism among business and knowledge elites. In a brilliant book that provides the indispensable historical background to American professionalism, Burton Bledstein has pointed to the pervasive influence of science on nineteenth-century American life and to the way in which science contributed to and helped legitimate unequal power relations.[11] The emerging culture of nineteenth-century America was everywhere animated by the rationalizing tendencies of American capitalism. By 1870, the surge of American industrialization and its diversifying occupational system had everywhere presented opportunities for more efficient ways to conduct business and to conquer or contain evil. Efficiency appeared in the mass distribution of books, through subscription and effective marketing techniques. The important lecturing business was rationalized. Spectator sports were professionalized, with the first professional baseball team appearing in 1869. Even college sports were professionalized, through the development of varsity sports guided by expert coaching staffs. During the last decades of the century, professional associations appeared in a wide variety of fields; for example, the first national professional association in law was established in 1878. A wide variety of professional schools appeared: dentistry in 1867, architecture and pharmacy in 1868, school teaching and veterinary medicine in 1879, accounting and business in 1881.

By the end of the century, a huge array of associations and learned societies had appeared—for example, associations for historians (1884), economists (1885), and political scientists (1889). In all areas there appeared pieces of paper, issued either by the state or private groups, signifying that an individual had the competence and the legal right to practice an occupation.

The essence of the new professionalism, continues Bledstein, is the mastery of nature's principles so as to acquire a mastery over the chaos of experience. Theoretical and applied knowledge (over specialized slices of worldly phenomena) gave the professional the ability to identify and control the seen and unseen factors in areas as diverse as mining, bridge or skyscraper construction, commercial farming, the treatment of diseases in all parts of the body, justice, poverty, rational management in business and government, the rationalization of politics, and even diet, hygiene, sex, dress, and recreation.

Armed with knowledge, the professional was a truly free, independent, autonomous individual and thus in harmony with a central theme of American culture. But, says Bledstein, the freedom of the professional had deeply conservative consequences. Professional claims—augmented by rituals, costumes, technology, and physical settings—to competence resulted in marked dependence on the part of the professional's clients. In all of life's spheres, the public was told that it faced one evil after another: crime, strikes, political uprisings, foreign threats, diseased bodies and minds, financial losses, legal calamities, and so on. Professionals preyed on and cultivated the insecurities and fears of the public. In the larger context, industry, technology, and science were upsetting the world while also offering themselves as the solutions to the world's problems. In particular contexts, Allan Pinkerton in 1870 was extolling the virtues of the professional private detective in the war against the professional criminal; journalists were warning the public about the menaces in their lives and claiming to have vital information about them; reformers were rationalizing politics and the labor movement. Even the struggle against poverty was professionalized; a national association of social work appeared in 1874. The net result was to make ordinary persons dependent on their betters and accept on trust that the experts knew better.

The emergence and establishment of this power relation in business, private professional practice, and in the polity (politics, government, and law), then led, says Bledstein, to the emergence of professionalism as an orderly lifetime career. The role of higher education in all this was to persuade the public that those in high places were competent and thus trustworthy. By standardizing admissions, prescribing formal courses of study, giving examinations, and conferring degrees, higher education proclaimed that the intelligent were rising to the top and that the country had a way to overcome family inheritance, political favoritism, and subjectivism.

Technocratic Liberalism and Corporate Capitalism

By the closing quarter of the nineteenth century, the essentials of the American industrial system were in place, and the liberal professions and disciplines emerged to do two things. First, the applied professions emerged to grapple with the practical problems of the everyday world on a pragmatic basis; each problem was taken at face value, and efforts to solve it were undertaken with little effort to relate it to anything else. A prime example is applied psychology, which began in World War I when psychologists introduced testing to help the military evaluate recruits and place them in the niches for which they were best suited. During the 1920s, applied psychology expanded and began to advise corporations, schools, universities, and government on how to evaluate individuals and fit them in to hierarchies, which were themselves unexamined and presumed to be entirely satisfactory. They also began to advise parents on how to raise children, and to advise individuals on how to solve personal problems. They became "architects of adjustment" who simply took society for granted; ignored workers, women, and minorities; and, using Darwinian ideas, thought of the human psyche as something that should adjust to its environment.[12]

Second, the theoretical disciplines arose to provide the metaphysical legitimacy that all power systems seem to need. By the last quarter of the century, the American economy had no accountable connection to wider social functions, and economics and administrative professions had emerged to tell us, respectively, that economic behavior reflected the law of nature and that the administration of corporations was a science. Property-based American political and legal systems were in place, and political science, public administration, and jurisprudence arose to formalize them. Political theory was on its way toward becoming a philosophical discussion of political (often referred to as "perennial") issues in the abstract, in isolation from an unproblematic civil society. Psychology emerged to provide the underpinnings in human nature for an economic system that needed a more cerebral approach to economic and other social tasks. Its supreme achievement was the IQ examination—or rather, its distortion of an intelligence test that France had developed to evaluate not students but its educational system. Academic psychology, testing specialists, educational psychologists, school boards, teachers, and university admissions officials all foisted on the American people a highly arbitrary test that gave an enormous advantage to the upper classes in the scramble for scarce benefits.

At length, certain liberals sensed the emergence of corporate capitalism without understanding its real nature. This can be seen in the work of Arthur Bentley, whose book *The Process of Government* was enormously influential in the field of political science.[13] In this creative focus on group life and group struggle, Bentley extended America's understanding of its polity by examining pressures exerted on it by economic and other groups. But, arguing pointedly against socialism, Bentley to some extent created the impression that private groups were not only important in understanding political life but an unalterable, eternal fact of life—that is, that collective, political action to bring America's groups into line with its ideals was neither possible nor desirable. In this seminal work can be seen the main ideological bias of American political science of the twentieth century.

In sociology, William Graham Sumner, Charles Horton Cooley, and W. I. Thomas helped establish the "late liberal" view that individuals are decision-making actors in groups (or situations); all three scholars made creative contributions to our understanding of small groups (and local situations). But on the whole, these thinkers helped to perpetuate obsolete ways of thinking. Their thought continued the focus on the individual-as-cause that has been such a marked feature of Anglo-American liberalism, and they sustained the traditional American emphasis on ideational causation. Collectively, they developed as the main American tradition in sociology a social psychology variously known today as functionalism, symbolic interactionism, phenomenology and ethnomethodology, social action, or exchange-rational choice theory.

What the work of America's mainstream knowledge elites amounted to was the professional investigation of society *in terms of its own assumptions.* Above all, their thought everywhere complacently assumed that American society was a naturally adaptive system and that the function of social research and thought was to learn more about its natural processes in order to help it along. Along with other segments of mainstream social science, and together with other professions and elites, America's knowledge elites were part of the larger technocratic meritocracy that emerged as the solution to the perceived diversity and instability of American society. In a broader sense, late liberalism accelerated the abandonment of the idea of a rational individual (which had formed the foundation of liberal democracy) by emphasizing the nonrational, emotional, and group nature of behavior. By stressing the need to study society professionally instead of asking that society be reorganized to promote rational individualism, the liberal social sciences were in effect endorsing the power structure of corporate capitalism.

As Ross has shown so brilliantly, all the anxieties generated by an industrial-urban system, beset by one problem after the other, helped feed a commitment to *scientism,* the faith that a professionalized science would lead America out of the temporary wilderness in which it found itself.[14] Nonetheless, the United States displayed considerable economic and political ferment in the decades that ended the nineteenth century and began the twentieth. In those years a strong minority radical conflict tradition, running counter to mainstream thinking, emerged—represented by, for example, Thorstein Veblen. All manner of other protests about the consequences of the disruptive industrial system occurred. There was even a huge outpouring of utopian literature, always a sign of a combination of social misery and an absence of political outlets.[15]

News, the News Media, and Journalists

The importance of information, or "news," to a complex society is apparent even in agrarian society. It was especially important to capitalist society, even in its opening centuries. Print journalism as we know it today emerged strongly during the nineteenth century, thanks to advances in printing technology. The major new developments from 1850 on can be listed:

1. Newspapers and magazines became national and helped in the development of a national economic market by carrying the advertising of national corporations and stories for a national political public.
2. Journalism slowly gave up the openly political style of reporting events and by the 1920s had adopted the ideal of objectivity. Here it followed currents in the other professions and science, but the result was blandness and inadvertent subjectivity, a politics that favored the status quo.
3. Journalism became highly concentrated from the latter part of the nineteenth century on, again following the basic trend of corporate capitalism. Editorials remained openly political and tended to favor business over labor, professions over clients, and nationalism over common sense.
4. Journalists began to specialize, as did all other professions. Matching journalism's specialization, on one hand, to the reality of the world and to the interests of the public, on the other, became a chronic problem.
5. Newspapers and magazines began to develop features to appeal to mass audiences even as they began to reflect the hierarchy of social class.

Sustaining Myths: The Garden of Eden and the Frontier

The nineteenth century believed that science would eventually demythologize society and usher in a bright new world of reason. This has not happened. Myths are still a very large part of how Americans communicate. Lester Kurtz argues that complex myths, such as the Garden of Eden story, can both manage conflict and help forge new boundaries or identities among conflicting groups.[16] The Garden of Eden myth holds two contrary images: a humanity free of social and physical constraints (freedom) and a fallen humanity punished by work and subjection to the authority of God. Kurtz shows how groups in Jewish, early Christian, and early American history used different aspects of this myth to promote their legitimacy, manage conflict, and establish new identities.

The Garden of Eden myth focuses on ultimate identity and downplays class, gender, political, and other issues. The myth helped to reduce internal divisions and establish the Jewish identity vis-à-vis the surrounding gentiles, as well as to quell the factionalism of the early Christians. In American history, Edenic imagery worked to increase, not reduce, conflicts; it was used to emancipate Americans from the Old World as well as from Calvinism and the corruptions of urbanism. The Eden myth was framed in agrarian terms by eastern literary figures and was combined with the frontier myth to create an image of a bright future of independent, free individuals. The Calvinist clergy fought this interpretation by emphasizing the Fall and the need to submit to the authority of God. But all parties debated the great question—Where is industrial capitalism taking America?—in terms of this familiar myth. By and large, Left liberals saw politics and government as a way to realize the freedom implied in Edenic imagery, while Right liberals tended to emphasize that government's role is to maintain order and punish deviants. But regardless of emphasis, the religious imagery of a Garden of Eden and divine revelation played an important role in the creation of the master American myth that the United States is a revealed society based on a pristine human nature.[17]

The cultural historian, Richard Slotkin, argues that the beliefs and values of a culture emanate from historical experience, not from mental archetypes or the biases of language. These beliefs and values are sometimes stated openly as creeds or constitutional declarations, but they also receive mythological expression. A myth, says Slotkin, is a highly compressed, emotion-laden story accepted by a population as somehow given and natural, a story that evokes a rich store of associations (to which one can add, but against which counterstories cannot easily arise). Myths arise from the historical experiences and salient concerns of a population. As instruments for coping with experience, they must bear some relation to reality; if circumstances change, the myths must be updated. They are not updated in the abstract, says Slotkin, but are framed by particular classes of people, who use them to mobilize populations in support of the dominant ideologies of societies.

Slotkin's three-volume work on America's "oldest and most characteristic myth," the myth of the frontier, traces the use of this master metaphor through the colonial period ("the white settler-state or colonial outpost of the European metropolis," roughly 1600–1820), the period of rapid economic growth (1815–1870), and the period since the 1890s.[18] These periods were marked by modernization difficulties, and the frontier myth helped cope with the unique features of each. The frontier myth of the colonial period emphasized the menace to civilization of the "savages" (Native Americans) and the need to defeat another outsider, the unjust authoritarian regime of England. The frontier came to signify separation, regression, and renewal through redemptive violence. The boundaries between evil and good were sharp; the stakes were total victory or total defeat. To project the survival and progress of white colonial settlements outward was to project outward with them the internal conflicts of white settlers and thereby avert class warfare. All this was aided by Protestant theology.

The frontier myth was updated to reflect the needs of the rapid and novel economic growth from 1815 to 1870. As we saw with the Garden of Eden, a myth can support different political positions. The Jefferson ideal of a nation of freeholding farmers was supported both by the idea and the opportunity of westward expansion and "bonanza" economics. But the myth was used primarily by those who wanted to wed the resources of the West to the industrial East without interference from the masses. The reality of westward expansion was a corporate capitalism able to amass the capital, technology, and organizational skill to link the factories of the East and Midwest to the natural resources of the rest of the continent.

The frontier myth allowed all this to take place without contradicting the myth of democracy. The frontier did more than beckon all to new opportunities—the myth was used to misdefine the serious economic and political problems that had arisen by the 1870s, many of which revolved around freed slaves, immigrant workers, and Native Americans. These latter groups were resisting incorporation into the discipline of the corporation. Instead of open discussion and negotiation among equals and a link between progress and a wide dissemination of property, American elites used the frontier myth to invent a "savage war" against a combined set of lower-order beings: freed slaves, immigrant labor, and Native Americans. Combined with the ideology of social Darwinism, the new frontier myth became a central part of the legitimating ideology of corporate capitalism, the Progressive movement. Some historians have argued that the Jeffersonian version of the frontier myth was ended by the closing of the frontier in the 1890s (the Turner thesis). But while other academics have been occupied with Turner's thesis, Slotkin has argued that the frontier myth concocted by Theodore Roosevelt to assert corporate ideology not only against domestic "savages" but against those outside was far more important.

Slotkin's focus on the use of communication technology to establish and transmit each version of the frontier myth is a particularly valuable part of his analysis. By the late nineteenth century, a huge outpouring of popular culture, made possible by new communication technology, had enabled American power groups to envelop the American population, not only in updated versions of the frontier metaphor but in a wide array of myths.[19] Throughout, Slotkin emphasizes, elites made political use of myth, and myth played a role in defining and establishing the American nation-state as it struggled to become an independent society, grow into a highly concentrated corporate colossus, commit various imperialist acts, and cope with boom and depression (1920–1940), the Second World War, the Cold War, and the Vietnam War.[20] The surge of popular culture that occurred in the late nineteenth century has become a flood (for a full analysis, see chapter 8).

Legitimating Imperialism: Ethnographic Exhibitions, the Novel, and Anthropology

The enhanced transportation-communication capability of the West opened up the world generally to European imperialism as early as the fifteenth century. But much of the planet was still outside the reach of European powers as late as the nineteenth century, a state of affairs that would soon end. As the French moved to gobble up parts of Africa, there appeared in France from the 1870s through 1900 a continuous series of ethnographic exhibitions. These were private operations that catered to the public's thirst for entertainment. By and large, these exhibitions painted a false and unfavorable picture of Africans, establishing, in effect, racist and imperialist attitudes among the French masses.[21] The same took place in other European nations as well.

Significant portions of the Western novel, perhaps especially in Great Britain, also furthered imperialism by establishing a mythology about the undeveloped parts of the planet.[22] Western social science, especially anthropology, also helped promote imperialism. Though the major thrust of anthropology was antiracist, its latent thrust was to justify imperialism under the guise of scientific objectivity. The general indictment of anthropology is that during its early and maturing professional stages it explored and reported on the outer world not objectively, as it claimed, but in terms of the sociopolitical concerns that anthropologists acquired as members of their home countries. The use of Western ideas, values, and concerns, which varied depending on changing social conditions at home, yielded deeply biased pictures of the non-Western world. This pattern has been richly documented by Kuklick's history of the most developed national anthropology, that of Great Britain.[23]

British anthropology was explicitly connected to the political concerns of the British upper classes from the early nineteenth century on. It engaged in all traditional questions of liberal social theory. What is legitimate political authority? How does change occur? What are the rights and duties of individuals? It offered itself as a way to make reform at home and the management of colonies easier. The general thrust of its scholarship varied with Britain's fortunes. As Britain prospered in the early to middle nineteenth century, anthropology saw progress as a universal law, of which primitive peoples were a part. By World War I, British optimism had declined with the decline of its economic fortunes. As political turmoil at home increased and the British masses increased their demands, British anthropology separated the idea of economic growth and the good life. The non-Western world now represented a good life without a growing material base. During the 1920s and 1930s British functionalist anthropology crystallized, thanks especially to A. R. Radcliffe-Brown (1881–1955) and Bronislaw Malinowski (1884–1942). The school of Functionalism adopted the concept of culture as a fundamental process of social control and stability through custom (mores). Functionalism redefined individuals to make them part of a functioning whole; because faith in progress had been abandoned, Functionalism abandoned history. Kuklick suggests that since World War II, anthropology's major new contribution to knowledge has been its discovery of its own biased history.[24]

Advertising and the Construction of a New Social Order

The advertising of one's wares and services is an integral part of a market economy and polity. It represents communication between sellers and buyers, and between candidates and voters, who are strangers to each other. American advertising goes back to the prerevolutionary eighteenth century, when significant advances in forms and techniques occurred. Its fortunes followed the contours of American capitalism. By the second half of the nineteenth century, advertising consisted of both words and art, and it appeared in many forms: outdoor signs, newspapers, directories, magazines. Between 1850 and the 1920s, advertising as we know it today emerged in tandem with the onrush of the corporate economy. Major corporations used advertising to establish their names and products on a national level, thus helping to undermine localism. National magazines, such as *Harper's* and *Saturday Evening Post,* and mail-order catalogs by Montgomery Ward and Sears Roebuck led the way. Needless to say, the U.S. Post Office (along with the railroad) played an important role in tying the nation together, not least through the delivery of catalogs and goods representing the orientation of manufacturers to a continental market.

Norris argues that advertising helped further economic concentration by promoting mass consumption. The old advertising had simply informed people about products; the new advertising was designed to create wants beyond the necessities of life. To accomplish its mission, advertising associated consumption with the American Dream. One of its main strategies in this regard was to model consumption on middle-class values, thus catering to the widespread hunger among Americans to rise above the working class. Norris ends his analysis by asserting that while advertising is not all-powerful, it can help solve social problems, including environmental problems, if it is part of a well-planned campaign.[25]

Stuart Ewen's analysis[26] of the development of modern advertising is far more critical than Norris's. Ewen associates advertising with a conscious attempt by business and allied thinkers to construct a new social order. Business needed to sell the products that corporate capitalism had begun to spew forth. But this was only part of a larger set of problems confronting property owners in the latter part of the nineteenth century. Workers with rural backgrounds, whether native-born or immigrant, were not readily conforming to factory work. Neither scientific management, coercion, nor the factory experience was working. Mass consumption was seen as having more purposes than simple disposing of the fruits of mass production; it was also a way to build a reliable labor force. The male would become dependent on the wage income needed to consume and eventually become resigned to the loss of craft skills and economic autonomy. All this was seen as part of transforming the American family from a production to a consumption unit.

Advertising eagerly responded to the task. Labor outside the home needed to be made legitimate; the male as patriarch had to give way to the worker who brought home income; it was business that should determine how people should live. In turn, women were to become a civilizing force, administering the home according to up-to-date principles and using modern products. Youth too was a legitimate target of advertising in the creation of a new social order. Youth not only had special consumption needs but lacked the obsolete values of the old society and could help bring about the new consumption-oriented family.

To further consumption, says Ewen, advertising instilled fear by publicizing the world's many menaces and at the same time offered protection against them (the reader will recall that the developing professions were doing the same thing—for the same pattern in journalism, see chapter 7). To further consumption, advertising insinuated that people should separate themselves from others as well as from their past; it did so by offering both specialized and standardized products. Leaders of corporate America (along with many others) also saw a need to Americanize immigrants who had brought their preindustrial values with them to America. Advertising was used by business to coerce the foreign-language press to accept the economic and political direction of business and to refrain from publishing contrary views.

The business world consciously sought to turn its perspective into a universal truth, continues Ewen, even as it used advertising to hide the truth of the factory system (the loss of skills, the domination of work and daily life by the clock) and to promote a way of consuming that could hide the fact that one was a worker. Mass consumption was clearly seen by business as a way to gain control by controlling antisocial impulses and anticapitalist sentiments and beliefs (class politics, socialism, Bolshevism). A wide choice of consumer goods would become in itself America's essential political process, as consumers in effect voted for their favorite corporations. All this would be part of a larger process of co-opting the demands of resisters to corporate capitalism. Resisters wanted to use industrial progress for human betterment while also preserving worker autonomy and control, values that were in fundamental conflict with corporate capitalism.

Business leaders, in keeping with leaders in education, psychology, and the social sciences, stressed building a new social order[27] based on facts, by which they meant knowledge—that is, a world of truth with no conflict. The facts they were interested in, says Ewen, were those of mass production, and the facts they ignored were those of craft traditions, traditional family values, rural lifestyles, communal self-sufficiency, and local popular culture.

Ewen concludes by arguing that while the new corporate capitalism was established in the 1920s, its real development got under way in the 1950s after the interruptions of the Great Depression and World War II. Writing in 1976, Ewen cited developments that foreshadowed the ubiquitous sway of commerce that was coming. For example, radio and television, which had previously stopped broadcasting at 10 P.M., began to stay on the air around the clock; the idea that there was "time and space inappropriate for commercial penetration began to vanish."

In any case, by the opening decades of the twentieth century, advertising, augmented by national radio networks, was a fully established adjunct of corporate capitalism. By the 1920s, it was ready to do its part in inaugurating the era of mass consumption, using what are now familiar techniques:

> Identification of unique qualities of given products (even if in fact there were none)
> Repetition to establish brand names
> Association of a product with values other than the product.

By the 1920s advertising had clearly gone beyond being informative and was associating capitalist production and consumption with happiness and the rest of America's values. By the 1920s it was also offering images that substituted (at least until purchase) for the actual satisfaction of the products and services themselves. It had also helped to legitimate the connection of income with consumption—that is, widely differing levels of class consumption.

Well before television augmented the power of advertisers to deceive the public, serious charges were leveled at advertising. As early as 1936, Kenner listed nine unethical or illegal advertising practices:

1. Misleading statements implying value or service not in the product;
2. misleading suggestions (not founded on science) that products could cure diseases or enhance health and beauty;
3. misinterpretation of scientific facts;

4. invasion of privacy or violation of decency;
5. dubious testimonials;
6. misleading price comparisons;
7. predatory price-cutting and baits;
8. unproven sales claims; and
9. unfair attacks on competitors.[28]

Advertising contributes in various ways to the substantial and growing divorce between American symbolic culture and historical reality. We have already pointed to a divorce from reality in education, professionalism, journalism, and to the prevalence of America's mythology of the Garden of Eden and the frontier in popular culture and politics. In later chapters, we will continue to outline how mainstream American social science helped to forge a fictitious view not only of communication but of American society and the rest of the world. All this is raised here in the context of advertising because many of the deep criticisms of American culture in the latter part of the twentieth century by Marxist theorists (for example, Herbert Marcuse) and postmodernist theorists (for example, Jean Baudrillard) would focus on consumerism as their takeoff points.

Advertising in this formative period also embraced racist, gender, and age biases in its depiction of reality—or rather, it used existing biases because they conformed to public ones. These biases still exist, despite the rise of significant antibias movements. Incidentally, the underrepresentation of male and female African Americans in both print and television advertising bears no relation to white audience preferences—whites have no negative feelings about the use of black models. Women are still depicted in advertising primarily in feminine roles. They are still used to sexualize commodities. They are still used to uphold unrealistic standards of beauty for women. Corporate control over advertising is being matched by a control over content, and even determined publishers have been unable to break the trend; Gloria Steinem's account of *MS* magazine's losing struggle with advertisers is a case in point.[29]

Advertising soon led to marketing. Profiting from the growth of empirical research and the use of statistical sampling in the 1920s and 1930s, advertising firms were able to construct campaigns for selling things with a certain degree of success. From that time on, messages to consumers were tailored to demographic targets, especially with respect to income, age, and sex. The success of advertising in these early years developed pressures on the media that blossomed at the end of the century. Media became heavily dependent on advertising revenues, and businesses paid a premium for media content aimed at specialized audiences. Thus, both in advertising and media content, business values came emphatically first.

Political advertising is business control in another guise. Political advertising was clearly evident as early as colonial days, though of course its first boom period occurred only with the introduction of mass suffrage after 1850. Political advertising was later augmented by radio, but its new heyday emerged with television. Regardless of the communication technology employed, however, the messages have been similar—populist, antipolitical, patriotic, and personal, as far away from being informative, deliberate, or an invitation to participate interactively in public policy as possible. One can easily speculate that James Madison would agree with contemporary Marxists and postmodern critics in this regard. (For a fuller discussion of contemporary political advertising, see chapter 5; for the failure of the news media, foundations, and think tanks to promote democracy, see chapter 7; for current antidemocratic trends in advertising, see chapter 9.)

Organized, Civil, and Popular Religions

America's religions are extremely diverse. While the United States is overwhelmingly Christian, there are deep divisions among Protestant, Roman Catholic, and Eastern Orthodox Christians. Each of these in turn is diversified in terms of doctrine, economic level, ethnicity, and often race. Jews are the largest non-Christian religious group, followed closely by Muslims, and both are also internally diversified. In addition, the United States has small numbers of Buddhists, Native American religions, and exotic cults of various kinds. The main reasons for this diversity are immigration, slavery, conquest, national expansion, and deep economic diversification and inequality.

The rationale for establishing a capitalist society (the liberal nation-state) in the United States was supplied, to a large extent, by Protestantism. A society based on the free individual was not an appealing prospect. Individuals are likely to choose self-interest over the social good, likely to quarrel rather than work in harmony. Protestantism reconciled the public good with the free individual by assuming that individuals were in service to God. It declared the New World the Promised Land, Protestant New Englanders the Chosen People, and society to be a covenant at once among believers and between believers and God. The affinity between the Protestant worldview and the liberalism of Jefferson and Madison is apparent. In the years after the American Revolution, the Puritan image of society was secularized—or perhaps better said, liberalism was sacralized. The tension between religion and secular society remained, but it was transmuted, by and large, into the service of liberalism, providing what one author calls a "Christian industrialism."[30] Eventually, the free individual was reconciled with social order and the welfare of society, not only by Providence but by the providential market.

The wedding of religion and liberalism eventually became what Bellah has called a *civil religion,* a celebration of American institutions using vague, nondenominational religious terminology.[31] Through its civil religion, the United States seeks to identify itself with both the natural and the supernatural worlds. Through civil religion much about the United States passes beyond conscious thought into that which is taken for granted.

Civil religion has a number of sources. Christianity supplied the concept of a single God with special plans for the United States. The early secular leaders of the republic turned this into deism and evoked the concept of a concerned God to buttress the American social order. The Civil War spurred the development of civil religiosity. Memorial Day, Arlington National Cemetery and local cemeteries, and a variety of public monuments imparted sacredness to the Civil War. Today, Presidents Day, Veterans Day, the Fourth of July, and Memorial Day celebrate America and promote solidarity. American exceptionalism rests in large part on the belief of Americans that God has specially favored them and their way of life.

Civil religion, then, is a pervasive auxiliary to secular institutions, a celebration and reinforcement of the American way of life. Public bodies and artifacts (for example, legislatures, courtrooms, coins) and public occasions of all sorts, from presidential inaugurations to baseball games, evoke the sanction of the divine. Americans are the most religious of all the industrial nations, on the bases of church attendance and stated beliefs in God and an afterlife, but it is clear that Americans do not take religion seriously enough to let it interfere much with the pursuit of liberal (secular) values. What Americans worship, in short, is Americanism.

Interesting and important trends in contemporary religion are the decline in the membership of established middle and upper-class churches (and a general decline in attendance in those churces, which is much lower than is believed) and the simultaneous growth of fundamentalist religion and the proliferation of exotic religious and quasi-religious groups. Viewed in terms of power relations, the revival of informal, fundamentalist religion is a powerful force for conservatism. Conventional religion among the upper classes has long provided a justification for the status quo. The status quo, or protection of existing power relations, is also served by other religious expressions. Fundamentalist (evangelistic, pentecostal, revivalist) Christianity distracts the lower classes from the source of their troubles (the American system of social power) and focuses it on themselves. Well-organized fundamentalist religious denominations (most of them based in the South) promulgate a simple religion based on love and the need to surmount individual sin. The world's troubles, they argue, come from a sinful humanity, and the only way to escape them is to be born again. Behind this simple, soothing message are the forces of modern communication technology (radio, television, printing press, airlines, computer).

Religious developments since 1945 seem contradictory. On the one hand is the general decline of religion, and on the other (starting in the 1960s) is the revival of the pentecostal, total-commitment type of Christianity (and other religions). A sociological explanation encompassing both phenomena is possible. The period after 1945 was one of unprecedented prosperity. Those who rode the wave of American economic expansion either lost their religion or joined churches that expressed little tension with or criticism of the world. Those who failed during the growth of the American economy or were bypassed or threatened by it (especially in the industrializing South) joined (or established) sects that provided personal identity and comfort through religious certainty, fellowship, and world rejection.[32] Events abroad also unsettled Americans as modern communication technology brought home perceived threats to the American way of life, and the clash of rival gods and moralities.[33]

It is clear that religious commitment can act as a safety valve to release pressure on an overloaded society. Oppressed groups have a long history of finding solace in religion. The revival of fundamentalist Christianity is helping small-town, rural

Americans make the transition to world-market capitalism. But there is more to it than this. The sociologist of religion knows that religion often misdirects society's moral energies. Some fundamentalist religious groups call for a withdrawal from the world into spirituality, in effect allowing "burly sinners" (John Dewey's phrase) to have their way. Other fundamentalist groups want to cleanse society and (aided and abetted by right-wing political groups) are politically active. Their attempt at moral regeneration is appealing, but its significance is widely misunderstood. Movements to regenerate morally the world have been a conservative, even reactionary, force since at least the time of Cato.[34] Whether promoting complacency among the affluent, withdrawal from the world, or moral zeal, therefore, religion in the United States plays a considerable role in misdefining social problems ranging from abortion to taxes, and from economic policy to foreign policy.

Religion also misdirects America's moral and intellectual energies in another way. Beyond organized (supernatural) religion and beyond civil religion lies *popular* religion. Here power groups use religious motifs to help them model social processes. But while they use secular and even scientific language, the effect, more often than not, is to hide society from view.

Popular religion operates when worship, faith, and miracles occur but participants are not aware they are in church. In popular religion, religious themes permeate secular life, clothed in secular terms. The social sciences have long had a religious dimension. The concept of Providence was smuggled into economics during the eighteenth century to become the magical "market." The concept of a golden age (the Garden of Eden), the idea of heaven, and the idea of the Second Coming were transformed by the French Enlightenment into the liberal (capitalist) concepts of perfectibility and progress.[35] Popular religion is also found in America's family-centered holidays in which a diffused religiosity celebrates and supports family life. The mass (and elite) media are saturated with religious themes in secular garb. Recent decades have seen more than the usual number of supernatural thrillers, science-fiction morality plays, and disaster films in which inexplicable evil is overcome by individuals displaying faith and courage against great odds.

Peter Williams argues that there is a religious dimension throughout American culture.[36] Religious figures have achieved celebrity status through television, propagating a "middle-class common sense" and an "ecumenical moralism." The advice given by religious broadcasts is very similar to that given by "Dear Abby" and similar columns in the print media. Mass-circulation tabloids such as *National Enquirer* have recurring "religious" motifs: miracle cures, astrology and predictions about the future, lottery winners, and the worship of celebrities, individuals who "seem to live in a world of their own in which the rules that govern and restrict mortals are suspended." Popular religion has a powerful voice in the *Reader's Digest*. Williams finds a continuity between the *Digest* and the McGuffey *Readers* that were so influential in nineteenth-century education. In each, "a system of values derived from implicit religious assumptions is disseminated as an unspoken frame of reference which underlies all of the other aspects of culture and society that are dealt with explicitly."

Further, both are linked to the inspirational literature that has had such phenomenal success in the United States.

Reader's Digest is obsessed with order, according to Elzey.[37] It affirms the ordinary and accepts the social order, asking only that individuals adjust so that they can fit in. In the *Digest* an idealized social order is squared with its contradictions, not through intellectual analysis but through inspirational anecdotes or, to use the biblical term, parables. Medicine, science, and technology are good; failures are due to the defectiveness or evil of individuals; anyone who wants to can work. The police and the Federal Bureau of Investigation are good, because they uphold the law and public order, but the Internal Revenue Service and welfare programs, along with labor unions, communist and socialist countries, and a vague something called "Asia," are outside the normal and natural. The *Digest's* "unforgettable characters" turn out to be ordinary people who always manage to summon the inner strength needed to prevail against adversity. One can always find stories in which "the elements of violence, defeat, death, and persecution are blended in such a way that they become occasions for recollecting the timeless values and reaffirming the providential logic of history." Overall, concludes Elzey, "the presence of the invisible (and visible) Hand of Providence in the 'world's most popular magazine' marks it as a work of Scripture, second only to the Bible in sales and influence. It is a religious text because it markets a distinctive and alluring picture of the logic of American life."

National Events, Holidays, Monuments, and Artifacts

The enhanced communication capability of the nineteenth century helped complete the creation of nation-states and gave added fire and focus to nationalism. Everywhere, governing elites sought to identify the masses with pieces of geography, imbue them with sacred myths about their peoplehood, and get them to believe that the economic and political institutions that the elites had created were anchored in the nature of things. Nationalistic emotions and beliefs are highly self-centered and are invariably defined in opposition to other national identities, thus making communication among peoples exceedingly difficult.

The creation of nation-states and the development of emotions and beliefs about society as a special cluster of cosmic values ensconced on a special piece of geography occurred at many levels. It involved the family, religion, local government, voluntary groups, and public education as well as national political parties and government. During the nineteenth century all the countries of the West developed a host of symbolic justifications and rituals for promoting social cohesion and institutional legitimacy.[38] The British monarchy, long held in low regard, was removed from politics and given ceremonial duties; it soon rose in public esteem. The United States also developed many civic ceremonies, national holidays, and public monuments to celebrate itself, especially its wars. Also, as Hobsbawn points out, this was also the era of mass sports and the start of the modern Olympics. Great events in the emergence of society were recorded and celebrated. A host of physical entities evoked society's name and glories—the flag, coins, currency, and public buildings and monuments.

The governing classes of complex societies have long used buildings, monuments, and defined spaces to objectify their subjective definitions of the world. Palaces, temples, tombs, statues, and public arenas and plazas are the more obvious ways in which meanings about power, hierarchy, justice, and legitimacy are established and communicated on a daily basis. No less obvious are towering corporation headquarters, marketplaces, residential areas, museums, theaters, and the like.

Edelman has used this idea to discern how meaning-infused buildings, monuments, and spaces (objects that have no intrinsic meaning) communicate and reinforce social hierarchies in contemporary complex society.[39] The Capitol, White House, Supreme Court building, and all their inner trappings, evoke a common political heritage, while the FBI building and the Pentagon are massive monumental structures that connote defiance of disorder. Edelman also calls attention to the plush offices that members of the upper classes enter when they deal with government, in contrast to the squalid welfare and unemployment offices experienced by the lower classes.

The nation-state received additional support during the twentieth century, much of it as the implicit consequence of furthering family and business interests. Along with industrialization, the growing movement by women into the labor force, and perceived threats to family stability, the United States developed an elaborate cycle of family celebrations. Mother's Day was deliberately created, along with Father's Day and more recently Grandparents' Day. Significantly, many of our religious and national holidays have been transformed into family celebrations having special reference to the role of women as mothers and wives. Religious holidays such as Easter, Halloween, and Christmas, and such national holidays as Presidents Day, Memorial Day, Independence Day, Veterans Day, and Thanksgiving have all been transformed into family-centered holidays.[40] Needless to say, most of these holidays are also occasions for heightened commercial activity.

Nationalism received added force with the advent of radio and film. Television has now made it possible for the public to participate directly in events of national importance. In a fascinating study of "media events," Dayan and Katz identify the positive functions of the "live broadcasting of history."[41] In a frankly neo-Durkheimian spirit, Dayan and Katz argue that broadcasting such events as Anwar al-Sadat's journey to Jerusalem, the Olympics or Superbowl, presidential debates, John F. Kennedy's funeral, the pope's visit to Poland, royal weddings and coronations, and the Watergate hearings serve multiple functions: they promote "mechanical solidarity" by giving all a shared experience; they define society in ideal terms by highlighting one or some of its central values; and they (perhaps) promote pluralism (the liberal world of equality, achievement, and rule of law). The scripts of these events, Dayan and Katz argue, fall into three categories, all exemplifying "turning points" in the career of a hero: the first serves to "qualify" the hero (the Contest), the second "shows the hero reaching beyond human limits" (Conquest), and the third recognizes and glorifies the hero (Coronation). The authors suggest that these events "can be considered enactments of Max Weber's traditional, rational-legal, and charismatic forms of legitimating authority."

Dayan and Katz acknowledge that their argument about the positive effects of the live broadcasting of history is not based on empirical research and ask us to consider their work as a set of hypotheses (an appendix situates their analysis in the tradition of communication research). Their book is carefully and elegantly written, and filled with insights; its main defect is that it somehow manages to depoliticize what its authors know to be highly political events. Their functional analysis of live media events contrasts sharply with the conflicting account by Chaney of three major events in Great Britain: the victory parade of 1946, the Festival of Britain in 1951, and the coronation of 1953. Chaney argues that all three events ignored the history-making victory of the Labor Party that had taken place at the same time, a victory that had established a socialist government with a clear mandate to restructure British society.[42] Media events undoubtedly do what Dayan and Katz say, but how much different their book would have been had Weber (or Marx), not Durkheim, been their guiding spirit? It might have become a sociopolitical analysis that asks how media events legitimate illegitimate (obsolete, contradictory, inept) power structures.

NOTES

1. For the transition from the proprietary-competitive market stage to the corporate-administrated stage of American capitalism, see Martin Sklar, *The Corporate Reconstruction of American Capitalism, 1890–1916: The Market, the Law, and Politics* (New York: Cambridge University Press, 1988).

2. William G. Roy, *Socializing Capital: The Rise of the Large Industrial Corporation in America* (Princeton, N.J.: Princeton University Press, 1997).

3. For in-depth studies of creative administration by various American corporations and its role in the success of American capitalism, see Alfred D. Chandler Jr., *Strategy and Structure: Chapters in the Industrial Enterprise* (Cambridge, Mass.: MIT Press, 1962) and *The Visible Hand: The Managerial Revolution in American Business* (Cambridge, Mass.: Harvard University Press, 1977).

4. William Appleman Williams, *The Tragedy of American Diplomacy*, rev. ed. (New York: World, 1962).

5. *The Transformation of American Law, 1780–1860* (Cambridge, Mass.: Harvard University Press, 1977).

6. Christopher L. Tomlins, *The State and Unions: Labor Relations, Law, and the Organized Labor Movement in America, 1880–1960* (New York: Cambridge University Press, 1985). The history of trade unionism in the United States since 1960 is one of decline since the 1980s. The United States undermines labor's power by maintaining surplus labor in a variety of ways: toleration of significant levels of unemployment; antilabor rulings by a pro-business National Labor Relations Board; union busting and hostility by business (expressed especially by neutralizing strikes with replacement workers, a tactic made possible by threats to relocate and the existence of surplus labor); the globalization of American capital (which pits American labor against labor in the developing world and sends American technology

abroad, lowering the skill and income levels of Americans); opening American markets (often to serve foreign policy objectives) much more widely than does any other Western industrial society (which puts American businesses and labor at perpetual risk); reduction of social services, which, combined with low wages for males and marital breakups, forces many women into the labor market; and allowing the entry of large numbers of legal and illegal foreign unskilled, skilled, and professional workers.

7. For a valuable in-depth study of the numerous thinkers who helped update American exceptionalism in the light of industrialization, see Dorothy Ross, *The Origins of American Social Science* (New York: Cambridge University Press, 1991).

8. For an insightful sociology of the railroad, see Wolfgang Schivelbusch, *The Railway Journey: The Industrialization of Time and Space in the 19th Century* (Berkeley, Calif.: University of California Press, 1986; originally published in 1977).

9. See Daniel W. Rossides, *Social Stratification: The Interplay of Class, Race, and Gender*, 2nd. ed. (Upper Saddle River, N.J.: Prentice Hall, 1997), chap. 9.

10. Ernest Pascarella and Patrick T. Terenzini, *How College Affects Students: Findings and Insights from Twenty Years of Research* (San Francisco: Jossey-Bass, 1991).

11. Burton J. Bledstein, *The Culture of Professionalism: The Middle Class and the Development of Higher Education in America* (New York: Norton, 1976).

12. Donald S. Napoli, *Architects of Adjustment: The History of the Psychological Profession in the United States* (Port Washington, N.Y.: Kennikat, 1981), especially chap. 2. Also see Michael M. Sokal, "James McKeen Cattell and American Psychology in the 1920s," in *Explorations in the History of Psychology in the United States*, ed. Josef Brozek (Lewisburg, Pa.: Bucknell University Press, 1984), 273–323. Loren Baritz, *The Servants of Power: A History of the Use of Social Science in Industry* (Middletown, Conn.: Wesleyan University Press, 1960), focuses on how industrial psychologists served the interests of corporations.

13. Arthur Bentley, *The Process of Government* (Chicago: University of Chicago Press, 1908).

14. Dorothy Ross, *The Origins of American Social Science* (New York: Cambridge University Press, 1991), chap. 10.

15. For a valuable analysis, see Kenneth Roemer, *The Obsolete Necessity: America in Utopian Writing, 1888–1900* (Kent, Ohio: Kent State University Press, 1976).

16. Lester R. Kurtz, "Freedom and Domination: The Garden of Eden and Social Order," *Social Forces* 58 (December 1979): 443–65.

17. For the role of religious imagery in the politics and theory of the West, see Michael Walzer, *Exodus and Revolution* (New York: Basic Books, 1985).

18. Richard Slotkin, *Regeneration through Violence: The Mythology of the American Frontier, 1600–1860* (Middletown, Conn.: Wesleyan University Press, 1973); *The Fatal Environment: The Myth of the Frontier in the Age of Industrialization* (New York: Athenaeum, 1985); and *Gunfighter Nation: The Myth of the Frontier in Twentieth-Century America* (New York: Athenaeum, 1992).

19. For a fascinating analysis (in which a superhuman hero saves the threatened community) of the Edenic myth in American popular culture, see Robert Jewett and John Shelton Lawrence, "The Birth of a National Monomyth," in *The American Monomyth*, 2nd ed. (Lanham, Md.: University Press of America, 1988), chap. 9.

20. Richard Slotkin, "The Significance of the Frontier Myth in American History," in *Gunfighter Nation: The Myth of the Frontier in Twentieth-Century America* (New York: Athenaeum, 1992), 1–26.

21. William Schneider, *An Empire for the Masses: The French Popular Image of Africa, 1870–1900* (Westport, Conn.: Greenwood, 1982).

22. Jonah Raskin, *The Mythology of Imperialism: Kipling, Conrad, Forster, Lawrence, Carey* (New York: Random House, 1971).

23. Henrika Kuklick, *The Savage Within: The Social History of British Anthropology, 1885–1945* (New York: Cambridge University Press, 1991).

24. For valuable essays, providing concrete details about the rise of Western ideas (for example, such Western legal concepts as rights, duties, and property), as well as an emphasis on how Westerners, including anthropologists, themselves created the tribal identities they claimed existed and changed their ways of formulating their depiction of colonies to suit economic interests and to create the illusion that the gap between colony and home country was narrowing, see George W. Stocking Jr., ed., *Colonial Situations: Essays on the Contextualization of Ethnographic Knowledge* (Madison: University of Wisconsin Press, 1991).

25. James D. Norris, *Advertising and the Transformation of American Society, 1865–1920* (Westport, Conn.: Greenwood, 1990).

26. Stuart Ewen, *Captains of Consciousness: The Social Roots of the Consumer Culture* (New York: McGraw-Hill, 1976).

27. It should be noted that the "new social order" envisioned by business and symbolic elites was really a movement from small-property to large-property capitalism. In this connection, see Martin Sklar, *The Corporate Reconstruction of American Capitalism, 1890–1916: The Market, the Law, and Politics* (New York: Cambridge University Press, 1988).

28. H. J. Kenner, *The Fight for Truth in Advertising* (New York: Round Table, 1936), xvii.

29. Sut Thally, "Image-Based Culture: Advertising and Popular Culture"; Robert Goldman, "Constructing and Addressing the Audience as Commodity"; Gloria Steinem, "Sex, Lies, and Advertising"; and Jean Killbourne, "Beauty and the Beast of Advertising"; all in *Gender, Race, and Class in Media: A Text-Reader*, ed. Gail Dines and Jean M. Humez (Thousand Oaks, Calif.: Sage, 1995), selections 10, 11, 15, 16.

30. For a fascinating picture of the organization of an early industrial town in Pennsylvania and of the role of Christianity in helping the propertied classes fight socialism and in providing religious support for the expansion and consolidation of American capitalism, see Anthony F. C. Wallace, *Rockdale* (New York: Knopf, 1978).

31. Robert N. Bellah, "Civil Religion in America," *Daedalus* 96 (Winter 1967): 1–27.

32. For background articles, see Charles Y. Glock and Robert N. Bellah, eds., *The New Religious Consciousness* (Berkeley: University of California Press, 1976).

33. For the impact of world (and domestic) development on the revival of religion in the American South and Southwest, see Robert Wuthnow, "World Order and Religious Movements," in *Studies of the Modern World-System*, ed. Albert Bergesen (New York: Academic, 1980), chap. 4.

34. Barrington Moore, *Social Origins of Dictatorship and Democracy: Lord and Peasant in the Making of the Modern World* (Boston: Beacon, 1966), 491–96.

35. Marxism has its own version of these themes, but it requires a separate treatment.

36. Much of the following is indebted to Peter W. Williams, *Popular Religion in America: Symbolic Change and the Modernization Process in Historical Perspective* (Englewood Cliffs, N.J.: Prentice Hall, 1980), esp. chap. 4.

37. Wayne Elzey, "The Most Unforgettable Magazine I've Ever Read: Religion and Social Hygiene in 'The Reader's Digest,'" *Journal of Popular Culture* 10 (Summer 1976): 181–90.

38. Eric Hobsbawn, "Mass Producing Traditions: Europe, 1870–1914," in *The Invention*

of Tradition, ed. Eric Hobsbawn and Terence Ranger (New York: Cambridge University Press, 1983), chap. 7.

39. Murray Edelman, *Space and Social Order* (Madison: University of Wisconsin Institute for Research on Poverty, 1978).

40. For an interesting discussion, see Theodore Caplow et al., *Middletown Families: Fifty Years of Change and Continuity* (Minneapolis: University of Minnesota Press, 1982), chap. 10.

41. Daniel Dayan and Elihu Katz, *Media Events: The Live Broadcasting of History* (Cambridge, Mass.: Harvard University Press, 1992).

42. David Chaney, "A Symbolic Mirror of Ourselves: Civic Ritual in Mass Society," in *Media, Culture, and Society: A Critical Reader,* ed. Richard Collins et al. (Newbury Park, Calif.: Sage, 1986), 247–63.

II

COMMUNICATION, MEDIA, AND CONTEMPORARY AMERICAN SOCIETY

observers have even gone so far as to call the economy monolithic, but this idea should probably be resisted.

Is There a Monolith Called Business?

The United States is characterized by an oligarchic economy, but it cannot be conceived in the same terms as in the agrarian oligarchies of the past. A feudal elite was made up mostly of hereditary landlords, though there is some differentiation. There were great landlords and smaller landlords; some of the nobility specialized in government or military service, others in religion or scholarship. On the whole, however, a serf or slave faced a monolithic entity, the nobility.

Power in an industrial society is different. Aside from abstract capitalist values and beliefs, there is no all-embracing business interest that unites small manufacturers and big manufacturers, small banks and big banks, or small anything versus big anything. The economy also has divergent interest groups within big manufacturing—for example, steel, aluminum, plastics, glass, and lumber all compete for the same customer. The same is true of big service industries, such as railroads, airlines, and trucking companies. Small farmers do not have the same interests as the large agribusinesses. Established firms, big or little, are threatened by the emergence of firms riding the crests of new technologies—for example, the "free" television networks versus cable, direct satellite television, and home videotape machines. Some businesses fear foreign competition (for example, textile, automobile, and steel manufacturers) and want protection, while some do not (manufacturers of medical technology and entertainment programs).

In general, then, the economic and professional groups of capitalist society are neither united nor homogeneous. This does not mean that America is a pluralist society. Nor does it mean that the state is autonomous or that politicians and civil servants do not make policies on behalf of the upper classes. It is clear that when its interests are threatened, business can mobilize and reassert its dominance. The United States is and has been a thoroughly capitalist society, which means that labor and the economically and politically weak receive benefits only after business and professional interests are satisfied. However, over the past half-century, perhaps especially in recent decades, something new may have occurred—American capitalism may be flourishing as never before, but American society may not be.

The Shift to a Service Economy

Communication technology has also furthered the seismic shift in the American economy from manufacturing to services. Manufacturing pushed farming aside during the nineteenth and early twentieth centuries, only to see the rise to prominence of the service sector. Services now make up a dominant portion of the gross national product; more than 70 percent of the labor force is engaged in providing them. The economy's shift to services has caused many dislocations, and it requires a major change in how we think of American capitalism. The rise of new occupations has put pressure on educational institutions to supply new programs and reorganize old ones. Changes in the nature of work mean that American youth must develop skills and aspirations that are vastly different from those of their parents.

The service sector has overshadowed the rest of the economy, but what exactly is it? Doctors and lawyers are certainly part of it. So are physicists and chemists, professors, economists, and public-policy analysts. The diverse economy also includes large numbers of "service professionals" who are better thought of as skilled workers: nurses, school teachers, computer programmers, police officers, and so on. It includes semiskilled clerical workers and salespeople, professional athletes, religious workers, elected officials, pilots, prostitutes, criminals, advertising personnel, designers, financial specialists, entertainers, journalists, hotel managers and workers, gambling casino workers, brokers and financial advisers, prison guards, workers in public relations and consulting firms, research workers, and so forth.

The Knowledge Society as Ideology

Some have referred to the shift to a service society as the rise of a "knowledge" or "information" society. Others have spoken of the decline of a "property-based" economy and the emergence of a "postindustrial" society. Some theorists (for example, Talcott Parsons) claim that a "managerial revolution" has occurred in which educated managers have replaced property owners as the central force in capitalism. The basic image proposed by postindustrial theorists is that of a knowledge-based society presided over by highly educated managers and professionals. But this image is faulty. Far from producing a knowledge-based economy, corporate capitalism gives every sign of separating the American people into a small group of highly skilled workers and a huge mass of semiskilled and low-skilled ones. The facts about the American labor force are clear—highly educated professionals still make up only a small percentage of the American labor force, and there is no indication that their relative size is growing. It is a mistake, therefore, to think of the service-centered economy as one characterized by the reduction of drudgery and the growth of challenging mental work. Indeed the service economy has many deeply embedded inefficient, ineffective, wasteful, harmful sectors—for example, health care, law enforcement, the military, education, advertising, political campaigning, and gambling. It is certainly premature to think that the United States is under the direction of educated elites who know what they are doing or where they are headed.

The idea of a postindustrial society shares a basic kinship with the computer movement and technocratic liberalism (see below, "Computer Movements as Technocratic Liberalism"), as well as the belief that society is leaving behind the period of ascription, property, factory work, and centralized power and is entering an era of achievement, rational administration, strategic management, and a pluralist power structure. The Internet in particular has reinforced the fiction of the United States as a postindustrial, knowledge-based society. If being a knowledgeable or educated person means knowing what is needed to deal with the complexities of the contemporary world (as opposed to mere years of schooling or degrees), then the United

American corporations, accelerated after World War II. A new phenomenon, *direct investment* (ownership of businesses in other countries, developed and developing), replaced colonial imperialism. This process has itself evolved into a new stage—whereas earlier the multinational corporation had been *polycentric* (operating in a number of countries), it has now become *geocentric* (operating on a global basis).

The last few decades have seen a third trend. International trade in services (financial, law, consulting, accounting, insurance, brokerage, entertainment and news, tourism) has outstripped trade in goods, commodities, and raw materials. While it is not clear that world trade has a bigger share of the American economy than in the past (see below), much of what is new and unsettling about world trade arises from the fact that it now affects every sector of the economy.

The fourth trend, in large part a consequence of the other trends, is the growing difficulty that governments have had in understanding, let alone regulating and tax-ing, the world economy (off-shore banking and free trade zones are only part of this problem).[6] The mobility of capital means that governments cannot control or even keep track of the astronomical sums of money that flow across national bound-aries—one and one half trillion dollars per day.

The U.S. economy has always been dependent on the movement across national boundaries of raw materials, processed consumer goods, capital goods, and various kinds of labor (at various times settlers, slaves, immigrants, illegal aliens, migratory labor). Today, the United States depends heavily on foreign trade to supply it with raw materials, inexpensive consumer goods, capital goods, and labor. In turn, it needs foreign markets in which to sell the products in which it is competitive (food, lumber, tobacco, airplanes, computers, medical technology, arms, mass media, and entertainment materials). On the whole, it has been buying more from abroad than it is selling, and its now chronic trade deficit has made it a debtor nation, a situation bearable only because other nations have even more serious economic problems.

American economists and policy makers, unable to understand the international economy any more than they understand the domestic economy, simply espouse a free trade philosophy, the counterpart on the international scene of domestic laissez-faire economics. They have been even less able to understand the rapid evolution of geocentric corporations (also referred to as "global" or "stateless" corporations). In an astute analysis with an insightful title, Robert Reich has distinguished between American-owned companies that conduct much of their business abroad (including high-technology manufacturing and research and development) and foreign-owned companies in the United States that employ mostly Americans and do high-technol-ogy manufacturing and research and development in the United States. The latter category (for example, Philips and Thomson Electronics, Honda), says Reich, is bet-ter for America's economic competitiveness than the former (for example, IBM, Whirlpool, Texas Instruments).[7]

The World Trade Organization has tended to enforce free trade even if the activi-ties run counter to domestic environmental laws.[8] So far, even explicit provisions about labor standards and the environment in regional treaties—for example, the North American Free Trade Association (NAFTA)—have not been honored. The world-market economy also makes domestic politics difficult to understand. Foreign companies have domestic lobbyists who often make proposals good for the United States, while American interests make foreign-trade proposals that are good for foreign countries but not for the United States. The many and varied global corporations are also difficult to regulate or tax. An American corporation goes to Mexico to escape environmental laws, and its pollution drifts north, falling on the United States. The global mobility of capital allows it to avoid or even evade taxes and to operate in countries with substandard protection for workers. A Japanese plant in the United States exports to Europe and escapes European restrictions on Japanese cars. If a Japanese company manufactures VCR parts in Thailand, assembles in Malaysia and exports them to the United States, the transaction does not show up in U.S.-Japan trade accounts.

The international economy has had an important effect on the United States in that the flow of capital abroad means poorer jobs at home. It means that American labor is pitted against cheaper labor in other countries.[9] Mobile stateless companies move when confronted by labor unions. The new global economy means that educated foreigners can come to work in the United States (the brain drain) and that foreign students can study in the United States (approximately 20 percent of the undergraduate students at MIT are foreigners, and foreigners make up 25 percent of American graduate students). Since World War II the United States has legally permitted an average of three-quarters of a million immigrants, many of them skilled and professional workers, to enter the United States every year (for example, 25 percent of American hospital doctors are foreigners). Another quarter of a million enter illegally, many of them students or those with work visas. Even as business and higher education interests oppose labor-force planning, business demands the importation of cheaper skilled and professional labor. There is even a special visa program that brings in temporary (six years) professional labor (195,000 per year for 2001–2004), most of them for computer companies (which, critics say, are discharging or not hiring higher-priced American workers). This program also includes architects, engineers, professors, and so on. Also, of course, a great deal of professional work is done by foreigners for American companies abroad, and a growing amount is being done on the stateless Internet (for example, by computer scientists in India working directly for American companies at home and in other countries).

Free Trade (Globalization) as Ideology

It is accepted wisdom (unconscious presupposition) among most business and academic economists, the Republican Party and many Democrats, the federal government, and many think tanks and policy groups that rapid movement to greater free trade and full capital mobility, coupled with less government spending, privatization of public enterprises, better accounting, and the enforcement of contracts will mean economic growth and rising living standards for both developed and developing countries. The advent of the multinational corporation is seen as spearheading this movement toward a better world. That is, it will allow all countries to reap the benefits of comparative advantage, based on the idea that each country doing what it does best is good for all.

The reason all this is ideology (empty words serving power interests) is that the historical record flatly contradicts it. Economic growth has not lifted living standards in the past thirty years in the United States, and the same is true in the developing world, except in a few places that have ignored American ideology (the Asian economies that have raised living standards have done so by adopting government-led economic policies). Nonetheless, the United States, working alone and through the International Monetary Fund, is pushing hard for free trade and its ancillary supports. One significant aspect of America's mania for free trade has been its success in undermining public service media in the developed world and in blocking a more balanced and independent news media in the developing world.

Robert Gilpin, a mainstream analyst and a leading authority on the international economy, favors free trade. What separates him from the mainstream establishment is his knowledge. In a careful assessment of the literature, Gilpin argues that free trade does not exist globally—the bulk of trade takes place among the developed countries and a handful of developing nations. Second, no country, including the United States, permits free trade—there are many protections for domestic economies throughout the world, and no increase in free trade has occurred as a percentage of domestic economies over that which existed in the nineteenth century. Three, free trade increases are occurring regionally, not globally: the United States in North and South America; the European Union in Central Europe, Russia, and the Balkans; and Japan in Southeast and East Asia. Four, the international economy is deeply deficient in its political norms and procedures; there are no established rules governing trading, exchange rates, or capital movement. To work, the international economy needs fixed exchange rates, full capital mobility, and national autonomy in developing macroeconomic policy. These, says Gilpin, constitute a "trilemma," an "irreconcilable trinity." National economies are extremely diverse, and it is very difficult to forge agreements. Agreements on one or two are possible but not on three, because they work against each other. Five, the multinational corporation does not reign supreme above nations but behaves largely in terms of the economic and political interests of its home country. Actually, the multinational corporation uses other countries to achieve comparative advantages, and there has been a dramatic increase in intercorporate alliances across national boundaries, giving a new meaning to the term *competition.*

All in all, Gilpin says, there is no convergence toward the American model of capitalism (which, it should be remembered, is also far different in practice from its ideology). The pressures of international trade and competition, however, have helped to tip the scales against labor in the United States and have heightened pressure against labor in Japan and Europe (and, one might add, in Canada and other developed and developing nations).[10]

The term *globalization* became popular in the 1990s, but as the foregoing suggests, there is much misunderstanding about it. Commentators rightly point to the roles of computer communication and of new, fast, cheap transportation in fostering world trade. It is also true that more and more of the world has adopted capitalist ways. But claims that an integrated competitive world economy has emerged lack empirical support.[11] Trade in goods and services is not higher in comparison to gross domestic product (GDP) than in the past, if current prices (as opposed to misleading constant prices) are used. Foreign direct investment as a percentage of total investment is smaller than is thought and not much larger than in 1913. In analyzing investment abroad, it is difficult to distinguish between mergers and acquisitions, distribution and advertising networks, and investment in new productive facilities.

The number of firms that operate internationally has grown enormously, but claims that a small number of giant firms control big portions of world GDP are widely exaggerated. The top one hundred corporations produce 5 percent of the world's output, own less than 5 percent of the world's capital stock, and employ 1.4 percent of the world's paid labor force. The top two hundred firms generate only 10 percent of value-added production. There is little empirical evidence that integrated production (companies that use a number of countries to research, design, fabricate, and market a product) is a growing characteristic of the world economy. Intratrade among branches of a firm is substantial, but much of this trade may be by marketing subsidiaries rather than integrated production. Finally, cross-border lending and transactions in stocks and bonds have exploded in recent years, but much of this activity may be changes in portfolio distributions rather than new ownership of productive assets.

Sutcliffe and Glyn argue that exaggerated claims of globalization may have generated a sense of political impotence on the part of the Left, since globalization implies that only an international movement can counter a globalized capital and a de facto international state. Local and national politics are still important, they argue, though there is also a need to extend politics to the international arena. Actually, argues Ellen Meiksins Wood, the Left should take heart from globalization, because it is using up capitalism's last escape valve (the developing world) without eliminating its self-destroying contradictions.[12]

Resistance to globalization has increased in recent years. The vehement protests (that culminated in violence) at the World Trade Organization meeting in Seattle in 1999 revealed much more popular opposition to unregulated free trade than most had been aware of. There were more vehement street protests when the major developed countries held an economic summit in Genoa in 2001. A steady, more diffused resistance has occurred in the United States and elsewhere using various and ingenious forms of communication (for example, changing billboard messages, holding festivals on busy streets).[13]

All this raises the question of why globalization has become an all-purpose concept that permeates American public discourse, even though it lacks concrete definition. A probable answer is that globalization meshes well with America's other empty abstractions, especially its master myth of abstract progress through abstract economic growth. The latter continues strong despite mounting evidence that economic growth without social planning does not necessarily lead to higher living standards or solve social problems. American-style capitalism cannot exist without the mythology of abstract economic growth and its supporting ideas such as *free trade, competition, markets, smaller government, more savings,* and *more democracy* in developing countries. Globalization also has a kinship with the American frontier myth. With the fall of communism in the Soviet Union and the commitment by Communist China (and Vietnam) to the world market, the United States needed a new rallying cry. What better way to try to submerge internal differences based on class, race, ethnicity, gender, and region than to invoke the idea that the nation is confronted by capitalist challenges from abroad that only domestic capitalists know how to deal with? In a wider context, the main source of capitalism's power and legitimacy is its claim that it can provide economic growth and a rising standard of living. The ideology of globalization is a way to avoid having to deal with stagnant living standards in the West, declining living standards in most of the world, environmental degradation, an aging population at home that requires huge unproductive expenditures for its upkeep, large military expenditures that protect the grossly unequal status quo, and claims for better education, health care, housing, child care, and a redress for past mistreatment by minorities.

THE SHORTFALLS OF THE AMERICAN ECONOMY

American society believes in the potency and rationality of free markets (the free enterprise economic system, the efficacy of electoral markets, meritocratic educational-professional markets). In recent decades, questions have been raised about the ability of the overall market system to solve problems. Not only does the market economy not provide full employment, reduce poverty, absorb minorities, provide housing, food, and health care for all, or protect the environment, but over the past thirty years or more it has been unable, despite growth, to raise living standards. In addition, political markets appear stalemated and irrelevant, while education is now a many-sided failure.

The Failure to Provide Full Employment

The main economic and social problem facing the United States is the lack of full employment. So far, those who make economic (and political-social) policy have been unable to provide a stable growth environment for farmers and businesspeople, for workers, or for local, state, and federal governments. Like most official figures, the low unemployment rate of the late 1990s (between 4 percent and 5 percent) was a fiction. It included temporary workers without health or pension benefits and did not include "discouraged" workers, the millions who had given up looking for work. It also counted anyone who worked part-time as employed, seriously distorting our understanding of underemployment. American business now employs part-time workers, managers, and professionals, most without health or pension benefits, in large numbers (businesses are planning their labor needs precisely, thanks to the computer, even as they denounce social planning). As astute analysts have pointed out, unlike other capitalist countries, the United States "manages" its labor force by relying heavily on incarceration. America's low unemployment rate in the 1990s would be significantly higher if the 1.8 million Americans in prison (mostly able-bodied males, disproportionately black) were counted as unemployed.[14]

The main reason for America's high level of business failure and worker unemployment and underemployment is that America's elites have persuaded the rest of the country that inflation is a bigger problem than unemployment (inflation erodes the value of property, makes business planning difficult, and hurts creditors, as well as people on fixed incomes). But perhaps the main reason why America's elites are not interested in full employment is that to achieve it requires public planning and a reduction of their concentrated power.

Our Less-than-Useful Productivity Rate

The Index of Output Per Hour, or Productivity Rate, measures the output of the nonfarm private business sector. It is used as an indicator of efficiency, or ability to produce more without more input (capital, labor, raw materials). Increased efficiency makes possible a higher standard of living. Unfortunately, it is computed on the basis of the gross domestic product, which counts all economic transactions, useful or otherwise (for example, the costs of crime, divorce, environmental clean-ups, preventable accidents and diseases, and so forth). The index rises and falls with economic growth, and it is almost impossible to tell which factors are decisive. The boom years of 1996 through 2000 lifted the productivity rate a small amount (below historical rates),[15] but not necessarily through increased efficiency. In the same period Americans worked more hours per year than workers in any industrialized country. Having experienced decades of stagnant wages and job insecurity, Americans took to working longer and probably harder, not the best prescription for a real or lasting improvement in efficiency. Most Republicans and many Democrats argue that economic growth and increased productivity (efficiency) require competition, lower taxes, a reduction in the budget deficit and national debt through reduced government spending, and an increase in our low savings rate. These are all debatable; competition is hugely wasteful, lower taxes should be carefully targeted, government spending often constitutes wise investment. In addition, the claim that we are saving too little is false. The real issue in regard to productivity is what is being *done* with savings.[16]

To understand productivity one must understand the following: our heavy social overhead; an educational system not geared to producing citizens or effective professionals or workers; the growing cost of natural resources; capital investment's failure to match productivity needs; the flow of capital overseas; and immigration (which, together with a lack of public services and the declining economy itself, provides an abundant supply of cheap labor and thus lowers the incentive to invest in new machinery or practices). Understandably, efforts to increase productivity consist largely of supporting business through direct subsidies or lower taxes, and abstract talk about competition and better education. Almost despite ourselves, we have produced some useful policies; for example, copying Japanese work practices and on-time inventory management. But many important steps that can be taken to increase productivity are ignored (for example, fostering cooperative and equitable labor relations,[17] regulating capital investment, establishing economic priorities on necessities rather than luxuries).

Economic Growth and Declining Social Welfare

Economic growth is the all-purpose problem solver of American capitalism. In a pioneering combined quantitative and qualitative cost-benefit analysis, Xenophon Zolotas challenged the master myth of capitalism—that economic growth leads to social welfare. Carefully and undogmatically, Zolotas subtracted the overhead costs of economic growth (economic activities recorded in the gross national product, GNP, that do not promote welfare—for example, crime, wasted resources, pollution, loss of time and money spent in commuting, and 50 percent of advertising, higher education, and health expenditures) to yield a "social welfare index."[18] His conclusion was that between 1950 and 1977 economic growth continued upward but that the social welfare curve grew far more slowly and became increasingly separated from economic growth as such. Zolotas has also speculated about the relation between economic growth and subjective quality-of-life factors (for example, longitudinal surveys asking people how happy they are) and crime, mental, and physical well-being rates. His conclusion again is that economic growth has ceased to have a direct payoff in social welfare.[19]

Zolotas's analysis has been confirmed by Marc Miringoff's "index of social health." The index traces sixteen indicators of the quality of life and of socioeconomic well-being between 1970 and 1996. Combined into a single number, the index in 1996 stood at forty-three out of a possible hundred, down from its peak of 76.9 in 1973.[20] Using a curve of nine indicators and matching it against the curve of GDP between 1959 and 1996, the divorce between social welfare and economic growth appears dramatically.[21]

Some of the indicators in the index of social health are improving (infant mortality, life expectancy at age sixty-five, poverty at age sixty-five or more, the high school dropout rate). Some indicators are unstable (teenage drug use, teenage births, alcohol-related traffic fatalities, affordable housing, unemployment). Some indicators are worsening (child abuse, child poverty, youth suicide, health care coverage, wages, income inequality, violent crime).[22] The Miringoffs' summary analysis of American social welfare data takes on added value because they place it in an international context—the U.S. record in regard to almost every indicator is the worst in the industrialized world.

The Miringoffs provide valuable background on the history of attempts to develop indexes of social health; they recommend that the United States adopt an official index as almost all industrialized and some developing countries have done, as well as the United Nations. They also think it would be a good idea to develop a council of social advisors to the president, and for journalism to develop a social health "beat." Many American communities and one state, Connecticut, have already established a variety of indexes of social health.[23]

The index of social health is extremely valuable but is not complete. Though it provides good coverage of age groups, it makes only passing mention of race, ethnicity, or class. Almost all data take on heightened significance when analyzed in terms of social class. The index of social health is probably designed to avoid controversy and political fallout (a curse of all American social science), but it should include data about inequality of wealth, crime by the upper classes, our plutocratic political system, class education, and of course, the natural environment.

The Decline of Worker Satisfaction

In the early 1970s two books on work appeared that attracted widespread attention.[24] Based on a 1969 national survey by the Survey Research Center of the University of Michigan, as well as other studies, both books emphasized that work in America was far from satisfying, especially among blue-collar workers and more especially among males, the young of both sexes, and blacks. Two key complaints (aside from inadequate income and fringe benefits) were the lack of control by workers over the work process and isolation from fellow workers.

The Survey Research Center repeated its 1969 study of worker satisfaction in 1973 and again in 1977, revealing a clear trend.[25] Worker dissatisfaction remained stable between 1969 and 1973 but increased significantly between 1973 and 1977. Workers in upper occupations were still more satisfied than workers in lower occupations; more broadly, white-collar workers were more satisfied than blue-collar workers. But significantly, worker satisfaction declined among *all* occupational, racial, sexual, age, and educational groupings.

The reason for the decline in worker satisfaction across all levels during this period appears not to be recession, stagflation (low economic growth combined with inflation), or a deterioration of the quality of work itself. The authors of all these studies concluded that a change in worker expectations was the major cause of worker dissatisfaction. Judged in long-term historical perspective, it appears that younger workers want work to be satisfying in itself and not merely a means to biological existence. Work once meant getting enough food and protection from the elements to stay alive. Given a century of abundance and a democratic ethos stressing individuals as of value in themselves, today's workers expect more from work than mere subsistence.

Significantly, college-educated workers are among those who have experienced the greatest decline in work satisfaction, with approximately one-third saying that they are in jobs that do not require a college education.[26] Though younger workers are the most dissatisfied, considerable dissatisfaction exists, as noted, among all age groups. Some reforms have appeared (quality circles, flexible hours, child care), but so far American employers have yet to realize that meaningful work is more efficient and productive than what they now provide.

Since the above studies, conditions in the occupational system have worsened. In 1990, two studies revealed the depth of work dissatisfaction among doctors and lawyers. In the first, 40 percent of doctors reported that they would not go into medicine if they had it to do over again. In the second, 41 percent of lawyers said they would not go into law if given a second chance. Interestingly, deep and pervasive dissatisfaction was found among lawyers at all age levels, among both sexes, and at all levels of practice.[27]

Fraser has documented the adverse consequences on white-collar workers (lower-level clerical through middle management and professional levels) that came out of the mobilization of American capitalism from the 1970s on.[28] American corporations embarked on relentless cost-cutting: layoffs (even when profitable), increased working hours, stagnant pay, reduced health, pension, and other benefits, and extensive use of temporary workers. Much of this occurred because of competition from abroad and at home, new technology that made it possible to monitor workers and to make them available around the clock, and the growing power of Wall Street, which punished companies (their stock value) if they failed to generate acceptable profits. To become efficient, corporations paid their top executives lavishly. The results, however, were far from efficient. In point of fact, says Fraser, companies that did not engage in ruthless anti-worker behavior not only didn't suffer but actually showed improvement when they treated workers fairly.

Writing and concluding her book during the boom period of 1995–2000, Fraser's analysis ends weakly. Probably impressed by the labor shortages that developed in that period, Fraser saw hope in the future from personal resistance, farsighted employers, and Wall Street analysts who understand the value to a company of good worker-management relations. Nowhere does Fraser (a financial journalist) put the horrific stories and data she recounts in the context of a capitalist social system that *must* exploit labor at all levels. Nowhere does she indicate that American-style capitalism has given more power to property over the past three decades. Nowhere does she point out that blue-collar workers suffered along with those in white collars, that personal debt grew erroneously, as did personal bankruptcy.

Work Inefficiencies: The Trust Gap

The decline in work satisfaction is only part of a huge, many-sided problem associated with work in America. Dissatisfaction with work (largely a function of deep, degrading corporate controls over the work process), combined with the American individualistic success ethic, leads to a pronounced pattern of job hopping, which has especially negative consequences among executives and professionals. (Unlike in Japan, those in upper-level jobs do not stay and identify with the groups they work for, leading to lack of commitment and responsibility.)

Work is also associated with high levels of stress and burnout, which in turn generate poor performance on the job and enormous damage to human health (and, of course, cause higher health costs). All struggle to cope and find security (golden parachutes, featherbedding, embezzlement, the big score, protectionist legislation for businesses, drugs and alcohol).

The United States appears to have a large layer of unnecessary managers in business and unnecessary officer staff in the military. These supervisors, claims Wright, act as a buffer between the owners-controllers and the working classes, allowing the upper classes to be routinely uncreative and enjoy unwarranted security and income.[29] We know that they are unnecessary (and thus costly and hardly satisfying to those forming the buffer) because other capitalist economies and armies do not have them. Also, when American industry had to compete against foreign economies, it fired huge numbers of middle managers, increasing both production and productivity to lower its costs, and actually increasing its efficiency, apart from reduced costs. The American workplace is also the source of many of our handicapped, and it causes many deaths. Laws on occupational safety are not enforced, and the Workman's Compensation system, which pays small amounts to injured workers and denies them the right to sue their employer, undermines any incentive to make work safer.

The structure of work can be characterized as a "trust gap."[30] Management, far removed from its workers, has no idea of what workers want (respect, higher management ethics, recognition for employee contributions, honest communication between employees and senior management). Study after study finds worker morale low and ebbing. Most managers do not survey their workers, and when they do, they do not follow through. Messages from management are sharply discounted, if not ignored. Management goals and direction are not spelled out. Workers are suspicious of the motives behind mergers and acquisitions. They do not understand or accept the widening gap between their pay and that of management. Top management is not only mainly white, Protestant, and male, but its experiences are far removed from those of ordinary Americans. All this is not only a drag on productivity but leads to overt sabotage.

Old and New Forms of Poverty

The United States has had no success in curbing poverty and today has as much of it as in 1960. In addition to old forms of poverty, it now has a huge number of one-parent (mostly female) households living in poverty, plus large numbers of working poor, sizable levels of homelessness, and a large percentage of its children living in poverty (making it the first society in history with more children in poverty than adults).

The stagnation in living standards from the 1970s on is unique in American history. Is it temporary, or does it herald a more permanent condition? The easy optimism that has marked America's past, an optimism derived from unprecedented economic growth, may be a false guide. The United States may be facing a future that its past does not prepare it for. In a few decades, traditional energy sources and various other planetary resources will become increasingly scarce. The United States may no longer have the flexibility it once had as a white, Protestant, middle-class, male monopoly. Today, a vast new array of groups are clamoring for their shares of America's benefits, and the American polity appears overloaded with demands. For the first time in its history, the United States cannot buoy its fortunes on a dependable supply of victims: the poor, racial and ethnic minorities, women, the young and the old, the handicapped, and gays.

THE DEFINING TECHNOLOGY OF
THE AGE: THE COMPUTER

Turning Human Meaning into Electrical Flows

A computer is a maze of electrical circuits that carries data in the form of electrons. By running rivers of electricity through gates and switches that correspond to human meaning (software, program, language, code, thought structure), a computer obeys human intelligence even as it extends and supplements it.

Computers were invented by humans, and it is not surprising that they resemble humans. Computers can talk, listen, and see with increasing skill. They can also store huge amounts of information and process it according to human instructions (meanings). While they cannot approach the free capabilities of the human being, they can do two things that humans cannot do: store huge amounts of information with great reliability and process it with great speed. Used during its first half-century as a calculator and filing cabinet, the computer underwent a momentous change in the 1970s when it became a communication device. From the late 1980s on, it underwent another momentous change—it also became a switching device that connects or integrates other forms of communication. With the advent of small, powerful, relatively inexpensive personal computers (PCs), ownership spread. Given its new capability, the computer can be in touch with other computers either in a one or two-way conversation, with or without wires (e-mail, chat rooms). Given its capability, it can tap into a permanent, expanding store of information (data banks, Web pages, catalogs, written and musical materials, and so on) put there by individuals and organizations on a global basis, to be used for commercial, educational, recreational, or public purposes (the Internet) by all users at the same time (see below for a discussion of the Internet).

The Many Uses of Computers

Computers do many different kinds of work. A computer can store data (customers' names, addresses, and purchases) and can compile and mail monthly bills. It can store and match profiles of individuals who want to meet other individuals (dating services). It can match employer with employee or scholar with scholar. It can analyze data (to determine which customers are tardy in paying bills, which customers might buy a particular product, which scholars ought to meet). Computers can be asked to analyze data on a moving object (say, an enemy missile), compute a trajectory that will intercept the enemy missile with another one, release the interceptor, detonate it, and so on. A computer can screen income-tax returns to identify those that look suspicious and may need auditing. It can write personalized letters to potential customers, clients, voters. It can automatically telephone customers to tell them their orders are in or call parents to ask why their children are not in school.

A computer can process large amounts of data so quickly that it makes possible better weather prediction, code breaking, automobile and other aerodynamic designs (that can be tested without prototypes), oil and geophysical exploration, three-dimensional visual models that make medical scanning of the interior of the body possible, and special effects in filmmaking. A computer can be attached to another machine and direct its operations—machines that shape metal, wood, and other materials; home appliances, engines, steel mills, and elevators; heating systems, alarms, a space shuttle, and the like. All automobiles today have computers that regulate their engines. Some high-speed, high-volume computers can monitor huge amounts of message-traffic data and thus help intelligence agencies separate useful from routine messages. A computer can help composers compose and sailors sail. Doctors, lawyers, air traffic controllers, and so on are deeply dependent on computers in the performance of their jobs.

The computer makes possible a military advantage, not only because it can guide a variety of weapons and ferret out detailed information about an enemy's defenses, but because it can also be used to cripple or misdirect an enemy's communication networks.

The computer allows users to create images that seem real—indeed, are difficult to identify as artificial. The computer also has the world's history at its disposal, including all film and all photographs. Those who control computers can generate whatever picture of reality they choose. The ominous implications of this capability have already begun to emerge in politics, as we will see in chapter 5.

The computer makes possible precise inventory control. Companies, governments, indeed, organizations of all kinds need no longer stockpile the materials they use; they can order what they require as the need develops. This not only saves the money it would take to stockpile large amounts of material but it puts suppliers on notice that they must deliver quality goods or be blamed for halting production. Perhaps another benefit is that inventory control prevents overproduction, of which contractions tended to cause severe economic slumps in the past. The computer can also determine labor power needs with great precision. Inventory and labor control, together with the computer's ability to store and reconfigure huge amounts of data, could well provide the means for a planned economy and society. Of special interest in this regard are the advances being made in computer software that can generate accurate predictions.[31]

The computer also makes it possible to command and control ever larger organizations over wider and wider geographic spaces. In short, the computer climaxes the trend toward globalization that began with the early empires and was accelerated in the fifteenth century with the ocean-spanning sailing ship. The computer makes it possible for a corporation to operate routinely in fifty, seventy-five, or a hundred countries. It has made possible a full commitment by developed countries to a world-market economy.

The Information Speedup

People talk of an "information revolution" and an "information society," but these terms are misleading. What has happened is mostly an information speedup (perhaps an information overload). The computer is an important aspect of this speedup. Along with other machines, the computer makes possible an information flow of great volume and speed. Linked to the telephone, wireless or cable television, and printing machines, the computer can deliver oral or visual messages to a wide variety of people. Information, stored or freshly generated, can appear on a screen in words, pictures, or graphics and then be printed on paper. As a word processor, the computer can be used to write a book, a newspaper, or a letter, and deliver it directly to homes or offices via telephone (wireless or wired), cable television, or wireless television. There is no need to print the book or newspaper and no need for a postal carrier to deliver the mail. A printer or fax machine can be attached to your phone, television set, or home computer if you want a copy of a message. You can also respond to messages instantly or at leisure, using the same devices that brought them. A computer can be linked to other computers and can tap data banks of enormous number and variety. It can send its messages through the air via satellites, then through telephone lines into homes and offices. Alternatively, many telephone lines can be connected to the same computer so that a bank, for example, can have all transactions of its many branches recorded and coordinated. The new communication capability has shortened the time it takes to do things, thus also speeding up behavior. Ironically, however, the computer both saves time and makes it scarce.

The Computer and Research

A computer can store meaningless sets, even fragments, of data (for example, phone calls, purchases of dynamite, partial descriptions of individuals) and in cooperation with other computers produce profiles of criminals, spies, or customers, or detect patterns among seemingly unrelated events and people. The computer is a filing cabinet that can search itself along many different lines of inquiry, analyze itself (its stored data), and make associations (among stored data). A computer can do sociological research by delving into stored data (from censuses, surveys, and other research) in order to answer a variety of questions. Actually, computers can do research in many areas, since there are over 1,300 data banks in specialized subjects. Data banks summarize and abstract information from many sources. One, for example, contains abstracts or articles from two thousand technical magazines and journals. Some data banks are updated twice a year, some daily, one every minute. Data banks are useful because they are indexed and cross-indexed. Many data banks permit searches to locate words specified by the researcher. The emergence of the

Internet has greatly augmented the research capabilities of the computer (see below, "The Internet").

THE COMPUTER AND THE ECONOMY

The Computer and Work

It is common in a wide variety of disciplines to analyze phenomena in terms of communication. Biologists think of cells, genes, and other bodily phenomena as conveying information and instructions to each other. Advertisers, teachers, journalists, public relations experts, etc., also convey information. Corporations struggle to communicate effectively internally. Urban sociologists think of the physical layout and the buildings of a city as either facilitators of or impediments to communication. Sociologists explicitly or implicitly analyze human interaction as modes of communication. It is common to regard politics as effective or ineffective communication. Work itself can be thought of as humans communicating with each other and with materials, nature, and the public. Machinery can be understood as frozen knowledge; a lathe, horse collar, axe, and so on, are ways of communicating stored knowledge.

As a unique communication device, the computer poses many questions for the world of work. Has it contributed to the de-skilling of the work force that Braverman pointed to? Is it leading to a fully automated, workerless economy? In what ways does it affect work? So far, studies across a wide variety of workplaces (manufacturing, insurance, banking, health care) agree that the workerless factory or office is not appearing.[32] Machines cannot be programmed to handle every and all kinds of work or to solve each and all kinds of problems. Computers do displace workers, and they do de-skill some of them, but computer-driven automation actually leads to higher and more widely dispersed skill levels among remaining workers (specific impacts on workers and professionals are discussed at various points in this book— see the subject index).

Computer use in the workplace is associated with various difficulties, some of which developed before computers. In an empirical study of four manufacturing companies, Thomas argues that "objective" solo work by each of the components in the overall work process (designers, product developers, manufacturing managers and engineers, supervisors, and shop-floor workers) is not productive. Each type of worker sees the world differently, and the results do not mesh. Design (and presumably marketing) and product development are more effective when done in full collaboration (communication) with all members of the manufacturing force (otherwise products are hard to make, machines fail to work, and supervisors and workers set up barriers). The overall production process must be a continuous back-and-forth flow of communication. Different perspectives must be given full rein. Far from relying on the problem-solving-through-science approach, the social organization of the workplace must be "political"—a matter of reconciling different interpretations, interests, and skills.[33]

The artificial separation of people in the work process represents faulty communication in the name of objectivity. Another breakdown of communication occurs in the relation between workers and automated machinery. The assumption behind computerized machines is that no humans are needed. Rochlin believes that this is a dangerous and destructive assumption. Rochlin (along with many others) recognizes that computers cannot be programmed to foresee every contingency or perform every human skill. Workers are needed to apply tacit knowledge and intuitive judgments to the work process, no matter how sophisticated the machinery. The reliance on computer networks and computer-driven automation will degrade human skills, warns Rochlin, skills that can only be acquired through training and experience (for a fuller discussion, see "Computerization, Professional Practice, and Organizational Failure" in chapter 9).

Zuboff has also warned us about the negative effect of computers on work skills. She asks us to record the changes in personality and behaviors being caused by the computer before they are lost, as happened in the industrial revolution. She also argues that work is collaborative and cannot be done simply through computer monitors. Work succeeds when workers, supervisors, and managers brainstorm (communicate) rather than rely on the old hierarchical system, in which one person is responsible.[34]

The development and widespread use of rational administration (bureaucracy) in the nineteenth century was a technological breakthrough of the first order. But that technology became outmoded as the complexity of work increased and as the spirit of equality and democracy spread. Unfortunately, the acceptance of new ideas for organizing the workplace has not kept up with developments and sociopolitical values. Property owners have yet to understand that more equality, cooperation, and safety in the workplace is good for business. Indeed, resistance to social and natural science among the business, political, and even professional classes is one of the pronounced features of early twentieth-first-century America. What appears to have happened as the major trend of the late twentieth century was the augmentation of hierarchical control through the computer.

The maturing world of electronic communication means, as we have seen, that almost all of human culture can be stored for instant retrieval and use. It means that machines can do work of every conceivable kind, including repairing and replacing themselves. The mastery of electricity means that almost the entire range of human thought and emotions, human wants and fantasies, human diversity, certified knowledge and pseudo-knowledge, useful and nonuseful information, human uplift and human fraud, and morality and immorality can be put into electronic forms and turned into sight and sound. The convergence of all forms of communication may well have an impact on society in many ways comparable to that of such past communication technology as the railroad and printing press, and perhaps language and writing as well.

The capabilities of the computer have also led to a more intense and pervasive research effort, spreading out beyond universities and research laboratories and institutes to the work process itself. Corporations throughout the economy have inaugurated permanent in-house processes of innovation in order to generate new products and services, further standardize the work process, and eliminate inefficiencies of all kinds. Liberals and radicals (especially Marxists) interpret the meaning of the surge of electronic creativity in communication since the 1970s differently.

Both Right and Left liberals have hailed the computer as more evidence that the United States has become a knowledge society. The Democratic Party wants to put a computer into the hands of every student and wire up schools and libraries to the Internet. Right liberal members of the Republican Party see the computer as a way to realize the true market society of "frictionless capitalism." Liberals argue among themselves about how to shape the Internet to permit law enforcement and intelligence agencies to eavesdrop for public purposes. They also worry about pornography, fraud, and hate messages on computer screens. Some worry about how to tax Internet commerce to protect local revenues, while others worry that enforcing laws in general will be difficult because the Internet knows no national boundaries.

Nonetheless, computerization blends well with the liberal emphasis on ideational causation. It merges easily into the liberal faith in the rationality of self-interest and "free" markets. A long history of research that explodes this faith has not penetrated the upper classes (their contradictory behavior of openly managing markets and compensating for negative market consequences is interpreted as helping the true market society to emerge). Perhaps the most glaring gaps in the liberal position are, first, that most work, by far, does not entail the use of much knowledge, and second, that work and knowledge are socially, not individually, caused processes. Certainly the computer is far from enhancing the American political process with knowledge (see chapter 5).

The second, and radical (mostly Marxian), position sees the electronic stage of computerization as continuing the process of de-skilling and replacing workers with machinery and thus undermining capitalism's ability to generate profit or surplus value. Tessa Morris-Suzuki and Martin Kenney argue that the present stage of computerized or information capitalism is merely postponing the end of surplus value. Their emphasis is on capitalism's new emphasis on extracting surplus value from knowledge workers at all levels of the economy, as well as in education and government.[35]

Corporate Communication Networks and Concentration

Corporations in the developed world have extensive private communication networks or use private networks supplied by communication corporations such as IBM or AT&T. These networks give corporations communication control over their subunits, subsidiaries, and branches. They make it possible to control from a central point gigantic enterprises that extend around the globe. In addition, specialized communication companies (for example, GE Information Services, Dow Jones) supply business with worldwide business analyses and data.

Concentration in Communications

The nature of communication technology tends to make communication service corporations monopolistic.[36] Through much of American history, the government regulated (or pretended to regulate) communication services, including the telegraph, railroads, shipping, telephone, radio, trucking, airlines, and television. When America experienced economic difficulties in the 1970s, business mobilized against trade unions and demanded less government regulation in all of the economy—in the name of America's master myth, the free market. Thanks to lax enforcement of antitrust law, economic concentration, which was already pronounced, increased in all sectors of the economy, including all aspects of communication.

Today, nine media giants are dominant forces in television ownership, television production, television and Internet news, magazine and book publishing, film making, popular music, theaters, cruise lines, arcades and amusements parks, and sports, including sports teams.

Time Warner—$25 billion in sales, 1997 (owns CNN)
Disney—$24 billion, 1997 (owns ABC, ESPN)
Bertelsmann—$15 billion, 1996
Viacom—$13 billion, 1996
News Corporation—$10 billion, 1996
Sony—$9 billion, 1997
TCI (Tele-Communications, Inc.)—$7 billion, 1997 (purchased by AT&T, 1998)
NBC (General Electric)—$5 billion, 1996 (owns MSNBC with Microsoft and has an alliance with the *Washington Post* and *Newsweek*).[37]

These nine companies (along with many like-minded second-tier corporations in the United States, Canada, Europe, Latin America, and the Asia-Pacific region) dominate the giant U.S. market, as well as the global market in communications (not including telephone, newspapers, mail and package delivery, or computer communications, which are themselves highly concentrated).

Concentration in the mass media accelerated in the 1990s, when companies realized that hitherto separate businesses complemented each other and that it paid to own the businesses on which one depended for sales, supplies, and services. The above nine companies are strong in most of the sectors of mass communications, because each part of the firm contributes to the whole. One part of a corporation, for example, produces a movie, while another part plays it on television, and still another exploits its potential for music or toy sales. One part of a corporation produces a book, another publicizes it on talk shows, and another distributes it through book clubs. In addition there are tie-ins with public relations firms, advertising companies, and fast food, snack, and soft drink companies. A company's magazines publicizes films or television programs made by other parts of the company.

Publishing is also highly concentrated and has become more so in recent years.

Critics argue that giant publishing houses and giant retailers tend to gravitate toward mainstream readers and neglect offbeat or controversial subjects. This has already happened in publishing for elementary and high school students, because state school boards adopt texts for entire school systems (large states in less developed parts of the country influence the rest of the nation, because publishers are loath to produce more than one text for each subject). In higher education publishing, there are only a handful of independent publishers left, threatening the main sources of innovation and critical thinking for college faculty and students (university presses are now hard pressed and have reduced their output of scholarly works).

One result of media concentration has been the near-total commercialization of daily life, as the airwaves, television, computer screens, stadiums, racing cars, supermarket carts, buses, clothing, magazines, and newspapers, etc., are used to deliver commercials. Together with the actions of the rest of the economy and their advertisers, the overall result is to lock Americans into high-level (and not always satisfying) consumption—that is, to lock them into the labor force to earn the money to consume. The incessant incitement to consume undoubtedly contributes to crime, bankruptcies, and personality pathologies among the many who cannot.

Another result of media concentration is that professional journalism has suffered severe budget cuts, because it is expensive and unprofitable. Television news, along with the highly concentrated newspaper and magazine businesses, now tends, even more than in the past, to give short bursts of news and long bursts of human-interest fluff. Gone are the documentaries and attempts at in-depth coverage. Advertisers openly censor content, and articles in magazines are difficult to distinguish from advertising. News that embarrasses or is unfavorable to the corporate owner of the network goes unreported (for example, the seventy-billion-dollar giveaway of digital frequencies to broadcast companies by Congress went virtually unmentioned by television news).

If newspaper ownership is analyzed separately, the same pattern of increasing concentration appears. The most influential newspapers—say, the *New York Times* and the *Wall Street Journal*—are now national in scope (with foreign readership) and provide much useful news and in-depth coverage of public issues. But their editorial pages correspond respectively to the liberalism of the left-center wing of the Democratic Party and the laissez-faire liberalism of the Republican Party. Together with the fact that the overall media are right-center and right wing in their politics means that Left liberal, not to mention radical Left views, are not available to the public (or for that matter, to our leaders). Despite the widespread notion that journalists themselves are liberals, a careful survey of Washington-based bureau chiefs and reporters (who cover national economic policy and politics) revealed that they are to the political right of the public on every issue except the environment.[38]

Telephone communication was a "natural" monopoly until recently, either regulated (the U.S. pattern) or government owned (in most of the world). In pursuit of the mythology of competition, AT&T became only a long-distance carrier, and five regional short-distance carriers were set up during the 1980s. Though there is now more long-distance competition (and lower prices), no breakup of local phone

This move made sense for both companies—one had content, and the other had a solid base in providing Internet services. Aside from the fact that each benefited immediately, the larger goal was to gear the Internet for mass entertainment. AOL Time Warner envisions—once the technical difficulties are overcome (and a full array of copyright protections are in place)—an interactive world of households ordering entertainment directly into their homes.

Nonetheless, in addition to having to figure out how to create profitable businesses, the Internet faces formidable technical difficulties before it can become a mass commercial operation on an interactive basis. The Internet now works like a gigantic telephone party line that millions can use simultaneously for different purposes, because of special codes (protocols) governing electrical transmissions. To work better the Internet needs enlarged storage capacity and better transmission lines. But to serve the whole world it needs different code(s), otherwise excessive traffic will choke the party line. That prospect appears to be far off.

The Computer and Productivity

The pervasive use of the computer was heralded as an important way to enhance productivity, but this has not been the case.[41] The optimistic belief that the widespread use of computers in the boom years of the 1990s had ushered in a qualitative jump in productivity turned out to be unfounded. Revised rates in 2001 saw only a modest improvement, leaving the United States still below historical levels.[42]

In some ways, the computer is similar to labor-saving devices in the home. When the latter devices were introduced, they did not reduce labor (and thus "costs," to yield more productivity in relation to a set amount of work) but rather made housekeepers more productive in the sense of being able to do more and better work. Houses were kept cleaner, clothes were washed more often (and kept softer and starched), more time was spent on fancier recipes, and so on. The computer has done much the same: fancier work complete with graphs and elegant type, reliance on written (more detailed) messages that are more time consuming than oral communication. The computer also increases the volume of communication, fragmenting the employee's workday. To a researcher's surprise, it was found that the major variable that leads to more productive computer work teams was support staff to answer the phone and prevent work interruptions.

The computer's amazing ability to handle data creates a presumptive need to use it (to justify its cost) and also demands for more information for ever more refined applications, not all of them essential to the enterprise in question. In addition, administrators overestimate the accuracy and value of computer models (based on quantitative questions and answers), leading to an "illusion of control" and "cognitive conceit." In general, administrators are not better at administrating, and they become overworked; not knowing this, they continually press to upgrade the abilities of their computers. In addition, while lower-paid workers are laid off, a large increase takes place in the numbers of better-educated, computer-skilled, higher-paid workers. The computer, it should be added, is also subject to "viruses," and its "health care" costs are very high. The Y2K problem (fixing all computers to correct fifty years of using only two digits to designate the year) cost a hundred billion non-productive dollars to avert before New Year's Day of 2000.

The promotion of the computer by various technocratic movements continues strong, though some welcome attempts to assess its worth to society have at last begun. That this was not done sooner represents an adaptive failure of major proportions.

The Electronic Sweatshop

Using an ad hoc collection of interviews, Barbara Garson has brilliantly captured a hidden trend in the general process of industrializing work, the use of the computer to de-skill the American workforce.[43] In what she never claims is a full scientific study, Garson roams from the bottom to the top of the occupational ladder to show how owners are continuing to dominate workers through computers, not for efficiency and profit (Garson states that she knows of no studies showing more efficiency through computerization) but for the sake of sheer control.

The thrust of the trend, says Garson, is to do to white-collar workers what has already been done to blue-collar workers: "Make them cheaper to train, easier to replace, less skilled, less expensive, and less special." This trend does not affect merely lower-level workers. The computer controls not only how long McDonald's french fries must be cooked but the overall operation of the store. It specifies the kind of conversation airline reservations clerks should conduct, it automates the social worker (who is replaced by several low-paid specialties, such as financial assistance worker and eligibility technician), and it provides software systems to take over the work of professionals—not just automatic pilots for airlines but software that does some of the work of doctors, lawyers, psychologists, brokers, military officers, bank loan officers, federal probation officials, workman's compensation judges, and managers—to which one can add the elimination of skills of automotive tune-up mechanics, bank tellers, and musicians.

The computer, warns Garson, also yields a close monitoring of work both to control workers and to provide owners with precise information of their labor needs. Knowing how much labor is needed for the various times of the day and the days of the week, month, and year has led to a huge increase of temporary and part-time, low-paid, no-benefits workers, some of them professionals. The computer also reduces contact between human beings. The computer is increasingly becoming normal, warns Garson, though it is not too late to prevent what happened in the past when the factory system, with its arbitrary features and severe drawbacks, eventually became part of the normal, taken-for-granted world.

Other Negative Aspects of the Computer

The computer is vulnerable to interception, and thus criminals can steal money or information. Business and professional fraud is common on the Internet. Computer security codes, while effective in most cases, can nonetheless be broken (with the aid of a computer). The highly interdependent sociopolitical world, made more so by the computer, is now subject to massive failure, either through error or sabotage.

The computer also means that individual privacy is difficult, if not impossible, to protect. Vital data on all individuals is now accessible electronically by anyone. Individuals with medical or genetic problems can be denied employment; individuals with embarrassing secrets can be blackmailed; and individuals with special habits, weaknesses, or needs can be targeted by both legitimate and illegitimate businesses and professionals. In addition to making it possible to supervise workers closely, the computer has also led to the political manipulation of voters and to widespread, continuous surveillance of students, workers, and citizens (see "Computers That Analyze, Manage, Correspond, Talk, Awe and Can Scold and Intimidate: The New Mass Politics"; and "Communication Technology and the Culture of Surveillance," both in chapter 5).

The computer is not as environmentally friendly as is sometimes supposed. Computer shopping and computer work at home may save energy spent in commuting to malls and work, but so far electricity use continues to rise; the computer, a voracious user of energy, now uses 13 percent of all electricity.[44] Disposing of old computers is an environmental headache.

The computer both disperses activities and increases hierarchic control. The computer makes possible, and has led to, an ominous increase in economic and political concentration. The computer also makes it possible for a corporation to operate in scores of countries—that is, to search the globe for the cheapest labor and resources and to become relatively stateless. Avoiding (and evading) taxes and regulations everywhere, corporations become market forces undermining community and public authority. The computer has also both augmented and undermined worker and professional skills, and it has put certain organizations at risk (see "Computerization, Professional Practice, and Organizational Failure," in chapter 9).

THE COMPUTER AND THE PROFESSIONS

America's Unique Professions

America's professions are different from those in all other countries in significant ways.[45] Their demand for total autonomy is perhaps the essence of their uniqueness.

By the late nineteenth century, a large number of American professional groups had claimed jurisdiction over special fields of knowledge. Various disciplines and professions emerged, each with its own association, subject matter, credentials, research journals, and special methods (within the overall world of empirical science). Each claimed to have knowledge about a special area of behavior and a special cluster of problems; each sought to restrict entry through a system of credentials and state licensing; and each struggled to obtain jurisdictional monopoly, high income and prestige, and autonomy from forces either to the side or below. From across the spectrum of professions and disciplines came similar statements and claims: "We are neutral, altruistic, objective searchers for and dispensers of knowledge"; "We can be judged only by our fellow professionals, since we possess a high and difficult-to-obtain knowledge base"; "Since knowledge is power and yields virtue, our activities will be service oriented"; "Whatever our deficiencies, we are the best guarantee of both knowledge and an improved society." The fact that these claims have all been rejected by research has had little effect on the professions.

The rise of the professions followed the trajectory of national socioeconomic development. The most important difference among national professions is the one between those of the United States and of all other countries. In both the liberal and authoritarian capitalist countries as well as in czarist Russia and later the Soviet Union, the state actively promoted the professions and employed them for both elite and public purposes. Itself clearly associated with functions deemed important to national development, the state openly established schools to conduct research and train scientists and other professionals. The state also employed professionals in large numbers, either directly or indirectly through state welfare programs. Even in England, the country that most closely resembles the United States, the professions were part and parcel of England's aristocratic traditions—elitist, public-minded, ambivalent about working for money, generally corporatist in outlook.

The professions in the United States rose without explicit state sponsorship and without a clear identification with social functions. America's professions grew up in a society with an entrepreneurial environment, an open economy, and a decentralized polity with limited responsibilities for performing social functions. Accordingly, the professions sponsored themselves; it is for this reason that they formed associations, helped establish schools and curricula, and engaged in politics to secure legal sanction for the standards they were creating. Accordingly, the American professions were deeply geared toward securing income from private clients and private employers, especially schools.

In all this, the American professions participated in the national hypocrisy, along with business and farmers, of advocating competition and the gathering of nonpolitical knowledge while pursuing government subsidies and legal monopolies. The overall pattern saw powerful groups denouncing politics and government while busily using both for their own ends; the net result was to deny the masses the ability to use government for their ends. Seen in another way, the American professions, along with business and farming, were given strong support by government, but with no explicit compact that the public would receive services in return. The ideology of laissez-faire made it unnecessary that the public's exchanges with private groups be of the same order as exchanges between private parties—an exchange of equivalencies.

The United States is unique compared to other capitalist societies in another respect as well. Lacking a political system that can generate collective purposes, the United States is now an international anomaly. It has the highest crime rates, the worst infant mortality rates, the highest teenage pregnancy rates, the highest divorce rate, and the worst health care system in the developed capitalist world.[46] None of this is surprising, however, given America's myth of exceptionalism. This myth, at the core of American culture, is the unexamined assumption that America has unshackled human nature and placed society on the path that releases the creative, if unequal, rational tendencies in human beings qua human beings. What is surprising is that America's knowledge elites should have believed in this fantasy for so long. Perhaps the explanation is that they too benefit from the utopian image of laissez-faire, or that in any case they are too busy securing their places in the overall system of power to have much time to think about fundamental political and social questions.

Instead, America's knowledge elites live in a partial version of the Enlightenment's worldview. That view committed Western elites to empiricism and secular progress. So far, said the Enlightenment, humanity has been subject to error and evil, but now, thanks to science, it has the means to analyze and master the factual world directly. But in pioneering the West's commitment to empirical science, the Enlightenment fully realized the deep problem in its perspective: how can knowledge (truth and virtue) be based on, or be derived from, the empirical world if that world is characterized by error and evil? Here the United States parts company with the Enlightenment (and the supposedly corrupt Old World). In practicing the empirical method, Americans believe, they are studying not error and evil (the past) but American society—not as a product of the past (which, of course, it surely is) but as revealed human nature making its passage out of the past (which it surely is not). Thus the abstract and nonpolitical nature of American social science and its ineffective and biased account of reality are due largely to its mistaken teleological presupposition that the United States is either reality or reality in the making.

Professionalism also occurred in education, completing the formalism that characterizes America's knowledge elites. As with the private world, which speaks the language of competition and markets but works hard to achieve the security of monopoly or government regulation, academics also avoid competition, by demanding tenure and establishing unnecessary credentials for job entry and success. By and large, academics soon professionalized and began to think of their goods and services as comprising just another sector of the capitalist economy. But academics get tenure and other benefits only by promising to be nonpolitical in their teaching and research.[47] To remain nonpolitical, social research had to be narrow and abstract, and thus began the process of professional fragmentation, by which specialized theorists talked to each other—and not about politics, the economy, or society. Just as there is no longer a referent to concepts such as *doctor* and *lawyer*, there is no longer a referent for economist, sociologist, political scientist, and so forth.

On the surface there appears to be a healthy clash of ideas in academe. But ideas do not have much impact if they are not propelled by politics. In addition, there is a profound segregation of academics and other knowledge creators into separate associations, caucuses, institutes, think tanks, advocacy groups, and types of colleges-universities. The lack of a clear social mission also means that all academic specialties and their infinity of topics become, rather than competitors, a tolerant overall brotherhood [*sic*]—or rather, a congeries of loosely coordinated brotherhoods, a democracy of oligarchs. Each and every discipline is worthy of respect; while some are considered more important than others, the distinctions are informal. The same applies to courses and research. Indeed, there appears to be no way to prevent the multiplication of subjects that need to be taught.[48] There is no way to criticize the unnecessary courses required to succeed as an undergraduate or to get into graduate-professional schools. Eventually, the distinction between academic education and the pursuit of professional careers disappears.

The fragmentation of knowledge elites was legitimated by the magic of laissez-faire. Bits and pieces of knowledge could be generated by career-oriented academics because somehow, sometime, the fragments would all come together. Thus there was no need for the various disciplines to talk to each other, let alone to require that no one spend more than, say, five years at a time in any one discipline (the magic of interdisciplinary studies and distribution requirements for students would solve this problem). Commentators have also noted the decline in the influence of intellectuals and the gradual fragmentation of the public sphere into an array of private worlds, something that can be linked to the emergence of artificial, specialized disciplines in academe.[49]

To its credit, American social science has generated the empirical research on which the above is based. As an example worth repeating, all claims by professionals to justify their power and rewards have been refuted by empirical research. Academic education has been found to be relatively ineffectual *even when it is done right*—that is, higher education, including elite schools (perhaps especially elite schools), cannot show that they have any impact on student aggregates that affects behavior after school, let alone show that they are producing better citizens or workers.[50] At the same time that empirical research shows its creativity, it also displays its impotence if its results run counter to liberal professionalism—little has appeared in our education, textbooks, or politics that reflects these findings.

The Various Uses of the Computer in the Professions

No profession can get along today without the computer. What lawyer, for example, would willingly forgo the ease and efficiency of quick reviews via the computer of all cases that have come to trial in a particular area? Doctors can talk to patients, record pertinent data, and check symptoms on computers to help diagnose illness. The computer helps many professions and agencies process a wide variety of special people: patients, customers, clients, students, voters, and taxpayers.

Intelligence agencies use computers to amass and analyze huge amounts of information in particular areas and to cross-check them with seemingly unrelated information. Computer voice recognition (already well started) will make it possible for computers to monitor all telephone calls (now very expensive in labor power). Speech recognition would allow a machine to ignore people in whom a power group is not interested; once a machine can understand speech and language, it can concentrate on "interesting" speakers (those discussing political strategy, industrial and trade secrets, subversion, espionage, crime).

The computer can extend the human imagination. Creative professionals often must imagine things that do not exist. The computer can be programmed to do the same, imagining a world without sex or money, a theatrical production without known human motives (or with various stars or script endings), a war between the United States and country *X,* and a world that does not obey physical laws. A computer can show you what the United States would be like without prostitution (more divorce?) or pornography (more sex crimes?). It can imagine the United States without a housing shortage, crime, poverty, or disease. The computer is already doing practical work about meteorology, crop shortages and surpluses, inflation rates, and environmental problems. Computers are valuable adjuncts in all fields of knowledge; they are uniquely able to do data processing for a number of applied fields, from weather forecasting to nuclear weaponry.

Computers have, as noted, displaced many unskilled and semiskilled workers. The word processor has already taken over a great deal of clerical work. Millions of industrial robots and other machines run by computers are already hard at work. Where all this will lead is hard to predict. Computers have been developed to "experience" the behavior of others and imitate them (pattern recognition). Once this capacity is fully developed, it will be possible to give computers many tasks that now require skilled and professional workers. Computers may one day be attached to our bodies in order to acquire the skills necessary to use a lathe or play the piano. It is conceivable that computers may one day be constructed not only to sense brain waves and muscle tension but ideas; thus minds might one day communicate directly with other minds via computers. Perhaps ordinary citizens will have computers for doctors.

The use of computers throughout the apexes of American society has tended to reinforce, even increase, the separation of elites and masses. In later chapters we will see a variety of elites at work. In chapter 5, political elites and their supporting professions will appear (pollsters, political consultants, public relations and marketing experts, lobbyists and think tank policy analysts). The separation of elites and masses will be addressed in chapter 7 (journalists and academic policy specialists) and in chapter 8 (entertainment specialists). The theme continues in chapter 9, where the communication deficiencies of the professions are also outlined ("Communication and Professional Practice"; "Computerization, Professional Practice, and Organizational Failure").

Social Power and the Computer

The computer is a remarkable machine, but it has no set purpose. This does not mean it is value neutral; like other machines, it is used by humans to serve human ends. We now know that technology is not always good or on a fixed course of development. The computer does work defined by humans; its performance no better than the information and instructions fed into it. Computer people have a slogan, devised no doubt to prevent the easily awed from icon worship, "garbage in, garbage out"—to which one can add, "evil in, evil out."

A computer is only a versatile workhorse, directed by humans. What is its social meaning? What are the politics of the computer? Did the computer make possible the present society, which is not only large in size but has enormously increased the range, density, and volume of its transactions? Does the computer provide the command-and-control structures that enable the Pentagon to maintain a military presence around the globe? Would the huge volume of domestic and global banking and stock brokerage be possible without computers? Could giant corporations keep track of their businesses or provide services without computers? Could multinational corporations operate simultaneously in scores of countries without computers?

Ideally, the computer could make capitalism work the way it is supposed to. The individual, provided with full information about the relative costs of products and services, could become sovereign in all markets. Even stock and other exchanges could be replaced. Individuals even now can place orders for products and services tailored to their special needs—for example, custom-measured and custom-made jeans. The computer could help make representative democracy work, a teledemocracy. Individuals in full possession of needed information could evaluate candidates and policies quickly and easily. The computer could decentralize society by allowing more people to work, worship, and be entertained at home. It could lead to less crowded cities and abandoned shopping malls, yielding in turn huge savings on tires, gas, metal, concrete, and time spent commuting and shopping. The computer could help overcome isolation. It could humanize the professions and make their services and products cheaper.

Or is the computer another stage in the industrialization and dehumanization of work? Evidence has appeared that the computer is furthering the standardization and thus interchangeability of workers from the bottom to the top of the occupational hierarchy. Already, the computer has accentuated and extended the power of an already concentrated economy. Airline companies have computer reservation systems that favor themselves, which also furthers monopoly. Computer systems are expensive and like all capital equipment are purchased only by those who have money. The computer has already helped centralize national economies even as it undermines them. In addition to centralizing politics, the computer has helped centralize government and law enforcement. Communications businesses are becoming more concentrated every day. In 2000, the giant computer software company Microsoft was convicted of using its monopoly illegally; whether its behavior can be curbed remains unclear.

Seen from a different perspective, the computer could assist in developing a planned (capitalist or socialist) economy. Perhaps the vast, impersonal bureaucracies that computers make possible will erode individualism, private property, and private values and functions. Perhaps the computer will replace the market and the entrepreneur, and perhaps even the nation-state, as the vehicle by which human and material resources are allocated. Even now, a computer could replace the guesses and hunches (mixed with rational calculations) of private economic agents as they interact to form markets, introduce new products and services, and create recession and inflation. Above all, capital formation, now accomplished helter-skelter through

90 percent owned 17.1 percent (and had 60.8 percent of income).[52] Preliminary analysis indicates that wealth inequality has increased further since 1995.

American ideology attributes success and failure to personal attributes, but as always, reality lies in social institutions. Beyond the formalism of individualist ideology lies the group organized for economic action. Profit-oriented groups, especially corporations, dominate the American economy. A corporation is a legal entity, administered bureaucratically, that allows large numbers of people to pool their resources and thus engage in a scale of economic behavior they could not achieve as solitary individuals. The result is a responsive chain of command that allows the owners or controllers of the corporation to amass and focus large amounts of capital to produce desired outcomes. The responsibilities and liabilities of corporations are spelled out in legal norms—one provision protects the owners' other property in case the corporation fails (law of bankruptcy). In addition, the corporation enjoys legal immortality, continuing even though individual owners die or transfer their interest.

The most striking feature of the American economy is the pronounced cleavage between dominant and weaker groups; a small number of corporations dominates all sectors of the economy, and a small number of groups dominates economically related activities (professional associations, hospitals, universities, law firms, the mass media, and so on).

Wealth concentration and ability to save go together. Many save, but realistically the ability to save significant sums is restricted to relatively few people, basically those in high-income groups. To recognize this is to know a great deal about the basic class structure of American society. The fact that only high-income groups can save helps to explain the high concentration of wealth; conversely, the high concentration of wealth helps to explain high income. The ability of high-income groups to save creates extra income (dividends, interest, capital gains, stock appreciation), which in turn promotes the unequal ability to save, etc. This has been called the *Matthew effect*—"For to everyone who has will more be given" (Matthew 25:29, Revised Standard Version).

Further, the large majority of those who are wealthy either inherited their money or used an inheritance to make money. If we examine three factors—(1) the source of income from property, (2) the ways in which such income is protected against taxation, and (3) the ways in which estate and inheritance taxes permit the transmission of wealth from one generation to the next, certain relationships will become apparent that go far toward explaining the highly concentrated and highly stable distribution of America's material culture. An exclusive focus on, say, the four hundred richest individuals (as listed in *Forbes*) or on the hundred largest corporations *(Fortune)* obscures a fundamental fact. Rich individuals are parts of interconnected families; corporations are connected parts of a concentrated economy; and rich families are owners and directors of the concentrated economy. The fact that the individuals and families who make up the rich and powerful are not always the same, because of upward and downward mobility, should not be allowed to obscure the reality of the processes that produce a high, stable, and often illegitimate structure of wealth in the United States.[53]

Knowledge about wealth is important because it tells us who makes the investment decisions that determine how material and human resources will be used. It is also important because the wealthy are active in a wide range of groups outside the economy: Business people dominate the governing boards of foundations (conservative and liberal), charities, hospitals, universities, and museums, symphony orchestras, and other cultural groups.[54] It is important because it translates into political-legal power (see chapter 5 for an analysis of the role played by property in general, and by property in communications, in constructing and maintaining America's plutocratic political system). It is important because concentrated ownership of the news media, and also corporate advertising and sponsorship, effectively narrow the range of information and ideas that reach the American people and result in fictitious and obsolete images of American society (see chapters 7 and 8).

Income Inequality

The 1970s saw a new trend in income distribution. Reversing its previous history, the United States now appears no longer able to provide an expanding number of middle-income jobs. The American economy has continued to generate jobs, but interpreting the number and quality of jobs is not easy.[55] Looking at high versus low-growth sectors of the economy reveals some disturbing trends. Many argue that service occupations (which, as noted above, have been setting the pace of the American economy) pay significantly less than do skilled manufacturing jobs. In an early analysis, Blackburn and Bloom pointed out that the twenty fastest-growing businesses paid one hundred dollars a week less than the twenty fastest-declining businesses. Tracing the growth of family income between 1969 and 1983, Blackburn and Bloom found faster growth among lower and upper families as opposed to lower-middle and upper-middle families.[56] In 1988, the Senate Budget Committee issued a report showing that jobs with middle-level wages had shrunk considerably and that the majority of newly created jobs were paying poverty-level wages (for a family of four).[57] Since then, there has been a steady growth of temporary and part-time workers who, in addition to receiving poor pay, typically have no health or pension benefits.

The new household income structure is moving away from the big bulge in the middle that was once characteristic of the United States and toward a bipolar (hourglass, two-tier) shape. The United States may or may not be generating as many good-paying jobs as in the past, but even assuming that it is, the crucial question to ask is how these jobs are distributed by households. Double earners are now common at all levels, but better-paid individuals marry each other, and this means that middle-income jobs are no longer held by single breadwinners. In addition, the lower classes have more single-income households, largely because divorced mothers quickly find themselves at that level.

The structural reasons for the new distribution of household income are the surge toward service industries; the movement of capital to low-wage, nonunionized sections of the United States and abroad; the successful attack on trade unions by business; and active support of these trends by government. (That support expresses itself in such ways as deregulation, the reduction in tax progressivity starting with the large tax cuts of 1982–1983, rapid depreciation for tax purposes, the curtailment of public services and benefits, privatization, anti-union rulings by a business-dominated National Labor Relations Board, high rates of job insecurity, congressional spending caps, and explicit decisions not to raise the minimum wage.) The women's movement and the rising divorce rate have also contributed to the new trend toward bipolar family incomes. That is, the women's movement has opened up economic opportunities for the daughters and wives of the upper classes, who tend to marry, or already be married to, men with good jobs. But the general surge of civil rights, individualism (laissez-faire American liberalism), more permissive divorce laws, and an erratic economy have also led to high divorce rates. The major casualties of divorce, even in no-fault divorces, are women—thus, as noted, the swollen ranks of lower-level, one-parent female households.

The unprecedented combination of relatively high growth and low unemployment and inflation of the late 1990s not only did not reverse income trends but made them worse. With few trade unions, and with only a bare-bones welfare state to see to it that workers shared in economic growth, income and wealth inequality worsened. The "boom" years of the late nineties led to modest productivity gains (more output per hour), but not because the economy had become more efficient; the most plausible explanation is greater short-term plant utilization.[58] In any case, while wage levels rose slightly, there was little evidence that the stagnant standard of living of the past thirty years was being reversed. Comparing business cycles shows that median family income in 1999 only barely exceeded its 1989 level.[59] Preliminary data from the 2000 census indicate that income inequality worsened in the previous decade, with the rich becoming much richer, the middle 60 percent slightly worse off, and the poor a little poorer.[60] The huge ten-year tax cut of 2001, massively favoring wealthy families, will, if allowed to run its course, worsen income inequality considerably.

The mighty current of Right liberalism since the 1970s helped give propertied and professional groups a freer hand in dealing with labor. The Right liberal argument that giving private property a freer hand will lead to a higher standard of living and solve many social problems has not occurred. In addition, laissez-faire American capitalism has been outperformed by welfare European capitalism since the 1970s. European countries have had higher income and productivity growth rates and less poverty than the United States (and by the 1990s, France, Germany, the Netherlands, and Belgium had caught up to American productivity levels). The United States had either low or the lowest economic mobility rates for people at the lowest economic levels during the 1980s (the last years for which data are available).[61]

IS THE MIDDLE CLASS DISAPPEARING?

The American middle class has long since disappeared, if "member of the middle class" is defined as the owner of a moderate-sized business or as an autonomous professional. Today, property is highly concentrated, and Americans, including professionals, are largely employees of large bureaucratic corporations, government, universities, hospitals, foundations, voluntary groups, and churches.

The disappearance of the middle class was hidden from view by economic growth, especially from the late nineteenth century to the mid-twentieth. Economic growth created a new middle class of salaried professional and high-income semiprofessional and blue-collar skilled workers. The new economy of abundance also homogenized a great deal of consumption, creating both a real and fictitious mass of middle-class consumers. Labor segmentation, the creation of meaningless distinctions and gradations among occupations, also misled Americans into thinking that things were getting better.[62]

However defined, the new middle class that appeared in the twentieth century seems now to be shrinking. In assessing trends in household income, it is important to distinguish between "middle income" and "middle class." A middle income can be acquired in a household in which husband and wife both work in blue-collar jobs. Today, earning a middle income generally requires two workers. Both the nature of the work and family background mean that many families with middle levels of income are nonetheless working-class families. "Middle class," on the other hand, means a certain level of income but from a source that promotes an independent, self-directed personality. It means awareness about and desire to live in a certain way—owning a home with enough space for family members to have private lives, and enough appliances, including a second car, to service those lives. It means vacations, as well as saving for the future. It means expectations for future advancement at work. It means proper socialization of the young for future middle-class (or upper-middle-class) status, especially through a four-year college education.

In the 1970s and 1980s there were laments for the skilled workers in so-called smokestack industries. What few realized then was that during the same period millions of middle-level managers were being laid off by hard-pressed corporations (many were "hard pressed" by their own subsidiaries in cheap-labor countries). Layoffs and labor turnover rates (job insecurity) remained high through the 1990s, thus effectively curbing demands for higher wages and opportunities for the formation of middle-class households. From the 1980s on, it was clear that some high-tech industries and upper-level occupations were also being exported to Third World countries.[63]

Trends in the ownership of productive property, household income, and occupation indicate an erosion in the size and power of the historical American middle class. From the 1980s on, another change has taken place in the middle class—diversification. The middle class is now made up of singles, married childless couples, double earners with children, divorced and remarried individuals, and older couples and singles. The decline of the middle class and its fragmentation into many different subtypes has serious implications for American society. The broad, politically moderate middle class was the mainstay of American representative government. As we see later, American political life has changed for the worse, and this may be due to the change in the American middle class.

THE AMERICAN DREAM:
REALITY OR NIGHTMARE?

The modern world is essentially the outcome of economic growth. Economic growth from 1200 to 1800 produced a middle class that undermined feudal society and eventually shaped Western society and the globe in its own image. Economic growth yielded a diversified group and power structure that generated representative government and constitutionalism (first in England, the United States, France, and then in many other countries). From 1850 to roughly the 1960s, it yielded a rising standard of living. But since the 1960s, the United States (like many other mature industrial societies) has experienced slow economic growth and stagnant, even declining, living standards. Today, a large and growing social overhead (for example, crime, pollution, military expenditures, and wasted resources in curative medical care and ineffective education) prevents even the healthy economic growth of the late nineties from being translated into higher living standards.

The stagnation in the standard of living stems from low productivity growth from 1970 on. The slowdown in productivity is itself caused by many factors. The rising productivity enjoyed from the mid-nineteenth century to the 1960s may have been historically unique. Much of it was due to cheap human and material resources (much of that, in turn, generated by government policies), which could be combined easily to yield mass manufacturing through complex organizations (the corporation). That era has passed; economies are now far more complex and require expensive capital and raw materials. The giant bureaucracies that dominate our economy are difficult to manage, either internally or in regard to the outside world. A large number of new values (for example, equality for minorities, protection of the environment) must be added to old values (such as efficiency and profit). Labor skills for many reaches of the economy have gone up even as much of the U.S. labor force is degraded by being pitted against labor in the developing world. The accumulating shortfalls of the past lead to increases in the social overhead, further retarding productivity growth—and so on.

Changes in the American labor force have also been depicted as a rise in skill levels. Many argue that we are in a postindustrial age where most people work with their heads, not their hands or backs. The reality is otherwise—the main bulk of new jobs in the United States have been and will continue to be unskilled and semi-skilled; the labor force will continue to have shortages of trained people even at a time when there are surplus workers. There are as many sweatshops in America today as there were a hundred years ago. The image of a bright new world of high technology hides a dark, unchanging reality—the U.S. economy has always rested on cheap labor, and the future promises to be the same. The sources of cheap labor were vastly augmented with the enormous expansion of the world-market economy. Today, significant portions of the American labor force can be considered to be in the developing world. In addition, significant (legal and illegal) immigration has brought an average of one million (many skilled and professional) foreign workers per year into the United States since World War II, ensuring the continuance of what is certainly one of the most important overlooked features in American history—plentiful supplies of socially generated cheap labor.

The declining fortunes of American labor extend far beyond blue-collar workers. College-educated males have lost ground since the 1980s (educated women during the nineties), in terms of types of job held. In addition, the income of college graduates declined in the late 1990s. Casualties among managerial ranks have been high, and there is considerable hidden unemployment and underemployment among professionals; for example, 44 percent of all higher-education faculty are part-time or temporary workers with low pay and no benefits.[64] In addition, employment firms have experienced an enormous growth in the placement of professionals in part-time, temporary jobs.[65] There is an ominous trend (made possible by the computer) toward exact monitoring of all workers, including many professional practitioners, to prescribe exactly how they will work and to determine how tasks can be further specialized and labor costs reduced.

Ominously, the basic thrust of the American economy is toward a labor force in which the relative number of secure, well-paying jobs is declining and the number of temporary, part-time, low-skilled jobs is expanding. Corporate capitalism has already undermined the power of organized labor. Labor unions now represent only 13 percent of the labor force, down from a high of 32 percent in the 1960s. The strike is no longer an effective labor weapon, given the large numbers of unemployed and underemployed and the practice, accepted by government and judiciary (but by no other developed capitalist country), of replacement workers. Labor unions have been forced to give back many of their gains. The basic thrust of the Reagan-Bush administration of 1980–1992 was especially detrimental to labor. By lowering social-service programs, aid to cities, public housing, and aid to education, the new era of smaller government forced many into the labor market. Since the concentrated economy has drastically reduced the power of small business (including small farmers) and the self-employed, the historical middle class (augmented by a well-paid blue-collar, middle-income group) that formed the reality behind the American Dream may be on the way out.

NOTES

1. U.S. Senate Committee on Governmental Affairs, *Structure of Corporate Concentration: Institutional Shareholders and Interlocking Directorates among U.S. Corporations* (Washington, D.C.: U.S. Government Printing Office [hereafter GPO], 1980).

2. Manuel Castells, *The Rise of the Network Society* (Malden, Mass.: Blackwell, 1996), 198f.

3. Castells, *The Rise of the Network Society*, 32; also see 66f, 92.

4. Castells, *The Rise of the Network Society*, 473.

5. C. Wright Mills, *White Collar: The American Middle Classes* (New York: Oxford University Press, 1953).

6. For background, see Saskia Sassen, *Cities in a World Economy* (Thousand Oaks, Calif.: Pine Forge, 1994), and *Losing Control: Sovereignty in an Age of Globalization* (New York: Columbia University Press, 1996).

7. Robert B. Reich, "Who Is Us?" *Harvard Business Review* 90 (January–February 1990): 53–64.

8. *New York Times*, May 16, 1998, B1.

9. For a richly detailed picture of the nightmarish working conditions in the Cavite Export Processing Zone, the Philippines, and for an analysis of how giant corporations like McDonald's, Wal-Mart, and Microsoft aggressively fight unionization and contribute to the development of a low-wage, insecure labor force, see Naomi Klein, *No Logo: Taking Aim at the Brand Bullies* (New York: Picador, 1999), chaps. 9, 10.

10. Robert Gilpin with the assistance of Jean Millis Gilpin, *The Challenge of Global Capitalism* (Princeton, N.J.: Princeton University Press, 2000).

11. The following is based on Bob Sutcliffe and Andrew Glyn, "Still Underwhelmed: Indicators of Globalization and Their Misinterpretation," *Review of Radical Political Economics* 31, no. 1 (1999): 111–32.

12. Ellen Meiksins Wood, "Modernity, Postmodernity, or Capitalism," in *Capitalism in the Information Age*, ed. R. W. Chesney et al. (New York: Monthly Review, 1998), 27–49.

13. Klein, *No Logo*, passim.

14. Bruce Western and Katherine Beckett, "How Unregulated Is the U.S. Labor Market? The Penal System as a Labor Market Institution," *American Journal of Sociology* 104, no. 4 (January 1999): 1030–60.

15. Jeff Madrick, "A Tarnished New Economy Loses More Luster with Revised Productivity Rates," *New York Times*, August 30, 2001, C2.

16. *Personal savings* in the United States are low, but the level of *total social saving* by individuals, private groups, and governments is high, stable, and on the whole equal to that of other countries, for example, Japan. In this latter respect, see Fumio Hayashi, *Understanding Saving: Evidence from the United States and Japan* (Cambridge, Mass.: MIT Press, 1997).

17. A comparison of fifteen developed capitalist countries indicates a strong relation between workers' collective bargaining rights and increased productivity (holding capital investment constant). In this comparison, the United States, with its poor protection of workers' rights, fares the worst. See Robert Buchele and Jens Christiansen, "Labor Relations and Productivity Growth in the Advanced Capitalist Economies," *Review of Radical Political Economics* 31, no. 1 (1999): 87–110.

18. Xenophon Zolotas, *Economic Growth and Declining Social Welfare* (New York: New York University Press, 1981).

19. For a valuable criticism of the GDP indicator for lumping together positive and negative money exchanges, see Clifford Cobb, Ted Halstead, and Jonathon Rowe, "If the GDP Is Up, Why Is America Down?" *The Atlantic Monthly* 276, no. 4 (October 1995): 59–78.

20. Marc Miringoff and Marque-Luisa Miringoff, *The Social Health of the Nation: How America Is Really Doing* (New York: Oxford University Press, 1999), 25f.

21. Miringoff and Miringoff, *The Social Health of the Nation*, 40, chart 3.1.

22. Miringoff and Miringoff, *The Social Health of the Nation*, 150f, charts 7.1, 7.2. Violent crime has lessened in the late nineties, though it is still much higher than the 1970s.

23. Miringoff and Miringoff, *The Social Health of the Nation*, chaps. 2, 8, 9.

24. Harold L. Sheppard and Neal Q. Herrick, *Where Have All the Robots Gone? Worker Dissatisfaction in the '70s* (New York: Free Press, 1972), and *Work in America: Report of a Special Task Force to the Secretary of Health, Education, and Welfare* (Cambridge, Mass.: MIT Press, 1973).

25. Robert P. Quinn and Graham L. Staines, *The 1977 Quality of Employment Survey* (Ann Arbor, Mich.: Institute for Social Research, 1979).

26. Russell W. Rumberger, "The Job Market for College Graduates, 1960–90," *Journal of Higher Education* 55, no. 4 (July/August 1984).

27. *New York Times*, July 10, 1990, 1; August 17, 1990, B5.

28. Jill Andresky Fraser, *White-Collar Sweatshops: The Deterioration of Work and Its Rewards in Corporate America* (New York: Norton, 2000).

29. Erin Olin Wright, *Classes* (London: Verso, 1985).

30. For the following, see Alan Farnham, "The Trust Gap," *Fortune* 120, no. 14 (December 14, 1989): 56–78.

31. *New York Times*, August 17, 1999, D4.

32. Stephen Wood, ed., *The Transformation of Work: Skill, Flexibility, and the Labour Process* (London: Unwin Hyman, 1989).

33. Robert J. Thomas, *What Machines Can't Do: Politics and Technology in the Industrial Enterprise* (Berkeley: University of California Press, 1994).

34. Shoshana Zuboff, *In the Age of the Smart Machine: The Future of Work and Power* (New York: Basic Books, 1988).

35. For insightful analyses, see Tess Morris-Suzuki, "Robots and Capitalism" and "Capitalism in the Computer Age and Afterward"; and Martin Kenney, "Value Creation in the Late Twentieth Century: The Rise of the Knowledge Workers," in *Cutting Edge: Technology, Information Capitalism, and Social Revolution*, ed. Jim Davis, Thomas A. Hirschl, and Michael Stack (London: Verso, 1997), chap. 6.

36. For a key source on concentration in communication, see Ben H. Bagdikian, *The Media Monopoly*, 5th ed. (Boston: Beacon, 1997).

37. Robert W. McChesney, "The Global Media Giants: The Nine Firms That Dominate the World," *Extra!* November/December 1997, 11–18; reprinted in *Annual Editions: Mass Media*, 99/00, ed. Joan Gorham, 6th. ed. (Guilford, Conn.: Dushkin/McGraw-Hill, 1999), 49–55.

38. David Croteau, "Challenging the 'Liberal Media' Claim," *Extra!* July/August 1998, 4–9; reprinted in Gorham, ed., *Annual Editions*, 99/00, 6th ed., 72–77.

39. Amitai Etzioni, "E-Communities Build New Ties, but Ties That Bind," *New York Times*, February 10, 2000, E7.

40. John Markoff, "A New, Lonelier Crowd Emerges in Internet Study," *New York Times*, February 16, 2000, 1.

41. Douglas H. Harris et al., *Organizational Linkages: Understanding the Productivity Paradox* (Washington, D.C.: National Research Council, 1994).

42. Jeff Madrick, "A Tarnished New Economy Loses More Luster with Revised Productivity Data," *New York Times*, August 30, 2001, C2.

43. Barbara Garson, *The Electronic Sweatshop: How Computers Are Transforming the Office of the Future into the Factory of the Past* (New York: Simon and Schuster, 1988).

44. Edward Tenner, "Let's Not Get Too Wired," *New York Times*, July 22, 1999, A21.

45. For a fuller analysis, see Daniel W. Rossides, *Professions and Disciplines: Functional and Conflict Perspectives* (Upper Saddle River, N.J.: Prentice Hall, 1998).

46. For a full analysis of all aspects of "the most expensive and inadequate [health care] system in the developed world," see the eight-part series starting January 7, 1999, in *The New England Journal of Medicine,* 48. The United States probably also has the worst record in regards to employment and poverty (especially among children), but comparisons are difficult, because cross-national indicators are compiled differently.

47. Clyde W. Barrow, *Universities and the Capitalist State: Corporate Liberalism and the Reconstruction of American Higher Education, 1894–1928* (Madison: University of Wisconsin Press, 1990). Academics got tenure because they and the new professional and business administrators/owners of higher education all adopted a similar late-liberal outlook.

48. For background, see Burton R. Clark, *The Academic Life: Small Worlds, Different Worlds* (Princeton, N.J.: Carnegie Foundation for the Advancement of Teaching, 1987).

49. Russell Jacoby, *The Last Intellectuals: American Culture in the Age of Academe* (New York: Basic Books, 1987).

50. Earnest T. Pascarella and Patrick T. Terenzini, *How College Affects Students: Findings and Insights from Twenty Years of Research* (San Francisco: Jossey-Bass, 1991).

51. Rob Kling and Suzanne Iacono, "The Mobilization of Support for Computerization: The Role of Computerization Movements," *Social Problems* 35 (June 1988): 226–43.

52. Lawrence Mishel, Jared Bernstein, and John Schmitt, *The State of Working America, 1998–1999,* Economic Policy Institute Series (Ithaca, N.Y.: Cornell University Press, 1999), table 5.2, 258. For updated data on wealth, income, poverty, international comparisons, etc., see the data-zone section of the Economic Policy Institute's Web site (epinet.org).

53. For a fascinating analysis of how wealth accumulates over the generations, complete with a vivid collection of case studies showing an almost feudalistic concern with family, see Michael Patrick Allen, *The Founding Fortunes: A New Anatomy of Super-Rich Families in America* (New York: Dutton, 1987). Also see *Forbes's* special annual issue, "The Richest People in America," for vignettes illustrating the role of inheritance in the concentration of wealth.

54. For a comprehensive picture of social stratification in America, see Daniel W. Rossides, *Social Stratification: The Interplay of Class, Race, and Gender,* 2d. ed. (Upper Saddle River, N.J.: Prentice Hall, 1997).

55. It cannot be said too often that the unemployment rate is not a reliable indicator of how many people are out of work.

56. McKinley L. Blackburn and David E. Bloom, "What Is Happening to the Middle Class?" *American Demographics* (1985): 18–25.

57. Senate Committee on the Budget, *Wages of American Workers in the 1980s* (Washington, D.C.: GPO, 1988).

58. Lawrence Mishel et al., *The State of Working America, 1998–1999,* Economic Policy Institute Series (Ithaca, N.Y.: Cornell University Press, 1999), 29.

59. Mishel et al., *The State of Working America,* 90.

60. Janny Scott, "Boom of 1990s Missed Many in the Middle Class, Data Suggest," *New York Times,* August 31, 2001, A1.

61. Mishel et al., *The State of Working America,* chap. 8.

62. David M. Gordon, Richard Edwards, and Michael Reich, *Segmented Work, Dividing Workers: The Historical Transformation of Labor in the United States* (New York: Cambridge University Press, 1982).

63. For a fascinating picture of downward mobility in the American middle class (defined

broadly to include managers as well as a blue-collar community), based on 150 in-depth interviews (not a random or representative sample), see Katherine S. Newman, *Falling from Grace:
The Experience of Downward Mobility in the American Middle Class* (New York: Free Press,
1988).

64. *Chronicle of Higher Education,* June 14, 1996, A13.

65. *New York Times,* May 23, 1996, A1.

5

✧

Communication, Media, and the American Polity

I n earlier chapters we showed the vital connection between forms of communication and the nature and development of both society and state. The emergence of writing, for example, played a large role in the creation of agrarian civilization. Writing and the Greek alphabet, along with small-scale farming, urban pursuits, and extensive interaction with other cultures, led to the democratic city-state and the creation of a rational worldview in ancient Greece. A system of roads and maritime routes made the Roman Empire possible. The development of commercial routes along the coasts and rivers of Europe, along with the printing press and the oceangoing vessel, helped create the unique world of capitalism. In American history, all of these plus the steamboat, railroad, Pony Express, newspapers, advertising, catalogs, telegraph, telephone, radio, television, and computer have been vital forces in the dynamic expansion and consolidation of American capitalism. In this chapter we want to understand the role played by communication in contemporary American political institutions.

THE POLITY: A DEFINITION

The *polity* (or state) comprises an entire network of political institutions. Complex societies generate public norms (laws) and values to defend themselves and to control, guide, support, reform, or curb the behavior of their members and groups. An important set of laws (taxes) raises the money to pay for these functions. Tax and other laws are implemented by tax collectors, the military, court officials, and other civil servants (the government). Thought of as an action system, the modern polity is essentially a struggle (politics) by power groups to control the public mechanisms

113

(legislature, government, courts) that decide which laws and which values will prevail—in Lasswell's famous phrase, "who gets what, when, and how."[1] Framed differently, the state is an important mechanism by which individuals, groups, and society solve their personal and collective problems. Thinking of the state as an adaptive, problem-solving institution is not easy for Americans, though in practice most of them try to use the state to their advantage, with only some succeeding.

KIND OF SOCIETY AND KIND OF POLITY

Simple Societies

A simple society does not develop a polity (a distinct sphere of public law and authority), because most of its members are the same and all have similar interests. In simple society, problems are solved either by all on a personal basis or by tribal norms that invoke a collective response.

Agrarian Societies: Feudal Authoritarianism

The state emerges in advanced horticultural society (Aztec, Mayan) and reaches its preindustrial peak in agrarian society (a society that has the technology to cultivate large fields). In an agrarian society, a hereditary nobility monopolizes the political institution, with one of their number emerging as a hereditary monarch. The nobility are landlords, and it is their economic power that gives them their political power—or rather, their specialization as landlords, warriors, clergy, civil servants, and royal advisers—and allows them to translate their economic power into a more thorough sociopolitical power.

The general causes of the emergence of the state are the increase in social complexity and social problems, and conflicts over how to deal with them. An important cause of state growth is the need to control powerful rivers and harness them for irrigation purposes, something that only central government can achieve. As society diversifies, unifying abstractions appear: God (or gods), king, ethics, moral codes, and royal law. The state is needed to enforce norms and to perform economic and military functions that would otherwise not get done.

Industrial Societies: The Trend toward Representative Government

The authority structures of modern society are similar to those of agrarian society but also strikingly different. The political institution is elaborated and, if anything, becomes a more important part of society. The struggle to enlarge formal access to political power finds its culmination. In England, this struggle, which surfaced in the seventeenth century, reflected the diversification of the English economy beyond agriculture and landowners. In essence, the struggle for representative government in the next two centuries would be between commercial and manufacturing interests and feudal landlords—in effect, an effort to translate the economic power of the historical middle class into political power. Common misunderstandings aside, the victory of Parliament in 1688, the establishment of the U.S. Constitution after the American War of Independence, and the French Revolution of 1789 all represent the success of the dynamic middle class (new propertied and professional groups) in changing the polity so as to favor their interests over both landlords and the propertyless.

The middle class took power in the name of the people, but the great bourgeois revolutions were a victory for the principle of *property in general* over the principle of landed property. The experiences of England and the United States are instructive on this score. Both countries became fully established capitalist systems (with the help of the central state, of which more in a moment) using a property qualification for access to political power. The extension of the franchise to the propertyless came *after* the political-legal system and the capitalist economy were fully in place (and after voting itself had come under the control of money, education, and organizational skills—that is, property in other forms).

The emergence of popular government and multiparty elections is a necessary development, given the growing complexity and conflicts of the maturing capitalist (industrial-urban) economy. The growth of representative government was gradual in the Western liberal democracies; England curtailed the power of the House of Lords only in 1911 and preserved remnants of the property qualification well into the twentieth century. The United States did not make election to the U.S. Senate popular, give women the vote, or extend effective political and civil rights to minorities until the twentieth century.

THE NATURE OF
REPRESENTATIVE GOVERNMENT

Representative Government: Parliamentary and Presidential Variants

Representative government in the United States has taken the form of a presidential system, as opposed to variants of the parliamentary approach found in Great Britain, Canada, and much of Europe. Under the parliamentary system, electoral districts choose among candidates representing political parties (themselves not actually part of the state but voluntary organizations). Those chosen assemble as a lawmaking body. The party having a majority forms a government, which can use its majority to enact laws binding on the population at large. The American presidential system separates executive and legislative functions; a president and a legislature (Congress) are elected separately. The result is often a stalemate, because the president and Congress can represent different political parties and thus a different mix of economic and social interests. The American polity is complicated further by its federal nature; though the Constitution has a clear function for strong, central government, the fifty states also perform important political-legal functions. The states vary widely in their socioeconomic development, and this unevenness is reflected in their legislatures, governments, and laws.

The Uniqueness of Western Political Institutions

The developed capitalist democracies have a number of unique features. The first is the idea of the *public interest* placed above private interest, a powerful and highly functional convention to which all appeal but that no one can define (for a fuller discussion of a related idea, the public, see chapter 7).

Second, all polities claim to be derived from the people and to act on its behalf. The Western polities demonstrate this principle by election to office through direct popular voting. It should be noted that the United States gives significant power in the Senate to its less-populated states (California, with over thirty million people, has two senators, the same as numerous states that have much smaller populations), while in the Electoral College each state gets one extra vote regardless of population. This latter deviation from direct popular rule resulted in a presidential victory for George W. Bush in 2000 despite defeat in the popular vote by 540,000 votes.

A third unique feature is the distinction between *delegates* (who carry out the wishes of others) and *representatives* (who act on behalf of others but who are permitted to think and act as they think best). The concept of *representative,* which is related to the idea of a public interest, allows for political behavior and thought not rigidly and narrowly bound to the service of a particular group, locality, or interest. It emerges from complexity and change and is a way to cope with them. Representative government encourages empathy and mental flexibility, promotes political creativity, and makes compromise morally acceptable (as does majority rule). In its origins, its characteristic mode of communication was face-to-face, door-to-door canvassing, and in-person oral discourse and debate, but increasingly the emphasis has shifted to formalized public debates and one-way oral communication via the mass media (the issueless campaign). Communication has also shifted to the exchange of written technical reports and courtroomlike committee hearings.

Fourth, the liberal democracies have sought to solve the problem of economic and social conflict also through *constitutionalism* (a basic code that stands above positive law, or legislation), responsible government, majority rule, a neutral speaker of a legislature (in Great Britain), government officials who are not political partisans, and an independent and impartial judiciary.

Representative Government: Are Its Thwarted Ideals a Permanent Condition?

The ideals of representative government are derived from ancient Greece, Rome, and the experiences of the historical middle classes of England, France, and the United States. Ideally, political power reflects the concerns and interests of all citizens. Ideally, political power is exercised according to law and by responsible public officials. Modern societies are ideally *rational-legal* systems of power (to use Max Weber's term), in which social problems are addressed rationally according to due process of law by all citizens, acting through individuals who reach positions of power through open, honest elections. Ideally, representative democracies adhere to constitutions (written or unwritten), submit to majority rule, empower legislators and government officials whose behavior is prescribed by law, and have impartial independent judiciaries. That these ideals are only partially realized is well known. Few, however, question whether they *can* be realized.

It is widely acknowledged that American elections are deeply influenced by the power of money—also that justice is something that one buys (by buying the services of a lawyer, for example) and that the judiciary and the law serve primarily to protect property interests. (To cite a significant example, in eight out of ten court cases in New York City involving landlords and tenants, only the landlord has a lawyer.) In the last two presidential elections, a bare 50 percent of the voters turned out; in other elections, 10 to 30 percent is the usual rate of voter participation. In the 1980s, "issueless campaigns" emerged in which those who said the least about social issues got elected. All observers of American politics know that legislatures pass laws that help established interests and that laws that go against such interests are not enforced. They also know that regulatory agencies work to help those they are supposed to regulate. Also, there is widespread corruption, from the White House through the entire executive branch, Congress, and (especially) at state and local levels. What is not so well known is that these shortfalls may be structural—that is, inherent in representative government, or rather, a capitalist polity. In any case, whether progress toward democratic ideals is possible cannot be known until the plutocratic nature of the American polity is eliminated.

The political institution in modern societies, therefore, cannot be understood unless naive notions of democracy, freedom, and equality are abandoned. No society, in the past or present, is a democracy (rule by and in the interest of ordinary people and the poor). No society is characterized by freedom and equality, nor is any society characterized by the rule of law. The stratified (or liberal, capitalist, plutocratic) democracies are systems of *representative government,* not true democracies. Even in England and the United States, which built on the unique experiences and ideals of ancient Greece and Rome, the emergence and operation of representative government makes more sense as the *prevention* of democracy than as its realization. Consider, for example, as we have noted above, that the United States did not hold an election until eight years after the success of its war of independence, and that when it did, it restricted the vote until the 1850s to white males who satisfied a property qualification. Long before the extension of the suffrage, the American legal system was shaped to benefit dynamic property groups.

Perhaps the most insightful way to get at the nature of representative government is to remember where government comes from. In advanced horticultural and agrarian societies, government resulted from the needs of economic groups. The complexity of society required systems to produce conformity and order. The symbolic systems of these societies quickly shifted away from particularism to universalism;

monotheism replaced polytheism, and broad abstractions arose to make sense of and unify an increasingly diverse world.

Representative government continues this process. The state becomes the unifying principle. There is an enormous development of abstractions, most of them empty or only partially realized ideals: the law, equality, freedom, rights, the people, progress. Representative government also depoliticizes itself by claiming that politics, government, the judiciary, the military, the police, and education are or should be nonpartisan and objective. In this it is supported by the professions and disciplines, which also claim the same for themselves.

Representative government initially provides a way for conflicting property groups to settle their quarrels without much interference from the masses. But over the past century or so, the propertied and professional classes have proliferated monstrously, probably beyond effective communication and consensus; in addition, they have been beset by demands from below that they have found difficult to meet or deflect. Empirical research by social scientists, public opinion polls, journalistic accounts, and elections provide America's power groups with knowledge about the classes below and give them feedback on the effectiveness of their policies. Nonetheless, representative government in the United States shows all the earmarks of social overload: political stalemate, a failure to solve social problems, surging volumes of litigation, and spending and consumption outstripping productivity.

THE AMERICAN POLITY

The Constitution: A Charter for or a Barrier to Democracy?

The U.S. Constitution, which emerged in the Newtonian era, represents the power of naturalistic imagery in how we think of society. The American polity is thought to be a great machine (separation of functions) in permanent equilibrium (checks and balances). It is a static instrument, in that it presupposes a fixed division of social labor; the polity referees the activities of a dynamic collection of private individuals and private groups. The Constitution controls government, but it also curbs the ability of the people to act ("Congress shall pass no laws . . ."). It presupposes that social differences will reflect natural differences in human beings. This is clearly indicated in James Madison's *Federalist Paper 10,* which constitutes the theoretical underpinning of the Constitution. Economic conflict, says Madison, is at the heart of politics. But, unlike Karl Marx's conflict theory, Madison argues that economic differences arise directly from "diversity in the faculties of men." Since economic inequality is natural, government's role is to maintain this natural order and mediate disputes.

After two hundred years, Madison's vision of representative government is still in effect. Under that view, unequal groups should compete to control government but never use it to change the natural economic order, and the people at large (society) are best served if public power favors private property and private solutions to public problems. When Adam Smith's concept of a natural equilibrium in the economy is wedded to Madison's politics, the depoliticizing, antidemocratic nature of the American political economy becomes apparent.

Voting, Interest Groups, and Other Forms of Political Participation

Politics in a liberal democracy is considered "open space," part of a larger area known as the "voluntary sector." Political parties, along with trade unions, business and professional associations, universities, reform groups (with a wide variety of interests), fraternal organizations, foundations, charities, and public-interest think tanks, try to influence the public and get government to do their bidding.

The essential ethic governing the relations of these groups is compromise, the conscious acceptance of the morality of trade-offs. Violations of this ethic have appeared frequently; Watergate (an attempt to undermine illegally the major opposition party) and Iran-Contra (an attempt to bypass Congress illegally) were violations of the essential spirit of liberal democracy. The absolutistic mentality displayed by these events has been matched by the growth of single-issue groups. These groups are focused on one cause and make no effort to relate it to other interests. Here we see an ominous threat to liberal democracy and one of the reasons for a stalemated polity, as groups emerge to focus exclusively on gun control, abortion, the whale (or redwood tree, or some other part of the natural environment), nuclear energy, animal rights, school prayer, or communism.[2]

Declining Political Participation

The American political process has never been based on mass political mobilization. American elites have created a negative view of politicians and government, and they have controlled the definition of public issues, essentially removing them from things that interest or involve ordinary people. The representation process has also failed to represent the American people (denial of the vote, grossly imbalanced electoral districts, the Senate and Electoral College, and the gerrymander). The power of private money (the political action committees, or PACs) has undermined party discipline because politicians in secure (gerrymandered) electoral districts can be directly financed by interest groups. These interest groups tend to thwart the desires of the American people on one issue after another: national health insurance, the environment, nuclear arms reduction, gun control, government action to help the poor or make the economy competitive, and so on. The reduction of political participation culminates in the issueless campaign. The increased formalism (empty abstractions and mind-numbing slogans) that appeared in politics in the 1980s rounded out the formalism that now characterizes American culture in other spheres as well. The apathy that appeared in politics was matched by a steady reduction in participation in all other forms of voluntary action. More ominously, claims Putnam, the drastic reduction of communicative experience by the American people has led to lower levels of social capital (trust, altruistic motives, skills at interaction), a lowering that no doubt contributes to decreased levels of civic involvement.[3]

Skocpol (with generous thanks to other scholars at the Civic Engagement Project she is coordinating at Harvard University) uses a more historical and sociological approach to understanding civic engagement. For much of their history, Americans have created groups to fight for the things they valued. Skocpol argues that the federated, mass-membership organizations of the past (from colonial times to the 1960s) have been replaced by memberless advocacy groups staffed by professionals and funded by the wealthy, by foundations, and through mailing lists. The earlier voluntary groups facilitated interaction between elites and ordinary citizens, linking the concerns of the latter to the corridors of political power. They provided mobility for local members and offered varied experience as individuals climbed the ranks. Participation in such groups not only generated social capital but, by creating the belief that participation meant something, generated participation itself.

The federated mass membership organizations declined, argues Skocpol, because of the civil rights, feminist, and antiwar movements of the 1960s. They were replaced by nationally based advocacy groups, paralleling the professionally run trade and professional groups that have also sprung up in Washington, D.C. The new advocacy-type groups can do without members because they do not rely on dues and they do not generate their policies through dialogue among members. Professional staffs are now oriented primarily to their counterparts in rival organizations. These advocacy groups engage in skilled lobbying to influence public policy and they reach out to mass audiences through television (talk show, news programs). All this, says Skocpol, contributes to clashing opposites, cynicism, and the withdrawal from civic life by ordinary people.

Skocpol is more focused on conflicts, politics, and group life than Putnam and she clearly refers to the domination of group life, both past and present, by America's upper classes. She is not above even suggesting that there is something oligarchic about advocacy groups. But her remedy is not much different than Putnam's: we should all do what we can to revitalize civic engagement.[4] Her analysis of the problem and her remedy would have been even more insightful had she assumed from the outset that the history of American voluntarism has been a struggle about creating a democracy, not an example of it.

Government in Action

Government does far more for society than Americans are aware of (or are allowed to understand). The specific functions of government are so numerous that a list seems best. The U.S. government provides:

1. security against external enemies;
2. espionage and intelligence services;
3. support for foreign trade, scientific exchanges, tourism, international mail, air traffic, American citizens abroad, aid of various kinds to other countries;

4. security at home against criminals, terrorists, rebels (beyond the obvious, there are many special programs—for example, to buy and destroy guns or provide money to colleges to curb sexual assault);

5. statistical and printing services that compile and disseminate an enormous range of information about the United States and other countries, and numerous pamphlets providing practical advice on many subjects (the U.S. Postal Service, long a government agency that provided subsidized communication services, is now an independent, unsubsidized corporation that must compete against private message carriers);

6. water for drinking, irrigation, and industry;

7. a comprehensive network of highways, bridges, dams, ports, and airports;

8. public train, subway, ferry, and bus transportation (other capitalist societies operate public air transportation as well);

9. public health and safety through health inspections; medical research and public health laws; fire protection, worker safety, consumer product safety, and coastal and waterway safety and protection;

10. some income security in old age or disability, and health care for the elderly, veterans, and the needy;

11. some income support for the unemployed and poor; rescue and relief services for disaster victims; insurance against floods and crop failure;

12. protection and restoration of the natural environment, provision and protection of public recreational areas (beyond the obvious examples, there are such special programs as monies given to farmers to take environmentally sensitive land out of production and to adopt conservation measures);

13. subsidies and other supports for a large range of private and public individuals and groups, such as farmers, corporations, small businesses, laid-off workers, ambulance services, groups and individuals in the arts, universities, public television, nursing homes, medical and mental health services, political candidates, researchers in all social and natural sciences, adoption services, sports teams, recreational facilities, urban, community, and rural development, and middle and lower-income housing (much of the above involves the central government helping state and local governments);

14. certification and licensing for a wide range of occupations; patent and copyright protection; monitoring of voluntary groups and pension plans;

15. law enforcement and regulations relating to power plants, gas, telephone, radio, television, computer-Internet, airlines, trucking, shipping, health care, education, sports, occupation, and finance (banking, investing, etc.);

16. establishment and protection of the civil rights of a wide variety of minorities (racial, ethnic, as well as women, the disabled, gays, the elderly);

17. influence on and protection of the economy exercised by adjusting its budget, raising or lowering taxes and interest rates, increasing or reducing the money supply;

18. weather information and warnings about impending storms, earthquake and weather research; and

19. the socialization of children and adults through formal education, by staging patriotic events celebrating national achievements and heroes, by honoring mothers and fathers with special days, and by drawing attention to achievements in private and public life and to America's wildlife and natural wonders (for example, through postage stamps).

Needless to say, the government does not do all of the above in so many words. It is halfhearted about some of what it does and fails to accomplish other things. Some things are done exceptionally well. Government-financed research accounts for over 70 percent of patents that increase economic productivity;[5] government initiatives are largely responsible for advances in computer technology, the establishment of the Internet, and reviving the computer industry against foreign competition. One reason government does not work as well as it should is that it operates in a context of false beliefs. Contrary to these beliefs, government is not getting bigger, taxes and spending are not rising, and the debt is not growing. (All such figures should be compiled as a percent of the total population or economy— when that is done, one finds great stability.)

Political Socialization and Legitimacy

Like other societies, the United States socializes its members to accept the legitimacy of the American political-legal system and the social order it serves. The family, school, mass media, religion, social science, and political participation itself serve to bring new generations into the American way of life and keep them there. Americans may ask for constitutional amendments or for new ways to finance political parties, but the overall sociopolitical order is taken for granted, and Americans rarely raise questions about it or consider alternatives to it. Social science, schools, mass media, and religion, in their own ways, promote a complacency about public power and the social order.

Political socialization in the United States has succeeded in giving liberalism (the Republican and Democratic Parties) a monopoly and in preventing alternatives from arising. But evidence has appeared suggesting important deficiencies in political socialization. America's socializing agencies have not been able to inculcate positive civic attitudes or behavior, overcome widespread political apathy, or prevent what appears to be a steady erosion of public confidence in politics, government, and law.[6]

The American Legal System

The *law* consists of a special body of norms enacted to uphold or realize a variety of social purposes. Law serves to integrate society, by establishing public order and by maintaining rights and duties. It also facilitates interaction between diverse groups, by enforcing rights. Law expresses a society's moral and ethical ideals. It confers legitimacy on the holders of power, insofar as it seems to pinpoint responsibilities, and it provides some measure of benefit to all.

In premodern society, legal and other norms openly enforce a *consensus* about the world. In premodern societies, law was not easily distinguished from morality, nor from religion or philosophy. In these societies, disputes were often settled by mediation or by open forums in which all values and beliefs were allowed free rein. Modern society separated law from other norms and made it society's ultimate boundary. Law becomes extremely complex and requires special people and groups to embody it and give it life. As Durkheim observed, law no longer merely enforces consensus (mechanical solidarity) but also restores and recalibrates rights and interests (organic solidarity).

Law today is an enormously varied attempt to serve a large variety of values and social purposes. Functionalist and conflict theorists see the law differently. Functionalists think of law as derived from consensus, the considered judgment of the community. The law, they say, serves vital social functions: stability, legitimacy, and adaptation. Conflict theorists also see the law as a stabilizing force but as one that protects both the good and the bad. Americans break the law precisely because it does *not* rest on consensus (businesspeople and landlords, for example, ignore laws designed to protect workers, the environment, or tenants). Law, for conflict theorists, means that the interests of the powerful prevail.

American law, argues Derek C. Bok, cannot be connected to the public interest. We do not know the consequences for society of labor law, antitrust law, or workplace-safety law. The American legal system, the most expensive in the world, does not protect the rights of most of its citizens.[7]

Creative Politics

The creative process in politics consists of separating concrete issues from all-embracing ideological programs and solving each one on a piecemeal basis. It is unlikely, for example, that the United States could have been established in the first place if the founders of the nation had not sidestepped the issue of slavery. The extension of the suffrage from the 1850s into the 1960s; the rise of the great regulatory agencies from the last decades of the nineteenth century on; the Wagner Act of 1935, establishing collective bargaining; the Social Security Act of 1935; the War on Poverty and the great civil rights acts of the 1960s—these are milestones of creativity in American history. From the 1930s to 1968, reform-minded business people, professionals, and voluntary groups, members of both major political parties, intellectuals, labor leaders, and leaders of racial and ethnic groups developed a working consensus (mostly elite driven) about how the United States should be run.

The Decline of Creative Politics

More recently, something new may have appeared on the American political scene—a decline of creative politics. Creative politics in American history reflected the dominance of a fairly homogeneous collection of property and professional groups. Today, dominant property and professional groups are far more complex and fragmented than they were before, say, World War II. Farm, manufacturing, and service interests, along with a wide variety of professions, are extremely heterogeneous. It is doubtful if they could escape stalemate even if they had no other groups to contend with. But, of course, America's property and professional groups no longer have a clear predominance of power. In recent generations, as noted, single-interest groups based on principles derived from morality, religion, or secular philosophies have appeared, whose causes include those of the working class and the elderly (since the 1930s), blacks and Hispanics, women, the handicapped, gays, environmentalists, and others. The United States today, years after the end of the Cold War, bears a huge peacetime military burden (which it shouldered, for the first time in its history, soon after the Second World War), and is providing military aid to a variety of foreign countries, as it struggles to defend its many and varied interests around the globe.

Each group—professional, ideological (single-issue), labor, black, Hispanic, women, handicapped, and other minorities—is internally diverse. Combined, they make a bewildering array of forces pulling and pushing the polity in all directions at once. These diverse groups have become a heavy burden for American political institutions to carry. Lacking consensus on fundamentals, they find it difficult to communicate. The reason America's political system exhibits rigidity and irrelevance may well be that it is overloaded by excessive and irreconcilable demands about how the country should be run and how the nation's resources should be allocated.

The failure of American capitalism during the Great Depression of the 1930s led to the creative politics of the 1930–1970 period. But since the late 1960s, there has been a growing tangle of postponed problems and half-solutions. Poorly framed legislation, the very expensive manned moon shot of the 1960s (the primary purpose of which was prestige, since the same knowledge could have been obtained through inexpensive machines), the expensive (and unpaid-for) Vietnam War, the dramatic increase in claimants on social resources during the 1960s and 1970s, the end of the era of cheap resources, the expense of protecting the environment, and the relative decline of the United States in world affairs came together to create a noticeable inability to solve problems. Each problem area and each proposed solution affects the others, making for a politics of drift and stalemate. Perhaps the best index of the loss of adaptive capacity in the United States is the steady decline of the political party.

The Decline of the Political Party

The political party is a prime mechanism for airing and reconciling sociocultural conflicts and contradictions.[8] When political leaders compete for election in a constituency of mixed economic, religious, ethnic, or racial groups, they are likely to search for common denominators and to pay attention to the problems of all voting segments. Political relations characterized by competition for support in a diverse electorate are likely to be both more creative and more responsive to public need. When like-minded leaders come together to combine their strengths in order to win majorities at various electoral levels, a political party is born. The party that garners a majority forms the government and can be held accountable by lay citizens. Putting political leaders in this relation to each other and the general citizenry is *the major achievement of Western political life.*

When parties are viable, there is a tendency to worry about the quality of candidates. Elected officials are eager to compile good party records. Party leaders have the organizational strength and resources to discipline wayward members but also protect creative mavericks. Strong parties prevent the fragmentation of the political public into rigid factions and groups based on absolutistic principles. Strong parties help prevent personal characteristics (charisma) from being the main factor in elections. A strong party can force those with a point of view or an interest to relate it to other points of view and other interests. Interest groups that fail to do this have little hope of success.

American political parties have never been strong. The antipolitical tradition in the United States has not made politics an attractive arena for most members of the middle and upper classes. Civil service reform, the emphasis on nonpartisan politics and government, and the general rise of the welfare state have robbed the party of its patronage, its reputation, and its ability to do favors and deliver benefits. Party reforms in the 1970s helped bring the political party to its knees. The party's control over candidates declined as the nominating process was opened up and many more states conducted primaries to determine who should run for office.

Campaign financing laws from the 1970s on curtailed contributions to the overall party organization, but a loophole allowed uncontrolled contributions (soft money) to assorted political entities, in effect, abolishing the effort to democratize elections. The Campaign Finance Reform Act of 2002 will help a little by curbing the flow of soft money. But it also increases the flow of hard money, keeping political influence still beyond the capability of most Americans. The decline of the party has also been furthered by the cumulative results of gerrymandering (which homogenizes electoral districts); by technological changes, especially in mass communication; and by the growth of professional political services performed outside the party by media experts, fund-raisers, advertisers, pollsters, and political consultants (with the hidden help of "nonpartisan" public interest groups, policy think tanks, and foundations).

The decline of the political party is reflected in and reinforced by a decline in voter identification with party (the rise of the undecided, the independent, the apathetic), by an increase at the state and federal level of split-party control of the executive and legislative branches, and by the growing practice of holding separate state and federal elections.

The decline of the party means a loss of problem-solving ability at the political level. Public life becomes fragmented and stalemated as it dissolves into single-issue groups, campaigns based on empty rhetoric and personality, and a divorce between political life and social problems. The overall trend also reflects and contributes to a significant new trend, the growth of mass political apathy. Since 1960, voter participation has declined steadily, reaching a steady low rate of about 50 percent of the eligible electorate for presidential elections (and much lower for off-year congressional and local elections). Strenuous efforts by both parties to stimulate voting have failed, and voter turnout in the United States remains far below that of the other developed capitalist societies (with the exception of Switzerland, whose low turnout reflects the unimportance of central government).[9]

The decline of the political party has not led to the decline of politics; if anything, the reverse is true. More time and money than ever are being spent on political campaigns. The bulk of the money comes from conservative groups, from the extreme Right to moderate Republicans, taking advantage of sophisticated computer-driven, direct-mail communication. The essence of the new political campaign is the packaged candidate who says little and thus offends as few as possible, who projects a pseudo-gemeinschaft personality and can disguise nineteenth-century norms and values with twenty-first-century words. The ability to produce this sterile form of communication between leader and follower has been enhanced by computer-driven audiovisual technology.

COMMUNICATION TECHNOLOGY
AND THE NEW POLITICS

The impact on politics of communication technology has been large and varied. The printing press, for example, did much to change Europe's politics by bringing about first a literate middle class and then a literate citizenry. In the United States, mass literacy (through mass education) and universal male suffrage both began in the 1850s.[10] Newspapers and magazines became important political forces during the nineteenth century. Public relations and advertising firms helped depoliticize the activities of business. In the 1930s, President Roosevelt used the radio to galvanize the American people in his effort to overcome the Great Depression.

Technology's impact on politics has continued in the age of television. The advent of television (along with other technology) may actually have introduced new and dangerous levels of control over American political life. For one thing, the dominance of television has turned politics away from written to oral discourse. No sane businessperson or professional would dream of conducting business primarily through verbal discourse, but radio and now television have steered the American political world away from writing to audiovisual interaction. The new audiovisual technology, in combination with other technology, actually makes it possible for people to see and believe in things that do not exist. The carefully arranged studio setting, the live shot in shopping malls and residential areas, and staffs of advertising and media experts, pollsters, and psychologists make it possible for political elites to package and *sell* a candidate.[11] What is sold is an image, an individual larger than life, one who corresponds to the public's hunger for a leader of heroic, unblemished stature. With careful editing, the leader always has a word of wisdom to offer. There is no fumbling or hesitation. By careful attention to props, the leader is associated with God, the flag, children, books, fireplace, and the current fashion in dress. The leader is against evil, is generous to the needy, and verbalizes society's highest values. The result is not politics but a civic religious ceremony.

The mobilization of opinion and voters takes place through political commercials and films that present an abstract (formal) political point of view. The selling of the candidate is supported by film shots of the candidate on the campaign trail. These are supplied free to the news bureaus of television stations. But the clips are carefully edited so that the candidate's mistakes and hesitations are omitted. Editing allows the candidates to appear with famous people—even when the famous people do not support them—and with large, adoring crowds (sparsely attended rallies and opposition heckling are carefully edited out). Film clips are geared to play on regional biases. Not only are commercials and news clips indistinguishable from one another, but seeing is no longer believing. Technology and its owners have created a vivid, plausible, but false reality (for a fuller discussion of the role of journalism in American politics, see chapter 7).

Kathleen Hall Jamieson has provided a comprehensive analysis, complete with vivid examples of campaign advertising, of what had become by the 1980s a skillful game of "deception and distraction."[12] Political commercials routinely use assertion and rosy description in place of argument, abbreviated but evocative images, pretended neutral reports, ordinary citizens voicing negative views of opponents, unidentified advocates and anonymous critics, and one-liners and anecdotes. These practices, says Jamieson, effectively prevent listeners from engaging in a reasoned, reflexive processing of what they are seeing and hearing. The political campaign not only lacks argument and fails to engage the listener cognitively but allows candidates to escape accountability for what they stand for and for what is said on their behalf.

Jamieson's conclusion is that dirty politics can be replaced—that argumentation can be offered rather than assertion, substantive engagement rather than storytelling, data rather than drama, and problem solving rather than candidates' strategy for winning—if the public insists that candidates and reporters restore the relationship between campaign discourse and governance (page 266). It might have been better, however, if Jamieson had said (even at the risk of generating cynicism) that reasoned public discourse in campaigns has never characterized American politics. It would have been better if she had argued that some improvement might be possible if Canadian and European practices were followed (wherein campaigns are much shorter, there are curbs on spending, significant public funding of elections is provided, political ads are much longer, and a great deal of time is donated by publicly owned mass media outlets). It would certainly have been better to question whether a rational focus on problem solving is possible in a plutocratic polity that has led to a gerrymandered system of representation in which 75 to 90 percent of the seats in the House of Representatives are not competitive and in which widespread apathy allows Congress and the president under ordinary circumstances to be elected by 26 percent of registered voters.

Television and other communication opportunities have spawned a new occupation, the political consultant. Sabato has provided a description of the growth of the many-sided world of political consultants, some of whom actually take charge of campaigns. Political consultants employ experts in various fields—nonstop pollsters, specialists in film and political advertising and in direct-mail campaigning and fund-raising. Sabato argues that the professionalized business of political consulting has changed the character of elections by weakening the ties between political parties and candidates and strengthening those between interest groups and candidates. Political consultants not only support interest-group politics (adding to the neglect of public-interest debate) but help to shape public policy by supporting candidates who are skilled at running for office but not at governing.[13]

Mayhew argues that professional political communication has eroded the public's ability to influence its leaders.[14] In superb summaries of the history and current status of advertising, market research, public relations, and policy groups, combined with a deft analysis of their use in mounting systematic political campaigns (chapters 7 and 8), Mayhew outlines how public opinion loses its moorings in social groups. Instead of rational deliberation about the concerns of the entire public, politics is now a way to mobilize core voters by using slogans, repetition, and euphemisms. Mayhew's solution is to develop public fora in which leaders and the led engage in meaty, meaningful dialogue.

Mayhew's objective is to augment sociology's (read liberalism's) response to radicals' critique of mass society. Along the way he provides insightful analyses of the thought of Talcott Parsons and Jürgen Habermas (chapters 3 and 4). But by and large, his overall analysis of what has happened to the public assumes a natural, unspoiled public that can be redeemed by ideas and ideals. What is missing from his liberalism can probably be expressed by the fact that his is a Left rather than Right liberalism, the latter providing almost all of his examples of how the public is being corrupted by professionalized communication. It never occurs to him to ask how a small minority of interest groups manages to thwart the wishes of the majority on almost all issues. It never occurs to him that Left liberals are doing much the same and that little would change in American life if their reforms were enacted.

There is little doubt that communication technology and those adept at using it politically continue to thwart the development of American democracy. Computerized campaigns, relying largely on television, have generated political apathy, lowered political skills and input by ordinary Americans, and generated distrust of and cynicism about politics and government. To understand this process fully, though, one must add to it commercial advertising and public relations (chapter 3), urban planning and architecture (chapter 6), journalism (chapter 7), and popular culture (chapter 8)—each does its part in depoliticizing the American people.

THE NEW POLITICS AND THE NEW COMPUTER-DRIVEN, INTEGRATED COMMUNICATION SYSTEM

Powerful groups have always used all the communication devices available to them. They have combined technologies for greater effect, as the previous section has shown. The computer introduces something new—a device that can integrate all forms of communication into one system, controlled from one command point.

Computers That Analyze, Manage, Correspond, Talk, Awe, and Can Scold and Intimidate: The New Mass Politics

Mr. and Mrs. John Q. Public are aware that a presidential election is coming. They are concerned about many issues but are now not sure how to decide on policies or priorities. Their number-one worry is how to pay for the college educations of their children, seventeen and eighteen years old. One day they receive what appears to be a personal letter from the presidential candidate of Alpha Party. They are flattered that an important figure would write to them, not realizing that the letter was written by a computer (*by* the computer, not *on* a computer). Their response is heightened because the letter focuses on the problem of financing college education. This makes them feel that the candidate cares about them—somehow they feel closer to the mainstream of American political life. They do not realize that stored in a far-away computer are data about the electorate's "hot buttons"—political slang for any issue that concerns a voter or interest group. They also have no way of knowing how many people around the town have received the same letter, but with slightly different wording to push a variety of hot buttons—taxes, abortion, crime, busing, and so on. They also do not realize that the letters are part of a large, complex, and expensive campaign the immediate purpose of which is to prepare their recipients for the candidate's impending visit to their city.

The candidate's visit has also been prepared by a computer that has all the relevant data: where to go, places to avoid; local dignitaries to invite to gatherings; local, state, and regional interests and biases; and what hotels and arenas to use. The computer has also been used to prepare political commercials and news clips to suit each locality and to see to it that they are broadcast in conjunction with the candidate's visit. The assumption behind the fake personalized letter is that Mr. and Mrs. John Q. Public's eyes will open and their ears will perk up when this candidate appears on television. Sure enough, the couple sees the candidate on television, both on the news and in commercials, in the days immediately following receipt of the letter. There are news shots of the candidate visiting shopping malls, talking to concerned parents, and eating ethnic food. These shots were not taken by the TV station but are film clips provided by the candidate. The clips have been carefully edited to eliminate all damaging material and to project a wholesome, concerned, grassroots candidate talking with ordinary people. Political commercials can be identified as commercials, but news clips cannot be. In any case, even commercials are hard to distinguish from news clips. The slick attention to image making, personality projection, and irrelevant associations tend to hide the fact that nothing of substance about policy or priorities is being said.

Four days after the first letter, another (written by the same machine) arrives inviting Mr. and Mrs. John Q. Public to meet the candidate at the airport (there are other letters arriving around town, inviting others to meet the candidate at the shopping mall and at the high school auditorium). At the airport, all is recorded on a digital camera, in a form that is easily edited and augmented (because a digital camera is an extension of the computer), and is made immediately available to television stations both locally and across the country, but especially to one in the candidate's next stop (the choice of stops is also made by a machine that is fed politically relevant data). An edited news release is prepared for newspapers and magazines. That night Mr. and Mrs. John Q. Public see the candidate on television being greeted by a crowd at the airport. They look to see if they are visible and are disappointed that they do not see themselves. But they are satisfied anyway—they have become part of the decision-making process.

Just after the local news, the phone rings, and a pleasant voice asks for Mr. or Mrs. John Q. Public. It says that it is calling on behalf of candidate John Wholesome to find out if there are any special concerns that John Q. Publics want to convey to him. You blurt out that paying your children's college education is really important right now, along with the need to defend the free world. The voice thanks you and then asks for a contribution, however small, to help the candidate carry the day against special interests. You pledge a hundred dollars and hang up, not realizing that you have been talking to a machine (*to* a machine, not *through* a machine). You are a little flushed and somehow wish you had not pledged a hundred dollars. Two days later a letter arrives with a pledge card and return envelope (all written and mailed by a machine) asking for your check. You delay sending it, and two weeks later the phone rings. A voice reminds you of your pledge and your promise to send it. If you say you don't remember, the machine is programmed to respond pointedly; it informs you that it has a recording, which it then plays. You hear your voice, and then the voice pleasantly chides you, reminding you how important it is to stay involved. The scolding and intimidation work. You sheepishly make out a check, which is processed by the same electronics that got you to make the pledge in the first place. Your candidate wins, and you feel good even though you do not notice much improvement in the way the country is being run (and you still can't pay for your children's education). Alpha Party at least explains why (there are too many special interests). You agree that special interests are a problem and resolve to stay involved.

So far the problem of power in American politics is not so much centralized control from one command point as the protection of the central power structure (private property) through a diffused collection of single-interest groups and the two major political parties. The computer may do no more than maintain the present system—but then again, maybe not.

Communication Technology and the Culture of Surveillance

Modern society has relied increasingly on impersonal mechanisms to achieve its purposes. Hierarchy, standardization, and specialization are key ingredients in the workplace, whether in private business, the voluntary sector, or government. As we saw earlier, communication technology has extended the ability of those who own and command bureaucracies to oversee employees tightly and to utilize labor in precise, cost-effective ways. But the oversight of American citizens goes far beyond such practices. Staples identified what he calls the *culture of surveillance* in a wide variety of settings in and beyond the economy.[15] New electronic technology makes it possible to obtain large amounts of information on all citizens as they bank, use their credit cards and telephones, or engage in transactions on the Internet or with public authorities. Video cameras provide security for buildings, malls, and residential neighborhoods, even entire commercial districts. Parolees are outfitted with electronic anklets that monitor their whereabouts. The use of security devices in schools is widespread. Schools extensively tape the behavior of students in order to evaluate them. Conversations are easily recorded. Beepers keep employees and professionals on short tethers. New data-gathering and storing devices enable private and public bodies to do a wide variety of testing: attitudes, beliefs, values, fingerprints, DNA, body fluids, and so on. Staples concludes by recommending that individuals resist this trend whenever they encounter it. One could add that this trend should be evaluated in terms of the essential dynamic of a capitalist world.

AMERICA'S PLUTOCRATIC POLITY

American public life (law, government, and politics) is dominated by the money and skills of propertied and professional interests. Efforts to regulate the flow of money into politics have succeeded somewhat with the ban on soft money but still do not match the superior electoral practices of the other liberal democracies. The plutocratic power of America's monstrously diverse interest groups has helped to undermine the political party, produce issueless campaigns, and generate mass apathy.

The Republican Party strenuously opposes campaign finance reform because it raises significantly more money than the Democratic Party (and may fear elections that are forced by limited money to focus on the issues). The Republican Party resorted to extraordinary efforts to block reform between 1998 and 2001 despite its promises and the fact that a clear majority of Congress and the American people wanted reform. Its behavior here is consistent with its efforts to thwart other reforms: health care, education, law enforcement, childcare, the environment, communication, and so on. All reforms help the Democratic Party and weaken the ability of the Republican Party to hide the fact that the interests it serves make up a minority of voters.

The U.S. Supreme Court, for its part, has continued it historical bias in favor of property and against democracy by ruling that the First Amendment (free speech) affords protection for those who want to use their money to advertise or to speak to the public.

Latent Structural Analysis: The American Polity as Unknown Familiar

Understanding the American polity, no less than other institutions, requires a strong application of *latent structural analysis*. Briefly, this means that things are rarely what they seem to be. American elections do not merely have rituals but have themselves become rituals, a way to disguise the fact that the acquisition and exercise of power takes place above and beyond the reach of ordinary Americans. As noted, a large majority of congressional elections are noncompetitive (and even more are in state elections); election outcomes in many are predetermined by gerrymandering, often through the collusion of the two major parties. Corruption in American public life is systemic, a way to make things work, not an aberration that can be rooted out through moral outrage. Reform in American public life largely benefits the upper classes and, by and large, effectively blocks social change. Reform often consists of "abeyance" processes—surplus people that cannot be accommodated are held in abeyance through make-work projects, imprisonment, welfare, and excessive education (the recently established program of national service by young people makes sense as an abeyance device). Incompetence in American government reflects the profoundly antigovernment stance of America's power groups, who systematically denigrate government while using it for their own purposes.

Making Things Worse through Competition: The Communication Act of 1996

The federal government has consistently pushed for policies, laws, and treaties that favor the use of public airways or subsidized media for private profit through competition.[16] In doing this, it has proclaimed that profit making in communication is compatible with broad public access to the media, with privacy, decency, quality, and with protection of the consumer. Because some forms of communication are monopolistic, the government has regulated them. It has also limited the number of other media that a media company can own, but this safeguard has broken down recently.

In a major rewriting of communication law in 1996, Congress deregulated most forms of media and relaxed the limits on ownership. The covering ideology was that competition would usher in new services and lower prices for consumers. But the opposite has happened, something that is an old story in the history of public protection through regulation versus competition. Deregulation has led to an orgy of mergers, bringing about the highest concentration ever in our media history, and rising prices (many of them hidden in the prices of the goods that Americans have to pay, thanks to high entertainment and advertising costs). In addition, the Republican Congress from 1994 to 2001 was openly unsympathetic to the Federal Communication Commission's attempts to broaden access to the airwaves for diverse voices and political debate[17] (after 2001 the FCC itself came under the control of the Republican Party).

The concentration of the media contains political dangers. The surge of mergers and purchases has created a small number of giant multimedia corporations, each of which has put elements of all aspects of communication, including the news media, under its roof (see chapter 4). Not only has local content in the media been reduced by national standardization, but strong pressure has developed to turn news and journalism into entertainment and ideological adjuncts of business.[18]

The mythology of competition as a beneficial and benign process, in conjunction with new communication technology, has concentrated the communication media as it has the rest of the economy. It has also led to sterile public discourse, a depoliticized, stalemated polity, and one-way communication between the upper and lower classes. Those interested in protecting and enhancing America's democratic values, argues Robert McChesney, need to fight for the following structural reforms:

1. Build nonprofit, noncommercial media.
2. Build a real system of noncommercial, nonprofit public radio and television.
3. Strengthen public regulation of private broadcasting to ensure public service in return for using public airways.
4. Strengthen antitrust law to break up the media giants.

These reforms by themselves cannot generate a mass movement, says McChesney, but could if they were combined with electoral reform, workers' rights, civil rights, environmental protection, health care, tax reform, and education (McChesney does not directly address the issue of a concentrated economy, of which media concentration is a part). Once media reforms are in place, concludes McChesney, American democracy will be able to scrutinize the activities of the powerful, be they on the Right or the Left.[19]

The United States has always been a society too complex for its polity to deal with easily. Despite post–World War II affluence and marvelous new instruments of communication, the disparity between social complexity (and its resulting problems) and the ability of the American political system to solve problems appears to have grown.

NOTES

1. Harold D. Lasswell, *Politics: Who Gets What, When and How* (New York: McGraw-Hill, 1936).

2. For a classic statement, see Richard Revere, "Single-Issue Politics," *New Yorker* 54 (May 8, 1978): 139–46 (widely reprinted).

3. For an impressive display of data indicating large-scale civic disengagement between 1965 and 2000, see Robert D. Putnam, *Bowling Alone: The Collapse and Revival of American Community* (New York: Simon and Schuster, 2000). Using a value-neutral, let-the-data-speak approach, Putnam catalogs every imaginable cause, settling for a guesstimate that blames the decline of civic participation on work (10 percent), mobility and sprawl (10 percent), generational change (50 percent), and unknown (5–15 percent). Lacking a sense of a power structure in need of revamping, Putnam concludes by calling on an abstract "everybody" in every sector of society to generate the civic participation, and thus the social capital, that the nation needs.

4. Theda Skocpol, "Advocates without Members: The Recent Transformation of Ameri-

can Civic Life," in *Civic Engagement in American Democracy*, ed. Theda Skocpol and Morris P. Fiorina (Washington, D.C.: Brooking Institution Press; New York: Russell Sage Foundation, 1999), chap. 13.

5. *New York Times*, May 15, 1997, A36.

6. Michael Oreskes, "Alienation from Government Grows, Poll Shows," *New York Times*, September 19, 1990, A26.

7. Derek C. Bok, "A Flawed System," *Harvard Magazine*, May–June 1983, 38ff. Bok is a former dean of Harvard Law School.

8. For a classic and incisive analysis on which much of the following is based, see Morris P. Fiorina, "The Decline of Collective Responsibility in American Politics," *Daedalus* 109 (Summer 1980): 25–45.

9. Robert W. Jackman, "Political Institutions and Voter Turnout in the Industrial Democracies," *American Political Science Review* 81 (June 1987).

10. However, an estimated 20 percent of the American population is functionally illiterate—that is, unable to comprehend relatively simple ideas through reading.

11. For a classic analysis of the 1968 presidential campaign on behalf of Richard Nixon, see Joe McGinniss, *The Selling of the President, 1968* (New York: Trident, 1969).

12. Kathleen Hall Jamieson, *Dirty Politics: Deception, Distraction, and Democracy* (New York: Oxford University Press, 1992).

13. Larry J. Sabato, *The Rise of Political Consultants: New Ways of Winning Elections* (New York: Basic Books, 1981).

14. Leon H. Mayhew, *The New Public: Professional Communication and the Means of Social Influence* (New York: Cambridge University Press, 1997).

15. William G. Staples, *The Culture of Surveillance: Discipline and Social Control in the United States* (New York: St. Martin's, 1997).

16. For a clear summary of this bias, see Sara Fletcher Luther, *The United States and the Direct Broadcast Satellite: The Politics of International Broadcasting in Space* (New York: Oxford University Press, 1988).

17. Stephen Labaton, "F.C.C.'s Rift with [Broadcasting] Industry Is Widening," *New York Times*, October 16, 2000, C1.

18. Ben H. Bagdikian, *The Media Monopoly*, 5th ed. (Boston: Beacon, 1997).

19. Robert W. McChesney, *Rich Media, Poor Democracy: Communication Politics in Dubious Times* (Urbana: University of Illinois Press, 1999), 304–19.

6

Communication, Media, and the American City

URBANIZATION AND THE STATE

The Urban Revolution: The Emergence of a Unique Density of Interaction

The emergence of cities was a profoundly important event for the human race. Human beings wandered the earth as hunters and gatherers for hundreds of thousands of years before there were cities. Settlements appeared with horticultural society, but a city way of life emerged only with the Agricultural Revolution. Agriculture (the cultivation of large fields using serf-slave labor) yielded a considerable surplus of food. Freed from the need to grow their own food, village dwellers expanded their activities. Their increased leisure led to new occupations and to creativity in many new fields: metalworking, astronomy, commerce, fine arts, and others. The expansion of specialized activities led to a unique density of communication or social interaction. Thus emerged the *city,* a social setting in which a large and varied population, freed from the endless drudgery of having to get its own food, can create new technology and symbols, and engage in far more intense and varied social relations than can villagers or nomads.

The City as the Center of Political and Economic Power

Cities are intimately related to the societies of which they are parts. But the relation between city and society has never been without tension. Cities are strongholds of economic and political power. In them, religion flourishes, but so do commerce, art, and science. Cities are difficult to run. The disaffected can communicate easily

135

among themselves and can communicate their discontent to others through riots and revolts. City streets can have barricades thrown across them and blood spilled on them. Cities always make elites uneasy; they seem always to be filled with unruly people and to be inherently unstable.

Historically, poorer city neighborhoods have spoken to more powerful neighborhoods through a variety of social movements. Urban political movements have been historically unique; women have played decisive roles in many of them; some have succeeded, and some have been crushed. The ability of the discontented to communicate and organize in urban settings has been a consistent feature of these movements.[1]

The Unique Western City

Early cities were feudal theocracies; power was in the hands of a priest-king (often a god-king) and a hereditary aristocracy. The uniqueness of the Western city derives from the Greek city-state and its successful break with the theocratic feudal tradition. The distinctive feature of the Greek city-state was that it was not derived from large-scale agriculture and thus was not part of a large, feudal, authoritarian empire. Ancient Greece had its share of feudalism and oligarchy, but its rocky, thin soil could support only small-scale farming. The social base of the Greek city-state was the small, independent farmer. This social base, in the relatively free atmosphere of maritime commerce, developed the historically unique ideal of a *self-governing community.*

Since the time of the Greeks, the Western city has always had a freer, more secular, intellectual, and political spirit than the non-Western city. Above all, the Western city has stressed its autonomy from outside forces. The Greek ideal of self-governance was continued by Rome. After Rome's fall, the ideal was revived in the medieval Western city. The West's self-governing city became a vital part of modern industrial Europe and of the United States (though as we see shortly, it is more ideal than real in the United States). The city is thus almost synonymous with the West's unique political tradition.[2]

URBAN SOCIOLOGY

The ancient Greeks made the first scientific attempt to understand the city. No other serious study of the city occurred until the somewhat tentative attempts of the nineteenth century and the more systematic ones of the opening decades of the twentieth century. Today, urban sociology is an important sociological field, and it has built up important knowledge about how cities work.

Sociology and the City

The sociological study of the city was an integral part of the development of sociology itself. As early sociologists struggled to understand the new society growing up around them, they also probed into the nature of the city. In seeking reasons for the rise of capitalism, Max Weber (1864–1920) cited the unique political (mostly urban) tradition of the West as a contributing cause. Ferdinand Toennies's (1885–1936) influential distinction between *Gemeinschaft* (communal, primary) and *Gesellschaft* (societal or secondary) forms of social interaction was actually a discussion of rural and urban populations.

Georg Simmel's (1858–1918) influential picture of urban life has important insights into how urban populations communicate. The city, said Simmel, promotes intellectual rather than emotional responses and values because of its "intensification of nervous stimulation" and its "rapid crowding of changing images." Consciousness and intelligence are by-products of the highly diversified field of sensory stimulation that makes up the life of cities. The money economy of a city promotes rationality (human behavior and interaction based on calculation of means and ends). Money is impartial, abstract, and anonymous; thus a money economy tends to undermine interaction based on personal qualities. The rationale of the city economy, argued Simmel, imparts an "unmerciful matter-of-factness" to life, requiring and getting from city dwellers "punctuality, calculability, and exactness."

The city represents a society's most advanced division of economic labor, Simmel concluded, and as such it insists on an "ever more one-sided accomplishment" on the part of its inhabitants. Whatever its faults, however, specialization still promotes individualism. The abstract, impersonal leveling of a city's money economy is offset by powerful urban forces that promote privacy, individual development, and personal freedom. Above all, Simmel adds prophetically, the city is cosmopolitan; it not only brings the world to its doorstep but reaches out beyond itself to capture the countryside, the small city, the nation, and even the world beyond.[3]

City residents receive messages continuously from signs, loudspeakers, buildings, spaces, authority figures (police), statues, and from their fellow citizens (even when the latter do not speak, they send signals by their dress, grooming, and demeanor). City dwellers interact with strangers, but much of their experience is in neighborhoods and informal networks (jobs are acquired through word-of-mouth communication, for example). Cities can gain new sources of information (ethnic radio or cable stations, for example) or lose them—for example, the neighborhood bar, once an important center of interaction, has declined. As Castells has shown, the city generates social movements, allows citizens to voice grievances, and tends to politicize people.

The Chicago School

Weber, Toennies, and Simmel greatly influenced the Chicago School, as we know the University of Chicago sociologists of the 1920s and 1930s who spearheaded the development of empirical sociology in the United States. Here again, the development of sociology generally is closely identified with urban sociology specifically. Pioneer sociologists such as Robert Park and Ernest Burgess, along with their colleagues and students, supplied sociology with rich descriptions of city life. They furthered urban analysis by using the ecological-functional model to explain how cities develop. They sketched influential general pictures (of which Louis Wirth's "Urbanism as a Way of Life"[4] is the most famous) of the city.

The Ecological-Functional Approach and Its Critics

The ecological-functional approach tried to explain the settlement patterns and dynamics of urban areas as adjustments to space (land). In this theory, the naturalistic model of biological adjustment to a natural environment was supplemented by the concept of the *market*. People, acting out of self-interest, would use land in terms of its greatest economic value. Such theorists as Park and Burgess argued that cities were subject to ecological successions; as areas decayed and revived, they were used for one purpose and then another.

The ecological school claims that the incessant exchanges of people responding to the challenges of their spatial environment were patterned. Various branches of the ecological school, however, found different patterns and came up with different theories: the concentric-zone model, the sector model (emphasizing transportation technology), and the multiple-nuclei model (specialized areas for manufacturing, residence, entertainment, finance, and so on). Despite its emphasis on economic factors and decisions, however, the ecological-functional school was deeply wedded to obsolete naturalistic models for interpreting social behavior. Also, notwithstanding its emphasis on economic variables, the ecological-functional school rested on the archaic assumptions of classical economics—that is, its theorists assumed that individuals are naturally self-interested and rational.

The abstract functionalism of the ecological school has been criticized by conflict theorists who argue that the city does not result from the free play of market forces. Economic markets are far from free; indeed, much of the city's structure is produced by economic groups that have managed to prevent market forces from operating. In addition, much of the city does not make economic sense—allowing, for example, valuable space in the center of cities to be used for parks. The city, argue conflict theorists, should be approached in historical, sociocultural terms. The city's shape and direction are not determined by abstract forces, either in nature or in human nature. Primarily, the city reflects the economic and political power of dominant elites. All attempts to explain the city's nature along naturalistic lines are suspect. In short, conflict theorists see the city as a center of power in which elites dominate both city dwellers and the countryside.[5]

The most important contributions of urban sociology lie ahead, because the policies of those that own or control cities are still generating disorder, destitution, disease, and despair. Politically concerned Americans face a formidable challenge: the heart and soul of civilization lies in the city, yet American elites no more understand their cities than their counterparts in ancient Mesopotamia, Rome, or China understood theirs.

The Preindustrial City

The first cities emerged in the fertile river valleys and deltas of the Tigris-Euphrates, Nile, Indus, and Yellow Rivers. Above all, the city results from plentiful water. The earliest cities flourished between five thousand and three thousand years ago and then declined. Cities rose again in Greece and Rome about 2,500 years ago. Eventually other cities grew in North and West Africa, Mexico, Central America, and Peru, again largely in response to plentiful water and thus food surpluses.

The preindustrial city was small by modern standards. With some exceptions, early cities were ruled by hereditary, landed elites and monarchs. Early cities were organized on the basis of kinship, and there was little spatial segregation by function. People conducted commercial and craft activities in their homes, in the streets, and in all parts of the city.

It was not unusual for cities to be parts of large empires and to contain conquered people or foreigners who had been invited in because they had needed skills. The preindustrial city was segregated along ethnic lines and in terms of estate-caste distinctions. Unlike in modern cities, however, segregation was practiced openly (was not disguised as conformance to zoning laws, for example). Unlike in modern cities, the populations of early cities were not separated from each other by well-defined residential areas or by deep economic specialization.

The Industrial City

The modern city had its origins in the economic expansion of Europe and ultimately the rise and development of capitalism. The medieval city grew along the trade routes of Europe and flourished as a commercial center linking Europe to the Mediterranean basin. Supplied with food from the outside, the city developed specialized trades in response to a variety of markets. From that point on, the Western city was marked by a growing, sustainable economic base—a productive agriculture to supply it with food, commercial and industrial expansion, and a large variety of services with important economic consequences (transportation, banking, retailing, research, education, medical care, and the arts).

The Industrial Revolution began the process of urbanization. "Urbanization" as a concept refers to the proportion of a given population that lives in cities and, in a broader sense, the proportion that lives a city way of life wherever it lives. Today, in most industrialized countries up to 80 percent of the populations live in urban centers, a point at which the curve of urbanization seems to flatten out.

Starting in the late nineteenth century, Western societies ceased being agrarian societies with cities and became urban societies. Today they are urbanized to such an extent that "industrial" and "urban" are interchangeable. However, an urban society is far more than simply a society of which a majority of members live in cities; it is one in which the special culture of the industrial city has drawn the whole of society within its orbit. The suburb, the farm, the town and village, and the small city are deeply imbued with industrial—or conversely, with urban—values, ideas, and behavior.[6]

Urbanization outside the West

The process of urbanization is now worldwide; the proportion of urban dwellers to farm dwellers is rising almost everywhere in the world. But there is no uniform pattern to this development; significant variations in city development exist between capitalist, socialist, and developing countries[7] (as it is also among the capitalist countries of the West,[8] a matter to which we will return). But the greatest contrast in urbanization is between the developed and developing countries.[9] Western urbanization was accompanied—one can say, caused—by economic growth, especially industrialization. In developing countries, urbanization is taking place much faster than economic growth, and is not supported or paced by industrial development. Cities there have grown because death rates have been lowered by more food, modern medicine, and better sanitation, and because rural populations have been displaced by mechanized export agriculture. While cities in the capitalist world have stabilized their growth through suburbanization and the development of smaller "satellite" cities, the developing world suffers from overurbanization in a few colossal cities and underurbanization in rural areas. For example, Bangkok, Thailand, is more than twenty-five times larger than the next-largest Thai city; similar ratios can be found in the Philippines, Brazil, Burma, India, and China.

Historically, urbanization in the developing world, including Eastern Europe, has reflected Western imperialism.[10] City growth in many developing countries reflects the cash-crop agriculture, settlement patterns, and centralized control once emphasized by colonial powers. The vast displacement of rural populations continued after independence, reflecting a continued shift from subsistence to cash-crop farming. In contrast to the West, cities in the developing world have yet to shake off agrarian influence. Some are mere clusters of different ethnic groups living adjacent to each other, almost as separate societies. Cities in developing countries are packed with the unemployed and underemployed. They lack transit, water, and sewerage systems. Many of them lack the vital ingredient of city life (besides water)—a dependable supply of food. Many are political or health disasters waiting to occur.

In recent decades, investment in manufacturing in the cities of the developing world has intensified. At first, Western factories produced for local markets, but in the past few decades another pattern has emerged: factories in a small number of developing countries (South Korea, Taiwan, Hong Kong, Singapore, Malaysia, Mexico) have intensified production for export back to the developed world.

There are two patterns in urban development outside the West. The developing capitalist countries have given their economies a relatively free rein, and their cities have grown in a spectacular but helter-skelter manner. As a result, cities segregated by race and ethnicity by former colonial powers have begun to disperse and rearrange themselves on economic (class) lines. In cities oriented toward development under private auspices, there are now marked contrasts between gleaming skyscrapers and fashionable shops, on the one hand, and the sweatshops, street stalls, and large numbers of unemployed and underemployed, on the other. Perhaps the sharpest contrast is between luxurious residential areas (often protected by walls and private security forces) and vast squatter neighborhoods without running water or sanitation. Perhaps the best example of runaway, urban growth in the developing capitalist world is Mexico City.

The other pattern in urban development is found in the formerly socialist countries (both in the developed and the developing worlds). Here the state controlled city growth by controlling population movement, supporting the farm economy, and helping smaller cities in the rural hinterland. (Whether the present socialist societies of China, Vietnam, and Cuba can contain urban sprawl remains to be seen.)

Cities and the Global Economy

Scholars have begun to distinguish between the imperialism characteristic of the West between 1450 and 1950 (the world economy) and the imperialism of the global economy.[11] The difference is fairly simple. After 1950, the multinational corporation (MNC) and the imperial state became "geocentric," or global. The top five hundred to a thousand multinational corporations now operate across the globe; with the collapse of state socialism in Russia and Central Europe and the entry of China into the global economy, these corporations became truly global.

Along with the growth of a global economy has grown a network of "state" forces to support and protect this new phase of imperialism. There has been an enormous growth of international governmental organizations (IGOs). These include organizations to regulate various forms of transportation and communication, such as traffic on rivers that traverse more than one country. They include organizations to regulate such commodities as coffee, tin, and petroleum (OPEC). Extremely important are the Western-dominated financial IGOs such as the World Bank, the International Monetary Fund, and various regional-development banks, all of which help non-Western development in the abstract but also aid in the penetration of such societies by MNCs. International nongovernmental organizations (INGOs) have also grown in one area after another (such as churches, charities, and fraternal, disaster-relief, and refugee-aid entities).

In recent years, the biggest of the developed capitalist societies have begun to hold annual economic summits to coordinate their activities better. Of course, these countries maintain strong military forces (with the United States leading the way) in an effort to protect their global investments and to curb political protests and rebellions against the governments of client countries.

The new global economy has produced new global cities. One prerequisite for qualification as a "global city" is to contain headquarters of global corporations. The ten global cities (with the number of global corporations headquartered in each, excluding banks) in 1984 were New York (fifty-nine), London (thirty-seven), Tokyo (thirty-four), Paris (twenty-six), Chicago (eighteen), Essen (eighteen), Osaka (fifteen), Los Angeles (fourteen), Houston (eleven), and Pittsburgh and Hamburg (ten).[12] The pattern is that while the developing world has many large, even huge, cities, all the global cities are in the developed (capitalist) world.

Global cities are communication centers that provide financial, entertainment, news, and other services. As Sassen stresses, these centers are not ivory towers but capitalist workplaces. Further, because the global economy has emerged in a rush, the upper-level occupations and the firms that supply them have reaped huge rewards, while the people who do the menial work (for example, clean office buildings, do clerical work, feed workers) have enjoyed few rewards. The surge of globalization has also made it difficult for governments to tax the world economy or to ameliorate its negative consequences.[13]

The global economy creates dependent societies and dependent cities. Even in the developed world, some cities have declined, due to their isolation from the world economy; the developing world is filled with dependent cities, themselves filled with squatter neighborhoods having no secure places or political identities. These neighborhoods generate large informal economies and, of course, new generations of exploitable labor and potential revolutionaries of all sorts. As such, they are needed (as well as feared) by authoritarian states, which themselves serve masters abroad.[14]

Cities and Communication

Cities are where symbols are generated and disseminated—indeed, where the bulk of all human creativity has taken place. Today's American cities are also specialized. For example, Washington, D.C., and Hollywood offer contrasts in types of communication; Washington commands overseas embassies and military bases; Hollywood (like New York) ships out large volumes of film, music, books, and television programs. American cities are corporate command centers—New York is a publishing center, Nashville is known for country music, and so on. The cities of the developed world send messages to the cities of the developing world but receive back little that is original from the outside world. American foundations and news corporations struggle to motivate Americans to do comparative international research or interest themselves in events in foreign countries.

THE AMERICAN CITY:
THE PROMISE FORESTALLED

The American Urban Experience

Haphazard development is the American city's most characteristic feature. The settlement of North America was profoundly affected by geographic, climatic, and technological variables (as well as, obviously, imperialist appetites). The first colonial cities developed because they had good sea or river ports and could serve as commercial, communication, transport, and military centers.[15] Later, the railroad helped determine urban development and land settlement across the continent. Still later, the trolley, the automobile, the airplane, and the elevator, along with other technology, further determined the shape, quality, and communication patterns of city life.

In colonial times, only a small percentage of the American population was city dwellers. That percentage grew somewhat up to the Civil War, but the real spurt took place during the northern industrial boom during the Civil War and continued to the 1960s (interrupted only by the Great Depression). The early urban period was characterized by industrial cities that were far from livable—boomtowns thriving on manufacturing, transportation, and cheap labor (the flow of immigrants but also migrants from the American countryside).

From 1900 on, the densely packed city was hit by another trend that has continued ever since—suburbanization. The advent of the automobile was one of the chief reasons for suburbanization. Cities that arose after the automobile—for example, Los Angeles—never developed industrial cores. In any case, throughout the country suburbanization soon blurred the identity of the core city. To help understand the suburbanized city, the Bureau of the Census developed the concept *metropolis*. The bureau uses as a unit of measure the "standard metropolitan statistical area," or SMSA, a city or suburb of at least fifty thousand people; the United States has almost three hundred SMSAs, comprising 73 percent of the population. Continuing urbanization has blurred the identity of the metropolis as well, and the Census Bureau has accordingly developed a new concept—the *megalopolis*, or "standard consolidated area" (SCA), a grouping of interconnected cities and suburbs. There are thirteen of them at present, the largest being "Boswash" (Boston to Washington, D.C.), which runs through ten states and has over fifty million people.

The Dependent American City

The problems of the American city stem largely from the fundamental thrusts of the American economy. The right of private capital to determine where profit can be made means that business firms can relocate, thus leaving the cities they vacate without adequate employment, credit, or tax bases. The right of professionals to practice as and where they please also causes problems. Large sections of American cities (and many rural areas), for example, lack doctors because doctors concentrate their practices in wealthier districts. In addition, the long-term shift in the American economy from manufacturing to services has had an adverse impact on the city, as has the shift of manufacturing from the Northeast and Midwest to the South, Southwest, West, and to other countries. Much of the decay and ungovernability of American cities reflects not only the value-free rootlessness of property and professional groups but also their ability to escape taxation, public regulation, and public direction. Capital is not only free to exploit opportunities for profit but to evade costs and responsibilities in various ways. The decay of northeastern and midwestern American cities in the 1970s and 1980s, for example, reflects the flight of capital to cheap-labor areas in the Sunbelt and abroad, protected by political power at suburban, state, and federal levels.

The decline of cities got worse under the Reagan-Bush administrations of 1980–1992. Intoxicated by supply-side economics, the Reagan-Bush administrations focused America's public resources on producers, by cutting taxes, reducing aid to the poor and cities, and undermining trade unions. They assumed that the resulting prosperity would "trickle down" to the working classes and the poor. They believed that states and localities should make decisions about public policy and that the federal government was usurping their prerogatives. The Reagan-Bush administrations were proven wrong on all counts. Prosperity did not occur, and what economic growth occurred did not trickle down. Choices by localities and states are limited by a wide disparity of resources, and in any case, federal actions result from the politics of the fifty states and from consultation with the states and localities. Not coincidentally, the actions of these Republican administrations hit cities, strongholds of Democratic strength, very hard.[16]

In 1999, the Federal Department of Housing and Urban Development reported that after seven years of unprecedented prosperity, major problems still existed in significant percentages of American cities: high unemployment, loss of better-off income groups, and high levels of poverty. Fourteen percent of cities studied faced two or more of the above troubles. Surprisingly, suburbs and communities in rural areas were also experiencing severe difficulties.[17] Acknowledging that many cities were better off, the report called for federal-state action to aid those in trouble. But aiding cities runs counter to the interests of most Republicans and of significant numbers of Democrats, and in all likelihood it will occur only in small increments, such as help for the homeless, nutrition programs, welfare-to-work programs, and the like. The growth of income inequality and the increase in economic and wealth concentration over the past twenty years will not be reversed any time soon.

The Reagan-Bush (and even the Clinton) administrations' preference for property over resource redistribution and public services was no historical anomaly. In the development of American society, the American economy gained the right to be let alone, or to be affected by politics only on its own terms.[18] The unique autonomy and dominance of America's propertied and professional groups explains much about American politics and cities, and about how Americans communicate about public issues. It is interesting that, unlike England, France, and Germany, the United States separated its economic and political capitals. American social theorists had developed a purer distinction between economy and society than had the capitalist societies of Europe; the federal government accordingly transferred the legislature and executive from New York to Washington, a new city created for that purpose. The artificial divorce between economic and political life that is such a unique and destructive feature of American ideology was thus given physical and symbolic embodiment early in American history. The net effect of this separation was to make it easier for business and professional elites to use the state for their purposes while simultaneously denouncing politics and government.

All in all, the weak, nondemocratic features of the American political tradition have had an adverse effect on the American city. People who make their money in the city tend not to live there. Starting with the wealthy Dutch families that moved out of New York City to develop feudal-like estates in the Hudson Valley, there has been a continuous exodus of the propertied from the American city. Throughout American history, the city's masses have been disenfranchised by unbalanced and gerrymandered electoral districts. Reforms in the system of representation in the

1960s (one person, one vote) came too late to help the city, since the process of suburbanization had already depleted it of economic power as well as of large portions of the middle and upper classes. By stressing geographic and rational market variables, early urban sociologists overlooked the real dynamics at work. They and all concerned about urban problems failed to see that the key variables affecting the city are economic (especially the profit-oriented firm) and political (especially a legal system that protects property and a legislative and governmental system responsive primarily to property interests). The early commercial city was a hodgepodge of social relations. Central urban areas were a locus for small, independent business people, workers, and professionals, who often lived and worked in close proximity. The later growth of cities in grids, concentric circles, and functional zones was no natural, spatial, ecological development but a process guided explicitly by land speculators who wanted to rationalize the urban land boom.

The industrial city from the Civil War until World War II developed because manufacturers needed a large pool of cheap labor. The core of the city became the center of manufacturing, a basic split between work and residence began, and cities expanded both in population and geographically as they annexed surrounding areas. In time, labor unrest made the city less attractive to business firms, and two related developments occurred: industry began to move out of the city, and the older cities stopped annexing adjacent areas as power shifted to the suburbs.[19] Older cities are still useful, as corporate headquarters and general service centers. As such, they are "redeveloped"—small businesses and the working and nonworking poor are dispossessed to make room for hotels, office buildings, convention halls, civic centers, research institutes, university and hospital expansion, and middle and upper-class housing. But the old pattern persists. Powerful economic groups continue to use government for their own ends, while a disorganized and apathetic electorate finds it difficult to confront and control the forces that determine their lives.[20] As such, the cities of the United States, says Katznelson, exhibit a "politics of dependency" in which the main objective of economic and political elites is not to solve problems but to control discontent and manage failure.[21]

Overcoming Bias: A Revised View of the City

American intellectuals have been profoundly biased against the city. Thomas Jefferson, Ralph Waldo Emerson, Henry Thoreau, Henry Adams, Henry James, John Dewey, Louis Sullivan, and Frank Lloyd Wright (individuals who were preeminent in their respective fields) denounced the city or had serious reservations about it.[22] Failure to accept or understand the city was also pronounced in early American sociology. Along with most of the city planning tradition, early sociology contained a deep bias in favor of rural, small-town life. Early sociologists and city planners who had grown up in small-town America during the late nineteenth century were appalled at what they saw in big cities, and this was reflected in their work. In their formative years, therefore, America's problem-ridden cities had to rely for leadership on an intellectual-moral tradition that at best was ambivalent and at worst was negative in its stance toward the city.

Ordinary Americans, however, knew something that their leaders did not. Actually, Americans have had a love-hate relation with the city. In both attitude and utterance, their view of the city is moderately negative. But their behavior is the opposite. They have streamed toward the city throughout our history, and even when they leave it, they do not want to go too far away. In recent years, urban research has caught up with the American people and has revised the negative view of the city that emerged in the Chicago School and Louis Wirth. Cities seem to have strong neighborhood communities. Family life is far from absent. Crowding does not appear to cause irritable, alienated people. In many ways, the city is liberating and promotes choice and privacy. It has services of every conceivable type. It provides enormous educational and economic opportunities. It is not a place filled with anonymity, and it does not produce robotlike people.

The city does have drawbacks. Noise and air pollution are more harmful the bigger the city. There is more crime and more fear of crime as the size of the community increases. But there appear to be no bad or even different personality features in urban populations. City people are not generally dissatisfied with their lot, they are not more likely to engage in mob behavior, and their behavior is not characteristically superficial or impersonal. Cities tend to be different from rural areas in the realms of values and beliefs; they are "deviant" (or innovative) in science, art, and morals. City people are somewhat less attached than rural people to their communities. But there seems to be much less difference between urban and suburban people than many think. Basically, people behave as they do not because of their spatial location but because of occupation, ethnicity, wealth, sex, and age.[23]

The Misuses of the Urban Potential

By common agreement, cities in capitalist Canada, Europe, and Japan are better run (and safer) than American cities. Why? One obvious reason is that the other capitalist societies have accepted government as a necessary and even primary factor in running society. Toronto, Ontario, for example, is a thriving, clean, and safe city. It has no slums like the notorious South Bronx in New York City; one is hard put to find even rundown areas. Why? One reason is that Toronto developed a federated metropolitan government to tackle the obviously interrelated problems of the region. Another and perhaps more important reason is that the wealthy, the upper middle class, and the broad middle class all live in the metropolitan area. Toronto's elites, therefore, are subject to any and all policies adopted to solve problems. They have immediate feedback on failed programs, because they and their families experience the failures. They can also see more clearly how policies adopted at other levels of government have an impact on cities, because they also have an impact on them.

American elites, in contrast, do not experience their policies firsthand. It is easier, therefore, for them to develop policies based on naturalistic, abstract, market conceptions (for example, the ecological-functional approach in sociology). American elites approach the city with the same ad hoc skills and practices that they use elsewhere (reliance on technology, management controls, public relations). But improved efficiency in administration, labor practices, budget controls, spending, and welfare expenditures have not arrested the decline of America's great cities; all such improvements do is slow the rate of decline. What they amount to is the energetic "management of failure."

The United States does considerable planning, but it largely benefits the middle and upper classes.[24] The great urban renewal programs of the 1950s and 1960s were transparently ideological—functional communities were uprooted for highways and to clear "slums," and the dispossessed were put in high-rise buildings that never stood a chance of becoming viable communities. In conjunction with federal mortgage guarantees, urban renewal brought an exodus of the middle class to the suburbs, eroding the city's tax base. It should be highlighted also that urban renewal had an explicit racial-segregation dimension, engaged in cooperatively by federal and local agencies, banks, and real estate developers. Planning to help the working and lower classes is woefully incomplete, underfunded, and fitful; overall, it compares very unfavorably with the capitalist democracies of Europe. American welfare programs also lag badly behind those in Europe. Neither in urban housing, planning, nor in welfare do the European countries deprive the upper classes while benefiting the lower. Their planning is better, they get more for their money, and consequently, the poor, though still poor, are better off.[25]

The American reform and planning tradition has always been elite run and elite bounded. Policy debates about the city have taken place largely among rival elites. Without questioning the basic thrust of American economic expansion (our heavy reliance on private initiative and private profit), American elites have struggled to control the city. Subject to a laissez-faire national and international economy, cramped by a fragmented governmental system, and lacking a vital economic and tax base, the urban center can neither control itself nor be controlled from the outside. Perhaps most striking is the way in which the urban center responds to all forms of technology, giving the technology of the past as well as that of the present and of the future an equal and unquestioned home. Thus the city is formed to suit the needs of shipping, the railroad, the automobile, the airplane, and construction technology (for example, the elevator). The result is not shape but shapelessness, at once short-term economic rationality and political-social disorder. Huddling their workplaces close together to take advantage of the division of labor, city elites and others radiate out to find suitable places to live. Ironically, they use city mortgage money and its construction technology to make possible the "suburban society," comprising those shapeless, problem-ridden agglomerates of better housing that are mere phases in the sprawling process of urbanization.[26] The overall thrust of the economy not only undermines community but also makes politics, government, and citizen action difficult. But "the economy" and "technology" are abstract terms; to understand the city, one must focus on the actions of concrete groups. The actor to hold responsible on the American political and urban scene is the business elite, in all its guises.[27]

The culture of capitalism (technocratic liberalism) means specialization and segregation (the functional outlook). It means self-oriented personalities and private orientations. It means the shrinkage of the *public sphere* (personalities that share common values and ideas; personalities that can interact in public places—streets, parks, plazas, public transit, neighborhood stores and services; personalities that engage in meaningful political dialogue because they live and work in pluralistic environments; personalities that can see the relevance of politics to their personal lives). Efforts to restore and revive the public sphere include the pursuit of common schooling, a return to religion (including in state activities), campaign finance reform, voter registration, broader, better public services, and so on. One important reform focus is the attempt to plan urban and suburban structures to facilitate improved interaction (communication) among citizens, protect the environment, and be more cost-effective. The essential thrust of the urban-suburban planning movement is to rely on pedestrian traffic, follow the bent of nature, and evolve mixed-use buildings, spaces, and services.[28] Many such efforts are under way, and their successes will surely change the way in which Americans communicate.

The Decline of the City's Unique Forms of Interaction

Lyn Lofland has assembled a huge and fascinating array of material on the city as a public realm that generates psychologically satisfying and sustaining interactions, largely among strangers.[29] Drawing on pioneering analyses by Gregory Stone, Jane Jacobs, Erving Goffman, William H. Whyte, and others, as well as upon her personal experiences, Lofland makes abundantly clear that the city is a rich store of familiar unknowns, one that deserves attention.

Unfortunately, the city has had many of its opportunities for interaction undermined by the deep anti-urban tradition (which Lofland shows has deep roots in Western culture). Many other causes contribute to its undermining: profit-oriented, one-way technology such as television and the VCR; the refrigerator and freezer (which cut back the need for daily trips to the market); and private developers and architects, aided by public officials and public planners. In addition, state-subsidized mortgages for homes in the suburbs and state-financed highways to get to them, huge buildings, and functionally segregated sectors deplete the city of resources, prevent pedestrian traffic, and deprive people of interaction with strangers (which is known to make people less fearful of cities). These forces also make it difficult to mobilize street rallies and protests. To these factors one can add that the Progressive era by the beginning of the last century, with its "good-government" program (bipartisan elections, complex electoral rules, commission reports, and so on) and the welfare state from the 1930s on, coupled with deep electoral discrimination against cities, all worked to undermine the health of America's urban centers. In short, major trends in America society have worked to stifle the ability of Americans to communicate with each other (creating perhaps a world of strangers, in the negative sense of people who fear and despise each other—a world epitomized by the explosive growth of gated communities and private police forces).

Communication Technology and the Decline of Community

Downtown Anycity, USA, began its decline with the giant surge of prosperity after World War II. The automobile made it possible for people to live in suburbs. People found it more convenient to drive to giant shopping malls on the outskirts of cities than to downtown stores. The automobile also led to fast-food outlets on the highways of America. Places like McDonald's give off an air of prosperous hustle and bustle, but critics charge that 83 percent of their revenues are siphoned out of the local community.[30] Community decline amid prosperity seems impossible, but faith in progress and in the automatic value of technology has begun to wane. The impact of technology (and other forces) on the common standards (moral norms and values) that make up a community has also been noticed. The story of John Moviehouse is a case in point.

John's father had prospered in downtown Anycity in the 1940s and 1950s as the owner of a movie theater. John, who inherited the theater, did well for a while, but in 1963 a shopping mall outside the city put in a theater with three showing rooms. Two other theaters also opened at suburban malls, and soon John was threatened with bankruptcy. But John was forty-three and had no prospects for earning a living in a different way. He decided to show X-rated films.

John's decision created an uproar. Church groups denounced his move and picketed his theater. The Parent-Teacher Association passed a resolution condemning it. The City Council discussed ways to stop "the flow of filth." A representative of a national women's group visited Anycity to speak against pornography. John's lawyer argued that any attempt by the city to stop his client from showing whatever films he wanted violated the First Amendment and its guarantee of free speech. Civic leaders were firm, though; the U.S. Supreme Court had ruled that it was permissible to stop expression that violated community standards. John was indicted and brought to trial.

The case caused an uproar for a week until John's lawyer realized something about contemporary communication that brought the agitation to an end. Four local appliance stores were selling X-rated videotapes and film for private collectors, a cable television company was beaming X-rated programs to Anycity, and the city had two adult motels. The case was dismissed once it became apparent that at least in this regard, there were no community (common) standards.

Chapter 5 called attention to the use of computers and television to "distract and deceive" the American electorate (especially pertinent in this connection are mind-numbing pseudo-gemeinschaft political speeches). Chapters 7 and 8 will call attention to the many ways in which communication technology undermines community by fostering specialized experiences—for example, entertainment programming and advertising directed at age, gender, racial-ethnic-language-income groups, and publishers directing specialized books and magazines at even narrower slices of the American population.

The American City and the Global Economy

The American city also reflects the various stages of development in the history of Western imperialism, as well as American imperialism. The present stage (1960 on) represents the linkage between American cities and the global economy (the political economy that links the core industrial states with the developing world).[31]

American cities have been hurt by capital movement and the reindustrialization that has taken place in suburbs or in other cities. They have been redeveloped as service centers, and their populations have been bifurcated into small, well-paid elites and large, low-paid workforces—the people who do the cleaning and feeding and other low-skilled jobs. The cities have large numbers of native white, black, and Asian Americans; sections of Hispanic Americans (largely from Puerto Rico and Mexico); newly arrived Hispanics (from the Caribbean and Central America); and many new immigrants from Asia and the Pacific. The new arrivals were dislocated by the corporate world-market economy and the various wars fought largely because of its spread and consolidation. Now located in the United States, these new immigrants enlarge the already large pool of cheap American labor.

None of this could occur without state action. Federal tax policies (especially rapid depreciation) help spur capital movement. Open markets for cheap foreign goods, antilabor policies, immigration policies, competition among state and city governments for business, and reduced public services provide the background for the new national and international mobility of capital.

The new global economy penetrates to the level of neighborhoods and households.[32] By upsetting routines and removing jobs and other resources, the global economy provokes protests and grass-roots movements as groups struggle for at least some degree of control over their lives. By reducing pay levels and breadwinner jobs, the global economy forces women into the workforce. By leaving city governments without tax bases and by pressuring state and federal governments not to raise taxes, the global economy reduces public services, thus forcing many to join the informal economy, to hold two jobs—and again, more women to enter the workforce. By privatizing social life and isolating groups from each other, the global economy makes it very difficult for the discontented to communicate, forestalling collective resistance to an economy that falls short of providing basic necessities for large numbers. Indeed, by legitimating a look-out-for-oneself culture, the global economy turns groups against each other, especially groups nursing ancient ethnic and racial animosities. It is no accident that the 1980s witnessed the beginning of an upsurge of bias and hate crimes.

The American city reflects international and national life; the unprecedented privatization of society that has absorbed political institutions at federal and state levels has also absorbed them at the local level. The United States lacks a viable public sector composed of a national civil service, explicit functions, and capital resources. Political and administrative functions and jurisdictions are badly fragmented; the antigovernment, antipolitical tradition is as strong as ever. American governments can never use capital directly (and thus plan) but must always distribute capital indirectly, through tax laws, subsidies, or bond issues. Federal economic policy and most federal legislation simply channel public money to private groups to use as they think best. The absorption of public functions by private bodies leaves the United States not only with many of the marks of an underdeveloped nation state but, like many new countries, with a political life deeply marred by corruption. Whether the United States can bring its cities under control is problematic. The city is a creature of the national and global economy and polity. Only when the national and global economy and polity are brought under control by a viable public will the city fulfill its promise.

NOTES

1. For fascinating case studies of urban social movements from sixteenth-century Castille though the Paris commune (1871), the Glascow Rent Strike (1915), the Tenants movement of Veracruz (1922), America's inner-city riots of the 1960s, the Neighborhood Mobilization movement in San Francisco in the late '60s, and the Citizen movement in Madrid in the 1970s, see Manuel Castells, *The City and the Grassroots* (Berkeley: University of California Press, 1983).

2. For the indispensable contrast between Western and non-Western cities, see Max Weber, *The City*, trans. and ed. Don Martindale and Gertrude Newirth (New York: Free Press, 1958).

3. Georg Simmel, "The Metropolis and Mental Life" (1902–1903); reprinted in *Urban Place and Process*, ed. Irwin Press and M. Estelle Smith (New York: Macmillan, 1980), 19–30.

4. *American Journal of Sociology* 44, no. 1 (1938): 1–24, reprinted in Press and Smith, eds., *Urban Place and Process*, 30–48. Wirth depicted the city in abstract terms as an outcome of size, density of interaction, and the heterogeneity of individuals.

5. Marxists are the most prominent among the urban conflict theorists. For two of the best sources of their work, see David M. Gordon, ed., *Problems in Political Economy: An Urban Perspective*, 2d ed. (Lexington, Mass.: D. C. Heath, 1977); and William K. Tabb and Larry Sawers, ed., *Marxism and the Metropolis*, 2d ed. (New York: Oxford University Press, 1984).

6. For good contrasts of the development and nature of the city, see Lewis Mumford, *The Culture of Cities* (New York: Harcourt, Brace, 1938) and *The City in History* (New York: Harcourt, Brace and World, 1961); Gideon Sjoberg, *The Pre-Industrial City* (New York: Free Press, 1960); and Lyn H. Lofland, *A World of Strangers: Order and Action in Urban Public Space* (New York: Basic Books, 1973).

7. For a valuable reference work on urban patterns in all parts of the world, see the two-volume work by Mattei Dogan and John D. Kassarda, eds., *The Metropolis Era: A World of Giant Cities* and *The Metropolis Era: Mega-Cities* (Newbury Park, Calif.: Sage, 1988). This collection suffers from not putting cities in the framework of domestic and international power relations and from not highlighting the enormous difference between urbanization in the developed and developing worlds. Nonetheless, these volumes contain analyses and meaty descriptions of cities in all parts of the world, including New York and Los Angeles, Tokyo, Delhi, Sao Paulo, Cairo, and Mexico City. For a valuable mainstream discussion of cities in "global society" (which also fails to put urban development in a power context), see Richard V. Knight and Gary Gappert, eds., *Cities in a Global Society* (Newbury Park, Calif.: Sage, 1989).

8. For a valuable analysis of the ways in which urbanization reflected contrasting forms of economic growth in Great Britain, continental Europe, and the United States, see Bryan

R. Roberts, "Comparative Perspectives on Urbanization," in *Handbook of Contemporary Urban Life*, ed. David Street et al. (San Francisco: Jossey-Bass, 1978), 592–627.

9. For informative discussions of this contrast, see Dennis McElrath, "The New Urbanization" in Press and Smith, eds., *Urban Place and Process*, 214–23; Stanley D. Brunn and Jack F. Williams, eds., *Cities of the World* (New York: Harper and Row, 1982); and John Agnew, John Mercer, and David Sopher, eds., *The City in Cultural Context* (Boston: Allen and Unwin, 1984).

10. For this perspective on world urbanization, see Byran R. Roberts, "Comparative Perspectives on Urbanization," in Street et al., *Handbook of Contemporary Urban Life*, 592–627.

11. For two critical studies, see John Walton, ed., *Capital and Labor in the Urbanized World* (Newbury Park, Calif.: Sage, 1985); and Michael Peter Smith and Joe R. Feagin, eds., *The Capitalist City: Global Restructuring and Community Politics* (New York: Blackwell, 1987).

12. Smith and Feagin, *The Capitalist City*, table 1.1.

13. Saskia Sassen, *The Global City: New York, London, Tokyo* (Princeton, N.J.: Princeton University Press, 1991), *Cities in a World Economy*, 2d. ed. (Thousand Oaks, Calif.: Sage, 1999), and *Losing Control? Sovereignty in an Age of Globalization* (New York: Columbia University Press, 1996).

14. For analysis and case studies in Peru, Mexico, and Chile, see Castells, *The City and the Grassroots*, part 4.

15. For an interesting example of urban development for underdevelopment, see David A. Smith," Dependent Urbanization in Colonial America: The Case of Charleston, South Carolina," *Social Forces* 66 (September 1987): 1–28.

16. Demetrios Caraley, "Washington Abandons the Cities," *Political Science Quarterly* 107, no. 1 (1992): 1–30.

17. Federal Department of Housing and Urban Development Report, "Now Is the Time: Places Left Behind in the New Economy," April 28, 1999.

18. For a detailed picture of the urban-based American upper class, see Frederic Cople Jahner, *The Urban Establishment: Upper Strata in Boston, New York, Charleston, Chicago, and Los Angeles* (Urbana: University of Illinois Press, 1982).

19. For a study showing a direct relation between unionization and capital flight, see David Jaffee, "The Political Economy of Job Loss in the United States, 1970–1980," *Social Problems* 33 (April 1986): 297–318.

20. For an insightful analysis of the development of the American city from a Marxist perspective, see David M. Gordon, "Capitalist Development and the History of American Cities," in *Marxism and the Metropolis*, ed. William K. Tabb and Larry Sawers, 2d ed. (New York: Oxford University Press, 1984), 21–53.

21. Ira Katznelson, "The Crisis of the Capitalist City: Urban Politics and Social Control," in *Theoretical Perspectives on Urban Politics*, ed. Willis D. Hawley et al. (Upper Saddle River, N.J.: Prentice Hall, 1976), 214–29.

22. In this connection, see Morton White and Lucia White, *The Intellectual versus the City* (Cambridge, Mass.: Harvard University Press, 1962).

23. Claude S. Fischer, *The Urban Experience*, 2d ed. (San Diego: Harcourt Brace Jovanovich, 1984).

24. For an early analysis of the federal government's highway and subsidized housing programs that enabled the middle and upper-middle classes to leave the city and thus erode its tax base, see Anthony Downs' "The Impact of Housing Policies on Family Life in the United States since World War II," *Daedalus* 106 (Spring 1977): 163–80.

25. Among the earliest to make this comparison are Susan S. Fainstein and Norman I.

Fainstain, in their "National Policy and Urban Development," *Social Problems* 26 (December 1978): 125–46.

26. For an excellent analysis of suburbia, see Robert Fishman, *Bourgeois Utopias: The Rise and Fall of Suburbia* (New York: Basic Books, 1987).

27. For a fascinating critical analysis and case studies of Louisville, Arlington-Irving-Richardson (Texas), Cleveland, Boston, Dallas, Chicago, Houston, Detroit, Wilkes-Barre, Hartford, Philadelphia, and Santa Monica, see Scott Cummings, ed., *Business Elites and Urban Development: Case Studies and Critical Perspectives* (Albany: State University of New York Press, 1988). For a mainstream analysis of poverty and the city sponsored by the Committee on National Urban Policy of the National Research Council, itself part of the National Academy of Sciences (the official science adviser to the federal government), see Michael G. H. McGeary and Lawrence E. Lynn Jr., eds., *Urban Change and Poverty* (Washington, D.C.: National Academy 1988). The background papers for this report provide some useful nonpolitical technical information on urban poverty. The report's summary of policy implications (pp. 51–54) takes the health and vitality of American society for granted, makes a few vague references to the need for more investment in human and urban infrastructure capital, and calls for more research.

28. For a politically sophisticated introduction to urban planning, accompanied by many useful illustrations, see Peter Calthorpe, *The Next American Metropolis: Ecology, Community, and the American Dream* (New York: Princeton Architectural, 1993).

29. Lyn H. Lofland, *The Public Realm: Exploring the City's Quintessential Social Territory* (New York: Aldine De Gruyter, 1998).

30. For a radical indictment of fast-food chains as detrimental to both human and community health, see Peter Barry Chowka, "Hamburger's Last Stand," *East West Journal* (June 1979).

31. For good case studies of Buffalo, New York City, Detroit, Houston, Los Angeles, and Pittsfield, Massachusetts, see Smith and Feagin, *The Capitalist City*. For good case studies of New York, Washington, D.C., Boston, and Baltimore, see Richard V. Knight and Gary Gappert, eds., *Cities in a Global Economy* (Newbury Park, Calif.: Sage, 1989).

32. Connecting the macrolevel global economy with national political economies, including state and local governments on down to neighborhoods and households, is a special strength of Smith and Feagin, *The Capitalist City*.

7

Journalism, Policy Science, Policy Groups, and Foundations: Undermining the Public and Contracting the Public Sphere

I nformation is valuable in all societies. Before capitalism, information was gener- ated by and for governing elites. Earlier societies also established elaborate commu- nication networks, both internally and between each other. Under capitalism, information is still generated by and for governing elites, but the generators are highly diversified and specialized. One of these, journalism, generates news, which has two characteristics not present in earlier societies—it is communicated to both elites and masses, and it is part of a profit-oriented business. Another information generator, the policy sciences, works largely for other elites, and its members tend to be employees of both profit and nonprofit organizations.

Our first step in understanding these two knowledge professions is to ask some questions about human thought. Is there a need to distinguish between information and knowledge? Under what conditions does knowledge arise? Does it take distinc- tive forms under different systems of society? What is the relation between knowl- edge and practice? Answering such questions is the province of the *sociology of knowledge*.

JOURNALISM, POLICY SCIENCE, AND THE SOCIOLOGY OF KNOWLEDGE

Thinking about Thought

The term *knowledge* (as opposed to information, data, facts) means knowing why things or people—the solar system, plants, the human body, a septic tank, consumers, voters, spouses, artists, scientists, theologians, groups, the human personality, society, and so on—behave as they do. Knowledge about causation is also a "capacity for action," as Stehr emphasizes. When, how, and why we act depends on sociopolitical conditions, as Stehr reminds us, noting that it is easier to act on natural-science knowledge than on social-science knowledge.[1] The policy sciences explicitly seek knowledge rather than information (raw data, facts that do not have context, origins, or purposes). Journalism supplies both information (financial data) and knowledge (background on everything from the weather to revolution). In analyzing these two knowledge elites, our main purpose is to determine how good they are at identifying the causes at work in American society and its outer world. In short, are they really knowledge elites?

The sociological specialty, the sociology of knowledge, strives for knowledge about how knowledge itself develops. In studying belief, moral, and aesthetic systems, it assumes that human creations, spiritual no less than material, and lodged in the personality or social relations, are social and historical phenomena. The sociology of knowledge also wants to know under what conditions knowledge is put to use. What prompts the "capacity for action" to become knowledge in practice? Does it make sense to think of society as organized, systemic ignorance?

The goal of the sociology of knowledge, therefore, is to explain an important part of human behavior (thinking, feeling, creating symbols, evaluating).[2] In seeking answers, the sociology of knowledge can take a broad historical perspective and study, for example, the social conditions that spawned modern legal and political philosophy, Protestant-bourgeois morality, or the modern professions and disciplines. Alternatively, it can assume a microsociological form and study the emergence of norms from play groups, explain the thought of social theorists by referring to their family experiences or religious backgrounds, seek to understand a natural science outcome in terms of social relations in a laboratory, or show how divorce law is constructed in part by the interaction of lawyer and client.

Analysis of the social sources of symbols is widespread and appears under various guises. The current term for it is the *social construction* of something, even of reality itself. Much of our understanding of social problems, for example, has resulted from sociologists' probing into socially generated definitions of crime, mental illness, mental retardation, disease, gendered occupations, and the like. Both reformers and radicals employ the constructionist perspective in an effort to show that a given phenomenon is not natural or fixed and can therefore be reformed or replaced (using a process of *deconstruction*). Conservatives are not likely to use this approach because of their reliance on human nature as explanation.

The social nature of knowledge has also been acknowledged by those who refer to the various empirical sciences as *interpretive* sciences. Interpretive philosophy has influenced a wide variety of sociological (and other) studies and represents the major creative current in all the sciences over the past few decades. Interpretive science argues that all human behavior, including that of professionals, is subjective (that is, based on experience and cultural assumptions). It also argues that those who study human behavior themselves employ assumptions—assumptions that tell them what to study, what evidence is relevant, and ultimately, what conclusions (interpretations) are warranted. One of the important things journalism has learned about itself is that it constructs the news—it does not discover or find it. The policy sciences, however, have yet to realize the limitations of the so-called objective method.

The Politics of Truth

To assume that knowledge and science are social in nature does not mean that the findings of science are not true. Those who emphasize the role of cultural assumptions in science or who employ the sociology of knowledge to study the symbolic world want to know how knowledge is created and what barriers stand in the way of additions to our knowledge. Therefore, in analyzing the social conditions that spawn knowledge (and bias, error, and ignorance as well), it should be remembered that the overwhelming majority of theorists in this field (for example, Vico, Condorcet, Saint Simon, Auguste Comte, Karl Marx, Emile Durkheim) have assumed that knowing how knowledge emerges is compatible with the idea of truth. Indeed, the major thrust of this perspective is that social conditions generate truth, usually over time.

The sociology of knowledge emerged from both the liberal and radical traditions. Radicals and liberals both think of knowledge as a by-product of a society committed to progress through science. Both ask a similar question: "If knowledge is dependent on social conditions, what is the best way to organize those conditions to produce better knowledge?" But liberals and radicals differ widely in their answers. Liberals believe that the fundamental conditions for progress in knowledge already exist: legal and political freedom (including safeguards for free speech and a free press), education, and scientific research. For radicals, a full body of knowledge, available to all, cannot occur under capitalism. The best known of the various radical perspectives is Marxism. Marxists believe that science reflects economic power—that at some point, science and the entire symbolic world of capitalism cease to be progressive (in the interests of all) and become ideology (the symbolic protection of an obsolete social system). Radical feminism, either alone or in tandem with Marxism, has also spawned an attack on what it considers to be a masculine (and thus biased and incomplete) body of contemporary knowledge. As we shall see, American journalism and the policy sciences (unlike their capitalist counterparts in Europe) are part of America's well-nigh monopolistic liberal worldview.

The emergence of the social constructionist perspective has generated a backlash among traditionalists, who accuse its adherents of being against truth. Suffice it to say that only a small minority of social or humanistic scientists say that truth and objectivity are not possible. Those who accuse today's creative scientific currents of being antitruth are generally those who are trying to uphold yesterday's truth—for example, creationists, politicized conservative scholars (the National Association of Scholars), and natural scientists who do not understand their roles as the servants of power, who have been stung by the doubts in science-as-salvation expressed by environmentalists (and others) and by the breakdown of their privileged world (that existed in World War II and the Cold War), experienced as cutbacks in federal financing and as unemployment and underemployment. The controversies about interpretive science that concern us, however, are those in journalism and the policy sciences. These controversies are between those who adhere to *positivism* (nonpolitical, objective, empirical analysis) and those who argue that a better pathway to objectivity is to employ an interpretive science (acknowledge the use of ideas, assumptions, and values in generating knowledge).

The Knowledge Professions and the Performance of Social Functions

The sociology of knowledge studies all forms of human symbolic creation, most importantly by the professions, including the academic disciplines, whether in natural science, social science, art, literature, theology, philosophy, or popular culture. Though our focus is on journalism and the policy sciences, we want to understand them as part of the American professions. The professions have been studied rather extensively over the past seventy-five years.[3] Scholars have sought to understand:

1. The rise of the professions;
2. their distinctive attributes;
3. the relation between formal and applied knowledge;
4. the social or class origins of the professions;
5. the status of minorities, including women, in the professions;
6. the internal differentiation and conflicts within the professions;
7. the struggle by each to carve out a jurisdiction (often in competition with other professions) through the elaboration of voluntary groups and ideologies, and through politics and law;
8. their relations with the state and with various kinds of clients;
9. conditions of work, in various contexts, such as solo practice, professional groups, nonprofessional groups, and small and large-scale organizations;
10. their efforts to establish an economic base, especially through the control of entry into their ranks;
11. the rewards of the various professions, especially income, and the relation of such motivations to the health of the professions and of society; and
12. the distinctive nature of the professions in various national contexts.

Most of the early studies of these issues were conducted in the nonpolitical, objective style of mainstream social science (functionalism), while later studies—say, in the past three decades—have been more political and critical. Many early studies investigated what the professions said about themselves or plumbed their attitudes through questionnaires or interviews. Many were case studies of particular professions and their immediate work circumstances. A trend in recent decades has been to criticize professional claims, especially when the professionals seem interested primarily in securing high and reliable incomes, openly engage in politics to secure their ends, do not have unique knowledge bases, or are ideological (biased in both their depictions of themselves and in their professional work).

A number of new developments in the study of the professions should be noted. First, the professions exhibit a considerable amount of deviant behavior. Scholarship in this area has gone beyond the conventional hand-wringing about the failure of the professions to curb wayward individuals, to a focus on institutions and organizations (in journalism, for example, systematic bias and underreporting by news organizations as opposed to made-up stories and plagiarism by individuals).

Second, scholars have also gone beyond noting how the professions are dependent on other elites and have begun to build a comprehensive picture of relationships among all elites. Here one notes the dependence of journalists on sources among the powerful and the dependence of the policy professions on their sponsors.

Third, scholars writing from various perspectives have noted that the professions do not apply knowledge in a direct manner to the problems they face. Some argue that professionals improvise and engage in artistic interpretation, while others say that professionals create reality. If the professions are not objective generators and dispensers of objective knowledge, then their claim to power and its rewards must be changed. In addition, society and human behavior also cease to be objective, natural entities and processes; serious consideration must be given to the idea that society and human behavior are merely human-historical creations.

Finally, an interesting finding in the study of the professions points to the neglected role of nationalism in how the professions have defined themselves and how it has skewed their vision of the world. What was and what is the role of the professions in helping to create and maintain the American nation-state? What nationalistic values prompted the professions? Is it possible to isolate notions of patriotism and national power from other considerations? Natural science, sociology, anthropology, political science, economics, history, psychology, and literary studies clearly show both intended and unintended contributions to, and a shaping of, subject matter to suit the needs of national development. This prompts us to ask whether American journalism biases its domestic and foreign news to serve a particular picture of the American nation-state. To what extent are the policy sciences, trapped inside American liberalism, unable to profit from practices in other societies?

While individual professions have been critically evaluated in terms of their services to individuals, groups, and categories of people, the question of how well the professions have performed their supposed social functions has been completely ignored. In keeping with the major theme of the book, this chapter revolves around a simple question: "How have journalism and the policy professions used communication technology either to *promote or retard the development of a responsibly organized democratic public* capable of consciously managing its affairs?"

In assessing the record of America's elites, either in or out of the professions, our book assumes that social problems can be solved only by a viable political system. Since the main thrust of modern professionalism has been openly antipolitical, it is unlikely that the mainstream professions will take the lead in raising questions about science and the professions in the political arena. It is also highly unlikely that they will ask the government to hold them to their promises of ever-improving service and solutions. This matter takes on special urgency when analyzing American society and its professions. The United States has gone farther than any other capitalist society in developing a (de facto) technocratic liberalism, and its version of professionalism may actually be working against the development of a democratic polity and society.[4] Questions must be raised, therefore, about the knowledge (both formal and applied) being generated by America's institutions and knowledge elites. Technocratic liberalism has shown that it can generate enormous amounts of knowledge (as did technocratic socialism in the former Soviet Union), but is it generating and implementing the knowledge needed to solve social problems? From all accounts, the answer appears to be no. (This is an enormously difficult question, and an answer in the negative is suggested at this point to balance the presumption, established largely by the professions themselves, that the answer is in the affirmative.) The key to understanding science and the professions is to see them in political terms—that is, as emerging and developing in given historical periods in response to sociopolitical conditions. Our first step toward understanding journalism and the policy sciences, therefore, is to illustrate briefly how symbolic activity serves the needs of power, and how, far from being transhistorical, it emerges, takes shape, and behaves in a manner consistent with historical power structures.

Modern Society: Industrialization and the Age of Empiricism

The advent of capitalism was a momentous event, comparable in importance to the Agricultural Revolution. By 1500, Europe had a thriving capitalist economy, anchored mostly in agriculture and commerce but not without the stirrings of industry. Between 1500 and 1800, England and France were transformed by their respective middle classes into unique capitalist societies. From 1800 on, these countries and others underwent processes of industrialization that were to usher in the contemporary world of developed capitalist societies and their distinctive professions and disciplines.

The first stage of capitalism (roughly 1500 to 1800) saw the advent of modern natural and social science. Basically, modern science began by abandoning the teleological worldview of the Greeks (and of the medieval period), but not their rationalism or deductive epistemology. Nature became, instead of a hodgepodge of qualitatively different entities, all responding to fixed inner blueprints, a set of abstract forces. To understand these forces, early modern science used mathematics, assuming, as had the Greeks, that reason was the way to get past the deceptions of experience and to penetrate nature's secrets.

The climax to this stage of science came in the seventeenth century, with the work of Isaac Newton. The Newtonian synthesis depicted nature as composed of material particles and abstract processes kept in orderly equilibrium by gravity—in effect, a huge machine, integrating the behavior of everyday matter as well as in the farthest reaches of the solar system. It should be noted that behind this grand act of reason lay centuries of European experience in struggling to harness the energy of wind and water through machinery (the humble but indispensable origin of the Machine Age).[5]

The eighteenth century established the Newtonian view of nature and human nature throughout Western culture. The eighteenth century also inaugurated the new stage of science, *empiricism*. The French Enlightenment took a revolutionary step and abandoned the Greek distrust of experience, the senses, and the world of facts. The phenomenal world, declared the *philosophes,* is orderly in and of itself and thus accessible to the thinking/sentient human being. The empirical outlook, which had been gathering for centuries, received full institutionalization in the nineteenth century. The nineteenth century also inaugurated the contemporary academic disciplines and the professions. Empirical research, the growth of knowledge, and the academic disciplines and professions cannot be understood unless they are placed in the context of the maturing capitalist society that spawned them.[6] (For an earlier discussion of the relation between capitalism and knowledge, see "Communication and Developments in the Symbolic Culture of the West," in chapter 2.)

Western society in the early nineteenth century was unique in a number of ways that bear on the West's commitment to empiricism and on the rise of the professions. Above all, the advent of significant economic changes, which ran the gamut from intensified capitalist agriculture to the factory system, generated a concern for the condition of the people, especially those subject to physical deprivations. Interest in the "social question" (as historians have come to call it) was a novel occurrence in Western politics and thought.[7] Obviously, thinkers and officials throughout history had concerned themselves with the general condition of the masses and had devised public policies to deal with it. What happened in the nineteenth century was unique in that both the holders and the near holders of power *saw their own fates* as bound up with the condition of the people. Previously, those in power had simply assumed a natural and fixed hierarchic order of things and human beings. The dominant groups took the people and their suffering for granted; whatever their condition, it was ordained by nature, normal, and familiar.

By the early nineteenth century all this had changed; powerful groups could no longer take their societies for granted. In addition, the widespread changes in social life had the effect of preventing the upper classes of Europe from directly experiencing their own societies—a situation that seemed to be politically dangerous to many of their members and must have been unsettling to almost all. An immediate result of this situation was a widespread desire to gain more knowledge about the social question, or the condition of ordinary people—thus a vast growth of intelligence gathering by the police, government bureaus, newspapers, and the emerging social sciences, and a proliferation of professions to deal directly with emerging social problems. The advent of organized empirical research in both the natural and social sciences was one of the more significant developments of this new social world. Against this background, a journalist or policy scientist must ask him or herself: "Am I generating knowledge largely to benefit the holders of power?"

The rise of the professions should not be seen only in terms of the ideology that accompanied it—that is, as progress toward democracy and an ever-expanding triumph over ignorance, hunger, disease, and exploitation. We must be especially careful not to take at face value the claim by the professions that they are the benefactors of humanity. The history of the relation between society and its professions shows clearly that the professions serve the economically and politically powerful. The claim that the modern world is under the sway of autonomous objective, progressive knowledge elites is highly problematic.

SOCIAL POWER, KNOWLEDGE, AND THE KNOWLEDGE PROFESSIONS

Since the ancient Greeks, Westerners have taken it for granted that:

1. Knowledge about the world can be obtained independently of time and place through the exercise of human reason (objective truth).
2. Knowledge can improve our personal and social lives.
3. There are special methods and people to provide and apply knowledge.
4. Knowledge will flow out from those who generate it to those who need to know (rulers, citizens, professionals, owners, workers, consumers).

The nineteenth century institutionalized the empirical method because powerful groups needed it and supported it. In its various embodiments (scholarship, originality, laboratory, the free press, education, learned societies, foundations, policy groups, research institutes, etc.), it was soon taken for granted that science held the key to progress, and perhaps of human perfectibility. By the end of the twentieth century some were arguing that the successes of science and professionalism had ushered in a knowledge society, signaling the end of ideology. The supposed new society has also been characterized as a *postindustrial, postmodern,* or *information society* (and in a related guise as the "end of history").[8] In an explicit expression of the evolutionary liberal tradition in sociological theory (like those, for example, of Emile Durkheim or Charles Horton Cooley), Talcott Parsons (1902–1979) announced the reality of evolutionary progress through symbolic (mental and moral) achievement.

Faith in the ability of science to produce transhistorical knowledge and to incorporate it into the life of society continues to dominate the social and natural sciences and education. It manifests itself in the liberal (Right and Left) reform tradition. It appears as the explicit planning tradition. It appears throughout the liberal professions, journalism, and the policy sciences. The fact that much radical thought, especially Marxism, also assumes some form of rational evolution makes it even more difficult to assess critically the West's deep faith in progress through ideational activity.

The Fiction of a Knowledge Society

This book assumes that the argument for a knowledge, or postindustrial, society is weak and that modern capitalism has not entered any stage that runs counter to its essence (private property as the source of economic, political, and social power). The United States is not in a postindustrial world, driven by or based on theoretical scientific knowledge; there is not even a discernible trend in that direction.

The idea of a postindustrial, knowledge-based society is deeply planted, and it has been reinforced recently by exaggerated, fanciful claims on behalf of computer-driven, integrated, interactive communication technology, the "information high-way." Nonetheless, the idea of a knowledge-based society must be resisted—nay, rejected. Perhaps the most sophisticated version of the fallacy of a postindustrial society is Harold Perkin's argument that English society, starting in 1880, left behind the class society of entrepreneurial England (just as class society left behind the aristocratic society based on land) to become a professional society.[9] Perkin argues that the professional ideal—occupation, income, and service by a certified meritocracy—has permeated society from the top almost to the bottom.

Perkin's argument is interesting and insightful to the extent that he has anchored much of it in the success that professionals have had in turning human capital (their expertise) into income-producing property. Nonetheless, his argument is deficient, and not merely because he cannot show that professionals have ceased using their power and privileges to prevent competition, or because his claim that a merit-based professionalism characterizes the basic occupational system is more than dubious. Perkin's argument is deficient because he does not recognize the co-supremacy of land, other forms of material capital, and human capital over society.

The best interpretation of the growth of white-collar occupations has occurred outside the liberal tradition. The classic analysis remains C. Wright Mills's.[10] For Mills, the new service, white-collar, or professional occupations represent a change *within* the historical middle class. Far from transcending class or industrial society, the new occupations are firmly embedded in economic, political, and social structures based on private property, managed markets, upper-level coordination, and bureaucratic administration. That significant portions of the new middle class are propertyless does not dilute their commitment (unconscious as well as conscious) to a property-oriented market society.

The belief in progress through knowledge raises two different questions: (1) Are the liberal professions supplying the knowledge needed to make the United States an adaptive society? and (2) have we entered a social stage in which knowledge animates power structures?

The answer to the first question is that they are not. The answer to the second is also no. But the damaging belief that we have become, or are on the verge of becoming, a knowledge society remains strong, though it is not always easy to identify, because it assumes various forms. To resist that belief, it is useful to also think of American society's symbolic culture (as with any society) as one of organized, systemic ignorance.

Symbolic Activity and the Needs of Power

Like all symbolic activity, empirical research is related to the structure of social power. Those who accept the conventional view of the development of empirical science and of liberal political institutions as collectively representing a growing emancipation from error and evil have themselves succumbed to the blandishments of power. Knowledge helps to make human beings free, but not all of them; indeed, the knowledge that sets some people free results in the nonfreedom of others. Knowledge about how a legislature works, for example, can result in laws that free some from tax burdens while placing heavier burdens on the weak and ignorant. Empirical research can certainly contribute knowledge and help in the clarification and realization of values, but its known historical forms cannot automatically be equated with truth, morality, or the common good.

What is referred to as "knowledge" is also suspect, because it is generated selectively and unconsciously, according to historically induced assumptions. The use of the *intelligence quotient* (IQ) test is a well-known example of how assumptions enter into empirical research and of how both are related to social power. Early research into intelligence quotients was conducted under the assumption that human beings are innately unequal. As a consequence, the science of IQs became a potent instrument for creating and maintaining a capitalist division of labor—especially when educational systems adopted the IQ as the measure of native ability, with the enthusiastic endorsement of the middle classes. Neglected was the counterassumption that the same facts about unequal IQs can be interpreted as functions of social power: People are made unequal in IQ, as well as in occupational skills, tastes, goals, and so on, by the hierarchy of social class. This assumption gives the user of IQs a very different view of the same facts.

The connection between empirical social research and social power originated with the absolute monarchy, especially during its mercantilist phase. The dynamics of internal and external power relations made it imperative that the state rationalize (bureaucratize) its operations. Hand in hand with routine administration, the keeping of accounts, the codification of laws, and the minting and printing of money went the development of intelligence-gathering: domestic and foreign spies and informers; police reports; inquiries and commissions concerning population; the state of the fishing or textile industries; surveys of public lands; and so on.

The case of England is especially instructive in understanding the power functions served by the institutionalization of empirical research. The symbolic development of England is essentially the record of the acquiring, consolidating, and employing of power by a dynamic middle class. In the seventeenth century, Hobbes and Locke shattered and displaced the feudal symbolic world in the name of an emergent middle class. In the eighteenth century, Adam Smith found rationality *in* capitalist society, not beyond it; Hume clipped the wings of reason, saying, in effect, that thought cannot be used to transcend or critically evaluate society. The nineteenth century saw the growth of a series of deductive disciplines, such as economics, political science, and sociology, all within the capitalist assumptions of laissez-faire economics, utilitarianism, progress, and social Darwinism. These disciplines eventually flowered as the *liberal arts*—liberalism's higher education. Alongside these symbolic developments, but not linked to them until much later, grew a tradition of empirical social research, a nontheoretical grappling with the problems of an established capitalist society rapidly becoming industrialized and urbanized (in the United States, the Chicago School in sociology in the 1920s and 1930s).

In the early nineteenth century, Britain had a well-established, though adaptable and somewhat open, set of ruling elites. There was an obvious need for intelligence, and it was assumed from the first that facts were to be used for purposes of formulating public policy. As Abrams has shown so well,[11] the basic form of research in Britain's centralized society was the massive government inquiry, and the basic roles that were encouraged were those of statistician, administrator, and reform politician. Most important is the fact that Britain's dominant classes held distinctive views about society, views that deeply influenced the nature of the research they sponsored—a deeply rationalist concept of society, a focus on the individual as the basic unit of analysis, and the idea of automatic social integration and consensus through the "invisible hand." Essentially, the purposes of fact gathering were to uncover the natural laws that constituted society, to expose artificial obstacles that impeded their operation, and to promote the consensual natural society through social legislation and government administration. Characteristically, researchers felt that there was no need for theory to organize their fact gathering. As Abrams points out, its characteristic units of analysis were

> the state, the individual (moral or immoral) and occasionally, the classes. What is missing is any developed concept of the social system, any extended or general analysis of structured interactions between individuals or classes, any theory of the social basis of the state. Where there is a model of society it is typically an administrative one suffused with moral judgment. . . . [T]ime and again the terms of analysis are the custodial state standing face to face with individuals in need of help, corrections, or regeneration.[12]

Here again, one is prompted to ask, "Is this how journalism and the policy sciences see American society and their role in it? Is this how they view fact gathering?"

Later in the nineteenth century, a late-liberal movement surfaced to spearhead a more positive and comprehensive program of social reform within the assumptions of an emerging corporate capitalism. The development of an empirical orientation in American sociology, along with its sociocultural emphasis and its involvement in social reform, identifies it as an aspect of late liberalism. With no laissez-faire tradition to overcome, French and German sociologists (for example, Emile Durkheim and Max Weber) developed an even more pronounced sociocultural orientation and became even more involved in the political issues of the day than was American sociology. In all countries, there was a clear recognition that empirical social research and social reform were positive forces that would act to prevent socialism.

It is clear that the main sources of the new interest in fact gathering during the nineteenth century were government, business, and voluntary groups, and that its motives were political, economic, humanitarian, and social—a fear of the masses and of socialism. In a classic essay,[13] Nathan Glazer has argued that the upper classes' new interest in facts stemmed from a feeling that they were surrounded by a society they neither knew nor could know, using such conventional methods as reading or personal experience. Glazer does not complete his insight, however. One of the main functions of the new interest in empirical research was to provide the dominant classes with the intelligence they needed to possess their society fully. The primary significance of the new passion for fact gathering is that it helped consolidate, update, and legitimate a particular system of social control (power). In this context, one asks, "Are journalism and the policy sciences unwitting adjuncts of the American system of power?"

The sanctities of government and politics; the moral cloak of voluntary organizations, including churches; the iron necessities allegedly governing economic life; and the prestige of science—all served to mask the essentially partisan nature of mainstream empirical research. If one views the activities of these institutions, however, as ways of developing private solutions to public problems, the generation of knowledge falls into place as another way in which the dominant classes solve their problems, invariably through solutions that create problems for the lower classes.

With the triumph of liberalism, starting in seventeenth-century England, philosophy and social theory no longer served a landed-clerical elite; symbolic culture no longer emphasized the next world and denigrated this one; and contemplation and transcendence were no longer feasible social ideals. In nineteenth-century England and twentieth-century America, organized empirical social research became the main way, in tandem with reform politics, to protect the status quo (capitalism). By camouflaging the status quo in the garbs of progress through problem solving, organized empirical research effectively preempted the future while safeguarding the present. In short, given the class uses of organized fact finding, one must resist associating it with truth, morality, and the common good, even when conducted by well-meaning professional bodies—including, as we shall now see, journalism and the policy sciences.

JOURNALISM: REPORTERS AND
NEWS ORGANIZATIONS

Journalism as a Profession

Journalism shares much with the unique American professions (see chapter 4). Like America's other professions, journalism emerged from entrepreneurialism and self-promotion. America's explicit constitutional protection of free speech made government sponsorship unlikely in any case. Journalism sometimes forgets, however, that the First Amendment's main purpose is not to secure the freedom of the press but that of the public at large.

Journalism's core identity comes from its claim that it can generate objective

knowledge about public affairs (pre-twentieth-century journalism was fiercely partisan politically, but in the 1920s journalism shifted to an avowed neutrality). Unlike
other professionals, journalists are not licensed or certified by government. Until the
1960s, the profession did not even require a college degree, let alone advanced
degrees. Journalists also differ from some other professionals in that they do not
receive their incomes from self-employment. Journalists are employees of profit-
seeking organizations—something that is becoming true of more and more of the
professions, given the spreading logic and practice of corporate capitalism. As we
shall see shortly, the employee status of journalists profoundly affects the processes
of fact gathering and news generation.

Like the educational programs of the other professions, journalism must keep up
with the fast-moving and ever more complex world. It missed out, for example, on
the environmental movement, because it had no "beat" that could respond to its
emergence—no one routinely covering such matters.[14] But like the social sciences in
general, its most important education goal is an old one—to bypass the mythologies
of power by providing an understanding of events in sociohistorical terms.

The Struggle for Autonomy

Brint argues that journalism and other professions have suffered a loss of autonomy
as markets have stripped away some of the protection that they once had against
such forces.[15] Brint's analysis is framed in terms of his overall thesis, that the once
nonpolitical, nonprofit professions, motivated by a service-scholarship ethic, have
become experts for hire, experts who are oriented toward markets and income.
Brint's thesis is a common one; it surfaces continuously in the individual professions
and is based on the dubious assumption that the professions were once separate from
and above the capitalist economy. It is closer to historical reality to see the professions as essentially capitalist actors who invented ideals of service, objectivity, and so
on to enhance their market capabilities. What Brint and others who want journalism
to live up to its ideals are observing is change in elements of a capitalist world that
is itself unchanging. Journalism is and has always been profit oriented, and more are
now aware of this, thanks to research and the fact that journalism is now embedded
in corporate, world-market capitalism. News organizations are not merely dependent on advertisers; they are big businesses in their own right, whether as separate
organizations or as parts of giant, and increasingly global, multimedia corporations.
Like the rest of the economy, the news media exhibit a strong trend toward
monopoly.[16]

Journalism has been able, by and large, to hold off attempts by government to
restrict or regulate its activities (thanks to the First Amendment). But the ability of
reporters and the news media to stand up to private interests has not been nearly as
successful. One reason is that corporations in the news business are profit seekers
and have much in common with advertisers and other private groups. Another is
that in recent years network news divisions have become smaller fish, as networks
have become parts of gigantic global corporations devoted to goals other than news.

A third reason is that the media and reporters are deeply dependent on their sources, which for the most part are powerful people or agencies in government and politics, people and agencies that in the last analysis are surrogates for private interests.

Journalism must also struggle against the powerful and insidious pull of American culture, especially the well-nigh monopolistic liberal worldview. Journalists are also socialized by education and probably undergo a loss of idealism in their advanced studies (as has been documented in medicine and law). There is further socialization as new employees absorb the culture that permeates news organizations.

Journalism also suffers a loss of autonomy through the operation of stratification processes. In his highly readable critique of journalism, Fallows points out that elite journalists are in the upper middle class, well above the people they are ostensibly serving. This, he says, negatively affects their treatment of such things as free trade (NAFTA), downsizing, and taxes; there is very little emphasis on the negative impact of such policies on ordinary people. Elite reporters are even farther removed from the world of ordinary people by their association with the rich and powerful on the lecture circuit, where they collect huge fees for saying nothing (their purpose is to fill seats).[17]

It is not wide of the mark to indict not only elite reporters but all news media, public or private—talk shows, news magazines, major newspapers, and programs like *Nightline* and the *Lehrer News Hour* (Robert MacNeil having retired)—for failure to solicit and vent the views of groups below the upper classes. Empirical studies of the kinds of people who appear on public affairs programs, on both private and public broadcasting, indicate a strong status-quo orientation; some are openly right-wing.[18]

The status-quo orientation of public television is the most disturbing. Conservatives have had a large, even predominant influence on PBS, largely through presidential appointments to the Corporation for Public Broadcasting, conservative programs, and incessant and successful efforts to keep federal funding at a disgraceful $1.06 per citizen—as compared to $32.02, $31.05, and $38.99 in Japan, Canada, and Great Britain, respectively (U.S. funding rises to $6.83 if donations and corporate and state funds are included).[19] Nonetheless, conservatives complain stridently that the news media, including public television, are biased toward the left. Their attacks are characterized by mere assertion and by obvious distortion (endlessly repeated, one suspects, not to persuade but to intimidate liberals and bolster the faithful); the few attempts by conservative scholars at serious analysis have failed to meet scientific standards.

The status-quo orientation of the news media, private and public, goes much deeper than the prevalence of openly conservative programs. Croteau and Hoynes studied the highly regarded ABC program *Nightline* and the equally regarded *Mac-Neil/Lehrer News Hour* in the late 1980s with disturbing results. Aware that trying to identify conservatives and liberals (in our terms, Right and Left liberals) by what is said is a highly subjective procedure, Croteau and Hoynes focused on the characteristics of guests: race, sex, nationality, occupation, whether they appeared alone, how much they spoke, and the subject matter of the program. Their conclusion is that these programs tend to equate the interests of the United States with those of the federal government, powerful economic interests, and selected experts (invariably identified as nonpartisan). News consists essentially of these categories of people telling audiences what everything means, with little input by ordinary people, or labor, environmental, feminist, gay-lesbian, or church-based groups (and when individuals from such groups appear, they are identified as partisans and are given little air time).

Croteau and Hoynes, with Kevin Carragee, also examined all public affairs programs on PBS (news, business, talk/interview, and documentaries) for one week each month during the first half of 1992. Here they found that men appeared three times as often as women, Republicans more often than Democrats, and that government officials, professionals (journalists and academics), and corporate representatives far outnumbered or outweighed members from the general public or activist groups. Of great significance was the fact that in economic coverage, corporate representatives far outnumbered journalists or academics. The result was that the great majority of economic coverage addressed audiences as investors and gave little coverage to people as workers, consumers, or citizens. In addition, there was almost exclusive attention to gross domestic product, stock market, and profit data (all accepted as nonproblematic); further, while unemployment was noted, there was no mention of underemployment or discouraged workers (the millions who have given up looking for work). The failure to give background on the narrow range of data that received emphasis was matched by a failure to provide historical background on the U.S. economy—to wit, when faced with competition from abroad in the 1970s, American business made a conscious effort to lower the cost of American labor by investing abroad, making jobs part-time, getting rid of benefits, lowering wages, and keeping the minimum wage low (not to mention by making a concerted attack on trade unions and using replacement workers).[20]

Croteau and Hoynes were undoubtedly helped in framing their studies by work done in the 1970s. Three studies from that period, to which we now turn, had uncovered a pattern similar to theirs, using different news sites and methods.

The Social Construction of News

The 1970s saw a creative burst of research that first established journalism's neglect of ordinary people. Three ethnographic studies by sociologists, all based on participant observation, reached the same conclusion—news is not about reality but is a skewed reality constructed by social actors in social settings. Tuchman, in a contribution to the developing interpretive sociology of the day, observed four news-gathering sites in the New York City metropolitan area. She argued that journalism's naïve empiricism, focused on the concrete, the contingent, and the present, turns [created] facts into objective [natural] facts and constitutes a protection of the status quo. That is, by accepting social institutions as legitimate sources of news, journalism legitimates them further. (For some reason, Tuchman concluded that she could not accuse journalism of bias, only of protecting the status quo.)[21]

Herbert Gans's study of newscasts by CBS and NBC, and by the news magazines, *Time* and *Newsweek*, is must reading for undergraduates. Gans's qualitative content analysis of the news created and disseminated by these media is carefully written, clearly indicating his reasons for whatever he says. His conclusions about the above news media were that they are oriented toward the upper classes and exhibit a glaring neglect of the bulk of the American people. Journalism (represented by these media) also uses a taken-for-granted cluster of values (in our language, the core presuppositions of American liberalism) to frame or construct reality: ethnocentrism, altruistic democracy, responsible capitalism, small-town pastoralism, individualism, moderation, social order, and national leadership.

Constructing the news, says Gans, is mostly about power (choice of sources) and efficiency (meeting deadlines); audiences are less important. The functions of the news media are to test leaders (especially political candidates), supply feedback for elected and appointed officials, bestow power (which may or may not be turned into political and economic power), and act as agents of social control (by helping to maintain order, warning against disorder, and acting as moral guardians). The above may be debatable, says Gans, but he is more certain about two other functions of journalism: the management of the nonfiction symbolic arena and, more important, the framing of events, using national values and a national context, to construct our understanding of the American nation and society. Gans, like Tuchman, unaccountably declined to call the media biased. He effectively did so, however, at the end of his analysis, by calling for more perspectives in the news than were available (multi-perspectival news).[22]

Our third report of news making from the perspective of the social construction of reality is a participant-observation, ethnographic study of a small-city newspaper in California. The paper's circulation included almost every household in the city (75,000) and metropolitan area (150,000). Fishman analyzed how the newspaper and its reporters turned the raw, diverse phenomena of daily life into news. His account revolved around two bureaucratic structures. The first, the newspaper, was driven largely by deadlines and revenue needs; the second, government bureaucracies, was driven by a need to let the public know that they were doing their job and that the world was operating normally.

The relation between these two structures, Fishman argued, is quite close, because they need each other. Reporters make their rounds: the city police, the county sheriff's office, the courts, public schools, council meetings, and ancillary sites, all of which have "certified status incumbents in structural positions of knowledge." By and large, government agency reports, which are already highly idealized and sanitized, become the basis of what appears in the newspaper. Everyone benefits: the newspaper gets its news copy free and prepackaged (at taxpayer expense), and government officials get to control how the public sees events and to sustain the public's belief that government officials are doing their jobs. In this overall process very little attention is paid to happenings outside bureaucratic routines and perceptions.

Fishman concluded that the resulting news is ideological, which he defined as the "procedures people use as a means not to know," and that news "legitimates the existing political order by disseminating bureaucratic idealizations of the world and by filtering out troublesome perceptions of events." Had Fishman used a full political economy approach, he might have added that journalism, acting in concert with government, was protecting a socioeconomic system. The term *ideology* means not only how journalism keeps itself ignorant but how it keeps everyone else ignorant as well.[23]

Thanks to these and other studies, we now know that objectivity in journalism is, like objectivity generally, a fiction invented by elites to protect themselves against each other.[24] We know that journalism has neither the time nor the money to cover the news fully or carefully (and still remain profitable). We know that often journalists lack the expertise and experience needed to get beneath the surface of substantive issues. We know that journalists become dependent on their sources, most of who are powerful groups and individuals. We know that journalists work in bureaucratic settings in a highly concentrated business.

We are also aware that the news media (perhaps especially television news) create dependency and undermine reflexivity, the ability to see oneself as an active participant in the formation and control of social reality.[25] TV news does not encourage viewers to understand social and personal problems in terms of causes in the larger socioeconomic world. Also, it does not present alternative public or private policies for viewers to choose from. Instead, it presents viewers with a taken-for-granted world, a fixed "objective" world in which people are acted upon. It unwittingly cooperates with professionals and government officials to instill fear and insecurity, in effect thrusting audiences into the arms of leaders (law enforcement, government officials, the military, doctors, and so on).[26] In this world, action takes place in terms of unquestioned cultural a priori propositions about the family, government, capital, labor unions, the legitimacy of experts, and other countries.[27] The basic causes in the world are different types of individuals, fixed and impersonal institutions, and sinister or unstable foreigners.

In this sense, TV news is part of the overall symbolic world that constitutes the basic outlook of all the theoretical and applied sciences and all the professions. As part of the larger culture, TV news does not control by imposing itself on viewers; perhaps more important is its ability to connect with the already fashioned personalities of its viewers and to involve them in a mythical world common to both sides.[28] Newscasts pretend to have authoritative pictures of what is going on in the world. They consist of fragmented bits of information in vivid word and picture; they appear omniscient because of their technical ability to conquer space and time. But all this undermines understanding and promotes passivity. Broadcast journalism rarely encourages action by its audience or works to empower it by situating personal troubles in public and private institutions. It rarely provides historical background that would allow the audience to learn from the past and locate itself in an ongoing process of social creation. In effect, journalism depoliticizes not merely by claiming objectivity (accurate, complete, authoritative knowledge) but by creating the *illusion* of objectivity.

Some of the above will be disputed. Many believe that improvements are possible and that journalism's ideal functions are in any case being served, at least to some degree—to act as a watchdog of the public's interest; to criticize wrongdoing by governments, private individuals, and private organizations; and to supply the public with the information it needs to make informed judgments.

Certainly, there is little doubt that many newspapers, television programs, magazines, and journals provide critical and meaty exposés or arguments on various sides of the American political spectrum. *Harper's* and *Atlantic Monthly*, for example, produce a steady stream of highly useful essays (it should be noted that both publications are tottering on the brink of bankruptcy, because the economics of publishing nonfiction are against them). Journalism as in-depth analysis of current issues and trends is a vital feature of newspapers, especially the *New York Times*, the *Los Angeles Times*, the *Washington Post*, and the *Wall Street Journal* (the editorials in these newspapers are another matter). Opinion magazines aligned with Right liberal (for example, *Commentary*, *Public Interest*) and Left liberal (for example, *The Nation*, *American Prospect*) causes and organizations also produce a heady mixture of ideas about current issues. The Public Broadcasting System has many useful programs that delve into various issues, as does National Public Radio.

The reader by now will have noticed, however, that in switching from television to the media that at least partially realize journalism's ideals, we have been talking about media that cater to America's upper classes. Once the focus switches to publications aimed at the broad public, journalism's effectiveness declines. The public's interest in network news has declined in recent decades, though increased viewing on cable and the Internet may have made up some of the difference. Documentaries have disappeared from network television, and news of any kind has virtually disappeared from commercial radio. To counter all this, journalism in television and newspapers have begun a noticeable trend to give the public what it wants: domestic rather than foreign news, sensationalist news (scandals, especially involving well-known individuals), natural disasters, medical developments, uplifting stories, news about eccentric people, and sports.

Behind these developments is the logic of a capitalist economy in which news organizations are pressed hard to seek profits as high as others not merely in their field but in all fields—to drive up profits and prices of shares incessantly, lest investors move to more lucrative areas. A special squeeze on news makers may develop, now that more and more of them have become small parts of giant entertainment companies.

Little doubt exists that advertisers have significant power over the news (and even over nonnews content). Combined with the fact that news organizations are profit-seeking big businesses in the first instance, a great deal of self-censorship occurs as news organizations socialize new members into their "master narrative" (every event is stereotyped according to American mainstream values and beliefs). Leadership positions in news organizations are filled from within. Reporters still have considerable autonomy to gather news, and they still feel they have the freedom to do so. But what they gather must go through a dozen others (gatekeepers), and the finished product is often different from what reporters intended.

Perhaps the biggest deficiency in journalism's educational programs, the research we have canvassed suggests, is the absence of social-structure analysis (the ability to see, and assign meaning to, an event or trend in terms of the society that spawned it). Given the monopoly of American liberalism, even well-educated Americans take America for granted and think of it as the outcome of what an individualized human nature does. This is why the basic, creative ideas in sociology and social science—especially the idea that there is no human nature, only society and history—had to come from abroad (Karl Marx, Emile Durkheim, Max Weber).[29]

Journalists as Ethnocentric Servants of Power

Journalism fails the American public in reporting foreign news, in three ways. The first is by neglecting it. The second is by reporting it in a biased manner. The third is its failure to compare American with foreign practices—for example, contraceptive technology practices are more advanced and effective in Europe than in the United States; France has a world-class child-care system; and so on.

Analysts have shown that the news media are distinctly ethnocentric and provide a false picture of the world at large, especially of the developing world.[30] The two American international news agencies (Britain, France, and Russia have one each) routinely support U.S. and Western interests in their news reporting. In an early analysis, Elliott and Golding found that the British news media (they imply that the same is true of news media in all capitalist countries) created a typical image of developing nations:

1. Developing countries are depicted only in terms of political, military, or economic crisis.
2. Direct British interests are highlighted in any news from a developing country.
3. Events are invariably framed in an East/West Cold War perspective.
4. The structure of the developing country is simplified; countries are seen in terms of their national leaders, and conflicts are reduced to tribal or religious disputes. National, regional, and racial stereotypes are also widespread.
5. Foreign news stories are framed within a narrow range of story cycles that limit the possibilities open to the developing country.

Western news media assume that it is normal for a developing country to strive to meet Western standards. Because of their reliance on Western news agencies and journalism training, developing countries devote more attention to the developed world than to other developing countries. Further, as is done in the West, they focus mostly on political leaders, defining political action as that of elites and equating official diplomacy with the substance of international politics and conflict.[31] Examples of biased foreign reporting by the American media are pervasive, as the next section shows.

Journalism and Biased Political News

Political news makes the most sense, and is most useful to a society with democratic ambitions, when it explains events in terms of power. But for the reasons cited above, journalism rarely achieves this ideal. In too many instances to attribute to error or incompetence, journalism actually falsifies. Journalism falsifies by accepting facts as presented by politicians and representatives of interest groups. It collaborates with the efforts of political figures and police departments at budget time to create false crime waves.[32] It falsifies by omitting facts. For example, in reporting on elections in El Salvador in 1984, it hailed the large turnout as a victory for moderation, omitting to note that voting in El Salvador was compulsory. Journalism falsifies by discussing a limited range of reform proposals as the only set of choices open to Americans. Journalism falsifies by faithfully reporting what government officials have to say. It falsifies the status of minorities (see below). Journalists who report on science consistently portray it as humanity's best hope and fail to raise critical issues about its social consequences.

The (witting?) collaboration between the news media and political interests is dramatically illustrated by the falsification of drug use. Reinarman and Levine show how the crack "epidemic" (or "plague") of the late 1980s was an invention of the news media and right-wing groups spearheaded by the Republican Party.[33] With no empirical evidence to go on, the various news media and both political parties competed strenuously to show that they were in the forefront of the war on crack, a plague that, they warned, threatened all American institutions. In the late 1980s, a huge outpouring of drug-related stories emerged from all outlets: TV newscasts by naturally known anchors, TV news magazines, *Time* and *Newsweek,* and the *New York Times* and *Washington Post.* President George H. Bush even made a national address on the scourge of crack; brandishing a pack of crack, he claimed the drug was even being sold outside the White House (it was later revealed that federal officials had not been able obtain any crack themselves, because its use was confined to poverty/black neighborhoods, and had had to bribe a black youngster to get them some for the president to use as a visual aid).

The fictitious crack epidemic must be seen as part of a larger ideological agenda by the New Right and the Reagan-Bush administration to focus on individual moral choice and to blame social problems on morally deficient individuals rather than on structural deficiencies in American institutions. By 1992, the drug-scare binge had subsided, as evidence appeared that addiction was not occurring at the reported rates, that crack was confined to poverty areas, and because a huge institutionalized war on drugs was now in place to distract people from serious problems (like teen smoking and drinking) and structural problems (for example, political stalemate, persistent high unemployment, and crime in decaying urban areas).

Perhaps the greatest act of falsification in American history was the way in which the U.S. government, including Congress and other branches, used the media to lie to the American people about America's support for France's recolonization of Vietnam (1945), its support for France against Vietnam's struggle for independence

(1945–1954), and about all aspects of America's direct political and military involvement in Vietnam.[34] Franklin's account shows how the lies and half-truths were continued after America's defeat to establish a fictitious memory of what had happened between 1945 and 1975. Now gone from America's memory is the fact that large numbers of Americans besides college students and hippies actively opposed America's involvement in Vietnam. These included merchant seamen in 1945; soldiers, sailors, and pilots, who either deserted in significant numbers or committed serious acts of mutiny and sabotage; and civilians at all levels of American society.

Even as he condemns the American power structure, Franklin celebrates the ability of American society to generate resistance to it. This included the skillful establishment of an alternative media, both in and outside the armed forces, to organize resistance and counter the mainstream media. Franklin's concluding chapter shows how the U.S. government made demands about prisoners of war and service personnel missing in action that it knew Vietnam could not fulfill, giving it an excuse to refuse Vietnam the aid that it had promised at the peace accords. The phony POW/MIA demand then became a powerful myth (aided by numerous Hollywood films) for twenty-five years that served to demonize Vietnam and help falsify America's behavior toward it.

Falsification (not necessarily intentional) can take place in numerous ways. In an important empirical study of the impact of TV newscasts on public opinion, Iyengar has found that the *episodic* framing of the bulk of news casting (the depiction of particular acts by individuals, particular events, individual perpetrators or victims), as opposed to a *thematic* format (putting the episodes in an explanatory context), reduces the public's ability to attribute acts and events to societal factors or to the actions of elected officials.[35] Hundreds of acts of terrorism, for example, were reported during the 1980s, but there were virtually no reports on their socioeconomic or political antecedents. In addition to terrorism, crime and poverty were reported episodically, but racial inequality featured both episodic and thematic reports, and unemployment was primarily thematic. With the exception of unemployment, the public was sensitive to the format employed. The influence of the format used by TV news is offset by other variables (for example, party affiliation and political ideology, but not level of education). Nonetheless, depending on the format it uses, TV news has the power to raise or lower the public's ability to hold political officials accountable. Iyengar's conclusion is that TV news lowers the public's ability to hold elected officials and social factors responsible for social problems, not least because it prevents the public from seeing the interconnections among "episodes"—for example, unemployment and crime.

Another careful study, this time of the personality of elite journalists (in the context of the national media), reports that they are fairly homogeneous in origin (upper-middle class, eastern urban, nonchurchgoing) and in personality (they are politically liberal and alienated from traditional norms and institutions; to the left on such social issues as abortion, gay rights, and affirmative action; and would like to strip power from traditional holders and empower black leaders, consumer groups, intellectuals, and the media).[36] All this leads them to give the news a Left-liberal slant, as judged by long-term coverage of nuclear safety, busing, and energy issues. The slant given to these questions (which occurs on all issues, say the authors) can be seen in two ways. First, American executives consistently see all issues differently than do journalists (as shown by tests); second, the journalists veer toward the left in comparison with experts on nuclear safety, busing, and energy.

The authors tend to conclude that journalists cannot be objective—that is, the authors do not make the mistake of criticizing them for not being objective. But their book creates the impression that executives have sounder judgment than journalists, and it assumes that the experts are objective. Instead of realizing that executives and experts are no different than journalists (one or another form of liberal bias), the authors seem to discredit journalists, not so much for displaying bias as for being biased on the liberal left. Somehow journalists are "biased" because personality tests reveal that they are anti-authority and their need for power is stronger than their need for achievement. The authors would also have been wiser to be suspicious of tests and of experts in testing in the first place (for a study of national journalists that found them to be largely to the right of the public, see "Concentration in Communications," in chapter 4).[37]

Journalism's failure to create and disseminate political news that resonates with the public has hurt it. Public confidence in newspaper and television news has dropped significantly in the past decade or so (part of a general loss of confidence by the American people in their institutions and professions). Journalism's loss of public confidence is at least partly explained, says Kathleen Hall Jamieson, by its focus on campaign strategy (that is, by emphasizing winning and losing by self-interested, often deceptive candidates) instead of focusing on the need to discuss substantive issues. Journalism too readily follows the polls and reports, and too often comments on what campaigns say in political commercials (such commercials, Jamieson points out, consisting largely of "deception and distraction"). By so doing, journalism blurs the distinction between itself and politics, in effect becoming much like the political candidates, thus alienating the public.[38]

In another empirical study, Jamieson and her coauthor Joseph Cappella identify a "spiral of cynicism." Journalism's cynical focus on strategy is necessary, say journalists, to reflect what politicians are doing. In turn, politicians say they behave as they do because that is all that journalists are interested in. The spiral continues— polls show that the public is cynical about both politics and the press—and completes itself in the conclusion of politicians (and their consultants) and journalists that the public is interested only in a horse race, will respond only to deception and distraction, and will not heed reasoned discourse about issues.[39]

Cappella and Jamieson argue that breaking the spiral of cynicism will require a consistent change in political discourse toward issues, a consistent commitment by the press to cover campaigns as a politics of issues, and a commitment of citizens to pay attention to the resulting discourse. Cappella and Jamieson rightly see a need to improve political discourse and to improve the reporting of politics, but the problem of bad political discourse and bad political journalism goes far deeper than their simple remedy suggests. At the risk of sounding cynical, the real causes of bad political campaigns and bad media coverage of them are the private financing of the campaigns of both major parties by the upper classes, the gerrymander (75 to 90 percent of the seats in the Hours of Representatives are noncompetitive), and the fact that the media are profit-making businesses. One can perhaps go even deeper and point out that America's politically active groups typically engage in deception and distraction both before and after campaigns.

Journalism, perhaps especially TV news, is politically biased despite, or perhaps because of, its strenuous effort to be objective and nonpartisan. To achieve objectivity, it searches out and affirms the broadest area of agreement. By focusing on social consensus, it neglects conflict, special points of view, and the possibilities for change. The world it creates appears unchanging and unchangeable. News masquerading as investigative journalism (for example, *60 Minutes*) focuses on rotten apples and ignores the barrel (the institutions of capitalism). In-depth coverage of issues (the news documentary) has all but disappeared from television; it represents a loss of profit, it only causes controversy, and the prime-time public is not interested. The demise of the Fairness Doctrine (the requirement that different positions on issues be given) means that the discussion of public issues is wholly subject to the power of money. Journalism—again, especially television news—has become an integral part of the new politics, the ability of candidates to create a false world through a careful management of symbols—privately produced film that is presented as news, and staged news events and photo opportunities at which little of substantive value is said.[40] (For a fuller discussion, see chapter 5.)

The emergence of public, or civic, journalism in the elections of 1994 and especially in 1996, spearheaded by grants from the Pew Foundation, is certainly welcome. Here news organizations determine what issues the public is interested in, stress them in their election coverage, and prod the candidates and parties to discuss them (see below for a further discussion).

The press may show signs of resistance to power, but by and large, the press clearly is an integral part of internal American power relations,[41] transmitting national news from the standpoint of the upper-middle class and from a distinctively American value standpoint. In general, the press depoliticizes social problems even as it promotes a corporate liberalism at the national level and an entrepreneurial liberalism at the local and regional level.

Journalism and Racial, Ethnic, and Gender Minorities

An analysis of how the Los Angeles riot of 1992 was reported by the *Los Angeles Times,* the *Chicago Tribune,* the *Atlanta Constitution,* and the *New York Times* exemplifies the problem faced by African Americans (and all other racial-ethnic minorities) when it comes to news reporting. By focusing on the event itself, with little positive, offsetting coverage of African Americans, the reports tended to blame blacks. That is, there was very little causal explanation of why riots take place.[42]

African Americans have a long history of publishing their own newspapers and other vehicles of information, but such efforts cannot overcome the biased image created by the white press, since white America does not read the black press. The biases of the white news world will not be overcome until more African Americans hold decision-making positions in newspapers and newscast organizations.[43]

Newspaper coverage of African Americans increased from 1960 on, but by and large, the coverage focused on crime, celebrities, and black politicians, with little time for or explanation of black protests about their problems. Also noteworthy was the tendency to depict black politicians in negative terms as special-interest pleaders (as opposed to white politicians, who were seen as spokespersons for the general interest).

The Republican Party's onslaught, starting in 1995, against the federal welfare system and affirmative action—matters of considerable concern to African Americans (and other minorities)—was discussed in the media largely by white males. Of particular interest was the implicit indictment of African Americans as innately immoral because of their illegitimacy rates. Throughout, nary a journalist pointed out that marriage presupposes a structured world, a sound economic base, and ownership of material assets that are worth passing on to heirs—things missing in large parts of the African-American population and, for that matter, among many non-black Americans who also have significant illegitimacy rates.

Journalism is not as biased with Native Americans, Hispanics, Asians, Muslims, Pacific Islanders, gays, or disabled Americans as it is with African Americans, largely because it does not spend much time covering them (which, of course, amounts to a considerable bias in itself). Here again the tendency is to focus on lawbreaking or controversy, with little explanatory background.[44]

Women are prominent in reporting the news on television, but they are not very well represented in decision-making positions in journalism. White women in the upper classes tend to have considerable class resources and thus wield a certain measure of political power. What this means is that issues important to them get aired in American politics and journalism.

The Failure to Promote Democratic Politics and Citizenship

A summary report on research on the mass media in general states as the consensus of scholars that journalism and popular culture (for the latter, see chapter 8) not only do not promote democratic citizenship but retard it. "The overwhelming conclusion is that the media generally operate in ways that promote apathy, cynicism, and acquiescence, rather than active citizenship and participation." The mass media, in short, renders societal power relations obscure and invisible. Though there is room for contrary interpretations and oppositional movements, the present pattern continues strong.[45]

In a later summary of political communication–effects research (focused on journalism), McLeod, Kosicki, and McLeod similarly conclude that mass media news does not promote democratic citizenship or politics.[46] Matching research against eight standards characterizing democracy (see table 7.1), they found the American

Table 7.1. Democratic Standards for Mass Media News, Constraints and Conventions, and Allegations of Performance Deficiencies

Democratic Standards	Constraints and Conventions	Media Performance
Surveillance of relevant events	Budgetary constraints; personnel limitations; audience maximization	Routinized coverage of politically irrelevant events for their high entertainment value; pseudo-event
Identification of key issues	Institutional organization of news nets; need for interesting video and photos; lack of news staff specialization	Issue coverage follows institutional agenda; emphasis on events not issues; decontextualized and ahistorical coverage
Provision of platforms for advocacy	Ideologies of objectivity and press autonomy; belief that the media must control "air time"	Media access is difficult for marginalized groups; mainstream groups must conform to media practices by "running the news value gauntlet"
Transmission of diverse political discourse	Reliance on official sources; ideology of source legitimacy; concern for audience composition	Mainstream content ignores "deviant" groups and less attractive audiences (e.g., the poor and elderly)
Scrutiny of institutions and officials	Interdependence of media and other powerful institutions; high cost of investigative reporting	Limited coverage of systemic problems; blame is focused on individuals not the system
Activation of informed participation	Ideologies of objectivity and press autonomy	Lack of mobilizing information to avoid accusations of bias
Maintenance of media autonomy	Corporate media ownership, particularly by nonmedia industries; "bureaucratic subsidization of news"; advertising revenue	Content reflects on elite agenda and elite perspectives; as politicians adapt to news imperatives, media transmit official propaganda as news
Consideration of audience potential	Audience maximization; consumer-driven news production	Existing preferences and abilities are seen as natural, not learned; news as entertainment

Source: Jack M. McLeod, Gerald M. Kosicki, and Douglas M. McLeod, "The Expanding Boundaries of Political Communication Effects," in *Media Effects,* ed. J. Bryant and D. Zillmann, (Hillsdale, N.J.: Erlbaum, 1994), 128. The democratic standards are derived from M. Gurevitch and J. G. Blumler, "Political Communication Systems and Democratic Values," in *Democracy and the Mass Media,* ed. Judith Lichtenberg (New York: Cambridge University Press, 1990), 269–89. Reprinted with the permission of Cambridge University Press.

news media systematically wanting. Nonetheless, the authors assume throughout that the eight democratic standards are possible to achieve, at least in meaningful approximation; in other words, they assume throughout that American representative government (plutocracy) can become a democracy. Their report on research into the failings of journalism is consistent with mainstream social science research. The authors say that normative considerations should be part of empirical research, but what they mean is that ideals should be explicitly stated, to see how the facts measure

up. Here again they are consistent with mainstream liberalism. To introduce normative considerations in a straightforward political manner, the authors should ask,
"Are capitalism and its journalism compatible with democracy?"

Is There Really a Public Out There?

The development of capitalism saw the emergence of a distinction between "private" and "public." Today this distinction pervades the way in which Americans
think (and stop thinking) about the world, despite the fact that it is very difficult to
define or to reach agreement about what it means. A sociological perspective, for
example, breaks down any distinction between government as public and the economy as private; these interpenetrate so much that it is impossible to tell where one
begins and the other leaves off. Is the family private when it is subject to invasion
by the mass media, or when its children must attend public schools? Are consumers
making private decisions when they purchase products that are publicly regulated?

From another perspective, it is clear that no "public" corresponding to C. Wright
Mills's definition exists. Following Mills, in a public as many people express opinions as receive them, public communications are so organized that publicly expressed
opinions can be effectively answered, public discourse readily leads to social action,
and structures of power do not penetrate the public, which is essentially autonomous.[47] But the *idea* of a public is central to journalists' identity. Without such an
entity, there would be no target at which to direct their professional services. Journalists are aware that the public is difficult to find and may even be a phantom,
prompting some scholars to believe that one of journalism's purposes is to help
revive the public, perhaps even to create one. Schudson, for example, has argued
that no public existed either in the eighteenth or nineteenth centuries, if measured
by participation by those eligible or by whether or not public discourse was rational
and critical. No public exists today, even though it is a democratic fiction useful to
those who want to improve the world. The news, Schudson says, serves a vital democratic function even if no public is "out there." The news creates a symbolic world
that in its easy accessibility becomes the property of all. The news is *public knowledge,* a resource available when people are ready to take action.[48]

In the late 1980s and early 1990s, a public or civic journalism movement
emerged, largely among regional newspapers and some broadcast stations, and
encouraged by foundations. The key idea behind the movement was that journalism
had to take responsibility for its actions; the mere reporting of news, especially about
political campaigns, was not only turning off the public but making it disgusted
with both politics and journalism. Accordingly, some newspapers conducted surveys
to find out what was on the public's (not just their readers') mind. Of particular
interest was the movement's emphasis on getting political candidates to address the
public's concerns.[49]

By 2001, public journalism had taken hold, and earlier objections to it as a threat
to professionalism and objectivity had subsided. A survey revealed that the senior
editors of 70 percent of the nation's 512 newspapers with circulations of twenty

thousand or more were increasing their interactions with the public and were writing the news with community concerns in mind. A substantial majority of newspapers have widened their sources, broadened their coverage of community affairs, made it easier for citizens to contact reporters, given reporters time to develop stories, and placed more emphasis on solutions and explaining the news and less on conflict and government.[50]

A variation on public journalism consists of trying to find the best way to reach the public by finding out how viewers and listeners respond to the news. Three political scientists, using a constructionist approach, have sought to understand how audiences actively construct meaning from a variety of media sources. The authors found a poor fit between what the mass media emphasize and what the mass audience says is important and relevant to their lives. They found that audiences respond with special enthusiasm when they receive information about how to do something about, or take control of, public issues. Incorporating civic action into the news thus seems warranted. Audiences also frame issues in moral terms, whereas journalists do not, sticking to an impersonal, objective stance. Journalists might do well to enhance democratic competence by providing contrasting pictures of events and contrasting analyses of issues.

This survey of how audiences learn found that television was more effective than print media in conveying information about topics of low salience to the audience (because it grabbed their interest, surprised them, and gave stories human interest). Print media were superior in communicating information with high salience. The survey's central finding is that people do learn from exposure to the media, especially over time and especially if they *want* to get news. The media, conclude the authors, bear the democratic burden of making news about public affairs accessible and inviting.[51]

Multiple Perspectives, or Alternative Media

Public journalism could well improve how journalism connects with the public, and its growth is encouraging. A common thread in public journalism and other reform proposals is to provide viewers and readers with more perspectives. By providing more perspectives, however, reformers rarely mean going outside the liberal worldview. The idea of multiple perspectives continues the supposition (stemming from the French Enlightenment) that something called the "public" or the "people" is a real force in society and that all will be well if it is given more ideas and information. This view underestimates the American power structure. One need only look at the fate of the attempt to provide free television time to political candidates to see what happens to real reform; paid political advertising became a torrent once a loophole in the election laws was exploited. As Lewis points out, political campaign news has become scarce, and he cites a reason advanced by Robert McChesney—that the media have little incentive to cover candidates when not doing so forces candidates to pay to publicize themselves. Lewis documents the enormous sums spent by the media to block legislation giving free time on television to political candidates and to pressure (successfully) the Federal Communications Commission to relax ownership rules.[52]

Multiple perspectives or alternative media? In pondering the question, readers should look at the annual publication of Project Censored (sponsored by the Department of Sociology, Sonoma State University, California). Using large and varied panels of referees, evaluators, and student interns, the project highlights each year's twenty-five most important but overlooked or underreported stories. The 1999 issue also has chapters on censorship in Canada, the politics of alternative versus mainstream news, and valuable appendices, especially the 1998 report of the American Library Association, "Less Access to Less Information by and about the U.S. Government," and Project Censored's large directory of alternative media.[53]

Another way to answer our question is to remember that communication flows and technology always serve primarily the powerful. The media may offer multiple perspectives, but that will rarely amount to equal time or go beyond the dominant American spectrum of Right to Left liberalism. At present, American journalism is not generating the knowledge that America needs. The social conditions (power structure) needed to generate a fuller spectrum of knowledge are lacking. A focus on power suggests that vibrant alternative media are not likely to arise without a vibrant pluralistic power structure. At present the media are keeping the upper classes informed about *their* society and the masses ignorant, ensuring the continuation of existing power relations. It is those relations that must change—a different matter than asking the news media to change them by changing itself.

THE POLICY SCIENCES: CURRENT PERSPECTIVES

To understand the policy sciences (or journalism, or any of the professions and disciplines), two things should be recalled about the relation between social structure and knowledge: (1) The elites of all complex societies generate universalistic explanations of themselves and their societies, seeking to legitimate their power with abstractions that link it to forces in supernature, nature, and human nature, and (2) the complex society of the West generated a universalistic and distinctive—namely, rationalistic—way of addressing the world.

Universalistic explanations are those that rely on broad generalizations to explain where everything comes from, why humans are here, how they got here, why they suffer and die, and so on. Universalistic explanations are transhistorical and transsocial; they transport people out of time and place into some version of supernature, nature, and human nature. The result, of course, is to anchor a particular power structure in forces that are permanent—that is, outside politics or the ability of deliberate human action to solve problems. The West, it should be noted, from the ancient Greeks to the present, has shared this characteristic with the non-West, even though its way of generating abstractions relies on human reason.

By and large, the rationalism of the West has focused its energy on finding universals (or laws or principles) directly in nature and human nature. The valid and potentially fertile idea that society is a human creation wrought half-blindly by power groups out of historical necessities and emerging opportunities has as little appeal to power groups in the West as it does to those in the non-West. The idea that society is a human creation (a political phenomenon) was first broached by Herodotus, only to succumb to the more alluring image (from Socrates) of the world developed out of logic. The goal of finding valid generalizations about humans and their world has continued into the modern period, and those who pursue it continue to shun the sociohistorical perspective.

The West does allow considerable scope for human effort and control over human destiny. This stems from its belief that the universe is rational and that its rationality corresponds to human reason. A corollary of this belief is that human nature and behavior are also rational and that knowledge about them can be obtained and used to construct a rational society. Accordingly, knowledge elites can be seen advising rulers in all phases of Western life.[54]

The search for a rational society was conducted deductively until the French (and Scottish) Enlightenment established the empirical method as the road to knowledge. The Enlightenment also gave rise to the modern social sciences, our foremost gatherers and transmitters of knowledge. In the following sections on the modern policy professions, we again encounter the power of the transhistorical view. As offshoots of the academic disciplines and as groups that want to establish themselves as professions, the policy sciences—and it should surprise no one, odd as it may seem—are profoundly antipolitical in how they define and conduct themselves.

Though lip service is paid by all to the importance of knowledge in formulating social policies, policy professionals (and groups) have decidedly different stances about how to acquire and use knowledge. The dominant liberal perspective has three subtypes: the openly conservative liberal, the laissez-faire or rational-choice liberal, and the reform liberal.

The Openly Conservative Liberal

The openly conservative policy scientist tends to limit the role of knowledge in the political life of society. This aspect of conservatism openly advocated can be seen most clearly in the inconsistent thought of Charles E. Lindblom.[55] Lindblom's argument is that society is essentially a system of "impairment processes." Both ordinary individuals and elites, as well as groups, are unable to act rationally (Lindblom emphatically includes professionals and social scientists among those impaired). Therefore, no attempt at shaping or guiding society should be attempted—despite its faults, society as it exists (something Lindblom refers to as the *self-guiding society*) is all we have. This society is based on markets, which Lindblom depicts not as rational systems for allocating resources but as processes of mutual adjustment. We do not know enough to manage or coordinate society, though we might help it work better if we strengthened free speech, civil rights, and education, and reduced gender and racial inequalities. Any attempt to base society on reason or science, however, whether derived from Plato, Marx, or reform liberals, is wrongheaded. Social science does not have "a single finding or idea that is undeniably indispensable to any social task or effort" (page 136).

Lindblom goes to considerable lengths to undermine all pretensions to efficacy or knowledge by economists, political scientists, psychologists, and professionals in general. He criticizes corporations as well as governments and acknowledges that we do not have a pluralistic power structure—in effect, rejecting rationality even as the outcome of markets. Why is all of the above inconsistent? Because Lindblom's thesis, that humans are not rational and that social science cannot supply knowledge for us to use in the management of our collective life, is based on a long grocery list of social science findings. It is inconsistent because Lindblom says some reform through politics and government is possible, while at the same time denying that reform is possible.

Laissez-Faire, Rational-Choice Liberals

Another form of conservatism (advocated by thinkers who do not think of themselves this way) derives from Right liberals who advocate free markets in all sectors of society to produce a society based on the rational choices (cost-benefit analyses) of self-interested individuals and groups. Right liberals are descendants of the Enlightenment; they believe that natural laws govern the economy and polity. Actually, they are still in the eighteenth century, mired in a static Newtonian world of eternal equilibrium. The vast bulk of Republicans and of American economists fall in this category. In sociology, exchange and rational-choice theorists also belong here.[56] A Nobel Prize–winning economist, James Buchanan, has influenced political scientists to think of politics in rational-choice terms. Another Nobel Prize winner in economics (Gary Becker) has used sociological analysis to influence rational-choice theory in economics.

Laissez-faire liberalism shades off into right-wing anarchism or libertarianism, exemplified by a Washington-based think tank, the Cato Institute. The fundamental otherworldliness of secular mainstream liberalism is revealed most fully in its right-wing utopian variant—otherworldly because of a failure to understand that human behavior and human society are sociohistorical in nature and that while human action can seek to shape institutions to realize human goals, it can never rise above history.

The reason why rational-choice advocates are conservative is that they believe in competition among individuals and groups but do little to make real (equal, fair) competition a reality. Advocates of rational choice think they are revealing real human nature and helping us move in the direction of maximizing choices, but by declining to tackle poverty, unemployment, and economic concentration they are merely defending the existing power structure (the upper classes have the choices). Rational-choice liberals are also inconsistent in that they use government for their purposes while denouncing government as inherently ineffective and wasteful.

Antirational Secular and Religious Perspectives

The nineteenth century generated a powerful Romantic current and produced the first of a series of antirational philosophers who were to have varied impacts on the twentieth century. Stretching from Nietzsche, Freud, and Pareto to the present, these thinkers have argued rationally that human beings and their society are essentially nonrational. Unlike reform liberals, who are aware of the powerful emotions that can govern human behavior but still believe that individuals can be socialized into rational behavior, the antirational perspective stresses the permanent nature of human fallibility. Antirationalism in itself would not be noteworthy if it did not get powerful reinforcement from Right liberals. After all, the basic assumption underlying the laissez-faire, anarchistic, free market, rational-choice perspective is that humans are not rational enough to construct collective responses to their problems.

Right liberals and antirational groups constitute American conservatism and together make up the core of the Republican Party. The secular laissez-faire segment of this coalition advocates economic growth through free markets and materialistic incentives and goals. The antirational segment is anchored in religion and tradition, and it is opposed to abortion, gender equality, birth control, and the sovereignty of individual choice guided by reason and self-interest. They uphold the traditional family and believe in the efficacy of the human spirit. Much of what they believe puts them at odds with their secular brethren, free enterprise liberals. In a broad sense, both are out of step with the basic thrust of science and the basic nature of American society. For this reason, the Republican Party, while able to achieve election successes, is not an effective governing party.

The Reform Liberal

Most social scientists have kept faith with the Enlightenment and continue to believe that research and knowledge will benefit and improve society. Most sociologists and political scientists are *reform liberals*—that is, they accept American society as a sound system but want it to work better. Liberals in this category see more of society in individual behavior than do other liberals. Left liberals stress that individuals are socialized to be evaluative, not clinically rational actors. Reformers are aware that some individuals are poorly socialized for participation in our society and need help. Reform liberals also stress the group nature of behavior, and this leads them to advocate ways to help the family, make corporations more responsive internally to minorities, enforce antitrust laws, and the like.

Reform liberals openly advocate the use of government to solve problems. They tend to be full Keynesians in regard to the economy—that is, they hold that the federal executive, Congress, and the Federal Reserve Board should use their tax, spending, monetary, and interest-rate powers to manage the economy. Reform liberals can be quite critical of American society; nonetheless, they remain liberals to the extent that they advocate nonstructural solutions.[57]

Radical Policy Orientations

The distinguishing mark of radicals is that they connect social problems to the basic structure of capitalist society, especially its economy. Radicals question whether private decisions about investment are compatible with a sound society. They argue that American capitalism is based essentially on the primacy of property over labor and that its institutions and public policies support this priority. A democratic society will emerge only when the organized public exercises control over capital investment.[58]

Radical feminists argue that patriarchy, or patriarchy plus capitalism, is the source of women's troubles and that only a restructuring of society will end women's domination by men, or the use by men of capitalism to dominate them.[59]

Radical environmentalists argue that the core ideology of capitalism, unending economic growth, is a deadly threat to both nature and society. Solving environmental problems piecemeal will not work unless the problem of capitalism is also tackled.[60]

THE FLOURISHING POLICY SCIENCES

The deliberate enactment of public measures to improve society in keeping with the latest scientific knowledge emerged as an ideal during the eighteenth century in both the French and Scottish Enlightenments. The credit for seeing policy as a more technical approach to updating society and running it more efficiently should probably be shared by Jeremy Bentham and Frederick the Great. Empirical research as the basis of public measures to improve society does not appear until the largely government-sponsored projects in nineteenth-century Britain—for example, Charles Booth's study of the people of London (1889–1991). No significant empirical research either in general or oriented toward the solution of social problems occurred in the United States until the Chicago School emerged in the 1920s. The United States lagged in developing policy research and policy-oriented social scientists because problem solving was long considered a local affair. The Great Depression and World War II changed all this; much of the responsibility for problem solving shifted to the national level. The policy sciences benefited from an influential set of readings edited by Daniel Lerner and Harold Lasswell in 1951.[61] But the real impetus to the policy sciences occurred when the Great Society reform programs were enacted in the 1960s; further impetus occurred during the 1970s and 1980s as American elites responded to an accumulation of unsolved social problems.

It is important to note at the outset that the policy sciences and the great reform movements of the past three-quarters of a century have been largely elite driven. Not only do policy sciences and reforms not originate in the lower classes, but the values and interests they serve go far beyond the problems of the poor, minorities, workers, or inner cities. Both manifest and latent analysis tell us that the policy sciences, wittingly or unwittingly, support the interests of the powerful even as they propose reforms on behalf of the downtrodden.

The contemporary policy sciences are flourishing in two senses. First, there are numerous policy-studies organizations, a large number of journals with the word *policy* in their titles, a large number of undergraduate and graduate public-policy programs, hundreds of policy-research centers both in and outside universities, and a declared interest in policy by book publishers, scholarly associations, and interest groups. Of great importance is the expressed interest in policy research and policy evaluation by local, state, and federal governments. The policy sciences are also flourishing in the sense that applied offshoots have appeared in all disciplines, part and parcel of the explosive specialization that has enveloped all of them. There are numerous applied journals in economics, sociology, psychology, and so on through the natural sciences. There is little doubt that the hunger for usable knowledge is there. Whether it is being satisfied is another matter.

THE PROFESSIONALIZATION OF REFORM, OR UNDERMINING PUBLICS

Reform, or the attempt to solve problems by changes in law and redistribution of resources, has become a routine part of liberal society. This is true of the United States as well as other developed societies, and as true of Republicans as it is of Democrats. The process of reform has also been professionalized—which is to say that reform has been defined in such a way as to guarantee failure. Also, liberal reform, American style, is inherently nonstructural—that is, it does not tackle the basic causes of problems. American reform liberalism is an ad hoc search for rotten apples and the depoliticization of the barrel. A basic reason for the ineffectiveness of reform is that Americans at all levels assume that they live in a natural, just, sound, pluralistic, and adaptive society, and that social problems come from social change (a progressive movement away from ignorance and obsolete ways) and from willful wickedness on the part of individuals and special interests.

The professionalization of reform appeared early in the nineteenth century in Europe, accelerated during the late nineteenth century, and came into prominence in the United States only from the 1930s on. Everywhere and at all times, it has been a "middle-class" movement. During its earlier stage, reform movements were in keeping with the nature of entrepreneurial capitalism (small-town, rural, small-business, solo practitioner, professional society). Here one finds the urban morality and beautification movement,[62] the Temperance movement,[63] and the sociologists who framed social pathologies in terms of human nature, Protestant morality, and abstracted, artificial situations.[64] More in keeping with corporate capitalism, one finds the growth of graduate schools (devoted to professional research and application), the beginnings of policy-research institutes, and the rise of the great foundations and philanthropies. The essence of corporate or elite liberalism consists of cloaking reform and the policy process in the garbs of science, neutrality, and professionalism. Today, elite liberalism has both a right and a left wing.[65]

The ideology of political reform dissolves the American people into individuals and emphasizes the need to facilitate their choices. The Republican and Democratic Parties have different versions of this ideology. The Republican Party emphasizes choice by parents (through vouchers) of where to send their children to school or where to rent apartments. They also emphasize choice on the part of business people (supported by government subsidies or by relaxation of regulatory laws) to go into various businesses, communities, or countries. Liberal democrats emphasize choice and the empowerment of ordinary citizens by emphasizing civil rights laws (including the right to choose abortion), income support for the poor, and more public services, including tax-supported lawyers for the poor. Neither party, however, says anything about popular choice over capital investment, full employment, or the huge welfare state for the well off and rich.

Both parties may stress the empowering of ordinary people, but this is more than counterbalanced by an emphasis on leadership and professional direction. It is clear, moreover, that the professionalization of reform has its sources in the dynamics of corporate capitalism; that is to say, it is now geared to the needs of large corporations and nationally oriented, upper-middle-class individuals. Essentially, the arguments about reform take place between a regionally diverse set of local property and professional groups and a set of elites who are nationally and internationally oriented. Indeed, much of what is called "reform" is really the extension of professionalization and a struggle among types of professionals.

The reform of education during the first half of the twentieth century, for example, was part of an effort to shift control of schools away from local communities to the state and federal levels.[66] The same is true of the general emergence of the federal interventionist-welfare state. By and large, the professionalization of problem solving at the policy level is part of the overall emergence of a national state to serve a national-international economy.[67] This is the background needed to understand civil service reform (the Pendleton Act of 1883), the establishment of the national regulatory agencies from the late nineteenth century on, the emergence of the Keynesian state from the 1930s on, and the proliferation of such professional advisory bodies as the Council of Economic Advisers, national security adviser and the National Security Council, the National Science Foundation, the National Science Academy, the National Health Institutes, and the National Endowments for the Humanities and Arts. The rise to prominence of elite liberal arts colleges during the same period provided ideological cover for the rise of professionalized academic disciplines and the applied professions.[68] Here too lies the meaning behind the interest within many professions and disciplines in improved statistical services—they need information about how the various actors of society are behaving in order to tackle their problems for them.

Finally, the professionalization of reform created a host of political-interest groups. In a real sense, the deeper meaning of the rise of the federal state is that it helped to legitimate—indeed, helped to create—the very business, farm, and professional groups that it ostensibly regulated and harnessed to the public interest. The federal state (no less than local and state governments) not only is in the service of property and professional groups but helps create and sustain them.

THE PROFESSIONALIZATION OF PLANNING, OR CONTRACTING THE PUBLIC SPHERE

Planning is an important characteristic of all societies in the contemporary world. By "planning" is meant the attempt to allocate and schedule resources to produce desired effects. Planning takes place in American society as it does in other countries, with one conspicuous exception. Alone among the developed and almost all the developing societies, the United States has no commitment to, or process for, national planning. American planning is done by private groups; when it is public, it is hidden by euphemisms and defined as nonstructural and nonpolitical.

The planning idea is strong in the United States, and it too has been professionalized. A number of professionalized approaches can be distinguished. In his informative history of the idea of planning in the United States, Wilson distinguishes between five approaches to planning: rational, incremental, mixed-scanning, general systems, and learning-adaptive.[69]

Planning also goes by other names: management science, information science, the planning-programming-budgeting-system (PPBS), strategic planning, risk assessment, cost-benefit analysis, and of course, central planning under state socialism. Professionals may argue about the virtues of these approaches, but beneath secondary differences, one theme stands out—planning is the attempt by elites to develop an efficient use of resources *to achieve vague goals without input from ordinary people*. Elites may develop specialized types of planning—say, for the federal government (PPBS), or planning software applicable to hospitals or universities. They may focus on the needs of a corporation, of a city, or a transportation system. But all these plans have two things in common—the overall structure of power (the position of ordinary people) is taken for granted, and the communication of research and policy options takes place among specialists and other surrogates for the upper classes.

Openly conservative liberals, like Lindblom, oppose planning, arguing that human beings are not rational enough to plan, that organizations are rife with habits and emotions, and that we should accept "muddling through" as our best strategy for rational action (incrementalism). This in itself reflects a false distinction—the so-called rational planning tradition is merely a variation of muddling through, or rather, a disguised form of laissez-faire. Basically, the liberal planning tradition rests on the uncoordinated, self-seeking behavior of a wide variety of social units, all in the faith that the combined effect will add up to the most rational possible society. Rarely do the professionals who discuss planning ever argue that the values and beliefs of all the relevant parties must be incorporated into the planning process. Rarely, in other words, do they ask that the political system be reformed so as to see what priorities the population has for capital investment, taxes, or public spending.

So far the planning process in both capitalist and socialist countries has been technocratic, something imposed on the bulk of the population by those who claim to know best.

POLICY SCIENCE: THE COMPROMISING
TIE TO THE ACADEMIC WORLD

The Policy Sciences as Warmed-Over Academic Disciplines

One would expect that if the academic disciplines are value free and nonpolitical, the policy sciences would be the opposite. This is not the case; the main thrust of the policy field, as is true of knowledge elites in general, is to depoliticize problems.

The public-policy (or social-policy) professions emerged in the nineteenth century in a hostile environment of radical laissez-faire. Explicit social planning is opposed by America's most powerful groups. Accordingly, the various specialties that emerged under the general heading of "public-policy professional" kept a low profile and employed euphemisms to camouflage their activities (for example, urban planning was located in schools of architecture). Throughout their development, these specialties maintained deep ties to the academic professions. Public administration and foreign policy/defense analysis are connected to political science. Housing, energy, transportation, foreign trade, and economic development are attempts at applied economics. Urban planning, law enforcement, penology, and social welfare (income maintenance, family support, etc.) are outgrowths of sociology. Public health is an outcome of medicine and sociology. Environmentalists have their footing in chemistry and biology, combined occasionally with a social science. Communication specialists draw on psychology, sociology, and academic programs in communication.

There are many hybrids. Military specialists have backgrounds in sociology, history, and political science. Statisticians have backgrounds in mathematics, economics, and sociology. Educators study psychology, administration, and sociology. Social workers have backgrounds in sociology and administration. There are subspecialties everywhere—for example, specialists in various kinds of crime, types of family pathology, or the various forms of communication.

Policy analysts agree that there is little consensus about what policy science means. There is also no agreement about basic terms or about requirements to ensure competence; the wide variety of activities and journals that call themselves "policy" in nature are extremely diverse.[70] Both as an overall field and as a collection of subspecialties, public policy shares much with the other professions. Like the other professions, it has identified an artificial area and staked a claim to it based on expertise. The result here, as in the other professions, is widespread ineffectiveness and failure.[71]

The Mania for More Research

The once-clear distinction between pure and applied research has blurred in recent decades as hard-pressed policy makers have called for usable knowledge to help them solve American society's mounting social problems. Higher education has been quick to respond and now contains a large number of policy and applied programs. So far, however, no great success can be reported. These programs and the research conducted in their name are largely disguised versions of academic programs. Harvard's Kennedy School of Government and the Lyndon B. Johnson School of Public Policy at the University of Texas, for example, focus on technical knowledge framed in value-free, apolitical terms. The failure to develop viable public-policy programs is perhaps the central failure of higher education, but none of the half-dozen higher education reports that appeared in the late 1980s even mentioned this problem. The reason is understandable. Our educators have an ahistorical (or academic) conception of knowledge that takes the usefulness of elite-generated knowledge for granted. To submit it to the test of usefulness would require a profound alteration in mental habits acquired over thousands of years.

Most research, therefore, is still framed in terms that policy makers cannot use. Increasingly, policy research has become a profit-making business; clients must be pleased rather than problems solved. The case of Lewin-VHI, a Virginia-based research institute, is probably typical. During 1994, at the height of a particularly heated discussion of health care reform, a number of Lewin-VHI research reports emerged containing diametrically opposed conclusions; indeed, the conclusions corresponded to the political positions of the interest groups that were paying for the research. What is of enormous significance is that *all the reports were objective and in keeping with scientific standards.* The explanation is that the sponsors specified what assumptions to use and what questions to ask in their respective projects.[72] Recent doubts about studies, conducted by drug companies themselves, comparing the comparative cost-effectiveness of drugs have highlighted the absence of standards in this field.[73] In addition, much of the research supporting the safety of drugs, airplanes, the workplace, and so on, is done for the government by the interested parties themselves.

When research appears that runs counter to the interests of powerful groups, it is simply denied or ignored (for example, research on smoking, pornography, strategic bombing, and supply-side tax cuts). Research appears to be largely a way to dodge problems and protect the status quo that causes problems. Research, for example, into the cause of cancer and its cure was spurred by President Nixon, rich individuals, and the American Cancer Society, effectively undermining efforts to *prevent* cancer by curbing chemical companies, putting scrubbers in smokestacks, and reducing our intake of high-fat food and exposure to the sun. A call for more research is the way that the Reagan administration forestalled action on acid rain for more than eight years. Research into a magical defense system ("star wars") was obviously a way to block serious arms control negotiations. A call by Education Secretary Bennett during the Reagan administration for more research in higher education (via a handpicked panel) effectively blocked the needed coordination and planning of American education that his department should have engaged in.

Liberalism began to develop the mania for value-neutral, nonpolitical research (and education) in the nineteenth century. Science not only worked with self-evident values but could no longer even pronounce on values. In one variant or another, this position is found in William Graham Sumner, Vilfredo Pareto, W. I. Thomas, and practitioners of mainstream American sociology, including theorists as dissimilar as George Lundberg and Robert K. Merton. In short, the emergence of empirical sociology helped to consolidate capitalist society by identifying and defining its problems with an eye toward nonstructural reforms, by improving its administrative structures, and by developing support systems for a private-property, profit-oriented exchange economy (a supportive state, better education, voluntary groups, etc.). At mid-twentieth century, liberalism in social science and sociology was characterized by narrow empirical studies and by abstract theories that more or less rendered the essentials of liberal democracy unproblematic. Science, argued social scientists, could take place without regard to values or politics; indeed, its knowledge was applicable to any kind of society. By and large, this is the position taken by policy analysts.[74]

POLICY GROUPS AND FOUNDATIONS: THE COMPROMISING TIE TO INTEREST GROUPS

Policy professionals work for America's one thousand private, not-for-profit think tanks, of which approximately a hundred are located in Washington, D.C.[75] Policy sciences and policy groups originated in the turmoil of corporate expansion that came to a head in the last decades of the nineteenth century. In these decades America was beset with monopolies, farm and labor unrest, disturbing revelations about child labor and urban poverty, a large influx of immigrants, and the like. In line with pragmatism and the professionalizing disciplines of economics, political science, and sociology, a number of research-policy groups emerged in the early decades of the twentieth century to help generate the knowledge needed to make America work better: the Russell Sage Foundation (1907), Carnegie Endowment for International Peace (1910), Twentieth Century Fund (1911), Brookings Institution (1916), and Hoover Institution (1919).

Think tanks and policy research groups have no precise definition. They range from large, permanent groups to ephemeral one-issue centers and ad hoc advocacy groups. Some are academic, others openly political, others are public-interest groups promoting public goods like clean air or consumer protection. Most are Left liberal in their research and tend to promote small or large reforms through state action. A smaller number, with an influence out of proportion to their numbers, are Right liberal. There is negligible representation from the radical Left, though there is some from the radical Right.

The "nonpolitical" councils, boards, centers, institutions, funds, endowments, committees, institutes, corporations, advisory boards, and foundations (such as the Carnegie Foundation, Council on Foreign Relations, RAND Corporation, Committee for Economic Development, American Enterprise Institute, and Heritage Foundation), which many policy professionals work for, however, are far from non-partisan.[76] These groups, which exercise great influence over domestic and foreign policy, are characterized by a narrow class composition and are funded by, and have direct ties to, specific business and professional interests.[77]

Some of these groups openly advocate Left or Right-liberal positions and glory in their commitment to private groups. Many of them, especially on the extreme Right—for example, the Heritage Foundation—easily arouse opposition because they make little effort to understand the vast world beyond their narrow frames of reference. Much more difficult to see as partisan and as noncontributory to a democratic citizenry and society are such supposedly nonpartisan organizations as Brookings, the Carnegie Endowment and Corporation, RAND, the Urban Institute, the Twentieth Century Fund, Russell Sage Foundation, Ford Foundation, and the MacArthur Foundation. A study of the Carnegie Corporation, for example, has shown how it steered policy making away from economic and political issues, injustice, and needed reforms toward an approach that stressed science, education, and elite culture. Within science and education, it favored certain approaches and fields of knowledge, thus helping to define the knowledge-producing elites (not just knowledge areas but also the racial, gender, and class attributes of the knowledge elites). The high-minded reforms promoted by the Carnegie Corporation should not blind us to the fact that corporate liberalism is merely one of alternative approaches to policy problems.[78]

Policy professionals also work for the "nonpolitical" undergraduate and graduate programs in public policy, social work, business, public administration, natural-science research, engineering, computer science, communication, and environmental studies. They work for government; for example, applied professionals work for legislative committees (as staffers), and for government directly as engineers, geologists, chemists, space scientists, lawyers, economists, and statisticians. Policy professionals also work for corporations and for for-profit research businesses, such as RAND, Battelle, and the hundreds of economic consulting firms.

The large flow of materials from think tanks exerts considerable influence on public life, as do, of course, public issue–oriented trade books and magazines, government statistical bureaus, and congressional and executive-branch research offices. But the messages carried by these materials are not framed to develop a public or a democratic citizenry. As Ricci[79] and others have pointed out, our policy groups and professionals treat Americans as an audience, not as a public. In this sense they are not much different from teachers, professors, clergy, journalists, and the mass media.

The creators of policy knowledge are eager to get their messages out to the public, especially its elite levels. Actually, marketing books and policy positions has mushroomed since the 1960s, with the advent of a wider voting and buying public. Of some interest is the fact that Right-liberal groups have been influential beyond their numbers because of their communication skills. These skills go beyond the marketing skills that even their opponents have begun to adopt: direct-mail expertise, public-relations savvy, and the cultivation of corporate, foundation, and individual funding sources. Much of their success also comes from promulgating repetitively a simple and nonrational grand narrative that resonates with broad American abstractions—freedom, optimism, individualism, morality, family, and faith in markets, rather than collective action through government. It makes no difference that markets in general are imperfect, says Ricci. It makes no difference that government has many accomplishments to its credit.[80]

Like right-wing, politically active religious groups, right-wing think tanks have a faith, not a scientific view. Indeed, their faith is consciously directed against American pragmatism and empirical science. As such it cannot be refuted, and its simple message often carries the day. In any case, they join Left liberals in keeping the policy sciences in the straightjacket of liberalism, together churning out knowledge within the narrow spectrum that the American power structure permits.

NOTES

1. Nico Stehr, *Practical Knowledge* (Newbury Park, Calif.: Sage, 1992).

2. For excerpts from or discussions about almost all the major contributors to the sociology of knowledge (with the exception of feminist theorists) and for many case studies suitable for student readers, see James E. Curtis and John W. Petras, eds., *The Sociology of Knowledge: A Reader* (New York: Praeger, 1970); Gunter W. Remmling, ed., *Towards the Sociology of Knowledge: Origin and Development of a Sociological Thought Style* (London: Routledge and Kegan Paul, 1973); and Nico Stehr and Volker Meja, eds., *Society and Knowledge: Contemporary Perspectives in the Sociology of Knowledge* (New Brunswick, N.J.: Transaction, 1984). For a feminist sociology of knowledge that indicts sociology and its objective, value-neutral method, by which it is biased and inherently unable to give women their due, see Dorothy E. Smith, *The Conceptual Practices of Power: A Feminist Sociology of Knowledge* (Boston: Northeastern University Press, 1990). For a similar theme in African-American feminist theory, see Patricia Hill Collins, *Black Feminist Thought: Knowledge, Consciousness, and the Politics of Empowerment* (New York: Routledge, 1991).

3. For an analysis of individual professions and disciplines, see Daniel W. Rossides, *Professions and Disciplines: Functional and Conflict Perspectives* (Upper Saddle River, N.J.: Prentice Hall, 1998).

4. "Technocracy" refers to the antipolitical emphasis (found in both liberalism and socialism) on giving political and social control of society to knowledge elites. For a valuable history of this perspective in the modern West and in the United States specifically, see Frank Fischer, *Technocracy and the Politics of Expertise* (Newbury Park, Calif.: Sage, 1990), chaps. 3 and 4.

5. For a Marxian analysis, which anchors Newton's theoretical synthesis in European capitalism's need to solve technical problems in water transport, industry, and war, see Boris M. Gessen, *The Social and Economic Roots of Newton's 'Principia'* (New York: Howard Fertig, 1971), with a new introduction by Robert S. Cohen; originally published in 1931. For both Marxist and non-Marxist analyses showing the social roots of modern science, see Lewis Mumford, *Technics and Civilization* (New York: Harcourt, Brace, 1934); Alistair C. Crombie,

Medieval and Early Modern Science, 2 vols. (Garden City, N.Y.: Doubleday, 1959); Samuel Lilley, *Men, Machines, and History*, rev. and enlarged ed. (New York: International, 1966); and Melvin Kranzberg and Carroll W. Pursell Jr., eds., *Technology in Western Civilization*, 2 vols. (New York: Oxford University Press, 1967).

6. This perspective has been obscured by Thomas S. Kuhn's enormously influential *The Structure of Scientific Revolutions* (Chicago: University of Chicago Press, 1962). Kuhn's work is a useful reminder that humans, including scientists, see and behave in terms of assumptions. Kuhn argues that when natural scientists change their assumptions (paradigms), revolutionary breakthroughs occur. But Kuhn tends to call all advances in knowledge *revolutions,* thus obscuring the real revolutions—changes from one worldview, or cosmology, to another (these are very rare). Kuhn also states that he has nothing to say about the world outside of natural science (p. xii), thus supporting the view that science is a self-explanatory force, when of course it gets its impulse and direction from society, especially government and the economy.

7. For an excellent portrait of this period and the social question, see William L. Langer, *Politics and Social Upheaval, 1832–1852* (New York: Harper and Row, 1969), especially chaps. 1 and 6 (vol. 14 of *The Rise of Modern Europe,* ed. William Langer).

8. Francis Fukuyama, *The End of History and the Last Man* (New York: Free Press, 1992).

9. Harold Perkin, *The Rise of Professional Society: England since 1880* (New York: Routledge, 1989).

10. C. Wright Mills, *White Collar: The American Middle Classes* (New York: Oxford University Press, 1953).

11. Philips Abrams, *The Origins of British Sociology: 1834–1914* (Chicago: University of Chicago Press, 1968), pt. 1.

12. Abrams, 48f. For further evidence of the (unintended) partisan uses of the empirical research that was established in this period and that is still with us, see M. J. Cullen, *The Statistical Movement in Early Victorian Britain: The Foundations of Empirical Research* (New York: Barnes and Noble, 1975), especially his conclusion.

13. "The Rise of Social Research in Europe," in *The Human Meaning of the Social Sciences,* ed. Daniel Lerner (New York: Meridian, 1959), chap. 2.

14. A. Clay Schoenfeld, Robert F. Meier, and Robert J. Griffin, "Constructing a Social Problem: The Press and the Environment," *Social Problems* 27 (October 1979): 38–61.

15. Steven Brint, *In an Age of Experts: The Changing Role of Professionals in Politics and Public Life* (Princeton, N.J.: Princeton University Press, 1994), 123–26.

16. Ben H. Bagdikian, *The Media Monopoly,* 5th ed. (Boston: Beacon, 1997); Robert W. McChesney, *Rich Media, Poor Democracy: Communication Politics in Dubious Times* (Urbana: University of Illinois Press, 1999).

17. James Fallows, *Breaking the News: How the Media Undermine American Democracy* (New York: Pantheon, 1996), chap. 3. Fallows's Left-liberal journalism savvy and easy writing style make this small book ideal for undergraduates.

18. An example of the latter is *Fox News Channel,* Rupert Murdoch's twenty-four-hour cable network; see *Extra!* August 2001 for empirical reports on the overall network and on *Special Report with Brit Hume* and *The O'Reilly Factor* in particular, based on types of guests and commentary.

19. For these figures and a detailed history of public broadcasting since its inception in 1967, see James Ledbetter, *Made Possible by . . . The Death of Public Broadcasting in the United States* (New York: Verso, 1997).

20. David Croteau and William Hoynes, *By Invitation Only: How the Media Limit Debate*

(Monroe, Maine: Common Courage, 1994), chaps. 3–5; originally published by FAIR (Fairness & Accuracy In Reporting), a national media watch group and publisher of *Extra!*

21. Gaye Tuchman, *Making News: A Study in the Construction of Reality* (New York: Free Press, 1979). Tuchman's prose makes for tough sledding, but the parts that describe workaday practices by journalists are accessible to undergraduates. Her analysis of how journalism failed the fledgling women's movement is also valuable.

22. Herbert J. Gans, *Deciding What's News: A Study of CBS Evening News, NBC Nightly News, Newsweek, and Time* (New York: Pantheon, 1979).

23. Mark Fishman, *Manufacturing the News* (Austin: University of Texas Press, 1980). The same linkage between journalism and government at the national level is seen as a culture of lying by Right liberal Paul H. Weaver—see his *News and the Culture of Lying* (New York: Free Press, 1994).

24. For how this occurred in higher education, see Clyde W. Barrow, *Universities and the Capitalist State: Corporate Liberalism and the Reconstruction of American Higher Education, 1894–1928* (Madison: University of Wisconsin Press, 1990).

25. Peter Dahlgren, "TV News and the Suppression of Reflexivity," in *Mass Media and Social Change*, ed. Elihu Katz and Tamas Szecsko (Beverly Hills, Calif.: Sage, 1981), 101–13.

26. For example, David Altheide, who has studied news reports about fear, concludes that their chronic exaggerations about crime lead to greater reliance on agents and agencies of social control, such as police, prisons, security systems; see his "Fear in the News" in Peter Phillips and Project Censored, *Censored 1999* (New York: Seven Stories, 1999), chap. 8.

27. For a fully developed analysis of journalism as part of the world it is reporting on and thus unable to avoid distorting the facts to suit American assumptions, see Alan Rachlin, *News as Hegemonic Reality: American Political Culture and the Framing of News Accounts* (New York: Praeger, 1988). To substantiate his argument, Rachlin provides case studies of bias in the way American journalism handled the downing of the Korean airliner in 1983 by a Soviet fighter plane (Canadian accounts were quite different and more objective), and in its coverage of labor unions at home and abroad (strikes at home are unwelcome interruptions, threats to society and its proper functioning, whereas the Polish trade union movement, Solidarity, was a welcome development in communist Poland).

28. Herbert I. Schiller, *The Mind Managers* (Boston: Beacon, 1973), chap. 1.

29. Social structure analysis, focused on the world of communication, is available (not without some effort) from Vincent Mosco, *The Political Economy of Communication: Rethinking and Renewal* (Thousand Oaks, Calif.: Sage, 1996); Kevin Robins and Frank Webster, *Times of the Technoculture: From the Information Society to the Virtual Life* (New York: Routledge, 1999); and Nick Dyer-Witheford, *Cyber-Marx: Cycles and Circuits of Struggle in High-Technology Capitalism* (Urbana: University of Illinois Press, 1999).

30. Oliver Boyd-Barrett, "Media Imperialism: Towards an International Framework for the Analysis of Media Systems," in James Curran et al., eds., *Mass Communications and Society* (London: Edward Arnold, 1977), 116–35; William Steif, "On the 'Objective' Press," *The Progressive* 43 (January 1979): 23–25; Edward W. Said, *Covering Islam* (New York: Pantheon, 1981); Soheir Morsy, "Politicization through the Mass Information Media: American Images of the Arabs," *Journal of Popular Culture* 17 (Winter 1983): 91–97. The enormously influential *National Geographic* invariably leaves out conflict, exploitation, civil war, and imperialism in its portraits of developing countries; Schiller, "The 'National Geographic': Nonideological Geography," *The Mind Managers*, 86–94.

31. Philip Elliot and Peter Golding, "Mass Communication and Social Change: The

Imagery of Development and the Development of Imagery," in *Sociology and Development,* ed. Emanuel DeKadt and Gavin Williams (London: Tavistock, 1974), 230.

32. Mark Fishman, "Crime Waves as Ideology," *Social Problems* 25 (June 1978): 531–43. For a fuller discussion, see Kevin N. Wright, *The Great American Crime Myth* (Westport, Conn.: Greenwood, 1985). The false crime wave is part of the widespread pattern in American professional and business life of identifying and exaggerating the dangers faced by the public, to make it all the more dependent on existing power structures (who are rarely identified as the cause of these dangers).

33. Craig Reinarman and Harry G. Levine, *Crack in America: Demon Drugs and Social Justice* (Berkeley: University of California Press, 1997).

34. H. Bruce Franklin, *Vietnam and Other American Fantasies* (Amherst: University of Massachusetts Press, 2000).

35. Shanto Iyengar, *Is Anyone Responsible? How Television Frames Political Issues* (Chicago: University of Chicago Press, 1991).

36. S. Robert Lichter, Stanley Rothman, Linda S. Lichter, *The Media Elite* (Bethesda, Md.: Adler and Adler, 1986).

37. See the sections on popular culture in chapter 8 for further discussions of journalism and TV news in the context of entertainment.

38. Kathleen Hall Jamieson, *Dirty Politics: Deception, Distraction, and Democracy* (New York: Oxford University Press, 1992).

39. Joseph N. Cappella and Kathleen Hall Jamieson, *Spiral of Cynicism: The Press and the Public Good* (New York: Oxford University Press, 1997).

40. For one of our earliest extended attempts to pin down bias in the news media stemming from a variety of sources, see Peter Golding, "The Missing Dimensions—New Media and the Management of Social Change," in *Mass Media and Social Change,* ed. Katz and Szecsko, 63–81.

41. Peter Dreier, "The Position of the Press in the U.S. Power Structure," *Social Problems* 29 (February 1982): 298–310; Bagdikian, *The Media Monopoly;* and McChesney, *Rich Media, Poor Democracy.*

42. Jyotika Ramaprasad, "How Four Newspapers Covered the 1992 Los Angeles 'Riots,'" in *Mediated Messages and African-American Culture,* ed. Venise T. Berry and Carmen L. Manning-Miller (Thousand Oaks, Calif.: Sage, 1996), 76–95. This essay has the added merit of providing a review of scholars and commissions, black and white, that since the 1920s have severely criticized news coverage of black behavior.

43. For informative histories of African-American journalism (and for more examples of biased treatment of blacks), as well as for data on the absence of blacks from positions of authority in journalism, see Jannette L. Dates, "Print News," and Lee Thornton, "Broadcast News" in *Split Image: African Americans in the Mass Media,* ed. Jannette L. Dates and William Barlow, 2d ed. (Washington, D.C.: Howard University Press, 1993), chaps. 7, 8.

44. For a detailed analysis of the deep (structural) bias by the press against Native Americans, African Americans, Hispanic Americans, the various kinds of Asian Americans, and Pacific Islanders, see Beverly Ann Deepe Keever, Carolyn Martindale, and Mary Ann Weston, *U.S. News Coverage of Racial Minorities: A Sourcebook, 1934–1996* (Westport, Conn.: Greenwood, 1997).

45. William A. Gamson, David Croteau, William Hoynes, and Theodore Sasson, "Media Images and the Social Construction of Reality," *Annual Review of Sociology* 18 (1992): 373–93. For the depoliticizing defense of the status quo by popular culture, see chapter 8.

46. Jack M. McLeod, Gerald M. Kosicki, and Douglas M. McLeod, "The Expanding

Boundaries of Political Communication Effects," in *Media Effects*, ed. Jennings Bryant and Dolf Zillmann (Hillsdale, N.J.: Laurence Erlbaum Associates, 1994), 123–62.

47. C. Wright Mills, *The Power Elite* (New York: Oxford University Press, 1956), 302–4.

48. Michael Schudson, *The Power of News* (Cambridge, Mass.: Harvard University Press, 1995), intro. and chap. 9.

49. For details and analysis, see Fallows, *Breaking the News*, 247–70. For a full discussion by one of the leading scholars advocating public journalism, see Jay Rosen, "Politics, Vision, and the Press: Toward a Public Agenda for Journalism," in Jay Rosen and Paul Taylor, *The New News v. The Old News: The Press and Politics in the 1990s* (New York: Twentieth Century Fund, 1992), essay 1.

50. *New Attitudes, Tools, and Techniques Change Journalism's Landscape* (Washington, D.C.: Pew Center for Civic Journalism, 2001).

51. W. Russell Neuman, Marion R. Rust, and Ann N. Crigler, *Common Knowledge: News and the Construction of Political Meaning* (Chicago: University of Chicago Press 1992).

52. Charles Lewis, "Media Money: How Corporate Spending Blocked Political Ad Reform and Other Stories of Influence," *Columbia Journalism Review* (September/October, 2000): 20–27.

53. Peter Phillips and Project Censored, *Censored 1999* (New York: Seven Stories, 1999). The American Library Association, Washington, D.C., publishes a semiannual report on efforts to restrict or privatize government. Seven Stories publishes the complete directory of alternative media compiled by Project Censored.

54. James Allen Smith, *The Idea Brokers: Think Tanks and the Rise of the New Policy Elite* (New York: Free Press, 1991), and David M. Ricci, *The Transformation of American Politics: The New Washington and the Rise of Think Tanks* (New Haven, Conn.: Yale University Press, 1993), both provide valuable background on this relationship, as well as on the burgeoning world of policy groups.

55. *Inquiry and Change: The Troubled Attempt to Understand and Shape Society* (New Haven, Conn.: Yale University Press, 1990).

56. Exchange theory in sociology has changed in recent decades as theorists—for example, Peter Blau—have come to realize that all social relations are mixtures of reason, knowledge, and a variety of values (emotions). An attempt to derive a sociological theory from rational choice theory is James Coleman, *Foundations of Social Theory* (Cambridge, Mass.: Harvard University Press, 1990).

57. Most social-problems texts in sociology, for example, have a reform liberal orientation.

58. For example, Herbert Marcuse, Michael Harrington, and Immanual Wallerstein.

59. For example, Dorothy E. Smith, Nancy C. M. Hartsock, and Kathy E. Ferguson.

60. For example, William R. Catton, Andre Gorz, and Murray Bookchin.

61. *The Policy Sciences* (Stanford, Calif.: Stanford University Press, 1951).

62. Paul Boyer, *Urban Masses and Moral Order in America, 1820–1920* (Cambridge, Mass.: Harvard University Press, 1978).

63. Joseph K. Gusfield, *Symbolic Crusade: Status Politics and the American Temperance Movement*, 2d ed. (Urbana: University of Illinois Press, 1986).

64. C. Wright Mills, "The Professional Ideology of Social Pathologists," *American Journal of Sociology* 49 (September 1943): 165–80.

65. For more on private research groups and foundations, see "Policy Professionals: The Compromising Tie to Interest Groups," later in this chapter.

66. David B. Tyack, *The One Best System: A History of American Urban Education* (Cambridge, Mass.: Harvard University Press, 1974).

67. For Alvin Gouldner's classic criticism of Howard S. Becker's essay, "Whose Side Are We On?" *Social Problems* 14 (Winter 1967): 239–47, for glibly rejecting the value-neutral approach without realizing that he was siding with national elites, see "The Sociologist as Partisan: Sociology and the Welfare State," *The American Sociologist* 3 (May 1968): 103–16.

68. For the relation between corporate capitalism and higher education, see Barrow, *Universities and the Capitalist State*.

69. For the characteristic of each in tabular form, see David E. Wilson, *The National Planning Idea in U.S. Public Policy: Five Alternative Approaches* (Boulder, Colo.: Westview, 1980), 118–19.

70. Milan J. Dluhy, "Introduction: The Changing Face of Social Policy," in *New Strategic Perspectives on Social Policy*, ed. John E. Tropman, Milan J. Dluhy, and Roger M. Lund (New York: Pergamon, 1981).

71. A content analysis of six prominent policy journals between 1975 and 1984 revealed that policy analysis had failed to live up to its stated ideals of being systematic, relevant, and multidisciplinary. Further, policy research displayed no movement toward such ideals, no integration of the field, and no noticeable differences between it and academic research. See David M. Hedge and Jin W. Mok, "The Nature of Policy Studies: A Content Analysis of Policy Journal Articles," *Policy Studies Journal* 16 (Autumn 1987): 49–62.

72. Hilary Stout, "One Company's Data Fuel Diverse Views in Health-Care Debate," *Wall Street Journal*, June 28, 1994, A1.

73. George Anders, "Doubts Are Cast on Cost Studies by Drug Makers," *Wall Street Journal*, June 28, 1994, B1.

74. This position is taken explicitly by Edith Stokey and Richard Zeckhauser, *A Primer for Policy Analysis* (New York: Norton, 1978), 4, and by default by David L. Weimer and Aidan R. Vining, *Policy Analysis: Concepts and Practice* (Englewood Cliffs, N.J.: Prentice Hall, 1989). The same nonpolitical approach is found in two leading political science texts on the practice of public policy: Thomas R. Dye, *Understanding Public Policy*, 6th ed. (Englewood Cliffs, N.J.: Prentice Hall, 1987), and Clarke E. Cochran, Lawrence C. Mayer, T. R. Carr, and N. Joseph Cayer, *American Public Policy: An Introduction*, 3d ed. (New York: St. Martin's, 1990).

75. These figures were compiled by Smith, *The Idea Brokers*, xiv. Smith's appendix of case studies of thirty leading policy-research organizations provides a good sense of the spectrum of orientation among America's think tanks.

76. For a pioneering set of essays on the political nature (corporate liberalism) of foundations, see Robert F. Arnove, ed., *Philanthropy and Cultural Imperialism: The Foundations at Home and Abroad* (Bloomington: Indiana University Press, 1980). For a focus on the foreign policy impact (corporate liberalism) of three powerful foundations, see Edward H. Berman, *The Influence of the Carnegie, Ford, and Rockefeller Foundations on American Foreign Policy: The Ideology of Philanthropy* (Albany: State University of New York Press, 1983).

77. William Domhoff has studied the latter phenomenon closely as part of his argument that the United States is ruled by a small upper class; see his *The Higher Circles: The Governing Class in America* (New York: Vintage, 1971), esp. chaps. 5 and 6. Also see Thomas R. Dye, "Oligarchic Tendencies in National Policy-Making: The Role of the Private Policy-Planning Organizations," *Journal of Politics* 40 (1978): 309–31. Also see G. W. Domhoff, "Where Do Government Experts Come From? The Council of Economic Advisers and the Policy-Planning Network," and T. R. Dye, "Organizing Power For Policy Planning: The View from the Brookings Institution," both in *Power Elites and Organizations*, ed. Domhoff and Dye (Beverly Hills, Calif.: Sage, 1987). Two studies have clearly established that the Right-liberal and

moderate-conservative think tanks are funded by a national corporate elite: J. Craig Jenkins and Teri Shumate, "Cowboy Capitalists and the Rise of the 'New Right': An Analysis of Contributors to Conservative Policy Formation Organizations," *Social Problems* 33 (December 1985): 130–45, and David Stoesz, "Packaging the Conservative Revolution," *Social Epistemology* 2, no. 2 (1988): 145–53.

78. For a full analysis of the Carnegie Corporation, see Ellen Condliffe Lagemann, *The Politics of Knowledge: The Carnegie Corporation, Philanthropy and Public Policy* (Middletown, Conn.: Wesleyan University Press, 1989).

79. David M. Ricci, *The Transformation of American Politics: The New Washington and the Rise of Think Tanks* (New Haven, Conn.: Yale University Press, 1993).

80. Ricci, *The Transformation of American Politics,* 233–35.

8

⟡

Communication, Media, and Popular Culture

The most important messages that Americans received until, say, 1850 were from the Bible and the pulpit (and of course from secular figures, especially during crises). From 1850 to 1900 religious messages had competition from newspapers, catalogs, and magazines. From 1900 on, popular culture began to make serious inroads on the kinds of symbols that Americans would consume. By 2000, popular culture permeated print communication and had ridden the wave of new communication devices to make up the bulk of messages received by Americans at leisure.

CREATING AND COMMUNICATING
POPULAR CULTURE

In the broadest sense, "popular culture" refers to the culture (symbols, emotions, things) of ordinary people as opposed to the culture of elites. Popular culture emerged with the advent of social stratification in the complex horticultural and agrarian societies, and it varies depending on type of society. Its most distinctive development occurred with the rise of capitalism, especially after industrialization. In the preindustrial period, popular culture was created by ordinary people for themselves. In the industrial era, popular culture was created by the upper classes for ordinary people and, it seems, for many in the middle and upper classes as well.

Popular culture appears to require no training. People respond to it easily, often giving a false appearance of spontaneity. But popular culture is part and parcel of how Americans are socialized, and people respond to it easily *because* of training. Of course, popular culture (unlike elite culture) does not require much *formal* training—but both elite and popular culture require participants who can respond to the sounds and sights projected through assorted technologies. By definition, therefore, all participants in popular culture are social actors who can decode the intricate symbols fired at them.

Much effort has been expended to determine the power of media messages over their audiences. Our analysis assumes that people and media are on opposite sides of the same coin. It assumes that popular culture consists of taken-for-granted ways of maintaining the present social system through the use of taken-for-granted symbols. Accordingly, we will attempt to politicize the media and their themes so that readers can more easily understand the coded messages that are sent their way and see how their choices are being limited. Almost everyone assumes that the media are powerful and almost everyone assumes that they can be changed for the better: political parties complain about the press, minorities about bias, parents about violence and sex, and so on. American academics also stress the power of the media and at the same time emphasize its limits and the ability of groups to resist.[1]

British scholars have emphasized the class, race, and gender themes that run through popular culture. But they too have argued that themes of popular resistance can also be found in popular culture.[2] Building on Gramsci, British culture studies have emphasized hegemony (as opposed to dominance), the continued need by the upper classes to negotiate their control of society with the lower classes. But Gramsci may have been influenced by his experience in Italy (and by his Leninism)—that is, his experience in a country that did not have a coherent governing class. The British, employing a "relativistic" outlook derived from Marx, phenomenology, and feminism, rightly insist that the powerful and the less powerful are in constant interaction and that hegemony is not mechanical or a one-way street. They quite properly point out that power relations continuously manifest themselves in new forms and that one must not reify such concepts as the *people* or *popular culture*. But this does not mean, as they broadly suggest, that popular resistance of any political significance takes place, at least not in the well-developed capitalist societies. While it is important to acknowledge that the masses know how to discount statements made by governing elites, that anti-authoritarian political jokes thrive under certain circumstances, and that anti-establishment music exists in American society, it is also important not to exaggerate the political significance of such phenomena.[3]

In studying popular culture, the wishful thinking of both radical critics and the mainstream must be avoided. One should be free, of course, to advocate popular resistance as a way to promote pluralism or an alternative society. Positive functions, such as stability or integration, can be identified and celebrated. But the "ought" world and the "is" world should never be confused. Art, both high and low, is now deeply professionalized and capitalized (though some areas are still open to amateurs and to people with little capital). The various arts require long years of schooling or training, expensive equipment and facilities; also, performers and creators of art must past muster by giant, profit-oriented corporations (see "Concentration in Communications," in chapter 4). Like the other professions, each of the arts develops as a specialty with its own journal(s) and association(s). All seek secure income either directly from a paying public or indirectly through tax-generated subsidies or tax deductions. In short, all the arts are thoroughly imbedded and integrated into the capitalist ethic.

THE ENDURING THEME OF
TECHNOCRATIC INDIVIDUALISM

Some think of popular culture as voluntary, spontaneous, diverse, unstructured, ever changing, as the opposite of enduring, classical art forms. But these are half-truths. Popular culture is highly structured and contains many enduring themes. Its many technologies (books, magazines, newspapers, painting, sculpture, stage, radio, pho- nograph, film, television, Internet, DVD) should not be confused with diversity of content. Its large variety of individual personalities, behaviors, and situations (romance, adventure, detective stories, espionage, fairy tales, sports, comedy, the supernatural, science fiction, and pornography) should not be taken as cultural plu- ralism or as the outcome of a diverse human nature. Despite its apparent multiplicity of subject matter and its inexhaustible fads and fashions, popular culture clusters around a few simple themes. To take perhaps the most important example, Ameri- can popular culture hews fairly closely to American liberalism—or rather, techno- cratic liberalism—with a decidedly nineteenth-century bias. Its main theme stresses individualism as both ideal and explanation. In keeping with the emphasis in the rest of American culture, including the disciplines and professions, popular culture celebrates the ordinary individual as well as the exceptional (either good or bad) individual.

For much of American history, the model individual was a young male confront- ing life and succeeding largely through force of character. The heroes in the Horatio Alger novels are a prominent example. Though poorly written, the Alger novels con- tained the mythic elements found in all complex cultures: a young male leaves home to achieve, performs a noble deed, is rewarded by a powerful figure, and rejoins the community by returning home and marrying. Using American materials (making one's fortune in the city, in conformity to the Protestant-bourgeois ethic), Alger succeeded because his stories were in line with the American tradition of individual mobility and success.[4]

Americans also respond to the loner, the outsider, and the inner-directed individ- ual. Sometimes the loner is portrayed as a man of action—self-employed, hard work- ing, and productive. A decisive leader, the loner is suspicious of bureaucrats and contemptuous of the well educated, who are always depicted as indecisive. From this perspective, the loner's struggle is a metaphor for moral purification and the restora- tion of unambiguous morality.[5] At other times, the loner is depicted as an outsider who deviates from social norms. Here audiences are invited to experience vicariously the actions of those who are not passive, who strike out openly at whatever bothers them. Sometimes those who are driven to break norms are defeated, in which case the lesson is clear—freedom from social constraints is bad.[6] At other times the loner is a vigilante hero (a staple of popular culture for over seventy-five years), who does good using bad means.[7]

In recent decades the heroic model has changed to resemble society's diversity. Popular-culture heroes now come in all ages, sexes, and skin colors and from all ethnic groups and economic classes. Heroes are physically diverse as well—tall, short, fat, handicapped, beautiful, and not beautiful. Some heroes are charismatic; others are mediators and brokers. Heroes win, lose, and draw. Some are clever, and some are befuddled.[8] Although heroes are recognizable social types, even when they are marginal or total strangers to society, they are rarely explained in social terms. This is especially evident in times of crisis; for example, during the Great Depression the individual achiever became a superhero, often superhuman.

Both popular culture and American culture in general also use individualism to explain evil, often by using the physically different as a metaphor for evil. Sometimes the evil individual is a metaphor for self-interest, corrupt government, or greedy corporations. For the most part, however, the clash of good and bad individuals is depicted as an emanation of human nature and tends to take the spotlight off society, its institutions, and its power groups.

A variation on individualism in popular culture is the priority given to achievement rather than love and family. Complex societies require achievers (heroes) who can solve problems beyond the home. A common theme depicts an individual (often male, often young) who must transcend an unsatisfactory family in order to achieve. Young males must leave home; adult males must forgo romance and sex, or leave wives behind.

America's technocratic liberalism is evident in popular culture's focus on technology and professionalism. Technology, real and imagined, is omnipresent in popular culture, busily solving problems in the expert hands of professionals. Popular culture's achievement theme depicts professional exploits in the hospital, law enforcement, space, the past, the future, or in foreign lands. The real problems of the day—achieving full employment, livable cities, a clean environment, a humane health care system, and so on—are not proper spheres for achievement (though problems from each of these areas are routinely presented, conventionally analyzed, and "solved" without raising questions about institutions or power groups).

THE CLASS NATURE OF POPULAR CULTURE

The class nature of all culture is an all-important feature of human history (after hunting-and-gathering society). The symbols of society and the explanation of where humans come from and where they are going have always reflected the problems and interests of the upper classes. This is as true of the rational culture of the West, including today's myths and universalisms, as it is of feudal-authoritarianism.

The cultures of the upper and lower classes were probably more differentiated prior to the twentieth century, at least before World War II. The upper classes consumed culture differently, having gone to school for longer periods. They went to churches that were more theologically oriented than the churches of the lower classes. They attended lectures, concert halls and opera houses, read more demanding books, magazines and newspapers, and were far more active in the politics of their day.

The upper classes have always translated their wealth into artistic and ideological supports for their way of life. Today, old class distinctions still hold, though significant changes have occurred. The upper classes are now diverse and highly professionalized. Despite broad differences in cultural intake, the era of mass communication has also tended to homogenize what the upper and lower classes experience, especially in entertainment. Nonetheless, the era of mass culture is still a class structure—that is, it upholds the worldview of the upper classes. The mass media's pervasive theme of individualism, for example, holds the working and lower classes in place and helps to socialize them to accept the world as it is. Individualism hides social structure as well as class structure. Everywhere superior individuals, often adept at using technology (gun, scalpel, spaceship, and so on), are effectively solving problems and protecting the postulated Edenic community (a marriage, a family, ranch, an urban center, the United States). Individualism hides social structure also by having individuals generate both good and evil, thus making it impossible for viewers to understand that social structure (and history) is responsible for both. From another perspective, the common participation of all classes in mass culture means that the middle and upper classes are also being depoliticized and thus rendered unable to govern effectively.

The mass media, both as entertainment and journalism, uphold a class-based society by not focusing on social class as such. Classes are portrayed, of course, but in a manner that denies their existence. The middle and lower classes are prominently portrayed, but only to become Everyperson. The problems of small business or semi-professionals are not discussed as such (except in elite newspapers or magazines); neither are the problems of the working classes or the poor. Everyone is depicted as an ordinary person coping with life through humor and improvisation. Or they are depicted as people with problems or as the causes of problems,—and whom professionals are needed to aid or thwart.

Soap operas are perhaps the best example of how class is asserted so pervasively that it is denied; working-class people are never seen, but solid upper-middle-class executives and professionals are everywhere, and they interact easily with the very rich. Also present is the Edenic theme that permeates American culture and politics; soap operas are usually set in small-town communities, they always assume an ideal marital-family world, and both community and family life are disrupted by some evildoer.

Roseanne: Workers without a Class

The television program *Roseanne* (1988–1997), about a working-class family, might seem to contradict the claim that the mass media neglects the working class. *Roseanne* touches on every problem faced by the working classes: lack of educational credentials, lack of employment skills, sporadic employment, cash-flow difficulties; children who consume beyond their means, engage in premarital sex, make bad marriages, continue their schooling through happenstance; and so on. The generational inheritance of class troubles is also fully outlined. Roseanne and Dan, who had unsatisfactory parents, are themselves depicted as parents who cannot provide their children with firm guidance. *Roseanne* raises all these problems only to make them seem the universal problems of every family, solvable by humor, cynicism, and ad hoc coping. Even Roseanne's small success at running a fast-food restaurant occurs only because of inherited money (from one of the despised parents).[9]

The Latent Class Functions of *Playboy* Magazine

On the surface, *Playboy* magazine appears to be an incitement to sexual passion. Its latent consequences, however, are far different. *Playboy* must be put in the context of America's pervasive commercialization of sex (advertising, hard and soft-core pornography) and of the overall devaluation of family values (mutual commitment to marriage and children). Beyond the commercialization of sex is the main theme of popular culture itself, the celebration of the individual-achievement ethic. Popular culture, from Superman comics to Walt Disney, from Doc Savage adventure stories to *Playboy* magazine, tends to have a common theme—sexual renunciation by males and segregation of males and females. Men are either indifferent to women or under siege by them.

As Jewett and Lawrence argue, *Playboy*'s focus on sex and nudity has nothing to do with love and commitment. Instead, it creates a uniform world of cool, faceless men and an image of lustful women imploring men to satisfy their needs.[10] Like popular culture in general, it makes clear that love and commitment between the sexes must not interfere with masculine achievements, all of which lie beyond home and hearth. As Jewett and Lawrence (and others) point out, *Playboy* is antisensual, amounting to a rejection of commitment to enduring sexual relations. *Playboy* separates the sexes, making women appear to want men, who themselves pick and choose like calculating consumers. Here one can also identify perhaps the major latent function of *Playboy*—that of a guide to consumption for upwardly mobile males (or those with disposable income) in the realms of cars, stereo equipment, clothing, dining, and reading.

Playboy magazine can also be placed in the context of structural trends in the American economy and class system. Barbara Ehrenreich has argued that the post–World War II period witnessed a flight by men from commitment.[11] From the 1950s on, the breadwinner ethic, the idea that men work for others, has declined. Men still want to work hard, but not for others. There are various signs of this: the new psychology of personal growth, criticisms of life in the corporate world, and warnings about the adverse health effects of the economic rat race. But *Playboy* magazine, which appeared in 1953 with an open rejection of marriage and family, is perhaps the best exemplar of the male "liberation" from commitment, argues Ehrenreich. *Playboy,* as primarily a guide to upper-middle-class consumption and in its attitude toward women and sex continues the tradition that sees the latter as barriers to the achievement of male values. Far from heralding the sex revolution, *Playboy* divorces sex from sexuality, commitment, reciprocity, and procreation. Putting this in a broader context, Ehrenreich suggests that the flight from commitment and the anti-feminist backlash of the 1970s and 1980s were really reflections of the decline of the breadwinner ethic. Few understand, says Ehrenreich that the decline has occurred because the economy is no longer generating single-breadwinner jobs.

Gail Dines has also spotted the consumerism of *Playboy* and has stressed its mean-ing for gender inequality. She also points out that *Playboy*, with five thousand employees and $200 million in sales by the 1970s, has successfully mainstreamed itself. Its role in maintaining gender and class relations has been achieved, in Dines's words, by its success in "commodifying sex and sexualizing commodities."[12]

The Adventure Story

The adventure stories in television programs, films, and print stress male achieve-ment through skill, heroism, luck, and technology. These stories focus on personal behavior while neglecting structural themes, in effect taking for granted all forms of inequality and adopting a rotten-apple (but sound barrel) approach to evil and injustice.

The basic adventure stories celebrate technology and use the frontier myth to promise progress against deviance and foreign enemies. They also sanctify the pres-ent, by setting stories in a mythical past (the days of King Arthur, Robin Hood, the American West) or a mythical future (*Star Trek* and its many sequels, science fiction in general). The adventure story relies on exotic locales to identify national enemies and often to justify (in the case of *Star Trek*, by depictions of intervention by a superior culture anywhere in the galaxy) American or Western intervention in Third World countries.

The adventure story also resolves the contradiction between absolute self-interest and the common good. Self-interest must always restrict itself to acceptable paths to success. Those who use immoral or illegal means (the villain) are depicted in deeply negative terms and die violently. This theme is central to the western film, as is the definition of the hero as an outsider and the depiction of ordinary citizens, govern-ment officials, and politicians as weak, cowardly, or corrupt (see below for a fuller discussion of the western). The antidemocratic bias of popular culture is especially apparent in the adventure story.

The film *Jaws* (1975) illustrates not merely the pervasive use of social class in popular culture but the way in which class myths remain invisible even as they suck audiences into the story. A prosperous resort (Eden) is shaken by a nonsocial disas-ter—a huge shark has eaten a young woman. The small-business people (America's entrepreneurial past) are frightened and unable to act except to keep the beach open. After another victim falls to the shark, they offer a reward for its destruction (capital-ist material incentive), and the oceanfront becomes a madhouse of bungling ama-teurs (the people are incompetent). An experienced fisherman (another small-business person but with a skilled manual trade) combines the reward with motives of revenge (sharks ate many of his navy comrades during the war). He fails, as befits someone with unworthy (material and moral) motives. To the rescue come a professional police officer and a wealthy fish expert (he owns a large boat with scientific equipment). Their motives are pure—duty and a disinterested search for knowledge. But even technology, knowledge, skill, and bravery are not enough; in the last analysis, they need luck (society cannot solve its problems through either personal or collective efforts).

All genres of contemporary popular culture have built-in ambiguities and token minority representation so that today's audiences can be reached. Until well into the post–World War II period, American popular culture openly used racist and sexist stereotypes to build audience-receptive stories. Open racist-sexist stereotypes are no longer acceptable inside the United States, and the importance of the foreign market to American producers of popular culture gives another incentive to avoid at least racist stereotypes. By avoiding open bias, by sprinkling minority individuals among both the heroes and the villains, and by inserting a certain amount of inconclusiveness in the story lines (though white males and liberal norms and values predominate), today's popular culture lends itself to various interpretations and allows various groups to find satisfaction in the same offering.[13]

Crime, Law, and Medical Stories

Crime, law, and medical stories could have been included in the adventure genre, but they have distinctive ideological aspects that need to be identified. Crime and mystery stories can no longer follow the structure found in Sherlock Holmes or Hercule Poirot stories, in which a crime is solved because the settled, highly predictable nature of society makes it possible to find clues and identify villains. Crimes today are not easy to solve, and they have many ambiguous features reflecting the ambiguity of contemporary society. But one function of crime stories remains—those who violate the Protestant-bourgeois ethic are deviants who deserve damnation and doom.

Law and medical stories also feature the white male achiever, technology, and problem solving in a world of rotten apples. Law and medical stories also display token assimilated nonwhites and women. What is distinctive about these stories is that many of the problems encountered by achiever-heroes are caused by ordinary citizens involved in everyday life. The overall impression created by the display of deviance up and down the class ladder is that problem behavior comes from a hard-to-control human nature.

The latent implications of crime, law, and medical stories go beyond the legitimization of American professionalism (also a function of adventure stories). These stories, along with the mass media and journalism in general, protect the American economy and American polity from scrutiny. They prevent Americans from asking why America's crime rate is the highest in the industrial world. Why doesn't the United States have a national health care system like the rest of the capitalist world (to get the same results at a 40 percent savings in cost)? Exactly what is required to construct a judicial system that generates equal, as opposed to class, justice?

Class, Film, and Popular Music

Early filmmaking companies were highly diverse and openly political but could not withstand the onrush of corporate capitalism in the entertainment business. The giant film corporations that came to dominate Hollywood in the 1930s steered filmmaking away from overt politics and toward two themes: True love can conquer all, including the chasm of class, and individuals can succeed, even against difficult odds. All in all, American films, like the rest of American culture, ignore the power of class over how resources and opportunities are distributed.[14]

Popular music also emphasizes the power of love and the American Dream but combines them with other themes—for example, laments about personal sorrow and poverty. While somewhat more diverse, popular music essentially reinforces the status quo ideology found in film and television. Of the top forty songs in the years 1955, 1965, 1975, 1985, 1995, only 4 percent were about economics or class.[15]

It should be noted that counting how many television programs, films, or songs belong in this or that category is not to establish empirical truth. The reason is self-evident—the construction of categories and the determination of what a cultural item means are interpretive acts, whether by scholars or laypeople. A given item can evoke very different responses, the classic case being the seventies series *All in the Family*—the Archie Bunker character was intended to expose bigotry to ridicule, but many viewers agreed with him. But overall there can be little disagreement that popular culture reinforces basic American myths and prevents Americans from gaining a realistic picture of their sociopolitical world.

DIFFERENTIAL CONSUMPTION OF SYMBOLIC CULTURE BY SOCIAL CLASS

Participation in "symbolic" culture can also be analyzed in terms of differential class consumption (and production) in the aesthetic and intellectual-moral sphere.[16] The main American pattern in this area is clear—Americans consume aesthetic, intellectual, and moral values in class-structured ways. The corollary to this pattern is the significant fact that the production of "symbolic" culture is also geared to class audiences. Perhaps of even greater significance is the fact that "symbolic" culture is now in an advanced industrial stage of production and consumption. In other words, organizations engaged in creating and distributing aesthetic, intellectual, and moral values are managed in much the same way as is the economy; they are characterized by narrow upper-class "ownership" and control, professional staffs that manage day-to-day operations, and benefits bestowed according to class.

A case in point is Edward Arian's analysis of the Philadelphia (Symphony) Orchestra.[17] Suggesting that forces at work in Philadelphia are found throughout the United States, Arian argues that the Philadelphia Orchestra Association is dominated through its board of directors by upper-class (old-rich) families, and that they and the upper classes are its chief beneficiaries. To combat mounting costs, the board instituted a rigidly bureaucratic, efficiency-minded mode of operations; this innovation enabled the board to retain control, especially since the orchestra's budget could still be financed by private wealth. One of the interesting by-products of this process is that the orchestra does not play before a wide spectrum of community audiences and performs little modern or experimental music.

Middle and upper-class dominance in the general area of aesthetic-intellectual-moral values makes for differences in the amount and type of enjoyment available to the various classes. Furthermore, control of prestigious forms of cultural activity by the upper classes strengthens and supports the general system of stratification by class. To the extent that high culture is thought to bear a special relationship to the integrity of society, the upper and middle classes are seen as its patrons and preservers. To the extent that the aesthetic-intellectual-moral realm has a bearing on social problems and issues, it is the upper classes that control its operations and compose its audiences, thereby deeply influencing the way in which issues and problems are formulated and solved. Finally, it is the upper and middle classes whose sensibilities are stimulated, and whose wits are sharpened, by offerings in the worlds of music, theater, painting, dance, sculpture, and quality publications—outcomes that are valuable in their own right and that have applications in the areas of class and power.

The relation between voluntary organizations in the field of "symbolic" culture and government is of growing importance and deserves much greater study. In addition to its growing influence on higher education, the federal government partially supports an extensive television network (the Corporation for Public Broadcasting and the Public Broadcasting System) and makes (relatively small) sums of money available to the arts and humanities (through the National Arts Endowment and the National Humanities Endowment). Framed in the image of the independent regulatory commissions, these public bodies resemble their predecessors; ostensibly nonpartisan, objective, and aloof from politics in practice, they dispense public monies and public prestige in a manner that coincides with the basic structure of class and political power.

An interesting review of some empirical findings in the mass media suggests that because the logic of economic life, and especially its technology, impels the mass media to attract mass audiences, very little content is specialized according to class. While blue-collar and white-collar families clearly tend to have different tastes and preferences in broadcast programs and print media (the former preferring more entertainment and less information), the interesting thing, according to Leo Bogart, is that the differences are so small. What the mass media represent, Bogart suggests, in his pioneering study, is a powerful instrument for inducing working-class conformity to a middle-class society.[18]

Pressure to conform is one thing; actual homogeneity of outlook and values is another. Despite the mass media, significant differences exist between the symbolic interests and skills of white-collar and blue-collar Americans. This is not surprising, given differences in the amount and type of reading (books, magazines, newspapers), formal education, socialization, travel, community participation, and occupational experience engaged in by the two groups.

The nature of the audience is much better known to those who devise programs to reach it (because they do market research) than it is to social science. The latter has studied the content of popular (and elite) culture and speculated about its ideology and its effects on audiences, but exact research on the class, age, sex, and racial-ethnic composition of audiences is scarce—largely because social science assumes a match between type of offering and type of audience. Herbert Gans's classic analysis of elite and popular culture, which identified five taste cultures, all deserving of equal respect, took it for granted that these cultures corresponded largely to class background.[19] Bogart, in his highly detailed *Commercial Culture: The Media System and the Public Interest*,[20] has much to say about audiences but reports little empirical research about audiences. Audiences reflect the daily rhythm of social life rather than conscious decisions about content. They reflect media opportunities that are richer in urban than rural areas. They reflect geography, sex, race, age, and class. The upper classes read more; the lower classes prefer television. Newspaper readership has declined, not only with the decline in the number of newspapers but because of competition by television (radio news has almost disappeared with deregulation). By and large, says Bogart, the American audience is both homogenized by the media and fragmented by them into specialized publics.

The creation of audiences through market research is important; the producers of culture create their markets just as the producers create soap, automobiles, and the like. In a sense, the concept of a *public* (a politically active citizenry) has been replaced by that of the *audience* (a depoliticized, skilled receiver of elite messages). The ability to track and reach audiences is now technologically highly advanced.[21]

Not surprisingly, audiences preferences for programs and printed material correspond to class, gender, race, age, and ethnicity. A good example is found in Radway's study of readers of romance novels, a study that provides evidence of class-based, gender-based, and age-based consumption of popular culture—readers tend to be working/lower-middle-class females between twenty-five and fifty (for details see the section "Romance Novels," below). Taste in popular music, television programs, and films also varies by age.

The interpretation of popular culture by a heterogeneous audience also varies by class, gender, age, and context.[22] Who one is with affects how one interprets a program—the very process that Lazarsfeld found in his classic voter study in 1940 (see "Awareness and Concern about Communication Technology," in chapter 9). Many, as noted, approved of Archie Bunker despite the program's purpose of ridiculing him. Also, of course, different cultures will interpret the same program (for example, *Dallas*) differently.[23]

Commentators have found opportunities in popular culture for resistance to social power. Soap operas, *Roseanne*, and romance novels could foster female resistance to patriarchy (though no significant evidence of this effect's actually occurring has been discovered). There is a long history of dissidents using communication ideology to mount criticisms of oppressive conditions, even against oppressive regimes.[24] Nonetheless, perhaps the most important thing about the class nature of mass media is that it supports, often unconsciously, the basic foundations of American capitalism. Sari Thomas argues that it is a mistake to think of television as mere entertainment around which advertisers target their audiences. Television programs show us how the world at all levels works; it has more to do with everyday life than does formal schooling. The idea that individuals interpret what they see is in itself individualistic ideology; actually, variations correspond to sociodemographic differences rather than to the uniqueness of individuals. The selling of products through advertising presupposes an audience housebroken to capitalist behavior. Entertainment programs help to generate acceptance of the general process of capitalism. All this is done almost invisibly, as part of background: spending is to be taken for granted, excess money is to be spent, saving is deviance, celebration is material, spending cures depression, big spenders get better treatment, being cheap is vulgar, hard work is the way to get money, and honest work is its own reward.

Television entertainment, Thomas points out, also propagates myths about social mobility; its focus on a world of middle-to-upper-class people makes it appear (contrary to the facts) that there is plenty of room at the top. Linked to this myth is the myth that anyone can achieve (most of the better-off on television come from humble origins). On the other hand, those at the top have a great deal of trouble, while poorer families enjoy love and harmony, enduring only minor problems solvable in half an hour (less commercial breaks). In short, if you want success, be hopeful, but if you fail be grateful that you don't have to pay its price.[25]

POPULAR CULTURE AND RACE[26]

Historical Trends

The early mass media (radio, film, and television) participated fully and openly in America's racism. African Americans were either invisible or depicted as lazy, stupid, or incompetent, as objects of comic ridicule, always in menial occupations. From the 1960s into the 1970s, changes occurred, and African Americans were portrayed in a more positive light. This change corresponded to a major shift in American (white) attitudes toward African Americans during the post–World War II period and to the realities of the civil rights movement. The changed depiction of African Americans has had its own shortcomings, however, and a new, more subtle racist stereotyping has appeared. The more "realistic" all-black shows are characterized by "irresponsible and absent black males, esteem given to bad, flashy characters, and a general lack of positive attributes in the Black community." Research since indicates that the media are still in this stage.[27]

Head Counts, Types of Roles, and Black-White Interaction

This is a good place to remind ourselves that experience is not always a good guide to reality. Whatever the appearances, research reveals that white males and females have increased their representation in television character roles in recent years, while black males and females are below their population percentages (with black females far below). As far as other racial minorities are concerned, America has none, if television is our guide. Native Americans, Hawaiians, Pacific Islanders, or Asian Americans are virtually nonexistent as far as the mass media are concerned (print media does have occasional stories about Native Americans and gambling casinos, and Asian-American achievement in school).

As for types of roles, black males lost ground in both major and supporting roles, and black females lost even more ground. Another major pattern on television is segregation. Whites and nonwhites do not interact much or on friendly, respectful terms in mixed-race shows, and the bulk of African-American representation on television is on all-black shows. Incidentally, there is also a strong tendency for whites and blacks to watch like-race shows. In one poll of top ten shows watched by black and white audiences, there was not one overlapping show!

Children's Programs and African Americans

Children's programs tend to have fewer African Americans and to depict them as inadequately as do programs for adults. Interestingly, audiences here, especially blacks, also identified strongly with same-race shows. It is noteworthy that public television has a much more positive portrayal of African Americans on children's programs than does private television.

The Mass Media and African Americans

Researchers report that Americans who watch entertainment programs believe that African Americans are much better off than they are, while those who watch television news programs think they are worse off than they are. Both here and elsewhere, an important reform in improving the depiction of African Americans would be to have more black reporters, commentators, and executives in the various media (where they are now very underrepresented). A striking example of racial bias by commentators is from sports—in a 1977 study, white commentators gave white players "more play-related praise and more favorable comments on aggressive plays, while blacks were more the subject of unfavorable comparisons to other players, and all eleven negative references to nonprofessional past behaviors were to black players."[28] The recent influx of black commentators into the broadcast booth has not been studied to see if improvements have occurred, but one can guess that they have.

Changes in the depiction of African Americans since the 1950s can be interpreted in terms of unintended consequences. African Americans are no longer uniformly depicted as inferiors, and there are many examples of blacks in high-achievement positions. But the special barriers to black achievement are rarely discussed, and blacks are uniformly depicted as assimilated, as a normal feature of a progressive society that is what it claims to be. This way of endorsing the status quo leads to a second way in which the media legitimate the present order of things and people.

Because blacks are sometimes shown in a positive light, the media cannot be accused of racism when they concentrate on African Americans as dangerous deviants. Since neither depiction is accompanied with explanations based on history or socioeconomic causes, viewers are confined to one (or a mixture) of two status quo interpretations, racist explanations or Right liberal explanations (all individuals are what they are by nature).[29]

POPULAR CULTURE AND ETHNICITY

Ethnicity is still presented stereotypically in the mass media, though not as blatantly as in the past, when Irish, Italian, Jewish Americans, and other of the earlier immigrants to America were openly denigrated. These former minorities are no longer economically depressed or segregated and have organizations to protect their images.

The new consciousness about minorities has also improved the way other ethnic minorities, such as Hispanics, are depicted, though some are still portrayed occasionally in negative terms. But the most important thing about ethnic minorities, especially new arrivals, is their virtual absence from the mass media. (For a fuller discussion, see sources cited in previous note.)

POPULAR CULTURE AND GENDER

The backlash against attempts to promote equality for women that was reported earlier has also appeared in the mass media. The trends in the area of gender are similar to those in the area of race and ethnicity. From the 1960s on, the blatant sexism of the media diminished. Women were better represented in achievement roles and as heroes [*sic*]. Women appeared as doctors, lawyers, detectives, and so on. That movement in the depiction of women has continued. The fourth sequel (1995) to the television program *Star Trek* has a woman as its central character, the captain. A 1995 episode of *This Old House* featured female plumbers.

But the overwhelming bulk of media characters and stories still feature males in achievement roles. Women are still depicted, and it seems increasingly so, as feminine—that is, as nurturing, engaged in household activity—and as defined by their appearance, including body shape, and by their relationships to others (mother, wife, and daughter).

Focusing on underrepresentation on television is not enough, and in any case, the idea of representing any aspect of American society accurately would not be entertaining and thus not profitable. The media not only reflect the American population's values and beliefs but sidestep problems and contradictions. For example, they may not be underrepresenting women in the medical or legal worlds, but they have little to say about the deep segregation of women in these professions into less rewarded, less prestigious specialties. When a woman does achieve standing in one of the high-profile specialties, she is apt to be referred to as, say, a *female* surgeon.

The biased depiction of women is difficult to see, because it is communicated through images that reflect unconscious assumptions of what is real and legitimate. This feature of gender bias, its pervasiveness, and therefore it obscurity, is addressed in many critical analyses. But many gender analyses, if not most or even all, especially textbooks, make literally no reference to social class. In addition, most gender analyses are liberal—that is, they are critical of the media or society for not allowing women full participation in American society. Mainstream feminism assumes that the United States as presently structured can generate equality and full participation by all its members; it does not ask, "Is the exploitation of women (and other minorities) a necessary consequence of the basic structure of power?"[30]

Soap Operas

The soap opera (from the 1930s on)[31] has stressed the importance of romantic interaction and the blossoming of true love, marriage, domesticity, and kinship values. The daytime soap opera presupposes and affirms an ideal family order: true love as the basis of marriage, having children as a woman's fulfillment, parent-child love and devotion, and generational continuity. All problems boil down to the need to maintain a happy, moral family life. Good people associate sex with love, marriage, and children. The world of everyday life is meaningful, and small decisions have big implications. Life is filled with the many different facets of human nature, all humans behave blindly, life is not always fair, but in the long run (which never comes) good triumphs and evil is punished.

Soaps have increased the number of women characters with careers, but theirs are token jobs, a ritual bow to the women's movement. (Actually, women characters on soap operas who devote too much time to their careers are punished.) Soaps are extremely popular and reflect family values that are deeply held (at least among women who make up the main bulk of the audience). In recent decades, the evening soap opera has developed the family theme (which dominates the day soaps) to include the world of big business, including the international economy. Here again, a variegated human nature reigns supreme, but unlike the day soaps the evening soaps have a greater tendency for individuals to do good and evil in personal relations as these bear on business relations, and vice versa.[32] The (small) movement of women into the business world and the growing importance of the international economy are also reflected in the evening soaps.

The soaps do not have straight narratives with strong patriarchal climaxes, and this has led some feminists to see the soap opera as a feminist text that can inspire resistance by viewers. But research has failed to produce such sophistication among soap audiences. As critics have pointed out, the soaps render the individual insignificant, and their multiple characters and plots make it difficult for viewers to identify with any of them. Soap operas show many limited egos in conflict; no character is able to take charge, because each is ignorant of what everyone else is going to do. Thus, far from inciting resistance to male power, the soap opera—with its format (narration without end); its themes of constantly thwarted ideal love, marriage, and family; its many-sided explanations for evil and failure; and its transgressions, which offer vicarious enjoyment for hidebound housewives—reflects the unsatisfactory lives of audiences and offers fake justifications and temporary solace for them. Unlike the masculine narrative, which depicts a strong character coping with his world, the feminine "story" is a never-ending mélange of episodic events in which self-oriented individuals struggle ineffectually in a world that is moral in the sense that people get what they deserve. Here one finds the social-action tradition of sociology, the rational-choice tradition in economics, and the interest-group politics of political science, that is, the capitalist world of eternal scarcity—except that in this case all, instead of most, fail.

Rating for soaps declined by 25 percent starting in the 1990s, a number have been canceled, and prime-time soaps have disappeared. The reasons are probably that more women are now working, are otherwise exceedingly busy, or have more viewing choices, including real-life "soap operas."[33] Another reason may be that working women, whether single or in two-income marriages, are experiencing a different sea of troubles than the characters in the soaps.

Romance Novels

The romance novel has a predictable formula and is easy for busy women to read (it is also inexpensive). Aspiring authors are given a tip sheet spelling out the formula. A vulnerable woman meets a powerful man who excites her sexually. They spar, she makes clear that she wants love with sex, they separate. She fears that she has lost him, but in reality he respects her. Plot twists threatens their relationship, but they finally declare their love for each other, presumably a love that will last forever.[34]

Like much of the mass media, romance novel publishing is a lucrative monopoly based on exploited female authors.[35] The readers are clear about why they read them—for escape. Janice Radway has studied a nonscientific sample of such readers and has offered contrasting interpretations of what the romance novel signifies. On the one hand, readers are escaping from patriarchal marriages into a world where love and commitment, not competitive pursuits for success, reign supreme. On the other, such reading and its content probably do very little to change the patriarchal marriages that the women must go back to—we will not be sure, concludes Radway, until we have traced what happens to readers and their spouses over time.[36]

Female Heroes

Popular culture has many females in heroic roles. A female in a heroic role in the gothic novel was a heroine because she triumphed over adversity pursuing a feminine goal, marriage to a man of substance. Today, females are heroic in male roles— for example, as detectives *(Cagney and Lacy, Murder She Wrote)*, journalists *(Murphy Brown)*, the *Star Trek* captain, doctors *(E.R., Chicago Hope)*, or predators *(Fatal Attraction, Disclosure, Thelma and Louise)*. Some have even interpreted *Roseanne* as a feminine text, because it features a housewife who openly ridicules feminine values.

Pornography and Slasher Films

Pornography is a ten-billion-dollar global business run by males for males; its revenues substantially exceed the seven-billion-dollar revenues of the mainstream American film industry. Once a furtive, minor business, pornography has had an explosive growth in recent decades, thanks to the anonymity made possible by new communication technology. Pornography can now be seen in homes (via cable, satellite, or video rentals), hotel rooms (40 percent of hotel rooms now make it available), and on the Internet (twenty-one million Americans visit one of its sixty thousand sex sites at least once a month). The companies that create and distribute pornography not only trade on Wall Street but are often subsidiaries of such major American companies as General Motors, AT&T, Time Warner, the News Corporation, and the Marriott and Hilton hotel chains.[37] Pornography depicts sex acts that men initiate and control. It is subject to attacks by both feminist groups and politically conservative groups. Feminists object to pornography in general, because of the overall male power relation that it helps to sustain, and to pornography with violence in particular, because, they claim, it leads to sexual violence against women in real life.

The evidence for the causal impact of pornography with violence is highly suggestive but far from conclusive[38] (the evidence is from experiments and registers attitudes, which of course are not the same as overt behavior). Beyond this, Gayle Rubin has argued that feminist antipornography campaigns are misguided. For one thing, pornography with violence is a very small part of the market and caters to a narrow clientele. The huge amount of violence in the media (films, music videos, television, books and magazines), much of it directed at women, has nothing to do with sex. Antipornography feminists, Rubin holds, should pay more attention to slasher films and less to pornography. (She implies that clamping down on pornography and prostitution, however desirable from one point of view, may prevent a more open attitude by all toward sex; in short, the opposition to pornography by pro-life, pro-family conservative groups on moral grounds is not necessarily in the best interests of women.)

In any case, Rubin argues, antiporn feminists cannot help women with the real problems they face, "of unequal pay, job discrimination, sexual violence and harassment, the unequal burdens of child-care and housework, increasing right-wing infringements on hard-won feminist gains, and several millennia of unrelenting male privilege vis-à-vis the labor, love, personal service, and possession of women."[39]

POPULAR CULTURE AND OTHER MINORITIES

Clustering these minorities into one heading should not be taken as a slight—these are large and often suffering minorities. The reason for combining them here is that little research exists on the mass media's depiction of these minorities.

Age

Television portrays age groups in a stereotyped manner, though there is some effort to show the middle-aged as heroes and heroines. Otherwise the pattern is to depict age groups in terms of class and gender biases and to slant programming toward younger groups, in order to please advertisers.

Disability

The disabled (15–20 percent of the population) are pictured largely as problems. There is still a tendency to use the disfigured or the physically different as symbols of evil or as villains.[40] The disabled are enormously varied, and it is difficult to generalize about how they are portrayed in film, television, or newspapers, except to say that it is seldom in positive terms (newspapers do have stories about the special services needed by the disabled and about their abuse by others). The disabled are absent from advertising. Children's programs do not differ much from other programs in how they depict the disabled.[41]

Gays and Lesbians

Gays and lesbians (1 to 5 percent of the population) were once uniformly depicted in a stereotyped manner and invariably ended up badly. Contemporary media are far more open and positive about gays and lesbians, though little appears that shows the wide diversity among them in terms of occupation and class. By and large, little research exists on how gays and lesbians are portrayed by the media.[42] But gays and lesbians have purchasing power, and advertisers have begun to target them in specialized markets and publications. In 1995, Hill and Knowlton, a major public relations firm, established a unit for marketing goods and services to gays and lesbians.

POPULAR CULTURE AND PERVASIVE DEPOLITICIZATION

The Taken-for-Granted Community

Though popular culture has been important throughout American history (thanks especially to print technology), the emergence of radio and film beginning in 1900 was a watershed with respect to its power. Combined with television at mid-twentieth century, mature computer technology at the end of the century, and new forms of print technology, popular culture may be a growing part of an unchanging power structure. Whatever its power, its main consequence is to uphold technocratic liberalism (heroes, leaders, individualism, professionalism, technology, competition, property) and to depoliticize social problems.

The process of depoliticization is still anchored in the pervasive theme of an assumed Eden and the frontier (see "Sustaining Myths: The Garden of Eden and the Frontier," in chapter 3). This theme blossomed during the 1930s as the old print technology combined with radio and television to develop our "national monomyth" (the archetypal plot pattern in American popular culture in which an Edenic community, threatened by nonsocial evil, is redeemed through nonsocial forces, especially superheroism).[43]

Popular culture invariably posits a community the peace of which is shattered by an evil of some sort. The evil can be a nature gone berserk (*Jaws,* disaster and horror films), incompetent or greedy businesspeople, criminals, the mentally ill, sinister foreigners, or some other threat. The assumption of a ready-made, natural social order appears in various ways. Often the focus is on primary groups—for example, the soap opera's obsessive focus on ideal kinship relations, and the situation comedy's focus on disruptions of the family routine. The orderly world of a family, a town, a business, or a ranch might be shattered by an act of lawlessness. Sometimes the notion of an orderly, benign, self-sufficient world is presented in terms of metaphor. For example, the spaceship *Enterprise* in *Star Trek* is a multiple metaphor that can stand for a smoothly running corporation, the United States, or American foreign policy. The various individuals who made up the members of the television series *M*A*S*H* represent the full spectrum of American statuses and values—they form a "family," resolve their minor conflicts, and thus say, in effect, "All's right with the United States."[44]

There is evidence, however, that popular culture no longer depicts society as orderly, benign, and rational. The classic detective story that emerged in the nineteenth century presupposed an orderly world in which a small, momentary disruption takes place. The detective can explain the disruption through observation and logic because he (always male until recently) can (like the rest of the newly emerging scientific, capitalist culture) assume an otherwise orderly and supportive world. The classic detective story has now been pushed aside by crime, espionage, and adventure thrillers in which action takes place in an essentially disorderly and unpredictable world.[45] Hence the increased reference to vigilante action and the need to fight evil with evil. Hence the kinship with soap operas with their double-dealing characters and seemingly random experiences. Hence the enormous emphasis on the breakdown of marriages or love relationships and on the untrustworthiness of others: spouses, roommates, nannies, coworkers, officials, friends, or neighbors. The enormous success of disaster and horror films is in the same vein. All of these themes strike responsive chords not only because they are in touch with how people feel about a social world that appears beyond individual control but because their exaggerations make that world appear secure and satisfactory by comparison.

Depoliticization is not just an outcome of fare meant for the masses. Most world-class productions (for example, *Masterpiece Theater*) and critically acclaimed film directors (such as Alfred Hitchcock) depoliticize more than we are aware of. Hitchcock supported the status quo by portraying a naturalistic, taken-for-granted social world, his camera acting as the eyes of the audience to observe gender rivalries, sexual tensions and repressions, espionage, mental obsessions and aberrations, violence, scams, and mixtures of normal and abnormal. What you see is all there is, he seems to be saying. The status quo is also safeguarded by his subtle catalog of anxieties, which match and allay the anxieties of the audience.

In an insightful analysis, Charles Simpson argues that popular culture helps individuals cope with their existential anxieties. In the social organization of premodern societies, these anxieties were managed more directly. But the processes of modernization have isolated individuals, made them feel powerless in an uncaring, unpredictable world, and deprived them of the easy connection with not only others but the universe at large. Popular culture allows for the safe discharge of the anxieties created by corrupt institutions and the loss of transcendental meaning. It provides specialized experiences for culture and age groups, enabling them to find identities that do not challenge the wider social structure. Simpson illustrates his analysis with a case study of Dashiell Hammett's *The Maltese Falcon*, a world in which nothing is what it appears to be, in which people lie and betray each other, "a marketplace with cash as its truth and love as its illusion." The hero, Sam Spade, works outside the ineffective and corrupt law. Mistrust is everywhere, and Spade must negotiate for scraps of information, knowing that his sources are probably lying. Spade's mind and emotions, and the outside world are never integrated. "Self-respect lies in being tough enough not to hide from the realization that passion or morality, or conventional routine are false courts of appeal; one acts on one's own." Sam Spade as hero is us, the hero who in many guises allays our anxieties about the absence of coherence and meaning in our lives.[46]

America's Nonpolitical Political Film

All films and all media content are political—that is, they are for or against something, occasionally even against society, whether the creators or audience are aware of it or not. The political film is an overt attempt at making a political statement. Genovese argues that American political films are decidedly different from the Western European political film. American filmmakers, such as Frank Capra and John Ford, presented a world of absolutes, simple virtues, simple problems, simple solutions, all of which are simply given to audiences, thus inducing passivity. The European political film, in contrast, is more complex, ambiguous, and balanced in its presentation of problems and solutions; audiences are asked to think about what is going on.[47]

The American political film is also antipolitical, in that the agent of redemption is always the heroic individual, and the cause of problems is always the evil individual. But a change can be noted. During the 1930s, American political films posited a sound American community with failed leadership. In Frank Capra's *Mr. Smith Goes to Washington*, a redeeming hero (nonpolitical outsider) confronts and defeats the bad leaders, and society becomes whole again. After World War II, this brand of idealism declined. The new perspective on politics was inaugurated by Robert Rossen's *All the King's Men* (1950), in which the hero is corrupted by power. The new image of the community and politics is of one that is permanently compromised and that can resist the efforts of the heroic redeemer.[48] Here too we may be seeing a reflection of the political dilemma faced by American elites. The United States needs a strong, positive, directive central government, but elites also know that such a government could become supportive of mass interests. Thus the United States remains politically enfeebled, the only developed country in the world without a positive tradition of central government. By and large, popular culture caters to elite prejudices by painting an almost uniformly negative picture of politicians and government officials. Here it builds on the paranoid style of American politics and on the laissez-faire, anti-authority traditions of both Left and Right liberals.

Robert Thompson suggests that Frank Capra's *Mr. Smith Goes to Washington* was popular with Americans because it declared that American ideals could actually be realized. All other American political films, all well made and far from dull, have been box-office disappointments. Americans know their ideals are far from being realized, do not want to be reminded of it, certainly not told that they probably cannot be realized. America's political mythology is deeply rooted and resistant to critical evaluation.[49]

Depoliticizing through Professionalism

Will Wright has made a brilliant contribution to our understanding of the media by analyzing the western film in sociological terms.[50] Wright employs the concept of *myth,* which he argues is a structure of principles—good and evil, right and wrong, courage and cowardice, love and hate, and so on. It is also a narrative and a model for social action, a code of advice on how to deal with our everyday world.

Myths have deep roots in a people's psyche, but myths change when society changes. The early western, says Wright, "corresponded to the individualistic conception of society underlying a market economy" (the stage of capitalist development characterized by small economic units, local markets, a small public sector, and self-directed individualism). The hero (always male) is autonomous, strong, decent, and resourceful. Invariably an outsider, the hero protects, and often saves, weak society (symbolized by women and old men) against evil (symbolized by another strong, but self-oriented, male). Once his mission is accomplished, the hero is eligible for love and sex. He marries and becomes part of a community of equals.

It is clear in the early western that the actors embodied principles. The moral in the narrative clash of principles is also clearly established—the safety of society rests on skillful, courageous, decent individuals with clear senses of priorities, placing the well-being of the community above personal interest or gratification. The hero is a private individual (who does not emerge from within the community, however); there is little emphasis on government as a problem solver; and the need for collective empowerment is ignored. Above all, the classic western resolves the problem of how capitalism can exist *if all individuals are pursuing their self-interest.* The reader should note that what makes all this myth rather than science is that the hero always remains an unexplained force. A social analyst must ask, "If society is weak and most of the human race is declared unfit, where does the heroic individual come from?"

After World War II, continues Wright, the *professional* plot emerged as the dominant mythic pattern in the American western film. The western changed, says Wright, to reflect a change from a market economy to a "planned, corporate economy," the stage of capitalist development characterized by large economic units, national and international markets managed by large corporations and government, and educated, professionalized elites. Accordingly, the western hero becomes a professional, often a member of a group of professionals (to correspond to the fact that corporate structures are run by boards, committees, and partnerships). Heroes are now technicians, and their relations to society have changed drastically. They now work for money, decide on their own what is needed to solve problems, remain aloof from society during and after the job, and get paid for what they do (often regardless of whether they succeed or fail). Elite values do not harmonize with other values, and professionals do not join the community when their job is done. Invariably, the problem faced by the elite group is presented as a technical problem amenable to professional skills. Elites are no longer motivated by personal values, and their actions are no longer connected to social functions or to the creation or protection of community values. Though still weak, society is taken for granted, more or less a going concern that supplies elites with enough problems to keep them busy. There is no suggestion that evil arises from the basic principles of society (private property embedded in individual self-interest), as in the classical western. Problems are now part of the *eternal human condition.*

The western declined in popularity during the 1970s, and its place was taken by the detective, adventure, medical, law, and espionage story. Unlike the classic detective story, the contemporary detective or secret agent is often an outsider or maverick (whether in private or public life) who is forced to break the rules (as exemplified by the movies *Dirty Harry*[51] and *Death Wish*).[52] A major break with the past is that social goals are now ambiguous, contradictory, and ironic. Like the later stage of the western film, the hero is now more professional and is often a "group" (to correspond to the specialization characteristic of advanced capitalism and to the policy-making committee structure of modern bureaucracies). The professional hero is also attached to or supported by complex organizations (hospital, law firm, supersecret government agency), a theme that subtly asserts the authority of those who own or control the powerful groups of our society.

The overlap and even confusion between entertainment and journalism is nowhere more evident than in the most popular show in television history, *60 Minutes*—a western film disguised as journalism. Here reporter heroes uphold heartland values (especially individualism as total explanation) by telling adventure stories about good and bad individuals (morality plays) in a world without institutions, groups, or social power. Since the professional reporter, as hero, has explained all in terms of rotten or good apples, there is no call for institutional reform or collective action.[53] The elite professional group also has women in it, different skin colors, and different ages (which makes it appear that society is open to achievement by all). Like the professional in westerns, heroes, whether individuals or groups, are not always fully successful; they often fail at their missions; since elites, and the organizations they represent, are assumed to represent the best in human talent and effort, the status quo is affirmed even so. The shift to this perspective in popular culture could well reflect, and be an apology for, the growing inability of elites under corporate capitalism to solve society-wide problems or perform society-wide functions.

Conflict themes permeate the mass media, but in ways that do not threaten fundamental power relations. Problems are aired and solutions presented within the existing social order, in effect updating rather than changing it. The great romantic comedies of the 1930s and 1940s signaled the emergence of the capable, intelligent woman (largely among the upper classes). The rise of the middle-class career women has been portrayed in the *Mary Tyler Moore Show,* and women can now be superheroes *(Bionic Woman, Xena: Warrior Princess).* The feminist movement, essentially a broadening of opportunities for middle and upper-class women, is reflected in popular culture in many ways. Women have been given new motives, personalities, and statuses, often conforming to male values and usually according to their social class.[54] Including women as professionals is necessary for another reason besides satisfying liberal feminism. Contemporary male elites are depicted as self-sufficient; no longer, as noted, do male heroes return to the community when their work is done. Since elites are no longer organically connected to society, it would not do to have males appear to be homosexuals given America's prejudices. Actually, elites engage in sex and romance during adventures, not after as in earlier heroic tales, thus creating the impression that the here and now is where everything worthwhile takes place (a reversal, obviously, of the Protestant-bourgeois, early capitalist theme stressing gratification postponement for the sake of a better future).

The Nancy Drew stories also suggest a new status for women, but they also compromise it. Drawing on the Horatio Alger tradition but reflecting the new world of corporate America, the Nancy Drew stories (along with the Hardy Boys series by the same male author) stress success through intellectual-professional creativity rather than character. But Nancy remains feminine and attractive and is thus a superwoman.[55] Here again popular culture, increasingly working through professionalism, mediates a conflict rather than solves it.

SPORT: THE TRIUMPH OF CLASS, RACIAL, AND GENDER IDEOLOGY

Upholding and Updating the Class System

The world of sport is constituted by norms and values that reflect the American class system: giving your all in a win-lose competitive struggle, being a good loser and gracious winner, playing fair, submitting to personal discipline and hard work, affirming group discipline and obedience, and not giving up. These values are openly espoused and openly declared to be good for people and society.

Sport also reflects the rationalizing and professionalizing processes that characterize American capitalism. The educational system openly fosters elitist sports programs (varsity teams) while neglecting participation by all. The corruption of college sports is pervasive and has defied all reform efforts. Colleges and universities are essentially part of the "farm" systems of professional teams. Television provides many hours of sports, further helping to turn the United States into a nation of flabby spectators. Also, sports are full partners in American corruption and hypocrisy—from the pervasive corruption of college sports to creative bookkeeping by team owners and huge, and often hidden subsidies to owners by public bodies.

Sport has followed the contours of capitalist development. The professionalization of sport started in the nineteenth century along with the general growth of professionalism, developed slowly, and accelerated after 1950. During this period, the strong tradition of amateurism declined steadily and today is no more. Amateurism had a twofold connection to precorporate capitalism: agrarian elites stressed versatility and participation in high culture and sport as leisure activities, and they shunned activities based on earning income if they implied the need to work. Early capitalist elites, who emulated feudal elites far more than we care to acknowledge, also stressed amateurism in sports and versatile participation in high culture as ways to gain prestige and hide the way they earned their money. Amateurism was also related to the form that individualism took under early capitalism; democratic and egalitarian, early individualism stressed the all-around, versatile, nonspecialized personality.

The movement to corporate capitalism diversified America's concept of individualism by stressing the value of specialization and expertise. Understandably, sport also changed in keeping with the change from entrepreneurial to corporate capitalism. (For example, as Eitzen points out, baseball, emphasizing the versatile individual, was superseded by football, based on the specialized individual embedded in a tightly coordinated group—to be discussed further shortly.) Football was originally played without rules. The emergence of rules for football at the turn of the century (at the initiative of Yale University and Teddy Roosevelt) bespeaks the transformation of a Darwinian laissez-faire economy to the managed economy of corporate capitalism. Sport became a big business in its own right after World War II.

Sport is now hard work, conducted according to all the imperatives of the economic world: special training, discipline, scheduling, standardization, and technology. The hard work (rather than play) starts early with Little League, junior high, and high school.

Sport uniquely supports the status quo, any status quo, simply by virtue of the fact that it emphasizes abstract character traits and alleges that rewards reflect human nature in a world of innate scarcity. In this way, sport blends easily with different power structures.[56] American sports reflect American capitalism—they are competitive, aggressive, impersonal, methodical, specialized, professionalized, and profitable. Sports are designed to yield a small elite—as are the economy, the other professions, the polity, and education. Sports also reflect changes in American society: women and minorities are now more prominent in sport; sport has diversified to accommodate all age groups; and there is no longer one national pastime—baseball must now share the spotlight with football and basketball, and to a lesser extent with auto racing, hockey, tennis, and golf.[57] Sport depoliticizes by allowing all to participate in the reenactment of American values, as if they had no contradictions or bad consequences. It depoliticizes by being nationalistic.[58] Sport depoliticizes by creating the impression that society, like it, is based on equal opportunity, that it promotes mobility and has clear winners and losers in a fair, refereed contest.

Sport also depoliticizes by providing variations on basic American values. Individualism, for example, is a highly ambiguous value, the source of much social conflict. Sport mediates such conflict by providing successful examples of individualism in a wide variety of contexts by a wide variety of individuals. For example, America's two major sports, baseball and football, provide different versions of individualism. As Eitzen points out, baseball is a nineteenth-century sport (entrepreneurial capitalism)—egalitarian, unspecialized, and leisurely, not bound by rigid time schedules. In baseball, players come in all sizes and shapes, play both offense and defense, and are judged as a composite of abilities (the all-around versatile individual). Football (a distinctively American game) is a game more appropriate for twentieth-century corporate capitalism. Here individuals are incorporated into a highly specialized corporate (team) effort. A military-like discipline spells out what is required under any and all circumstances. Players not only play only on offense or defense, but some only place-kick, some only punt, some play only on kickoffs or third downs. Here is the specialized, nonpolitical worker who turns a bolt, treats only kidney diseases, or teaches Chaucer, microeconomics, American politics, or a course on the family.

Michael Real argues that the Super Bowl (which decides which football team is number one) has become the central mythic spectacle—it may have surpassed the World Series—of American capitalism. Here Americans collectively celebrate a game that is openly aggressive, violent, and male dominated; a game committed to seizing territory through force, guile, and technology (a way to legitimate imperialism?); a game that is profitable big business, with ties to the corporate world and the polity; a game that openly associates itself with patriotism and the American way of life.[59] Perhaps more important, however, is the way football, together with baseball, monopolize the meaning of individualism within a common, American-style capitalism.

Professional sport as a mass opiate should not obscure the similarities and mutual supports that exist between sport and the rest of the American political economy. Elitism in sport has yielded world-class athletes and a flabby, overweight population. The U.S. Supreme Court gave baseball an exemption from antitrust laws and Congress has given professional sports generous tax subsidies. Local governments heavily subsidize stadiums and arenas for professional sports.[60] Professionalism in sport has yielded monopoly profits for many owners,[61] high incomes for athletes, modest incomes for auxiliary personnel, and dead ends for the hundreds of thousands of youngsters who fail to make big-time sport teams. (The huge salaries of professional athletes come from television revenue, which in turn comes from advertisers and thus ultimately from consumers.)

Sports organizations, athletes, and television networks combine to sponsor public service announcements extolling the United Way (a charity) as a solution for unemployment, poverty, and disability. Professionalism in sport receives massive support from the voluntary groups who sponsor Little League teams, from high schools and colleges; from cities, states, and the federal government, which provide massive subsidies through outright grants and tax laws; and from newspapers and television stations, which celebrate professionalism as a way of life, and as a given. The similarities with professionalism in all other sectors of society are apparent, forming a seamless political economy that is as powerful as it is invisible. Perhaps the most insidious disservice of that political economy is to support the myth that talent in all areas of life is scarce, as all sectors funnel undeserved income and wealth upward.

Sport and the Endorsement of Racial, Gender, and Other Inequalities

African Americans are prominent in many professional sports (basketball, baseball, and football, but not hockey, tennis, golf, auto racing, or horse racing). African Americans succeed in sports that are accessible to them—that is, in terms of class position. In addition, success of African Americans in professional sports belies their lack of success in American society. Perhaps the most bitter irony is that the success of a tiny handful of African Americans on the playing field took place at the same time that the American economy was moving away from muscular labor toward cerebral labor (beginning in the 1950s). The civil rights movement and integration of sports allowed professional sports teams to expand dramatically in the South and Southwest from the 1960s on—but they also allowed northern and midwestern corporations to move to the cheap labor of the nonunionized South and Southwest. One result was to leave many African Americans high and dry in decaying, older, industrial urban centers.

On a concrete level, "stacking" (segregation of positions by race and ethnicity) is still prevalent in sports. In addition, African Americans have not been able to move into managerial positions in sports. Basketball has a better record than baseball or football in recruiting African Americans into coaching and front-office jobs, but progress in all areas stalled in 1991, though occasional success since should be noted.[62]

As for the positive gains made by women in the field of sport, progress in giving girls and women equal opportunities in lower and higher-education sports had been slow since Title IX of the Education Amendment Act of 1972 guaranteed gender equality for schools receiving federal aid. Almost three decades later, women were still suing to get colleges and universities to provide them with equal treatment in sports. Because of the economic constraints faced by schools and resistance by male sports directors and organizations (resulting in slow-motion enforcement by the Department of Education), schools dragged their feet in extending equality to women.[63]

In an important empirical study, Don Sabo explodes a number of myths about female participation in sports. Contrary to some of them, females are healthier both physically and psychologically if they participate in sports. Women do not become "macho" by playing sports but expand their feminine personalities.[64]

Providing equality for women in sports has two latent consequences. Female athletes may not become "macho," but women athletes and programs have succeeded by imitating, not merely masculine behavior but class values. The second latent consequence of women's success, not only in school sports but in the professional world has been to demonstrate in almost every sport their inferiority in performance to men (the one exception is horse racing, where female jockeys do as well as men).[65]

Despite golf tournaments for seniors and Special Olympics for the mentally retarded, both male and female sports have had the latent consequence of emphasizing youth and health as the bases of achievement, thus distracting attention from the fact that 15 to 20 percent of the population is handicapped, that we have an aging population with special needs, that large majorities of Americans get no exercise, and that America's governing class is made up of white males aged fifty and older who do not operate in a world of clear-cut rules and results.

But perhaps the best way to see sports as a reflection and reinforcement of all forms of inequality is to read Douglas E. Foley's "The Great American Football Ritual: Reproducing Race [Ethnicity], Class, and Gender Inequality."[66] Foley's study of a small Texas town (80 percent Mexican American), based on participant observation and interviews, revealed a powerful, all-pervasive socialization process in which male athletes and their boosters promoted a way of life dominated by economically powerful white males. One need know little more than that coaches ranked higher than academic teachers in the high school and that principals and superintendents were drawn from their ranks to understand sports as a legitimating practice and ideology for an illegitimate class system.

Perhaps the best way to deflate the use of sports-supported arguments for widespread innate inequality is to note that experts have demonstrated that almost all of the ability that we observe in sports can be acquired by almost anybody, through long years of systematic training and practice. Daniel Chambliss has convincingly demonstrated this in regard to Olympic swimmers, arguing against the concept of talent as cause.[67] According to other experts, it appears that the same holds true not only in other sports but for fields as dissimilar as mathematics, sculpture, research neurology, chess, and violin playing.[68]

THE CONCENTRATION OF
CULTURAL PRODUCTION

Popular culture—which can include publishing (trade books, magazines, newspapers), advertising, public relations (including many aspects of political campaigns), as well as entertainment, sport, and television news and special events—is an integral part of corporate capitalism. Generating and distributing popular culture require large amounts of capital, and like the rest of the economy, large-scale organizations. Not surprisingly, the popular culture industries are heavily concentrated, a concentration that was accelerated during the 1990s by the prospect of a fully integrated system of communication—the projection of meanings through sight, sound, and print through combined wire and wireless media, interconnected through complex switching devices, fed by huge computer storage systems, instantly translatable into any language, and combining both production and distribution to any individual or place on the planet by one command structure (for details, see chapter 4).

TECHNOCRATIC LIBERALISM: NONSTRUCTURAL PROBLEMS, NONSTRUCTURAL SOLUTIONS

It is hard not to conclude that the use of the means of communication to create and distribute popular culture, in all its forms, has helped divert Americans from the real causes of their problems throughout the twentieth century and into the twenty-first. In this sense, popular culture joined hands with Keynesianism, the New Deal, and other assorted Band-Aid treatments of symptoms. An unproblematic national identity was bolstered by the establishment in the 1920s of a "national" literature (the male-oriented classics in undergraduate literature courses)[69] and by a developing tradition of ethnocentrism and gunboat diplomacy. A rich fantasy world emerged in which superhuman heroes and unexplained human heroes saved the otherwise sound American community from supernatural and other forms of unexplained evil. Radio comedy distracted Americans and helped them cope with unemployment and poverty.[70] Tough-guy detectives appeared who used bad means to good ends. Best-selling novels depicted Asians as inferior, and American films were racist and propagandistic, as befitted the times and circumstances.[71] The western film falsified American history for mass audiences, much as the high-school history text was falsifying it for America's youth.[72] Interestingly, the science fiction–utopian tradition declined drastically in the twentieth century, reflecting perhaps complacency, perhaps despair about contemporary industrial society.[73]

In their study of television crime shows, the Lichters found that these shows depict business people and professionals as criminals far more frequently than individuals from the lower classes. The Lichters conclude that television's creators, with their anti-authority perspective, "seek to move the mass audience toward their own vision of the good society."[74] A different interpretation is possible. The Lichters imply that television is biased toward liberal reform, but regardless of what television's creators want, their anti-authority perspective is common to a wide variety of Americans, including conservatives, right-wing ideologies, populists, and democrats who want a decentralized democracy. Americans believe in the private individual, in voluntary behavior as a solution to problems, in vigilante heroes. This populist approach is profoundly antipolitical and antigovernment, even when it espouses the need for government to do something. Far from a political bias, what the Lichters have found is the pervasive American focus on evil and good individuals (human nature) and the protection of American society (elites and institutions) from scrutiny. What better way to protect the American class structure than to focus on evil *individual* business people and professionals while leaving the institutions of the capitalist economy out of the equation? What better way to depoliticize social problems than to depict law enforcement officials as inept and unimaginative?

Popular culture's distortion of the world of business is a disservice to Americans. The business world contains many positive values that need protection. It also has shortfalls that need to be explored in institutional terms. Realistic pictures of American capitalism are also missing in economics and in business schools. Popular culture joins them in deflecting attention away from the basic source of American social problems and from the power base of American elites.

Popular culture also supports the status quo by extolling family and religious values. It celebrates ordinary individuals in family situations, focusing on the little things in life. It celebrates spiritual values and resorts to supernatural explanations, thereby deflecting attention from social power. Television programs invariably use a "family" format—a small primary group readily recognizable by the audience and to which it can relate. Whether on television or the *Reader's Digest,* popular culture's stress on family-personal values and the little things in life appeals to both sexes and all ages.

Popular culture joins in America's commitment to violence as a problem solver. Redemptive violence is found not merely in our celebration of war, the federal cavalry, the adept gunfighter, and the vigilante. Redemptive violence is inherent in competition in business (including violence against workers, through downsizing), in the relation between genders, in sports, and in the private and public treatment of minorities. Americans commit violence against nature, and we use the metaphors of violence in our approach to immorality, social problems, and disease (we conduct war on them).

Since the Great Depression, popular culture has followed other contours of the larger culture. It now gives a more prominent role to professionals, thereby supporting the new power structure of corporate capitalism. It forestalls real solutions by offering a wide variety of entertainment in which social problems are classless (for example, the upper classes have problems like everybody else) and solvable within the confines of existing institutions. Popular culture also reflected the changing position of women; the romantic comedies of the 1930s and 1940s had strong, intelligent heroines, and women today are often depicted as achievers (remember, though, that American culture dominates by being ad hoc, contradictory, and shapeless— thus women are also, and mostly, depicted along traditional sexist lines). Racial and ethnic minorities were depicted in a better light after World War II, especially as the export market for American popular culture grew.

The ever tighter grip on popular culture by the corporate economy and its ever greater (mostly unintended) use for political purposes are perhaps the best ways to see the similarities between all elements of American culture. Popular culture and the state join to develop a long list of family-centered (ostensibly religious) national holidays. Popular culture forms the stuff of up to one-third of our conversational material. By entering into everyday life, popular culture facilitates secondary interaction and renews primary attachments. As such, it both promotes and constitutes group solidarity and group integration.[75] Film, music, television, best sellers, and sports are big business, and its products are manufactured much as if they were shoes, steel, or soap.

Popular culture has become an important dimension of our political life. Movies, television entertainment, and news people all propound a deeply populist, anti-authority, individualistic (often vigilante) ideology that keeps the American people off balance and unable to use politics or government to promote their interests. The mass media also make possible a new phenomenon—politics and government by cliche. Thanks to television and the computer, political campaigns are now exercises in the manipulation of consensus-oriented formalisms. Mass-media celebrities not only endorse candidates but run for office and get elected; perhaps nothing better illustrates the false reality and limited choices in American life than this confusion among mass electorates between public leaders and celebrities. In 1980, the United States elected a cardboard president whom it recruited from popular culture to match the other cardboard figures in popular culture. Popular culture, in short, is part of the control structure of society. It helps to dominate people—it creates its stories out of liberal norms and values and helps push the basic presuppositions of capitalism beneath the level of consciousness. It helps in social control in that it evokes and reinforces the emotions that tie people to the status quo. It supports existing power structures by affirming and updating the popular beliefs that prevent people from holding institutions and elites responsible.

Popular culture is neither unitary nor homogeneous. Much of it is ad hoc and contradictory, because that is the sort of world its creators and audiences live in. Much of its power to control, therefore, lies in its shapelessness. Above all, it contributes to social control by translating social conflicts into personal problems, by providing a variety of fantasy identities, and by depicting fictional others who are experiencing all manner of hardship in nonpolitical settings, thus allowing for a safe discharge of socially induced anxiety, insecurity, and resentment.

Popular culture provides some choice and promotes some awareness, but its main thrust is to conserve a taken-for-granted world. Along with the rest of culture, it actually helps to create that world, including its false realities—for example, that there is more pluralism than there really is; that problem behavior is eternal, because its source is an unchanging human nature; that there is no social conflict (among social groups and institutions); and that social institutions and the elites they generate are not the causes of social problems.

Popular culture supports the same abstract, apolitical concept of culture that dominates the mainstream professions and disciplines. The politicization of all culture is long overdue. Culture is created by humans, especially powerful individuals and groups. It defines and defends a particular way of solving existential problems. Culture explains human behavior and makes human society possible. Culture also causes social problems (often the result of solutions imposed by elites). Culture expresses common interests, but also favors elite interests largely by putting the causes of social problems beyond society. Culture also prevents the members of society, including elites, from understanding any of this. Culture is always hegemonic even if it is not totally integrated; there is no better example of the power of culture to protect the status quo than its declared war on depoliticized problems.

Popular culture is part of the corporate economy; it is big business in its own right. It overlaps and blends with religion and political life. Its penetration of everyday life is pervasive and thus invisible. It helps to socialize each generation and reinforces acquired sentiments and beliefs throughout the life cycle. It caters to and blends with the American population by social class, sex, ethnicity, age, and race. It contributes to social control by mediating social tensions and bridging social discontinuities. It forestalls social explanations of conflict and problem behavior, and it prevents solutions through political action by depoliticizing the problems, largely through a ritual enactment of American myths.

NOTES

1. For example, William A. Gamson, David Croteau, William Hoynes, and Theodore Sasson, "Media Images and the Social Construction of Reality," *Annual Review of Sociology* 18 (1992): 373–93.

2. This double theme is expressed in the introduction and chapter 1 of Tony Bennett, Colin Mercer, and Janet Woollacott, eds., *Popular Culture and Social Relations* (Milton Keynes, Eng.: Open University Press, 1986), and is mentioned frequently in the essays that follow. But the main thrust of the essays is to show how British elites have dominated through popular culture and to offer little evidence of popular resistance. The one good example of popular resistance is provided by Stuart Hall's "Popular Culture and the State" (chap. 2), in which he discusses law, the press, and radio-television, all in relation to the state and economy (and of these the only area in which the masses have been able to assert some resistance and make some gains is law). Needless to say, it is stretching definitions to say that law is part of popular culture.

3. In her highly useful, empirically oriented study, Linda Holtzman, *Media Messages: What Film, Television, and Popular Music Teach Us about Race, Class, Gender, and Sexual Orientation* (Armonk, N.Y.: Sharpe, 2000), shows that critical music, while controversial, forms a very small percentage of popular music (see pp. 141–46).

4. Richard Wohl, "The 'Rags to Riches Story': An Episode of Secular Idealism," in *Class, Status, and Power*, ed. Reinhard Bendix and S. M. Lipset (New York: Free Press, 1953).

5. For this image in the literature of the political Right (the shrinking old middle class of individual producers), see Jack W. Sattel, "Heroes on the Right," *Journal of Popular Culture* 11 (Summer 1977): 110–25.

6. B. Lee Cooper, "The Image of the Outsider in Contemporary Lyrics," *Journal of Popular Culture* 12 (Summer 1978): 168–78.

7. Gary Hopenstand, "Pulp Vigilante Heroes, the Moral Majority and the Apocalypse," in *The Hero in Transition*, ed. Ray B. Browne and Marshall W. Fishwick (Bowling Green, Ohio: Bowling Green University Popular Press, 1983), 185–95.

8. For the latter, see Elizabeth S. Bell, "The Cultural Roots of Our Current Infatuation with Television's Befuddled Hero," in *The Hero in Transition*, ed. Browne and Fishwick, 188–95.

9. For an interpretation of *Roseanne* as a rare example of working-class life, along with a

review of the literature on class and prime time television, see Holtzman, *Media Messages,* 119–30.

10. Robert Jewett and John Shelton Lawrence, "Playboy's Gospel: Better Wings than Horns," in *The American Monomyth,* 2d ed. (Lanham, Md.: University Press of America, 1988), chap. 4.

11. *The Hearts of Men: American Dreams and the Flight from Commitment* (Garden City, N.Y.: Doubleday, 1983).

12. Gail Dines, "'I Buy It for the Articles': *Playboy* Magazine and the Sexualization of Consumerism," in *Gender, Race, and Class in Media: A Text-Reader,* ed. Gail Dines and Jean M. Humez (Thousand Oaks, Calif.: Sage, 1995), 254–62.

13. For a good introduction to the adventure story, see Gina Marchetti, "Action-Adventure as Ideology," in *Cultural Politics in Contemporary America,* ed. Ian Angus and Sut Jhally (New York: Routledge, 1989), 182–97.

14. For a review and analysis of the literature, see Holtzman, *Media Messages,* 131–40.

15. Holtzman, *Media Messages,* 140–46.

16. For an interpretive study that identifies various levels of "culture" in America and their relations to class, see Herbert J. Gans, *Popular Culture and High Culture: An Analysis and Evaluation of Taste* (New York: Basic Books, 1974). For dominance by the upper classes in the consumption of high art, see Paul DiMaggio and Michael Useem, "Cultural Democracy in a Period of Cultural Expansion: The Social Composition of Arts Audiences in the United States," *Social Problems* 26 (December 1978): 179–97.

17. Edward Arian, *Bach, Beethoven, and Bureaucracy: The Case of the Philadelphia Orchestra* (University: University of Alabama Press, 1971).

18. Leo Bogart, "The Mass Media and the Blue-Collar Worker," in *Blue-Collar World: Studies of the American Worker,* ed. Arthur B, Shostak and William Gomberg (Englewood Cliffs, N.J.: Prentice Hall, 1964), 416–28.

19. Gans, *Popular Culture and High Culture.*

20. New York: Oxford University Press, 1995.

21. Oscar H. Gandy Jr., "Tracking the Audience," in *Questioning the Media: A Critical Introduction,* 2d ed., ed. John Downing, Ali Mohammadi, and Annabelle Sreberny-Mohammadi (Thousand Oaks, Calif.: Sage, 1995), 221–37.

22. Ien Ang, "The Nature of the Audience," in *Questioning the Media,* ed. Downing, Mohammadi, and Sreberny-Mohammadi, 207–20.

23. Tamar Liebes, *The Export of Meaning: Cross-Cultural Readings of "Dallas"* (New York: Oxford University Press, 1990).

24. John Downing, "Alternative Media and the Boston Tea Party," in *Questioning the Media,* ed. Downing, Mohammadi, and Sreberny-Mohammadi, 238–54.

25. Sari Thomas, "Myths in and about Television," in *Questioning the Media,* ed. Downing, Mohammadi, and Sreberny-Mohammadi, 330–44.

26. The following relies on the superb summary of research on minorities and the media by Bradley S. Greenberg and Jeffrey E. Brand, "Minorities and the Mass Media: 1970s to 1990s," in *Media Effects: Advances in Theory and Research,* ed. Jennings Bryant and Dolf Zillmann (Hillsdale, N.J.: Lawrence Erlbaum Associates, 1994), 273–314.

27. African-American characters on programs that achieve, especially soap operas, are thoroughly assimilated into white society.

28. Bradley S. Greenberg and Jeffrey E. Brand, "Minorities and the Mass Media: 1970s to 1990s," in *Media Effects,* ed. Bryant and Zillmann, 289.

29. For an extended discussion of the depiction and participation of African Americans,

American Indians, Asian Americans, and Latinos in popular culture, see Holtzman, *Media Messages*, chap. 5.

30. For a fuller discussion of gender in popular culture, see Holtzman, *Media Messages*, 73–95.

31. The following is a composite interpretation of Deborah D. Rogers, "Daze of Our Lives: The Soap Opera as Feminist Text"; Karen Lindsey, "Reading Race, Sexuality, and Class in Soap Operas"; John Fiske, "Gendered Television: Femininity"; and Tania Modleski, "The Search for Tomorrow in Today's Soap Operas," all in *Gender, Race, and Class*, ed. Dines and Humez, 325–54.

32. Mary S. Mander, "Dallas: The Mythology of Crime and the Moral Occult," *Journal of Popular Culture* 17 (Fall 1983): 44–50.

33. *New York Times,* June 21, 1999, A1.

34. Marilyn M. Lowery, "The Traditional Romance Formula," in *Gender, Race, and Class*, ed. Dines and Humez, 215–22.

35. Richard Pollack, "What's in a Pseudonym: Romance Slaves of *Harlequin,*" in *Gender, Race, and Class*, ed. Dines and Humez, 223–27.

36. Janice A. Radway, *Reading the Romance* (Chapel Hill: University of North Carolina Press, 1984). The 1991 reprint has a new introduction.

37. Timothy Egan, "Technology Sent Wall Street into Market for Pornography," *New York Times,* October 23, 2000, A1.

38. For a summary of research, see Richard Jackson Harris, "The Impact of Sexually Explicit Media," in *Media Effects,* ed Bryant and Zillmann, 247–72.

39. Gayle Rubin, "Misguided, Dangerous, and Wrong: An Analysis of Anti-Pornography Politics," in *Gender, Race, and Class,* ed. Dines and Humez, chap. 28. For a counterargument by Andrea Devorkin, a leading antipornography feminist, see "Pornography and Male Supremacy" in the same collection, selection 27.

40. For the widespread use of the physically different to portray evil in popular (and elite) culture, see Bert Needelman and Norman L. Weiner, "Heroes and Villains in Art," *Society* 14 (November/December 1976): 35–39.

41. For a summary of research on the media and the disabled, see Bradley S. Greenberg and Jeffrey E. Brand, "Minorities and the Mass Media: 1970s to 1990s," in *Media Effects,* ed. Bryant and Zillmann, 273–314.

42. For the lack of quantitative analysis of sexual orientation, see Greenberg and Brand, "Minorities and the Mass Media," 302. For a discussion of advertising and lesbianism, see Danae Clark, "Commodity Lesbianism," in *Gender, Race, and Class,* ed. Dines and Humez, selection 19. For an insightful history of the depiction of homosexuality in film arguing that the more open attitude toward sexual difference is not really an improvement because it does not take gays and lesbians seriously, see Vito Russo, *The Celluloid Closet: Homosexuality in the Movies,* rev. ed. (New York: Harper and Row, 1987).

43. Robert Jewett and John Shelton Lawrence, "The Birth of a National Monomyth," *The American Monomyth,* chap. 9.

44. Peter J. Claus, "A Structuralist Appreciation of 'Star Trek,' " in *The American Dimension: Cultural Myths and Social Realities,* ed. W. Arens and Susan P. Montague (Port Washington, N.Y.: Alfred, 1976), 15–32, and Robert Jewett and John S. Lawrence, " 'Star Trek' and the Bubble-Gum Fallacy," in *The American Monomyth,* chap. 1; Roger L. Hofeldt, "Cultural Bias in M*A*S*H," *Society* 15 (July/August 1978): 96–99, and Peter Homans, "Psychology and Popular Culture: Psychological Reflections on M*A*S*H," *Journal of Popular Culture* 17 (Winter 1983).

45. Peter Rickman, "Quixote Rides Again: The Popularity of the Thriller," in *The Hero in Transition,* ed. Browne and Fishwick, 219–28.

46. Charles Simpson, "Shadows of Anxiety: Popular Culture in Modern Society," in *Art and Society,* ed. A. W. Foster and J. R. Blau (Albany: State University of New York Press, 1989), chap 3.

47. Michael A. Genovese, *Politics and the Cinema: An Introduction to Political Films* (Needham Heights, Mass.: Ginn, 1986).

48. Harry Keyisian, "Heroes in American Political Film," in *The Hero in Transition,* ed. Browne and Fishwick, 219–28.

49. Robert Thompson, "American Politics on Film," *Journal of Popular Culture* 20, no. 1 (Summer 1986): 27–47.

50. Will Wright, *Six Guns and Society: A Structural Analysis of the Western* (Berkeley, Calif.: University of California Press, 1975).

51. Carl B. Klockars, "The Dirty Harry Problem," *The Annals of the American Academy* 252 (1980): 33–34; reprinted in *Sociology: Contemporary Readings,* ed. John Stimson and Ardyth Stimson (Itasca, Ill.: Peacock, 1983), 167–76.

52. Robert Jewett and John Shelton Lawrence, "The Golden Way to Violence in 'Death Wish,'" in *The American Monomyth,* chap. 3.

53. For a rich descriptive analysis that bends over backward not to be too critical, see Richard Campbell, *"60 Minutes" and the News: Mythology for Middle America* (Urbana: University of Illinois Press, 1991).

54. By 1980, popular music had begun to drop the traditional sex-role standards that had prevailed in the 1960s and 1970s. See Kathleen L. Endres, "Sex Role Standards in Popular Music," *Journal of Popular Culture* 18 (Summer 1984): 9–18. (In addition, women rock stars, like Madonna, have assumed the aggressive, sexual, calculating, money-hungry swagger that had long been characteristic of male rock stars.) For other changes in the depiction of women, see Cornelia Butler Flora, "Changes in Women's Status in Women's Magazine Fiction: Differences by Social Class," *Social Problems* 26 (June 1979): 558–69, and Victor Gecas, "Motives and Aggressive Acts in Popular Fiction: Sex and Class Differences," *American Journal of Sociology* 77 (January 1972): 680–96.

55. Susan P. Montague, "How Nancy Gets Her Man: An Investigation of Success Models in American Adolescent Pulp Literature," in *The American Dimension,* ed. Arens and Montague, 99–116. For a study showing that college women have accepted the conservative image of superwoman, see Laura D. Cummings, "Value Stretch in Definitions of Career among College Women: Horatia Alger as Feminist Model," *Social Problems* 25 (October 1977): 65–74.

56. Fascist and communist dictatorships, past and present, have fully recognized the political value of sport.

57. For a good introduction to the sociology of sport, see D. Stanley Eitzen, ed., *Sport in Contemporary Society: An Anthology,* 4th ed. (New York: St. Martin's, 1993).

58. Individuals and teams from various countries now play on a year-round basis in almost all sports. The Olympic Games are especially nationalistic. The staged wrestling matches that are so popular on television also have a blatant xenophobic flavor.

59. Michael R. Real, "The Super Bowl: Mythic Spectacle," in M. R. Real, *Mass-Mediated Culture* (Englewood Cliffs, N.J.: Prentice Hall, 1977), chap. 6.

60. James Quirk and Rodney D. Fort, *Pay Dirt: The Business of Professional Team Sports* (Princeton, N.J.: Princeton University Press, 1992), chaps. 3, 4.

61. The average total return (profit) of baseball, football, basketball, and hockey owners

in the early 1990s was 27 percent, with half of the owners realizing above 30 percent. This is well above the return of the five hundred largest industrial corporations and can be considered a monopoly rate of profit; for the data see Gerald W. Scully, *The Market Structure of Sports* (Chicago: University of Chicago Press, 1995), chap. 6.

62. Richard E. Lapchick with David Stuckney, "Professional Sports: The Racial Report Card," in *Sport in Contemporary Society,* ed. Eitzen, 355–71.

63. For a history of how male athletic directors and organizations took over women's sports, including a marked reduction in women coaches and athletic directors, even as the number of female athletes swelled, see Linda Jean Carpenter and R. Vivian Costa, "Back to the Future: Reform with a Woman's Voice," in *Sport in Contemporary Society,* ed. Eitzen, 388–95.

64. Don Sabo, "Psychosocial Impacts of Athletic Participation on American Women: Facts and Fables," in *Sport in Contemporary Society,* ed. Eitzen, 374–87.

65. Margaret A. Ray and Paul W. Grimes, "Jockeying for Position: Winnings and Gender Discrimination on the Thoroughbred Track," *Social Science Quarterly* 74, no. 1 (March 1993): 46–61.

66. Eitzen, ed., *Sport in Contemporary Society,* 326–54.

67. Daniel F. Chambliss, "The Mundanity of Excellence: An Ethnographic Report on Stratification and Olympic Swimmers," *Sociological Theory* 7, no. 1 (Spring 1989): 70–86.

68. For a review of research in these areas, see Maya Pines, "What Produces Great Skills?" *New York Times,* March 30, 1982, C1, and Daniel Goleman, "Peak Performance: Why Records Fall," *New York Times,* October 11, 1994, C1.

69. Paul Lauter, "Race and Gender in the Shaping of the American Literary Canon: A Case Study from the Twenties," *Feminist Studies* 9 (Fall 1983): 435–63.

70. Arthur Frank Wetheim, "Relieving Social Tensions: Radio Comedy and the Great Depression," *Journal of Popular Culture* 10 (Winter 1976): 501–19.

71. Tom Engelhardt, "Ambush at Kamikaze Pass," *Bulletin of Concerned Asian Scholars* 3 (Winter–Spring 1971): 522–31; Daniel B. Ransdell, "Asia Askew: U.S. Best-Sellers on Asia, 1931–1980," *Bulletin of Concerned Asian Scholars* 3 (October–December 1983): 2–25; and Jay Weinstein, "Fu Manchu and the Third World," *Society* 21 (January/February 1984): 77–82. For a classic argument, first published in 1971, that Disney comics are an imperialist influence, see Ariel Dorfman and Armand Mattelart, *How to Read Donald Duck: Imperialist Ideology in the Disney Comic,* trans. and intro. David Kunzle (New York: International General, 1975). For an update on the extensive literature on the right-wing agenda in Disney films and a critique of recent Disney films (even as the heads of Disney Studios openly support the Democratic Party), see Eleanor Byrne and Martin McQuillan, *Deconstructing Disney* (Sterling, Va.: Pluto, 1999).

72. Paul Gagnon. "Why Study History," *The Atlantic Monthly* 263 (November 1988): 43–66; James W. Loewen, *Lies My Teacher Told Me: Everything Your American High School History Text Got Wrong* (New York: Touchstone, 1995). For a fuller discussion of the failure of high school history texts and the school itself to promote a democratic citizenry, see "Teachers and Professors," in chapter 9.

73. Donald McQuarie, "Utopia and Transcendence: An Analysis of Their Decline in Contemporary Science Fiction," *Journal of Popular Culture* 14 (Fall 1980), 242–50. By and large, science fiction, such as *Star Trek, Star Wars,* and *E.T.,* reaffirms the existing social order.

74. Linda S. Lichter and S. Robert Lichter, *Prime Time Crime* (Washington, D.C.: The

Media Institute, 1983); Linda S. Lichter and Robert Lichter, "Prime Time Crime: Who and Why," *Wall Street Journal,* January 6, 1994, 20.

75. Irving Lewis Allen, "Talking about Media Experiences: Everyday Life as Popular Culture," *Journal of Popular Culture* (Winter 1982): 106–15. As Allen reminds us, mass media material can also disrupt and disintegrate social relations.

9

Communication and Media Problems: The Need to Ask Foundational Questions

AWARENESS AND CONCERN ABOUT COMMUNICATION TECHNOLOGY

From roughly 1840 to 1940, Americans experienced an onrush of wondrous communication-transportation devices: the telegraph, railroad, camera, cheap daily newspapers, magazines, catalogs, postal service, transoceanic cable, telephone, transatlantic steamship, radio, automobile, airplane, and film (television and the computer emerged in the 1920s, but their social impact occurred after 1950). Communication technology itself helped to advertise and make the devices familiar—for example, through depiction in motion pictures. The new communication devices were also used for political purposes. The owners of newspapers used them to pursue overt political goals. President Roosevelt used the radio to soothe the depression-sore American public during the 1930s, and Adolf Hitler's Nazi regime employed the radio to blame imaginary enemies for the economic troubles of the German people.

Awareness about communication technology turned into concern and eventually into social-science research. The new research that emerged was funded by government (spurred by a concern over enemy propaganda) as well as by corporations eager to understand the ways in which the new communication technology could be used for commercial purposes.

The beginnings of empirical research on communication date to the heyday of radio. Researchers wanted to determine the impact of radio on American citizens. It was thought that the one-way communication process of radio to listener could dominate public opinion. The initial empirical finding was that audiences were influenced by ordinary group life more than by the mass media. The classic work that helped establish the relative power (or limited effects) of mass communication was the Lazarsfeld-Berelson-Gaudet field study of voters during the 1940 presidential election.[1] Through repeated interviewing of the same six hundred people in a county that had followed national voting trends throughout the twentieth century, the study found "personal influences" more influential than newspapers, magazines, or radio. Actually, the study found a "two-step flow" of communication, from print and radio to "opinion leaders" and from the latter to others. The authors' naïve concluding paragraph is:

> In the last analysis, more than anything else people can move other people. From an ethical point of view this is a hopeful aspect in the serious problem of propaganda. The side which has the more enthusiastic supporters and which can mobilize grass-root support in an expert way has great chances of success.

Limited versus Large Effects

The emergence of television in the 1950s and 1960s produced another major research thrust. The major finding of this research was that audiences interact with mass-media messages, thus yielding another version of the limited-effect perspective. It also connected media research with the symbolic interaction tradition in sociology stemming from Charles Horton Cooley and George Herbert Mead, thus keeping the discussion of media within the dominant liberal paradigm.

The debate between limited and large effects also took place outside scientific circles as public figures debated communication issues relating to government regulation, violence, sex, racism, crime, privacy, and political influence. That debate continues to the present, with issues relating to gender, pornography, and homosexuality added in recent decades. The surge of computerization since the 1970s has generated the same, plus new concerns (see below). All in all, awareness and concern about the uses of communication technology have produced a politics of single issues, a politics profoundly conservative no matter what side is taken, because it assumes that solutions can occur within the existing structure of social power. In this final chapter we will continue to distinguish mainstream thinkers from those who regard the foundations of society as the problem.

Communication Science: The Triumph of Professionalism

By the 1980s the booming field of mainstream media research had a solid base in the mainstream communication programs of American higher education. Communication research defined itself as a pure science, thus aping developments in the other academic disciplines and professions. It has many achievements, especially in specialized fields, and it has mounted significant criticisms of particular aspects of communication. On the whole, however, the main thrust of discussions of communications, not only in higher education but in politics, journalism, think tanks, and foundations, continues to focus on narrowly defined issues and is complacent about the role of communication in the structure of power. A few scholars, both liberal and radical, however, have gone to the heart of the issue and have clearly shown that the media are profoundly undemocratic (see "The Failure to Promote Democratic Politics and Citizenship," chapter 7). In this chapter we want to cover the spectrum of communication problems, putting them in the context of social power, and to prompt the reader to ask foundational questions.

Curiosity and research into topics or problems do not ordinarily lead Americans to social power, either in public discourse or academe. Communication is assumed to be amenable to technical analysis by communication science; it is considered to be an autonomous problem within the confines of American society, solvable by political science, journalism, and so on. As is true of other subject matter, communication is characteristically defined in abstraction from social power. In an interesting variation of this ahistorical perspective, Peters traces the history of the idea of communication, providing many fascinating examples of how philosophers, religious leaders, social and political theorists, literary figures, social scientists, and communication experts have thought about communication.[2] Peters provides a useful classification of these diverse figures by distinguishing between those who want communication to culminate in a full bonding between people and thinkers who take a more practical view. His own view is neither of these, though he takes particular care to reject the idea that communication can or should lead to communion among people. Indeed, his main thesis is that we should delight in our hardwired eccentricity, in our diversity, in our communication failures, and in the fact that our communication technologies produce as much miscommunication as understanding.

Somewhat overwritten, and thus not itself the best example of successful communication, Peters's work stays at the level of analyzing what various people in history have said. He notes that communication became an explicit problem in the 1880s and 1890s, and that the 1920s and 1940s exhibited creative surges in ideas about communication. But this information does not lead him or us to a useful sociology of communication, namely, *that the relations among human beings were massively changed,* by industrialization and other social phenomena, such as total war. Had the social nature of communication problems been identified in this period, Peters might have been led to conduct a social analysis of past thinking about communication. At some point, Peters might have realized that most talk about communication has been ideological, messages that divert attention form social power. He might have seen his own view—that we are unique selves, forever unable to connect fully with others—as a secular version of original sin, as merely another version of the mistaken but stubborn idea that there exists a human nature independent of history and society. In fairness, even as Peters stresses the eccentricity of the self and the ambiguities of language, he rightly points out that these do not prevent significant cooperation among humans. He is also at pains to point out that part of his objection to the goal of a full communion of souls is that it works against a healthy politics.

This book has tried to avoid the ahistorical, asocial thrust toward communication problems that have characterized both scientific and humanistic communication theories. Instead, it has assumed that *communication failures and successes are intimately connected to the division of labor and social institutions in general.* It is American society that divorces the symbolic world from social reality. More pointedly, communication studies, including Peters's analysis of the history of the idea of communication, take their place alongside our plutocratic politics, liberalism, the professions, and the professionalized social sciences as obstructions to our understanding of not only the relation between communication and society but American capitalism in particular.

COMMUNICATION IN PRIMARY GROUPS

The 1950s and 1960s saw considerable research into primary or small personal groups outside the family. Since then, research interests have moved into adjacent areas to explore communication issues in family life, conversation, gossip and rumor, graffiti, and neighborhood networks, as well as the special vocabularies and ways of communicating of particular groups (blacks, jazz musicians, teenagers, etc.).

Much of this research was typically American and in line with American liberalism, namely, a search for the sources of behavior in human beings as human beings. In addition, *qua* academic studies, they rarely connected these areas to the structure of power. For example, George Homans, Erving Goffman, and Harold Garfinkel in sociology explored the ways in which individuals as individuals interacted (communicated). There was little sociology in their work, but their influence on sociology was substantial. Their approach was essentially a dead end, a use of psychology (human nature) to explain behavior.

The world of communication in primary groups is more clearly revealed by focusing on people in various kinds of trouble. In a fascinating series of case studies, communication specialists have identified the plight of a wide variety of Americans who are cut off from effective ways of reaching help and who must simply cope with and endure their troubles.[3] For each of the following kinds of troubles, the authors show how individuals in various social statuses are disenfranchised and marginalized by biased and incomplete communication with others:

Gays and lesbians during an antigay referendum
The homeless
HIV patients in an inner-city clinic
Poor, ignorant women dealing with the possibility of breast cancer
Infertility
Adolescent cancer
Contested divorces

Caring for an elderly parent
Rape victims
Incest victims
Wife abuse
Sexual harassment
Losing a gay partner to cancer
Living with HIV and AIDS
Women with HIV and AIDS
Families coping with the death of the mother
Alcoholism at work
Working and living with disabilities.

These illuminating case studies give us vivid pictures of how people experience a wide variety of troubles. Though not their primary purpose, they also provide advice for those, like doctors and mediators, who communicate with the troubled. But while valuable, these case studies come perilously close to "blaming the victim" or asking that we (the abstract reader) empathize better with the less fortunate. What America needs, however, is to stamp out discrimination, homelessness, rape, incest, and sexual harassment. It needs to provide comprehensive, competent health care, to eliminate the many socially created causes of disabilities, and to shore up marriages and families; in short, it needs social restructuring, not better coping mechanisms.

COMMUNICATION IN SECONDARY GROUPS

Communication inside American secondary groups is hierarchical; messages come primarily from the top down. This pattern prevails in corporations, government, the military, schools (including higher education),[4] hospitals, and voluntary groups, including churches. The absence of two-way, pluralistic communication has many negative consequences—especially the reduction of trust (see "The Electronic Sweatshop," in chapter 4). It also leads to poorer policy making (for example, groupthink during the Cuban missile crisis) and to lower productivity through wasteful competition, excessive supervision, and lack of worker input (see below, "Managers"). Corporate America has yet to learn that workers who are kept informed and are in a cooperative structure of power (and who enjoy full collective bargaining rights) are more productive.[5] In the absence of these arrangements, workers generate influential sets of informal relations that often run counter to organizational blueprints. Management devices to control workers and to prevent unions from forming also prevent effective two-way communication and retard productive work.

Management and governing boards communicate easily with each other and with other organizations. They have similar class and educational backgrounds, belong to similar voluntary groups, clubs, churches, and professional-trade associations. There is a significant overlapping of membership on boards of directors of corporations and between corporate boards and the top levels of voluntary groups. The upper echelons of business and voluntary groups provide the overwhelming bulk of the personnel in high government posts. The growing privatization of knowledge and of knowledge production (even knowledge produced by taxpayer money) also means that corporate America is slowly gaining a monopoly on knowledge generation. Corporations specialize in producing research for other corporations; some do their own research; others commission research through universities or think tanks. Publishing and journalism are now parts of giant corporations. Public-policy groups, think tanks, and foundations, while often reform minded, tend to take the viability of the United States for granted. Corporate America is the main beneficiary of government research.

COMMUNICATION AND GENDER

Gender, Personality, and Communication Styles

Male, female, masculine, and *feminine* are sociocultural phenomena; thus the analysis of gender communication must focus on communication by occupants of socially created statuses. Communication between males and females is a very large area; we need to delimit our topic. Research has established, popular beliefs notwithstanding, that men and women are not as different as is supposed in their perception, listening, or empathy, though often their similar characteristics have different causes.[6] Significant differences do appear elsewhere—the socialization process generates a more limited self-image for women and lower self-esteem.[7]

Men and women also verbalize differently. Men are more direct and aggressive and seek dominance in conversation; women tend to use words and expressions that are more polite and less direct, and to take more responsibility for keeping a conversation going. These differences result from sex-role differentiation; we are especially prone to using vocabularies and ways of expressing ourselves that are derived from the types of work we do. Here, again, similar behaviors are often perceived differently.

Women and men use language that conforms to socially prescribed statuses. Men are instrumental, goal oriented, assertive, and so on, while women are caring, nurturing, and affiliative. But here we are really talking about role requirements, or rather, superior-inferior, autonomous-supportive social relations.[8]

Men and women also differ in their use of nonverbal communication: their definition of interpersonal and other spaces, eye contact, facial expressions, gestures, posture, bearing, touching, voice quality, control of conversation, and objects, especially clothing. Women are better at decoding nonverbal communication. Male nonverbal communication expresses autonomy and power, and the opposite is true for women; both conform to traditional social expectations. The fact that women are better at decoding nonverbal communication is a result of the need for social inferiors to pay more attention to relations of power.[9]

Gender also channels self-disclosure; men tend to disclose less about themselves than women. Gender also controls self-assertion in communication; men tend to be more assertive than women (and are more likely to be aggressive—that is, to prevent others from communicating). Though there are many variations on the above, the differences correspond to the basic personality types required of men and women in American society. Men are socialized to be economic, political, and military achievers, and to be goal oriented and competitive, all of which requires an assertive, open, direct communication style (but inhibited emotional attachments through self-disclosure).[10]

In analyzing gender communication, one must be careful to depict gender relations as power relations. Too often it is implied that gender differences are natural; too often commentators ask the sexes to be more empathetic and accommodating, thereby obscuring the power processes that produce the differences and the communication interactions that help maintain them. Without deeper alterations in the socialization process and the division of labor, mere changes in conversational style will only maintain the status quo.

Gender and Power (Institutional) Relations

Gender differences (and similarities) emerge from institutional settings. Males and females are socialized (family, play, mass media, education) to fulfill different roles for society. These personalities are reflected in the economy and in law, government, and politics.

Class background affects how one is socialized, and so does minority status, regardless of gender. Social change in the last century or so has changed many traditional roles and thrown others into disarray. In noting this change, one must be careful to focus on the personalities and the roles that the American power structure has deemed necessary in the age of world-market, corporate capitalism. Also, it must not necessarily be assumed that one can simply mix and adjust existing norms, values, and statuses. There is considerable evidence, for example, that a central capitalist value and belief, competition, has many negative consequences and few, if any, positive consequences for society.[11]

The core American value of competition is found everywhere. The institutional structures of America reflect masculine communication styles. Feminists have been critical of family life on this ground, just as they have criticized interaction styles in workplaces, classrooms, politics, and places of worship. Recently, women's communication styles stressing collaboration and mutual learning have found favor, in some corporations at least, because they have positive consequences.[12]

COMMUNICATION AND
PROFESSIONAL PRACTICE

The deficiencies of a number of professions have already been covered: political and other pollsters, political consultants, journalists, policy analysts, and popular culture producers. Here we analyze the communication deficiencies that have appeared in some other major professions.

Doctors

The mechanistic model that has dominated modern medicine from its beginning has had adverse affects on health care (medicine has still to learn that emotions are vital to physical health). Doctors receive little training in interviewing (communicating effectively with) patients—that is, it is assumed that communication is a one-way transmission of objective information, from doctor to patient. The medical world assumes that new developments in medicine will be transmitted to doctors via journals, publications by drug companies, and the like. It is not known how effective this transmission is, though there is evidence that many doctors lag behind medical knowledge (new computer software, by providing answers to specific questions, makes it theoretically possible for doctors to keep abreast of all medical research). Recently, health management organizations have put restrictions on medical practice, further limiting discussion of problems and options by doctors with their patients.

The lack of communication skills in doctors has adverse effects on diagnoses and treatment. It is known, for example, that patients who are able or allowed to talk about their medical or other problems tend to follow doctor's advice and treatment more faithfully. One study by Johns Hopkins University researchers also found that patients of all races and ethnicity found female physicians "less autocratic and more inclusive," probably because of their "better communication skills." In addition, all races and ethnic groups felt more like active participants when seeing doctors who shared their race or ethnicity.[13] Problems in doctor-patient communication are compounded by doctors' stereotypes about gender, ethnicity, race, and age. We know that doctors have different images of health for men and women. If women accept the doctor's image, mistakes occur; if women do not accept it, communication may break down. Doctors and other professionals have also begun to understand that universalism in professional practice (or failure to employ valid stereotypes about ethnic and racial groups) may retard professional performance in medicine, psychological therapy, law, and social work.[14]

Medical school does not provide doctors with important skills that present-day health professionals need: how to conduct business; how to negotiate with insurance companies, hospitals, and governments; and how to engage in labor organizing and politics. The emphasis on scientific testing and computer diagnosis may also be eroding medical skills in receiving messages from a patient's body through sight, feel, and sound.

The computer has also curbed the ability of doctors (and all professions) to maintain exclusive jurisdiction over information and problems. Health care information as well as health data on patients are widely available, involving new ways of communicating and relating among all those involved in health and health care. It also raises the issue of privacy—a matter arising in regard to individuals using professional services in all areas.

Lawyers

Lawyers also receive little training in interviewing (communicating effectively with) clients. They receive little training in courtroom procedure, and, under the assumption that lawyers will always be matched with clients from their own class backgrounds, they receive no training in communicating with diverse classes or ethnic and racial groups. When mismatches occur, lawyers do not act in accord with the requirements of law or their profession but fall back on harmful stereotypes.[15]

Lawyers have also been affected by the computer. Some simple (and maybe not so simple) legal work can now be done readily without lawyers. Controlling jurisdictional boundaries and keeping clients ignorant will no longer be easy as legal information becomes even more widely and easily available. Of course, the problems created by computers themselves will also change the world of law—for example, copyright issues arising on the Internet.

Psychologists and Mental-Health Therapists

Applied psychology began in World War I, when psychologists used testing to help the military evaluate individuals and place them in the niches for which they were supposedly best suited by nature. During the 1920s, applied psychology expanded and began to advise (especially through the use of testing) corporations, schools, universities, and governments on how to evaluate individuals and fit them in. They also began to advise parents on how to raise children, and individuals on how to solve personal problems. All in all, they became "architects of adjustment" who simply took society for granted, ignored workers, women, and minorities, and, using Darwinian ideas, thought of the human psyche as something that should adjust to its environment.[16]

Applied psychology hitched its wagon to testing in the early decades of the twentieth century and since then has resisted the knowledge that tests (IQ, SAT, LSAT, MCAT, GRE, and so on) are class based and might have more value if used in that light. But the idea that tests reveal the basic natural hierarchy of talented individuals is too useful to their clients (the upper classes, schools, corporations, governments) for psychologists to listen to criticism. Not only do tests not predict how individuals behave outside of schools, but their predictive power even about success or failure in school is weak. One study, for example, revealed that the GRE has almost no value in predicting success in America's graduate programs.[17]

Communication difficulties among applied psychologists (and teachers) and their clients can also be gleaned from several case studies. In the first, the way in which a group of male and female psychologists, school psychologists, and male and female public school teachers ranked fifty-three stressful experiences for teenagers (for example, the death or divorce of a parent, a car accident, moving to a new town or school, dropping out of school, being required to attend summer school) was compared to how teenagers (aged fourteen to seventeen) ranked the identical list. The results showed a wide disparity in how each group ranked the items. Not only does this cast doubt on professional competence, but the psychologist who reported the results of the study referred to the professionals as "adults" who were misinterpreting the experiences of the "young."[18]

In another study, young children and a group of adults (made up of child experts, teachers, and college students) rated twenty items in terms of stressfulness (for example, a new baby brother or sister, being caught stealing, having an operation, being sent to the principal's office). The adults tended to agree strongly, but their ratings were markedly different from those of the children. That is to say, the child experts were no different from teachers, both experts and teachers were no different from college students—all were wrong.[19] Erroneous stereotyping is rampant among elites and professionals, and perhaps worst in the field of psychotherapy.

A third study comparing school psychologists in an urban, bureaucratic setting with psychologists in a suburban, less bureaucratic setting found that the former stressed objectivity and testing and saw themselves as serving educators, while the latter focused on students and sought whatever information might be helpful in serving them.[20] The author stressed the influence of organizational setting and argued that suburban schools are part of a "moral community" that invite psychologists to tackle the various value and other conflicts in their work. The urban school psychologists, dealing largely with minority students, used allegedly objective tests to counsel students, in effect enacting the latent consequence of all tests (including the influential academic tests that students are subjected to)—social control in the name of the existing class system.

Counseling, which has its roots in American psychology, has been especially remiss in addressing the special needs of minorities. This failure has its first cause in the lack of minority representation in both the American Psychological Association and the American Counseling Association. Continued failure to redirect these organizations eventually led to a protest movement within counseling and then to the establishment of a separate group (the Association for Multicultural Counseling Development) and journal. This movement is significant not merely because minorities form one-third of the American population but because its focus on all forms of sociological phenomena, including social class, could benefit the rest of psychology. The multicultural movement in psychological counseling has climaxed its efforts with a valuable handbook.[21] Unfortunately, the movement has not been able to escape the scientism that mars mainstream psychology.

Mental-health therapists have discovered that to communicate effectively with patients they must often work in the context of the patients' other relationships (marriage, family, occupation/profession). Like their colleagues in physical medicine, they have begun to realize that they must take a patient's race and ethnic background into account.

Teachers and Professors

Teachers and professors face students who are subject to a wide variety of symbolic stimuli from the mass media and to pressures from family and friends. This makes it difficult to transmit knowledge far removed from their experience. Given the enormous growth of knowledge and specialized professions, it is understandable that the core curriculum has faded even at elite institutions of higher learning. The decline of the core curriculum has occurred, of course, because scientific knowledge about society and nature has evolved rapidly over the past four centuries, literally exploding in the past two. Science has also had to discard many classics (truth) as biased. Given all this, science has also raised serious questions about the possibility of truth (a finished system of knowledge). It was the simpler social world of the past, with its narrow elites in all fields, that generated the consensus that passed for truth, including the truth that objective truth was possible.

Communication in schools is also difficult because the personality and interests of teachers and professors are very different from those of students.[22] Understanding that communication technology determines much of what goes on between teachers and students is a help in this regard. Writing, both before and after the printing press, changed education from reliance on orality to the more disciplined world of reading and one-way orality (the lecture and teacher-controlled discussion) that became the norm in modern times. In the twentieth century, visual aids of all sorts, especially film and video, greatly augmented what teachers can do. The recent explosion of on-line courses also raises the issue of the effectiveness of interaction in a classroom versus that of distance education. It also raises the issue of who owns on-line courses, the teacher or the school—or do they own them jointly?[23] Another problem that has arisen for teachers and schools is that the computer has turned images (art, photographs) into commercial property, and computer companies and museums have made arrangements for their sale.[24]

The appearance of the computer in the classroom raises far more serious questions. The virtues of the computer for learning have been vastly overblown—there is little scientific evidence that computerized instruction actually enhances learning—and yet politicians, parents, and schools continue to give the computer priority over other educational resources and goals.[25]

On a deeper level, the computer has been rejected because it reinforces obsolete and harmful cultural assumptions. The computer, along with language and literacy, is a far from neutral technology, argues Bowers. Language is not a mere tool that allows human beings to express their thoughts or to communicate with others. All thought is formed by language, and the structure of language and its content *are* thought. Skill in reading and in using the computer, in reality, are ways in which children are socialized in the thought of the developers and owners of software (and textbooks). The computer should be seen as part of the mechanistic, Cartesian world, or scientism (in our terms, technocratic liberalism), that dominates modern society. As such, it reinforces the American belief that we are all autonomous, self-sufficient individuals. Its harm does not stop there. The computer gets us farther away from the teacher's first responsibility—to awaken in children a sense of the social and natural communities that they are embedded in and to instill in them the skills they need in those real worlds.[26]

Bowers's focus on "deep culture" (in our terms, raising foundational questions) gives us a different perspective on educational reform. Producing better-qualified teachers and professors means raising their political consciousness and through them the political skills of students. When the American economy suffered reverses in the 1970s, the business and other elites did not address the issue directly (that could have led to a loss of power). Instead, they blamed education, and their misdirection of America's attention, as well as their badly flawed view of education, has persisted to the present. The main thrust of reform, then as now, is to go back to the basics (to be certified by testing), vouchers, charter schools, and privatization. These reforms are directed at teacher unions, ensuring surplus quantities of literate, docile and thus cheap labor at all levels of the economy.

The most important need in education by far is to eliminate the dreadful conditions at the bottom of American society from which many students come. Inside schools, the first need is to focus on turning academic subjects into attention-grabbing, thought-stirring political options. Students should come to see themselves and the contemporary world as outcomes of sociohistorical causes. Though all subjects can be improved along these lines, none is more important than high school history. As Loewen (like others) has shown, on the basis of the twelve texts that dominate the field, American history is rendered boring and irrelevant. Subject to political pressures from the satisfied classes and to the logic of textbook publishing, these texts glorify and prettify American history. Heroes are presented without warts or deviant politics, and none have materialistic motives. The horrific treatment of American Indians and African Americans is barely touched on—in any case, it is "behind us." There is a great emphasis on presidents and the federal government but barely a mention of the imperialism and serious civil rights violations committed by both. There is almost no mention of the powerful force of social class or the conflict that has characterized the United States since its inception. Anyone who wants to can get ahead, say the texts, in effect blaming victims for their problems. All in all, high school history texts provide no sense of social causation and do not invite students to see themselves as both the product of and as shapers of an ongoing sociohistorical process.[27]

Beyond the overriding need to turn academic subjects into thought-provoking political options, the best way to facilitate communication in education is to raise salaries and lower class sizes. The current emphasis on high standards in reading and other academic subjects, to be established by testing and by privatizing public schools to foster competition, should be recognized for what it is—the protection of an inequitable and ineffective class system of education and the prevention of a better-educated democratic citizenry.

Managers

The science (and incipient profession) of management emerged in the United States in the 1830s and 1840s, in keeping with the practical problems of manufacturing (such as at the Springfield Armory, in Massachusetts, where mass production through interchangeable parts was introduced) and transportation by railroad. Building on the new system of education that graded individuals (using a hierarchy expressed by letters and numbers) on reading and writing through examinations (a system begun at Cambridge University in the late eighteenth century but perfected with a vengeance by the U.S. Military Academy at West Point between 1817 and the 1830s), the Springfield Armory and America's new railroads (West Point graduates were prominent leaders in these enterprises) began the practice of keeping precise accounts. This practice helped increase productivity and coordinate far-flung, multi-unit enterprises like railroads. It was the first time that accounts were kept in such a way that managing for the future and aiming for specific goals, including profit, could be attempted.[28] In the context of economic expansion in the early decades of industrialization, bureaucratization was also an important aid in generating efficiency and productivity; bureaucracy is one of capitalism's most important inventions. But with mature industrialization, the American version of bureaucratization developed many practices that now thwart efficiency, productivity, and accountability (or communicative effectiveness).

A *bureaucracy* (also known as a "complex organization") is a group organized to ensure efficiency and responsibility. Described in ideal terms, a bureaucracy is an administrative structure in which a hierarchy of statuses, separated from other statuses, is given specified duties and rights. The statuses are occupied by employees selected by stated qualifications. Employees are expected to establish careers—that is, make long-term commitments to the enterprise. The equipment and facilities that employees use to perform their duties belong to the group.

Actual bureaucracies deviate from this ideal. Behavior within corporations, schools, foundations, hospitals, law firms, the military, and government agencies varies somewhat from the enterprise's official blueprint. While different theories of complex organizations abound, the key idea for making sense of them is power.[29] Bureaucracies belong to or are controlled by somebody, and they represent not so much efficiency and responsibility as the power of property. Both private and public bureaucracies create images of nonpartisan public service, but in the final analysis they represent the heart of *corporate* capitalism.

A long scholarly tradition, from Frederick W. Taylor in the early part of the twentieth century to present-day public administration, business administration, and organizational theory, has sought to perfect the science of management.[30] These efforts, however, have helped to cloak the deep trend toward economic and political centralization and concentration. This trend has also been hidden by analysts who argue that corporate capitalism has undergone a managerial revolution—that well educated managers have replaced property as the organizing principle of capitalism. Of course managers are also property owners and share fundamental class interests with owners in any case. The trend toward a concentrated political economy is further obscured when it is called the End of Ideology, a Knowledge Society, a High-Information Society, a Postindustrial Society, the rise of Professional Society, or the End of History (see "The Knowledge Society as Ideology," in chapter 4, and "The

Fiction of a Knowledge Society," in chapter 7). Narrow, technical studies of organizations in a taken-for-granted world also obscure the trend toward, and the reality of, concentrated power.

The basic managerial style in the United States stresses individual responsibility within a hierarchical structure. Orders come from on high; responsibility is from the bottom up. Within this ethic, the manager is free to hire and fire (subject to some controls and labor union contracts). The corporation is the stronghold of the managerial ethic, but it is also the model for managerial styles in government, the military, religion, education, health care, and voluntary groups.

Hierarchy and specialization have their uses but also create problems. We now know that an efficient bureaucracy does not necessarily mean centralization or steep hierarchy. Workers must feel free to exercise skills and assume responsibilities. Cooperation among workers and worker participation in management yield better and more work. Excessive centralization, hierarchy, and specialization breed insecure workers, clog communication lines, and result in employees who "feather their nests" and carve out turfs.

In recent years, the managerial style of American corporations has been seen as a barrier to corporate innovation, productivity, efficiency, and long-term investment. The American executive is an individual careerist who moves a great deal among different companies, putting down few roots and developing only temporary loyalties, a practice that contrasts sharply with Japanese custom. The American executive is subject to pressures to produce profits every quarter and thus cannot take the long view or argue for investments that will take years to pay off. Again this runs counter to Japanese practice. Centralized control around one dimension leads to inefficiency, and the hierarchical structure promotes social distance between adjacent levels—and chasms between managers and workers. As a result, it is difficult to harness the experience and skills of those directly involved in creating products or providing services.[31]

Corporations strive to make their operations seem fair and just as well as efficient. Today the personnel director serves as the corporate conscience in this regard, in effect linking organizational behavior to broad concerns about social and individual justice in the outside world. Organizations have many features not directly linked to efficiency or work. But such things as company newsletters, titles, company bowling teams, and retirement parties are vital to fostering loyalty and commitment. The pretense that ranks, income, and benefits can be determined through scientific assessment helps to give the organization legitimacy in the eyes of its members. Nevertheless, and despite the claims of "scientific management" and "scientific personnel work," the process of recruiting, testing, interviewing, hiring, and training new members of an organization is largely a legitimizing facade, not science.[32]

In fact, the science of management, like the social sciences, is not so much science as *American* science. Generated in a culture based on universalistic, secular principles and supported by a gigantic continental market, American symbolic culture has stressed quantitative studies when it does research and universal principles when it reaches conclusions. Flushed with victory in World War II and able to take the functioning of society for granted, management science did the same thing as the social sciences—it concentrated on developing abstract, universalistic principles. This meant American phenomena were deemed somehow "natural." The result in management science was to validate American practices that had little to do with economic success. The economic boom of the 1950s and 1960s, when management science came into its own as a profession, was largely the result of the pent-up demand created by the Great Depression and World War II. It was also due to the fact that the other capitalist societies were either exhausted or in ruins—that is, America's postwar economic success was an artifact of monopoly.

American management science did little comparative work and failed to see that American practices were culture bound. Decades later, many American companies have become global corporations and the American economy faces serious competition from abroad, but American management science has still not engaged in comparative research to uncover other managerial styles or understand the cultures that spawn them (for a fuller discussion, see below, "Problems in Intersocietal Communication"). This no doubt is part of the explanation for the poor showing by American employees abroad—between 16 to 40 percent return home early (each premature return costing a hundred thousand dollars), and approximately 30 to 50 percent of those who stay in their overseas assignments are considered ineffective or only marginally effective by their firms.[33]

The deficiencies of management science are connected to deficiencies in business education.[34] In turn, business education is hampered by its reliance on mainstream economics.[35] Professionalized managers administer policies made by governing boards (or by policy-making committees, agencies, councils, etc., depending on the type of activity). By and large, policy-making bodies have homogeneous memberships, often despite laws requiring diversification. For example, no progress has been made by the U.S. State Department in obeying the Foreign Service Act of 1980, which requires that America's diplomatic corps be representative of the American people. Corporate boards, university trustees, hospital boards, and presidential advisory bodies[36] are still composed of like-minded individuals. The chances are high that up to 90 percent of the members of governing boards of American universities have had no training in education. Probably no one on the board or staff of a hospital understands where health comes from. Women, blue-collar workers, blacks, Hispanics, the handicapped, and gays are underrepresented on policy-making bodies throughout American society. Managers, therefore, are subject to policy groups that fail to generate the ideas needed for good decisions. Leaders in general are subject to a narrow pipeline of information, guarded by a narrow circle of like-minded advisers. All in all, homogeneous policy bodies; mechanically organized, one-dimensional bureaucracies; obsolete managerial style;[37] and connections among power groups across the apexes of society[38] are collectively a major reason for America's economic, social, and political shortfalls.

Despite the trend toward all-purpose administrators, the field of administration is split up into business, public, hospital, welfare, recreational, and voluntary (nonprofit) subfields. Of these, public administration is solidly established, with a large association and a journal. Nonetheless, all forms of administration fail to measure up to what we know about complex organizations. A simple question about American bureaucracies (collectively, corporate capitalism) yields an important insight. Why does the United States use so many college graduates in its private and public administrative structures, including the military, in comparison with other developed capitalist societies? The only reason is that unnecessary educational requirements and unnecessary layers of personnel act as buffers and camouflage to enable the top people to reap rewards far above those available to their counterparts in other developed capitalist countries.[39] It is a telling fact about the large corporations that make up the heart of the American economy that their executives pay themselves and that there is no relation between income and the size or performance of their enterprises, whether judged against other corporations or similar bureaucracies in public utilities, government, or the military, either in the United States or in other developed capitalist societies.[40]

Civil Servants

An array of communication problems exists in this area. Poor public services can be partly understood by the simple fact that local civil servants are often better educated and have higher incomes than the people they are expected to serve (for example, social workers, welfare workers, garbage collectors in barrios and ghettos, police in working-class and poverty areas). At the upper levels of government, specialized agencies and departments of the federal government tend to have direct communication with specialized constituencies, leading to secretive, selfish outcomes:

Department of Commerce—business
Department of Labor—labor unions
Department of Agriculture—farmers
Pentagon—defense contractors
Treasury—bankers
National Institutes of Health—natural sciences and medical professions
U.S. Army Corps of Engineers—local government, developers, farmers, etc.

Political and Other Public Figures

The class background and other experiences of political leaders and other public figures separate them from the people they want to lead. The communication problem to which this leads is compounded by gerrymandering. When diversified electorates must be addressed, one tends to use vague generalities. Thus, the issueless campaign and the transformation of the public (a partner in two-way interaction) into an audience (a receptor of one-way interaction). All these technocratic processes have been significantly augmented by the use of computers (see chapter 5).

Public figures that seek to influence the people at large (religious leaders, trade union officials, environmentalists) also find themselves gravitating away from addressing the general public and spending more time trying to influence other elites (or limited publics). This stance is already well established for think tanks, foundations, and policy groups (see chapter 7). This process further undermines local voluntary groups and leads to more reliance on elitist values and practices.

Communication Educators

The study of communication once excited sociologists, historians, and political scientists. The power of communication technology to influence behavior and serve power commanded attention. Academics explored this world, from the printing press to radio and film, sometimes in nonpolitical and sometimes in political terms. Over the past decades the study of communication emerged as an academic specialty in its own right—that is, it became nonpolitical and professionalized. Some scholarship in this area is still highly political, but the education of new members for the various occupations in communication has become a large, nonpolitical, vocational specialty, with a faculty larger than that in economics, political science, or sociology.

No exact studies of communication education exist; therefore, we are limited to impressions garnered from a perusal of texts and college catalogs. The first impression, however, is that the study of communication is no longer related to concerns about power but is largely a technical, nonpolitical introduction to an academic field. This applies even when the topic is the influence of the mass media in politics. The second impression is that the field is a technical introduction to either a set of new occupations or the improvement of existing occupations.

Research will probably also reveal that similar patterns have occurred in a host of related areas. Preparation for positions in film, television, theater, advertising, and public relations bears a deep kinship to trends in journalism, publishing, and museum management. Whether overall trends in the commercialization and professionalization of information, art, and entertainment are helping to produce a comprehensive closure at the apexes of corporate capitalism can only be suggested.

COMPUTERIZATION, PROFESSIONAL PRACTICE, AND ORGANIZATIONAL FAILURE

The Y2K problem (in the 1970s and 1980s especially, computers programs had omitted the "19" from years, and accordingly the advent of the year 2000 threatened to disrupt the functions controlled by the many computers of which that was true) was widely publicized. Less well known are the risks to the professions and organizations of automated computer networks. Rochlin has called attention to our widespread dependency on them at both the personal and institutional levels and to the special risks existing in a number of areas: running businesses, conducting financial transactions, flying airplanes, controlling air traffic, monitoring nuclear power plants, and commanding military forces, from a naval vessel to entire armies.[41] Based on actual events, Rochlin argues that extensive, comprehensive computerization erodes the skills of the professions in such areas by preventing them from learning through experience. Eventually, the human actors in charge are separated from real events by the computer and are thereby rendered unable to assemble full cognitive maps of what is going on. Because computer programmers cannot foresee every possible real-life scenario, situations arise for which computers cannot provide unambiguous information or solutions. It is not so much either computer error or human error that Rochlin is worried about as the errors that are made (he discusses a variety of cases) because of the *relation* of inexperienced managers, brokers, pilots, air controllers, nuclear power operators, and soldiers to their computer programs.[42]

THE CONCEPT HEGEMONIC CULTURE

Antonio Gramsci's concept of a *hegemonic culture* asks us to stop thinking of dominance in terms of only universal values, political control, and propaganda-ideology. The process of domination, argued Gramsci, is a pervasive and enduring part of our entire experience—at home, in school, in church, at work, at leisure, attending festivals, as well as in politics and government. But hegemony, he argued, is always problematic; elites and masses are always in a process of negotiating the terms of domination.

A hegemonic culture has its roots in the basic economy, from whence causes flow to embrace the polity, the voluntary sector, and personal and family life. Explaining the hegemony of culture consists of showing both relative unanimity among those at the top and how the masses are absorbed into elite thought forms. Herbert Marcuse and C. Wright Mills led the way in the 1950s and 1960s in developing the concept of a hegemonic culture by pointing to economic concentration and the absorption of the masses through ideology, fear, and consumerism (for Marcuse's thought, see below). Since Marcuse and Mills, many have contributed to the idea of a hegemonic culture, though the person most associated with the idea today is Herbert I. Schiller.

CORPORATE WORLD-MARKET CAPITALISM AND THE COMMERCIALIZATION OF CULTURE

Culture, Inc.

Schiller's analysis of culture rests on the assumption that the prime cause in modern society is the concentrated economy, and its auxiliary, the polity. Here Schiller is continuing the radical conflict tradition in American life that stretches from Veblen through Mills and Marcuse. Schiller's contribution to this tradition was in calling attention to the new trends in knowledge generation and transmission made possible by twentieth-century communication technology. Schiller's basis thesis is that the corporate economy, and its helpmate, the polity, has reached out to commercialize knowledge—indeed, all of culture, both at the macro and micro levels of society. The means by which this is done are parts of the economy itself—that is, the culture industries. These include "publishing, the press, film, radio, television, photography, recording, advertising, sports, and more recently, the many components that make up the information industry (database creation, production of software for computers, and various forms of saleable information)." The culture industries include "museums, art galleries, amusement parks (Disneyland, Sea World . . .), shopping malls, and corporate 'public' spaces." In addition, Schiller claims, the entire range of the creative arts, such as dance, drama, music, and the visual and plastic arts, have been separated from their group and community origins and turned into commodities.[43]

Schiller's focus on the direct buying and selling of symbols directs him away from the disguised manner in which symbols protecting and furthering corporate interests are generated and transmitted by political parties, public relations and consulting firms, academic education, the professions, research institutes, foundations, charities, and churches. Nonetheless, he provides many new insights into the deeper meaning of some well-known trends. In the corporate world itself, says Schiller, knowledge comes from the top and trickles down the hierarchy on a need-to-know basis, hardly a process conducive to the development of democratic personalities. Schiller (along with others) has also sounded the alarm about the strong trend toward the privatization of knowledge. In recent decades, a more explicit movement toward the privatization and commercialization of knowledge (as information) has occurred as private information businesses have multiplied and the federal government has shaped its data-gathering operations to accommodate them. The basic pattern that has emerged is that the government pays to amass data, restricts its own free distribution, and allows private companies to use its data free of charge as a profitable commodity.[44] Congress and the courts have helped in privatizing symbol creativity by extending the types of knowledge that are patentable,[45] and the U.S. Supreme Court has given the sanction of law to corporate power by protecting its right to speech, both through advertising and contributions to political campaigns.[46]

The computer has made selling data profitable. In particular, a thriving business has developed that provides information on the private lives of individuals. Computer searches of tax, bankruptcy, lawsuit, asset, lien, and other records are valuable to many businesses as they check potential employees or try to identify credit risks or new markets. Market research has long used survey methods, but few realize that polling on public issues is also a private business and that it tends to ask only the questions that its elite clients are interested in.[47]

Schiller is also insightful in pointing to the public mall as an extension of the power of private property (its owners can prevent political and intellectual expression even as they immerse citizens in commerce).[48] Sports and many cultural activities, including theater, parades, and festivals in parks and streets, along with public television, are now thoroughly encased in advertising and corporate sponsorship. By and large, the nonpartisan sponsorship of sports, art, and public television does more than provide corporate visibility and recognition, more than make the corporate world appear altruistic—it tends to create the false impression that these reaches of human expression have no social base and no politics.[49]

McAllister provides a superb, detailed extension of Schiller's insight into contemporary advertising, and like Schiller, he holds that advertising is antidemocratic.[50] The growth of competitive media and federal deregulation in the 1980s gave advertisers more control. In conjunction with market research and new techniques for constructing commercials, both aided by the computer, advertisers have worked hard to overcome a viewer's ability to "zap" commercials or graze across channels (for example, the use of celebrities, camouflaged ads, ads that tell stories or are humorous). They have placed ads everywhere: places of entertainment (movie theaters, arcades, sports arenas, and so on), travel, retail, health, and educational sites (not just television programs but on soda machines and donated teaching materials).

Advertisers also engage in cross-promotion, and on a large scale. Corporations arrange tie-ins between their activities (for example, United Airlines and McDonald's) by placing products in a movie or by associating products with a well-known places or persons. There is also cross-promotion within a giant media corporation, as various parts of it promote a program, movie, book, or record (see chapter 4 for an analysis of media giants and this practice). Advertising also takes place through sponsorship. A corporation will take credit for bringing you a program, implying that it is serving the public. But sponsorship is advertising, and it has now invaded public television. It is also undemocratic, in that it helps eliminate neutral public space and because it sponsors some cultural activities and not others, thereby influencing what ideas and values are circulated. A corporation will also sponsor a magazine, carefully targeted, in which it is the only advertiser, chalking up the costs as marketing for tax purposes. Corporations are increasingly sponsoring the development of entire programs, giving them not only self-promotion but control of content. Sponsored shows are sometimes openly politically conservative, but most choose to be apolitical. All in all, McAllister agrees that the new creative trends in advertising, intermixed as well as all-pervasive, do not promote but actually retard a democratic citizenry.

In a related argument, but one focused on intellectuals, Elliott argues that we are witnessing a "shift away from involving people as political citizens of nation states toward involving them as consumption units in a corporate [global] world." The result is to curb two-way interaction, restrict the public sphere, and undermine the power of politically aware intellectuals.[51]

The Globalization of Corporate Expression

Schiller (along with others) has called attention to the outward thrust of America's (and other countries') transnational corporations, to establish not only a free flow of capital and labor (and goods and services) but a free flow of information.[52] With the help of the American government, corporate capitalism mounted an onslaught against all nationalized systems of communication (including the well regulated, quasi-public monopoly AT&T in the United States) in both developed and developing countries. It worked hard to curb anyone who defended the need for public service broadcasting or to place communication systems under public supervision, whether at home, in other countries, or at the United Nations. Along with the transfer of communication technology and systems into private hands has come an elaboration of "intellectual property" law and its application to all countries and their interchanges.

At the end of World War II, the United States pushed hard to break the British monopoly on global communications. It emphasized the free flow of information, a phrase that had a democratic appeal but that was largely a way to supply giant American corporations the information networks they needed. The ability to transmit data about all the things that are vital to corporations (taxes, currency rates, personnel and inventory records, technical designs, etc.) effectively made capital mobile, ready to move wherever costs are lowest and profits highest. It also meant that Third World countries have little to say about how they will develop.[53] By the mid-nineties, the United States had not only effectively blocked Third World efforts to gain a degree of power over the world's communication networks but had succeeded in getting information transfer defined as a "trade service" and included in the new GATT (General Agreement on Tariffs and Trade) treaty of 1995. Global information was now in the service of global capitalism.

Far more is involved than the free flow of economic data. News, advertising, and entertainment are now also "free." The capture by corporate capitalism of communication around the globe means not only that all messages running counter to capitalism are reduced (often through misinformation, the deliberate creation of false realities) but that the marketing messages of consumerism now blanket the world. The messages are not merely transmitted formally by voice, picture, or print but permeate the atmosphere at international sporting events, from the Olympics to auto racing.[54] In addition, the international nature of scientific knowledge creation and exchange—whereby knowledge is assembled in global corporations, privatized, and wedded to profit—can be seen in the example of plant science. This process of appropriating the culture of others is far more extensive than is commonly understood.[55]

Some have argued that the U.S. preeminence in media production and exports is a form of cultural imperialism. But American media products are far from monopolistic, and even American products are screened by the meshes of local culture (see above, "Limited versus Large Effects"). Television programs are produced by a number of countries to serve geolinguistic regions and diasporas: India for South and Southeast Asia and elsewhere; Brazil and Mexico for Latin America and the U.S. Spanish-speaking market; Egypt for the Arab world; Hong Kong, Taiwan, and China for the Chinese-speaking world; and the United States, the United Kingdom, Australia, and Canada for the English-speaking world.[56]

One can add that American firms are globally important in other communication fields (film, books, advertising, consulting, news, data transmission, and telecommunications) but are in all cases far from dominant. What is dominant is the worldwide surge toward not merely capitalism but capitalism unhindered by public services, public regulation, or public-interest broadcasting.

PROBLEMS IN INTERSOCIETAL COMMUNICATION

Communication among Cultures

The cultures of the world differ profoundly in their views of reality and in their value priorities. Having different histories and inhabiting various stages of development, the countries of the world are structured differently, and their peoples interact and communicate differently. Andersen provides a valuable summary of research pointing to cultural differences in how people communicate. [57] A first step, he says, is to remember that much communication takes place without speaking or writing—that is, through nonverbal codes. The peoples of the world have very diverse ways of viewing and using time, interpersonal space, facial expressions, body movements, gestures, touch, dress, eyes, music, singing, and smell. Drawing on a wide variety of scholars, most notably Hofstede and Hall, Andersen argues that differences in nonverbal communication occur because cultures give different meanings to:

Immediacy and expressiveness
Individualism (as opposed to group orientation)
Gender (masculine and feminine values)
Power distance (or social stratification)
Uncertainty (or tolerance for ambiguity)
High and low context (or implicit and explicit communication).

Individuals abroad can experience many different communication difficulties. These individuals are a mixed lot: missionaries, explorers, traders, conquerors, tourists, aid teams, business and government negotiators, arbitration lawyers, technical personnel doing research, visiting scholars or students, or a variety of other professionals on assignment (for example, journalists, engineers, managers, consultants, film makers). Today, professionals from all sectors of American society must deal with other countries. Manufacturers, banks, insurance companies, brokerage houses, advertising firms, law firms, construction companies, sports leagues, charities, medical help groups, and film companies all operate beyond national borders. Many of these businesses are multinational organizations (MNOs), and how they communicate internally and how different nationalities in the same MNO communicate are important questions. Though each country has its special attributes, two detailed studies, of Japanese and Latin American MNOs, offer valuable broad orientations to Asian and Latin American countries.[58] Two other studies show the similarities and differences between two large MNOs from two different cultures, and the problems that arise when a MNO has workers of different nationalities.[59]

The Globalization of Professional Practice

Many kinds of professionals now work in cultural settings other than the ones in which they were raised and trained. This raises a host of communication problems in both personal and professional spheres. The growth of the corporate world market and intensified international relations of all kinds have generated a need for professionals who can function in countries where even professional standards are different. Sometimes professionals spend a short time in other countries (for example, a corporate consultant or government economic negotiator). Sometimes professionals go to other countries for extended stays (for example, business executives, government officials). Sometimes an American corporation will employ a professional from another country (say, a Mexican engineer) who must then adapt to American practices while helping to construct an automobile plant in Brazil. American corporations spend a great deal of time and money on training executives for foreign assignments (though not as much as Japanese corporations). One reason for this commitment of resources is the poor early return of executives sent abroad (see above, "Managers").

The American uninterest in comparative work has contributed to the astonishing lack of information about the professions in most countries outside the United States and Europe. There is understandable interest in standardizing educational credentials to facilitate the mobility of professionals and semiprofessionals but little interest in the socioeconomic backgrounds of professionals or their competence in different sociopolitical contexts.

National Negotiating Styles

Private and public styles of negotiation differ among countries. These negotiating styles reflect a nation's history, culture, national interest, and its bargaining strengths. Though each style has important nuances, it is useful to reduce them to two—the American versus all others. More than other developed capitalist societies, the United States has put economic variables ahead of all other factors. American negotiators stress sticking to business, not wasting time, doing technical analysis, and making quick decisions. Most other countries take a more leisurely approach and want to do business on a broader level of trust. Most other nations also have economic and political-cultural interests that are threatened by America's obsession with free trade.

Given its power and the pace of today's world, the American view is probably becoming the international norm. This is occurring, for example, in international commercial arbitration law.[60] But the practice of trying to get narrow empirical fixes and decisions has serious drawbacks. The United States is a huge country and has adopted universalistic symbols and objective standards to overcome its internal diversities. It is not historical minded, and it is not much interested in the outer world (a point that applies to its social science as well). Living in a world of empty abstractions does harm at home but, as the following example illustrates, abroad as well. American economists at the International Monetary Fund (IMF) (based in Washington, D.C.) set the conditions (abstract economic principles) for lending money to developing countries. Untrained in sociopolitical analysis and with little knowledge of client countries, IMF economists nonetheless feel free to tell these countries how to run their economies. Predictably, IMF conditions for loans create suffering among the masses. In Southeast Asia in 1997–1998 their conditions actually magnified economic problems.

American policy mistakes in the past (Vietnam, Iran) have had their roots in America's ethnocentric education and poor intelligence. America's governing elites go to America's best schools, where they see the world only through American eyes. The Central Intelligence Agency and other intelligence organizations also have American eyes, but they often make things worse by relying more on satellite pictures and other technical data than on reports from agents in the field.

Another example of "one" culture not understanding another is NATO's miscalculation in the Kosovo crisis of 1998–1999. NATO assumed that Serbia, confronted by the military of the industrial West, would back down when given an ultimatum. All historical experience tells us that national pride (and a government's fear of losing power) will prevail over prudence. Instead of patiently negotiating, NATO precipitated a one-sided war that caused enormous death, misery, and damage.

The Information Needs of the Developing World

The overwhelming bulk of communication capability resides in the capitalist West, especially the United States. Not surprisingly, many messages are sent to the developing world from America (and other developed countries), but the developed world receives few messages from Africa, Latin America, or most of Asia. In addition, Western journalism provides a very selective and biased picture of the developing world.

During the 1970s and 1980s, numerous international conferences on world communication issues were held under United Nations auspices. The Third World, working through the United Nations (the UN Educational, Scientific, and Cultural Organization, UNESCO) mounted a demand that communication capabilities be more equitably distributed (a "new world information order"). The right to communicate was steadily and emphatically asserted, and proposals were made to include it under the Universal Declaration of Human Rights or the Convention on Civil and Political Rights. The Western powers, especially the United States, dragged their feet and finally got their way—international arrangements about communication would be settled by free trade, not politically. The United States mounted an intense attack on UNESCO (eventually resigning from it) claiming (falsely) that the Third World wanted to stop the "free flow of information." In the 1990s nothing more was heard about a more equitable distribution of communication resources.

The American media also misrepresented Third World demands with selective coverage. In his detailed analysis of the history of international relations and agreements on communications, assessing how well they serve the human right to communicate, Hamelink concludes that dominant countries "pose serious threats to the freedom of information standard by their governmental and commercial forms of censorship and concentrated control over communication channels; they hinder the universal accessibility of common natural and human resources; they refuse liability for defective communication; and they deprive people of knowledge, cultural identity, and privacy."[61]

The dominant powers have generated many ways to further their interests against those of the developing world. Their various national anthropology disciplines created a distorted picture of developing societies, a picture in keeping with the needs of Western imperialism. The core social science disciplines have badly neglected comparative studies. In today's world, American companies routinely use data about the Third World to form investment and marketing strategies, knowing that their targets are weak, not least because they are information poor. However, the computer and the Internet have provided developing countries with ways to obtain scientific and other information more easily. What this will do to correct present imbalances in communication capabilities remains to be seen.

RATIONAL COMMUNICATION BEYOND CAPITALISM: MARCUSE AND HABERMAS

Eduard Bernstein, a German social democrat of the late nineteenth century, argued that welfare capitalism and a growing standard of living had muted class consciousness and had transformed the class struggle into a peaceful political process.[62] Marcuse built on this tradition by emphasizing a new development in the capitalist economy itself, the emergence of a highly effective and pervasive industrial communication technology that not only has pulled people into society but has turned them into willing conformists.

Marcuse argued that material technology, along with the spirit of *positivism*, or instrumental technology, has turned humans themselves into technology—that is, willing participants or cogs in the industrial (capitalist and state socialist) system.[63] What liberals were referring to as the "end of ideology" and the "postindustrial society" (based on knowledge) was to Marcuse a unique system of domination.

The main thrust of Marcuse's analysis is that the capitalist economy has evolved into a highly concentrated, intricately interconnected hegemonic system (much of its concentration and coordination made possible by communication technology) and that white-collar as well as blue-collar workers are caught in its web. But Marcuse wanted to know how a rational bourgeois culture can create mindless conformity. To fashion an answer, Marcuse built on Freud's psychology, namely Freud's emphasis on the deep impact on the impressionable psyche by socialization. The human need to satisfy pleasure urges are legitimately curbed and rechanneled by any society, and capitalism is no exception. Legitimate repression makes it possible for work to be performed and society to take place, but the capitalist curb on pleasure has gone beyond legitimate repression to "surplus repression."[64]

But Marcuse also used another part of Freudian psychology to help him answer another question. If capitalist rationality (efficiency) has caught everyone in its icy grip, then how will the liberation of humans take place? Marcuse's answer is that the economic and social repressions of capitalism will one day exceed what the powerful human drive for pleasure will tolerate. What Marcuse suggested is that in Freudian psychology lies a degree of hope for eventual liberation.[65] The powerful human drive for pleasure will one day help destroy the society that now denies it.

Despite his use of Freud, Marcuse maintained the Marxian dialectic as his central focus, even as he pointed out unique features of twentieth-century society that Marx could never have anticipated.[66] His ultimate position was that somehow an emancipatory process—now composed more of social movements led by students, minorities, and artists than of workers—would one day realize a genuine full-bodied human rationality. Contemporary capitalism had somehow been able to clog up the dialectic and its creative tension between existence and possibility, between the "is" and the "ought to be." By absorbing Americans in a world of commodities, alienated labor, and liberal ideology, the United States had made transcendence well nigh impossible. But Marcuse found hope, not only in practice (people need to experience the contradictions of a society) but in the rationality of the pleasure-driven aesthetic imagination as expressed by the dispossessed, especially students and artists. In this sense, Marcuse was pinning his hopes on Hegel, not Marx; on the intelligentsia, not the proletariat.[67]

Jürgen Habermas is one of many in the Marxist tradition who have tried to relate Marx to the contemporary capitalist world. Habermas has tried to wed the dialectic of Marx to interpretive science (whose fountainhead was the great German sociologist, Max Weber). Habermas, like Weber, does not seek to replace traditional empirical (or positive) science with a different way of achieving truth. There is a multiplicity of ways to achieve knowledge. But whereas Weber saw an irreconcilable cleavage between "instrumental knowledge" and "truth knowledge," Habermas seeks to unite them into one theory.[68] Traditional (empirical) science, he argues, stems from the human need to wrest a living from nature. Like the natural sciences, positivism gives predictions and thus control. In addition, there is the knowledge we get when we interact with others—interpretive, or meaningful, knowledge. Meaningful interaction is based on the fundamentals of language and presupposes full intelligibility among communicating (interacting) individuals. This form of knowledge has not yet been fully developed by historical societies, though there has been an evolution toward a more rational world. The critical or emancipatory standard toward which we must move is a society in which actors can reach a full measure of mutual understanding or consensus. Such a society will be based on *ideal speech*—that is, communication among individuals that is undistorted by the wrong types of knowledge (out-of-context empirical knowledge, understandings imposed by power).

Capitalism, says Habermas, is no longer characterized by class struggle between owners and labor. Welfare capitalism has muted this struggle, and labor now shares in the growing prosperity. The state provides many welfare services, promotes education, and manages the economy for the common good.[69] But capitalism has developed a different contradiction. Having allowed the instrumental science of the economy and the natural sciences to take over politics, capitalism is suffering from a "legitimization crisis." The state is now run according to norms of efficiency and cannot perform its main function, which is integration, through an elaboration of a meaningful moral order. The twentieth century witnessed the spread of moral claims (which cannot be satisfied in the economy) into the political arena. But the polity cannot satisfy them either, because it too is subservient to instrumental rationality. Emancipation is possible only if we steer ourselves toward a society that is characterized by ideal speech—that is, a society that has subordinated the economy and its instrumental reason to allow the (rational) individual to communicate (interact) with other (rational) individuals according to the logic of human language. When this occurs there will be consensus and thus a genuine society (community).[70]

Habermas agrees that objectivity, or universal truth, as a representation of reality, is not possible. He opposes the objectivism both of positivism and of phenomenology (in the interpretive tradition). He also opposes the relativism of the postmodernists. Echoing Max Weber, Habermas says we need knowledge rather than truth. Unlike Weber, that knowledge will be rational, because the possibilities of language will have been fully explored and agreed upon by social actors. The problem with Habermas's theory, of course, is that the capitalist division of labor does not permit, but actually opposes, such interaction.

Further questions about Habermas's position arise immediately. How different is it from Socrates' use of question-and-answer dialogue to elicit the rational? How different is it from James Madison's emphasis on the polity as a deliberative process? How different is it from Hegel's dialectical idealism? How different is it from liberalism's emphasis on free speech, science, and education? How different is it from positivism's belief in science as a self-correcting process? How different is it from American pragmatism's belief in the power of intelligence to grow with use? How different is it from rational-choice theorists who continue to promote the idea of a society based on perfect information when it is clear that society has always been the opposite?

To be different from all these, Habermas would have to attack the capitalist economy and the powerful communication media that have diversified modern populations far beyond the possibility of rational discourse. To be different, Habermas would also have to indict the business, political, and professional elites who maintain their power by keeping knowledge scarce, by developing biased social indicators, by tolerating premodern myths, and by practicing the liberal (formalistic) disciplines.

THE FRAGMENTATION OF THE PUBLIC SPHERE AND THE DECLINE OF INTELLECTUALS

From the ancient Greeks to the nineteenth century, the intellectual (known by different names, of course) was a leading professional. During this period, intellectuals dealt with a seamless world of causation. They were at once both metaphysical and practical, at home in both natural and social science. They could focus on literature, politics, or theology. Their expertise lay in their familiarity with both perennial and current issues and with the ideas required in dealing with them. Some of them defended the status quo, and some attacked it. Some generated knowledge, and others codified it. Despite their substantive differences, intellectuals were those who were at home in the world of ideas and who sought to persuade other educated people that their ideas were important to humans and society.

Intellectuals are here distinguished from scholars, professors, specialists, empirical researchers, nonpartisan social and natural scientists, and so on, who rarely focus their scholarship on trying to figure out what kind of society they belong to; intellectuals, on the other hand, tend to be consciously for or against the world they live in. They are also different from the Knowledge Class, the New Class, technocrats, or the intelligentsia, and all other such designations (these terms merely refer to educated people or to experts). Intellectuals claim the gift of prophecy. Like astronomer-priests forecasting the weather (so vital to crops in agrarian society) or social philosophers forecasting prosperity, depression, or war, intellectuals are those who predict about matters important to powerful publics.

A decline of the intellectual "profession" occurred from roughly 1850 to 1950. The decline occurred because of the onrush of science and its specialization (which is also the story of the development of higher education). Of course, the rise of science and the narrow, artificial disciplines of academe reflected the surge into industrialism and the end of the simpler ages of agrarianism and commercial capitalism. Today, forecasts and predictions are cast in more tightly circumscribed terms by academic and professional specialists: meteorologists, economists, military experts, and demographers.

Early professional social scientists such as William Graham Sumner, Lester Ward, and Thornstein Veblen were also intellectuals who involved themselves in the larger issues of the day. Early historians were prone to writing for the general public. But by the 1920s, the various disciplines had settled into the empirical investigation of smaller issues, including a concern for depoliticized social problems. Henceforth the trend was clear: under corporate capitalism, America's cerebral energies were being splintered into specialties, whose members wrote not for the general public but for each other.

American intellectual culture thrived from the 1930s to the 1960s, helped by the puzzling shocks of depression, fascism, communism, and Cold War.[71] Some segments of this intellectual ferment became disenchanted with the radicalism of the 1930s and became more centrist, even conservative, in regard to domestic and foreign policy.[72] After the 1950s, the world of intellectuals developed into its present pattern—a neoconservative or right-liberal wing, a left-liberal wing, and a radical left-wing composed of Marxists, radical feminists, radical environmentalists, radical ethnic and racial theorists, and politically charged academics who develop American Studies programs or espouse political interpretation of literature (the deconstructionist perspective). If one defines an intellectual in this way (as someone who is eager to change something in the sociopolitical world), then intellectuals are alive and well. No longer freelance writers living in Bohemia, they now work for research institutes, journals, magazines, policy institutes, reform groups, and so on. They even exist on college and university campuses.

The decline of intellectuals, however, can be argued on two fronts. One, they are now so scattered and diverse that their influence on the life of society may be much smaller than it once was. Small numbers of intellectuals writing (or creating) for a small and powerful set of elites, concentrated in Paris, say, or New York, may once have been influential. Today, American intellectuals are scattered in many cities, appear in many public journals from *Dissent* to *Commentary*, in many scholarly journals (such as *Public Interest, Telos,* and *Signs*), and in many newspapers (such as the *Wall Street Journal* and the *New York Times*). To frame the issue differently, there seem to be many small publics (audiences), focused around class, racial, ethnic, sexual, and environmental groups, and the like, rather than a large one capable of being swayed by broad intellectual arguments. These groups use a variety of ways to communicate: journals, newsletters, radio, church basements, talk shows, computers, and so on.

The decline of intellectuals may also be seen in the fact that many educated people, both as college graduates and as college faculty, consider themselves to be nonpolitical. There may no longer be a public for intellectuals to write (or create) for. Nothing better signifies the demise, or rather domestication, of the critical intellect than the fact that millions of students are busy acquiring abstract, nonpolitical knowledge under the direction of professional specialists in artificial, life-removed subject matter. Russell Jacoby has deplored the decline of intellectuals (evidenced, he claims, by the absence of young intellectuals and the continued prominence of intellectuals from earlier decades) and has attributed the decline to the explosive growth of higher education after World War II.[73]

A third argument, implicit in the others, is that the political economy of advanced capitalism, aided by communication technology, is transforming knowledge into private property and gradually absorbing public spaces and relations (including politics) with commercial artifacts and messages.

AMERICAN SOCIETY: THE ROLE OF COMMUNICATION IN CREATING A PERMANENT SEMI-DEMOCRACY

All societies depend on communication; indeed, they are constituted by it, if we remember to include all social interaction in its definition. Seen through the lens of communication (and others as well), American society appears to be in a permanent halfway house on the road to democracy. From chapter 3 on we saw how basic American institutions have thwarted the development of a democratic citizenry and politics. The basic engine driving American society is its supposed market economy and supposed market (democratic) polity. This political economy has generated diversity unparalleled in human history, a diversity that now clogs America's adaptive institutions.

American diversity stems from an economy far more complex than any other. It comes from religious differences, ethnic and racial diversities, from gender differences, and from regionalism. Underlying all of these are pronounced and enduring class differences. American public life is dominated by private groups—a thought that should make one pause when tempted to use words like *public* or *private,* as well as *civil society, private sector, voluntary sector, market, public interest,* and so on. Usage varies. The dynamism of American life is sometimes located in the so-called private economy, sometimes in the voluntary sector. The term "civil society" is not always clearly defined, but is widely thought to generate movements of social regeneration and political creativity (right or left wing). Civil society is held to be the natural arena of freedom, while government is artificial and compulsory. Close examination, however, reveals that civil society and government are both sociohistorical creations and cannot in fact be separated. In any final tally, civil society, either by itself or in tandem with government, merely updates or modernizes itself, and it cannot be said to be making progress toward realizing America's ideals or solving its problems.

Secular Americans debate their future and what to do about social problems using the above terms as well as others like *individualism, constitutionalism, science,* and *technology.* Without challenging any of the above, nonsecular Americans evoke the need to conform to supernatural norms. Racial, ethnic, and gender minorities create more vocabularies of desire, as do various style-of-life advocates, gays, the disabled, the aged, and others. The ability to communicate fruitfully across these social divisions is seriously compromised as incompatible perspectives multiply. The ability to reach or negotiate a consensus on the nature of social and natural realities declines further.

America's plutocratic polity marginalizes the bulk of the lower classes and effectively prevents a fuller democracy (chapter 5). Effective communication and community-building relations are thwarted by urban spaces that are specialized by function and segregated by class and race (chapter 6). A nonreflexive journalism that spews out episodic news with few causal explanations and little policy options retards the development of democratic citizens. The same is true of professionalized policy analysts and planners who share the views of their clients, the upper classes (chapter 7). The depoliticizing process that keeps America in the halfway house of liberal democracy is also evident in popular culture, with its themes of individual achievements (outside the home) and of Edenic communities, under siege by evil individuals and natural disasters, waiting for saviors from outside the community. Sports are perhaps the most insidious protectors of the status quo; by falsely appearing to reflect nature's hierarchy of talent in a world of strict rules and fair competition, they reinforce the ideology that the same is true of society at large (chapter 8).

Americans rarely have available to them ways of seeing the obvious (actually, the obvious is defined in ways that renders it something different). How can an individualistic society that encourages self-interest possibly become a community? How can the primacy of property in the economy and politics, and thus over family and private life, be compatible with democracy?

Nonetheless, there are countless ways in which effective communication takes place. The U.S. Postal Service, UPS, Federal Express, and smaller companies deliver billions of packages and letters intact and on time. Each day countless messages are delivered via telephones, fax machines, videotape, television, e-mail, magazines, and newspapers. Information is available around the clock from private companies and the U.S. Commerce and Labor Departments. Clergy and teachers send their various messages to their special audiences. Politicians send out huge amounts of mail and use all the media when campaigning.

America's messages keep America functioning, but they fall short when judged by how well they contribute to realizing America's ideals, creating pluralistic publics, or solving social problems. As for discussing the problem of society itself, they are almost all totally deficient.

COMMUNICATION, PLANNING, AND DEMOCRACY

Planning without Democracy: The Present Pattern

From town councils to the U.S. Congress, American legislative bodies are busy planning. Once taboo, the term "planning" is openly used (though there is no national office of planning and, unlike other developed capitalist societies, no national commitment to planning). But American planning is technocratic (planners allege that they are using objective knowledge to generate objective plans) and plutocratic (legislators, courts, and governments are subject to the power of money both private and public). The knowledge that American planners generate stems from liberal assumptions (the Democratic and Republican Parties, civil servants, professionals in public policy) and is, therefore, biased and incomplete. Private and public economic and social indicators and data are based on how the upper classes frame reality and define problems; even counting the population is ultimately a political act. Public-policy research, including polling public opinion, loses something by pretending to be objective, a pretense that denies the lower classes a full voice in decision making. Perhaps the most detrimental practice and barrier to democratic planning is rational-choice (or cost-benefit) analysis, the reduction of policy options to money choices. The growth of rational-choice analysis among policy groups, political consultants, government departments, and the social sciences goes hand in hand with instrumental reason and watered-down pragmatism. Together these protect the present power structure by pretending that it does not exist.

Planning as Democracy

Planning the direction of a huge and complex entity like the United States may not be possible. But the first and most important barrier to a planned (either socialist or nonsocialist) society is that the powerful and satisfied have too much to lose to permit national planning. A second barrier is that the United States is characterized by deep and crisscrossing conflicts, many of which are metaphysical and thus difficult to reconcile (for example, some forms of supernaturalism, absolutistic socioeconomic philosophies).

Democratic planners do not have to start with a blank page. The planning mentality is well advanced among the upper classes, though only in terms of planning the fortunes of families, enterprises, or voluntary groups, or of trying to coordinate public services, especially on a metropolitan or regional basis through various unelected authorities and commissions. Planning is deeply embedded in the American way of life (scientific management, Fordism, marketing campaigns, electoral campaigns, standardization, reinventing government, legislation to achieve goals, monetary and fiscal policies, and so on).

The federal government plans extensively but not explicitly, and not in a coordinated manner. Its armed forces plan singly, but their plans are not integrated, and the overall military is hugely wasteful and far from being as effectively organized as it could be. The Department of Transportation does not coordinate with the Department of Housing and Urban Development. Federal departments tend to be tied to congressional committees, which in turn are tied to interests in the private economy or the professional world. The independent regulatory commissions plan when they try to fight inflation or recession, promote drug and airline safety, etc. Congress plans when it passes legislation to fight recessions or to spur depressed economic sectors. It plans when it puts into place protections for the environment or against national disasters. Congress plans in a hundred and one other ways and reveals its commitment to planning when it demands that policies be evaluated to make sure they are working,

American planning, however, is done without democracy—that is, it is a thoroughgoing plutocratic process. In democratic planning, all kinds of people have effective voices in deciding the uses of human and material resources. It means continuous negotiations about the evolving shape of social reality. It does not mean searching for or conforming to the laws of history, the principles of society, or human nature (there are no such things). It means that whatever priorities are established, or changes to them, will command allegiance, because they are the products of open and equal deliberation.

American capitalism, or rather its governing classes, oppose national planning, intoning their faith in the rationality of markets. Most knowledgeable observers know that the idea of rational markets is a hugely wasteful and damaging fiction. Some who know this say that it is all that we can rely on, given the monstrous complexity of American society. The advent of the computer has led some liberals with technocratic bents to see the possibility of national planning. Other capitalist thinkers believe that the computer will yield an economy of perfect markets (because all actors will have perfect information) and usher in a "frictionless capitalism."

Radicals, on the other hand, argue that the computer makes democratic planning possible—perhaps under capitalism, perhaps under socialism. Pollack, for example, argues that the computer is now capable of tracking the entire economy and can generate a viable socialism. Citizens as well as economic and political actors have access to databanks with any and all kinds of information. Computer models can tell us what will happen if this or that policy is followed, with a net result that society can achieve its democratic goals of economic growth justly distributed.[74] But Pollack's "frictionless socialism" suffers from the same defect as do the models of those who promise a free market utopia through computers: property owners, including those with property in professional skills, are not interested in either perfect markets or democracy. Computers cannot solve value and belief conflicts, for example, while people who are concerned about developing a sustainable natural environment cannot accept the economic-growth philosophy of either liberals or socialists. Democratic planning can come only out of a pluralistic political process, and that can develop only if economic power over politics is reduced. Equalizing social power is the most important goal of social planning; unfortunately, concentrated power made possible by modern communication technology is the main barrier to democratic planning.

NOTES

1. Paul Lazarsfeld, Bernard Berelson, and Hazel Gaudet, *The People's Choice: How the Voter Makes Up His Mind in a Presidential Campaign* (New York: Duell, Sloan and Pearce, 1944); also see the preface to the second and third editions, Columbia University Press, 1948, 1968, for further lessons to be learned from the 1940 study.

2. John Durham Peters, *Speaking into the Air: A History of the Idea of Communication* (Chicago: University of Chicago Press, 2000).

3. Eileen Berlin Ray, ed., *Case Studies in Communication and Disenfranchisement* (Mahwah, N.J.: Lawrence Erlbaum Associates, 1996).

4. For an insightful essay that argues that collegiality or shared governance is a fiction in higher education, a façade to ward off unionization and to hide the power of the president/ administrators, funders, and trustees, see Ellen Willis, "Why Professors Turn to Organized Labor," *New York Times*, May 29, 2001, A15.

5. Public relations firms have developed specialties in management-employee communication and are being hired by some of America's largest corporations. See *New York Times*, July 25, 2001, C8. It is not clear if the communication will be two way.

6. Judy C. Pearson, Richart L. West, and Lynn H. Turner, *Gender and Communication*, 3d ed. (Madison, Wisc.: Brown and Benchmark, 1995), chap. 2.

7. Pearson, West, and Turner, *Gender and Communication*, chap. 3.

8. Pearson, West, and Turner, *Gender and Communication*, chap. 5.

9. Pearson, West, and Turner, *Gender and Communication*, chap. 6.

10. Pearson, West, and Turner, *Gender and Communication*, chap. 7.

11. For a superb summary of research and a compelling synthesis of the need to abandon even notions of "healthy" competition, see Alfie Kohn, *No Contest: The Case against Competition* (Boston: Houghton Mifflin, 1986). For a classic study of "grubbing" for grades instead of knowledge because of grade competition, see Howard S. Becker et al., *Making the Grade: The Academic Side of College Life* (New York: Wiley, 1968). For a summary report on experi-

ments and studies on cooperation and competition, focused on racial and ethnic relations, see Walter G. Stephan, "Intergroup Relations," *Handbook of Social Psychology,* ed. Gardner Lindzey and Eliot Aronson, 3d ed. (New York: Random House, 1985), 639–43. For the significant deviation from scientific norms generated by competition, see Daryl E. Chubin and Edward J. Hackett, *Peerless Science: Peer Review and U.S. Science Policy* (Albany: State University of New York Press, 1990).

12. For some incisive analyses, see the essays in Dana Dunn, *Workplace/Women's Place: An Anthology* (Los Angeles: Roxbury, 1997), unit 4.

13. *New York Times,* August 17, 1999, D8.

14. For the need to pay special attention to ethnic and racial cultural differences in these areas of professional work, see Monica McGoldrick, John K. Pearce, and Joseph Giordono, eds., *Ethnicity and Family Therapy* (New York: Guildford, 1982); Stanley Sue and James K. Morishima, *The Mental Health of Asian Americans* (San Francisco: Jossey-Bass, 1982); Jay C. Chunn II, Patricia J. Dunston, and Fariyal Ross-Sheriff, eds., *Mental Health and People of Color: Curriculum Development and Change* (Washington, D.C.: Howard University Press, 1983); Man Keung Ho, *Family Therapy with Ethnic Minorities* (Newbury Park, Calif.: Sage, 1987); and Joseph G. Ponterroto et al., eds., *Handbook of Multicultural Counseling* (Thousand Oaks, Calif.: Sage, 1995).

15. David Sudnow, "Normal Crimes: Sociological Features of the Penal Code in a Public Defender's Office," *Social Problems* 12, no. 3 (Winter 1965): 255–76.

16. Donald S. Napoli, *Architects of Adjustment: The History of the Psychological Profession in the United States* (Port Washington, N.Y.: Kennikat, 1981), esp. chap. 2. Also see Michael M. Sokal, "James McKeen Cattell and American Psychology in the 1920s," in *Explorations in the History of Psychology in the United States,* ed. Josef Brozek (Lewisburg, Pa.: Bucknell University Press, 1984), 273–323. Loren Baritz, *The Servants of Power: A History of the Use of Social Science in Industry* (Middletown, Conn.: Wesleyan University Press, 1960) focuses on how industrial psychologists served the interests of corporations.

17. James L. Wood and Amy C. Wong, "GRE Scores and Graduate School Success," *Footnotes,* November 1992, 6.

18. *New York Times,* November 29, 1983, B7.

19. *New York Times,* March 17, 1988, B9.

20. Carl Milofsky, *Testers and Testing: The Sociology of School Psychology* (New Brunswick, N.J.: Rutgers University Press, 1989).

21. Joseph G. Ponterotto, J. Manuel Casas, Lisa A. Suzuki, and Charlene M. Alexander, eds., *Handbook of Multicultural Counseling* (Thousand Oaks, Calif.: Sage, 1995).

22. High-school teachers in the experiment cited above about school psychologists also failed to understand what negative experiences meant to students.

23. Lisa Guernsey and Jeffrey R. Young, "Who Owns On-Line Courses?" *Chronicle of Higher Education,* June 5, 1998.

24. Patricia Failing, "Scholars Face Hefty Fees and Elaborate Contracts When They Use Digital Images," *Chronicle of Higher Education,* May 29, 1998.

25. Todd Oppenheimer, "The Computer Delusion," *The Atlantic Monthly,* July 1997, 45–62.

26. C. A. Bowers, *The Cultural Dimensions of Educational Computing: Understanding the Non-Neutrality of Technology* (New York: Teachers College Press, 1988).

27. James W. Loewen, *Lies My Teacher Told Me: Everything Your American History Textbook Got Wrong* (New York: Touchstone, 1996). Loewen is aware that he has not treated all "lies"—for example, about Hispanic-Americans and women.

28. For background and bibliography on the above as part of understanding the origins of accountancy, see Keith Hoskin and Richard Macve, "Writing, Examining, Disciplining: The Genesis of Accounting's Modern Power," in *Accounting as Social and Institutional Practice,* ed. A. G. Hopwood and Peter Miller (New York: Cambridge University Press, 1994), chap. 3.

29. Charles Perrow, *Complex Organizations: A Critical Essay,* 3d ed. (New York: Random House, 1986).

30. For a critical history claiming that Taylorism is ideology not science and cannot bridge the gap between management and labor, see Stephen P. Waring, *Taylorism Transformed: Scientific Management since 1945* (Chapel Hill: University of North Carolina Press, 1991).

31. For a summary of the many studies showing that the American managerial style generates bad work and bad morale, see Alan Farnham, "The Trust Gap," *Fortune* 120, no. 14 (December 14, 1989): 56–78.

32. Harrison M. Trice, James Belasco, and Joseph A. Alutto, "The Role of Ceremonials in Organizational Behavior," *Industrial and Labor Relations Review* 23 (October 1969): 40–51.

33. J. Stuart Black, Mark Mendenhall, and Gary Oddou, "Toward a Comprehensive Model of International Adjustment: An Integration of Multiple Theoretical Perspectives," *Academy of Management Review* 16, no. 2 (April 1991): 291. For practical advice on how to choose executives for assignments abroad, see J. Stewart Black and Hal B. Gregersen, "The Right Way to Manage Expats," *Harvard Business Review* (March/April 1999): 52–62.

34. For an indictment of business education as excessively specialized and out of touch with business realities, including the new global economy, see Lyman W. Porter and Lawrence E. McKibbin, *Management Education and Development: Drift or Thrust into the 21st Century?* (New York: McGraw-Hill, 1988). For an interesting radical feminist criticism of this report as merely reasserting the patriarchal values and practices characteristic of business, see Marta B. Calas and Linda Smircich, "Thrusting toward More of the Same with the Porter-McKibbin Report," *Academy of Management Review* 15, no. 4 (October 1990): 698–705.

35. For a wide-ranging critique of the negative results from business education's alliance with mainstream economics, see Milton Leontiades, *Myth Management: An Examination of Corporate Diversification as Fact and Theory* (Oxford, Eng.: Basil Blackwell, 1989).

36. In his study of the political leanings of White House staffs, John H. Kersel reports that the key advisers to President Reagan were extremely homogeneous, essentially Reagan clones, as reported in the *New York Times,* August 27, 1983, G7. William Domhoff, "Where do Government Experts Come From?" in *Power Elites and Organizations,* ed. G. W. Domhoff and T. R. Dye (Beverly Hills, Calif.: Sage, 1987), chap. 10, shows that the President's Council of Economic Advisers is drawn from the corporate elite and a narrow spectrum of elite foundations, think tanks, research institutes, and private policy organizations.

37. For a discussion of the powerful impact of the engineering profession on management during the formative period of corporate capitalism, see David F. Noble, *America by Design: Science, Technology, and the Rise of Corporate Capitalism* (New York: Knopf, 1977).

38. Michael Useem, *The Inner Circle* (New York: Oxford University Press 1984).

39. Articles criticizing excessive executive pay have appeared frequently in *Fortune.* CBS News reported (May 20, 1991) that chief executive officers in the United States are paid eighty-five times as much as average workers, whereas the ratio in Germany is twenty-three to one and in Japan seventeen to one. Since that time, American executive pay has accelerated "out of control," say Geoffrey Colvin, Ann Harrington, and Paola Hjelt, in "The Great CEO Pay Heist," *Fortune* (June 25, 2001), 64–70.

40. Erik Olin Wright and Luca Perrone, "Marxist Class Categories and Income Inequality," *American Sociological Review* 42 (February 1977): 32–55.

41. Gene I. Rochlin, *Trapped in the Net: The Unanticipated Consequences of Computerization* (Princeton, N.J.: Princeton University Press, 1997).

42. For additional examples of how computers can retard scientific understanding, see Todd Oppenheimer, "The Computer Delusion." For the way in which computers have come to form the heart of the U.S. economy as well as defense establishment, and the vulnerability of both to sabotage, see James Adams, "Virtual Defense," *Foreign Affairs* 80 (May/June 2001): 90–112.

43. Herbert I. Schiller, *Culture, Inc.: The Corporate Takeover of Public Expression* (New York: Oxford University Press, 1989), 30–31.

44. The American Library Association, in Washington, D.C., monitors this process and issues regular reports.

45. For a discussion of this process in plant science and biotechnology, see Jack Ralph Kloppenberg Jr., *First the Seed: The Political Economy of Plant Technology, 1492–2000* (New York: Cambridge University Press, 1988) and Martin Kenney, *Biotechnology: The University-Industrial Complex* (New Haven, Conn.: Yale University Press, 1986).

46. Schiller, *Culture, Inc.,* chap. 3.

47. Herbert I. Schiller, *The Mind Managers* (Boston: Beacon, 1973), chap. 5. A full-scale analysis of polling also shows that results (public opinion) emerge from the way questions are asked, their locations in the interview, and the class and racial characteristics of the interviewer; see David W. Moore, *The Superpollsters: How They Measure and Manipulate Public Opinion in America* (New York: Four Walls, Eight Windows, 1992). Moore's title is more radical than his book, which concentrates on the evolving science and profession of polling and its relative success in "monitoring the pulse of democracy."

48. A few states—for example, New Jersey—have extended free speech protection to shopping malls.

49. For a fascinating, richly detailed picture of how contemporary corporations are co-opting public space, as seen through their strategy of branding everything with their logos, see Naomi Klein, *No Logo: Taking Aim at the Brand Bullies* (New York: Picador, 1999), chaps. 1–5. Also valuable are chapters 12–18, which explore various forms of grassroots resistance to corporate advertising power.

50. Matthew P. McAllister, *The Commercialization of American Culture: New Advertising Control and Democracy* (Thousand Oaks, Calif.: Sage, 1996).

51. Philip Elliott, "Intellectuals, the 'Information Society,' and the Disappearance of the Public Sphere," in *Media, Culture, and Society: A Critical Reader,* ed. Richard Collins et al. (Newbury Park, Calif.: Sage, 1986), 105–15.

52. Schiller, *Culture, Inc.,* chap. 6.

53. Eileen Mahoney, "American Empire and Global Communication," in *Cultural Politics in Contemporary America,* ed. Ian Angus and Sut Jhally (New York: Routledge, 1989), 37–50.

54. For more on the global reach of sports, see the section, "Sport: The Triumph of Class, Racial, and Gender Ideology," in chapter 8.

55. For a fascinating collection of essays on the transformation of Third World folk wisdom, knowledge about plants, the plants themselves, art, songs, and artifacts into the private property of Westerners, including examples of and suggestions for a more equitable distribution of benefits, see the special issue "Intellectual Property Rights: The Politics of Ownership," *Cultural Survival* 15, no. 3 (Summer 1991). See also Kloppenberg, *First the Seed.*

56. For a background on the plural nature of world television program production, see

John Sinclair, Elizabeth Jacka, and Stuart Cunningham, eds., *New Patterns in Global Television: Peripheral Vision* (New York: Oxford University Press, 1996).

57. Peter Andersen, "Cues of Culture: The Bases of Intercultural Differences in Nonverbal Communication," in *International Communication: A Reader*, ed. L. A. Samovar and R. E. Porter, 8th ed. (Belmont, Calif.: Wadsworth, 1997), 244–56.

58. Alan Goldman, "Communication in Japanese Multinational Organizations," and Lecia Archer and Kristine L. Fitch, "Communication in Latin American Multicultural Organizations," both in *Communicating in Multicultural Organizations*, ed. Richard L. Wiseman and Robert Shuter (Thousand Oaks, Calif.: Sage, 1994), chaps. 4, 5.

59. Donald P. Cushman and Sarah Saunderson King, "Communication and Multicultural Organizations in the United States and Western Europe" (chap. 6) and Young Yun Kim and Sheryl Paulk, "Intercultural Challenges and Personal Adjustments: A Qualitative Analysis of the Experiences of American and Japanese Co-Workers" (chap. 7), in *Communicating in Multicultural Organizations*, ed. Wiseman and Shuter.

60. Yves Dezalay and Bryant G. Garth, *Dealing in Virtue: International Commercial Arbitration and the Construction of a Transnational Legal Order* (Chicago: University of Chicago Press, 1996).

61. Cees J. Hamelink, *The Politics of World Communication: A Human Rights Perspective* (Thousand Oaks, Calif.: Sage, 1994), 293.

62. Many Marxists after Bernstein, such as Louis Althusser and Nico Poulantzas, have elaborated on this theme.

63. Herbert Marcuse, *One-Dimensional Man* (Boston: Beacon, 1964).

64. Herbert Marcuse, *Eros and Civilization: A Philosophical Inquiry into Freud* (London: Routledge and Kegan Paul, 1956).

65. Herbert Marcuse, *An Essay on Liberation* (Boston: Beacon, 1969).

66. Marcuse, a distinguished interpreter of Hegel's philosophy, was influential in correcting the mistaken belief that Hegel was an authoritarian precursor of Nazism; see his *Reason and Revolution: Hegel and the Rise of Social Theory* (New York: Oxford University Press, 1941).

67. Marcuse, *An Essay in Liberation*.

68. Jürgen Habermas, *Toward a Rational Society* (Boston: Beacon, 1970); *Knowledge and Human Interests* (Boston: Beacon, 1975); *Theory and Practice*, trans. John Viertel (Boston: Beacon, 1973); *Legitimization Crisis*, trans. Thomas McCarthy (Boston: Beacon, 1975); *Communication and the Evolution of Society*, trans. Thomas McCarthy (Boston: Beacon, 1979); *The Theory of Communicative Action* (Boston: Beacon Press), vol. 1, *Reason and the Rationalization of Society* (1984), and vol. 2, *Lifeworld and System: A Critique of Functionalist Reason* (1988). John B. Thompson and David Held, eds., *Habermas: Critical Debates* (New York: Macmillan, 1982), provides useful commentaries on Habermas's thought.

69. Habermas is here referring to the European welfare state, which appeared in the United States in only a grudging and paltry manner. The essential nature of American-style capitalism (the legitimacy of an economy that has no political or moral responsibilities for the welfare of society, including the provision of material needs) reappeared as an issue in the 1970s and especially the 1980s. It should also be noted that in the 1990s the European welfare state experienced strong pressures for significant reductions of public benefits.

70. The idea that associates consensus with truth has a long and varied history. It blends into traditionalism (the wisdom of time-tested custom) and is also found in the evolutionary Christian liberalism of Vico and Lamennais.

71. Terry A. Cooney, *The Rise of the New York Intellectuals: 'Partisan Review' and its Circle* (Madison: University of Wisconsin Press, 1986), and Alan M. Wald, *The New York Intellectu-*

als: The Rise and Decline of the Anti-Stalinist Left from the 1930s to the 1980s (Chapel Hill: University of North Carolina Press, 1987).

72. Richard H. Pells, *The Liberal Mind in a Conservative Age: American Intellectuals in the 1940s and 1950s* (New York: Harper and Row, 1985).

73. Russell Jacoby, *The Last Intellectuals: American Culture in the Age of Academe* (New York: Basic Books, 1987).

74. Andy Pollack, "Information Technology and Socialist Self-Management," in *Capitalism in the Information Age: The Political Economy of the Global Communication Revolution,* ed. Robert W. McChesney et al. (New York: Monthly Review, 1998), 219–35.

Name Index

Abrams, Philips, 164
Adams, Henry, 145
Alger, Horatio, 202
Altheide, David, 195n26
Andersen, Peter, 257
Aquinas, Thomas, 28–29
Arian, Edward, 208–9

Babeuf, François-Noel, 32
Becker, Gary, 183
Bellah, Robert N., 55
Bennett, William J., 190–91
Bentham Jeremy, 185
Bentley, Arthur, 46–47
Bernstein, Eduard, 260
Blackburn, McKinley L., 104
Bledstein, Burton, 44–45
Bloom, David E., 104
Bogart, Leo, 209, 210
Bok, Derek C., 123
Bonnot de Condillac, Étienne, 30
Booth, Charles, 185
Bowers, C.A., 246–47
Brint, Steven, 166
Buchanan, James, 183
Burgess, Ernest, 137, 138
Bush, George H., 108, 143–44, 173
Bush, George W., 116

Cappella, Joseph, 175–76
Capra, Frank, 219, 220
Carragee, Kevin, 168
Castells, Manuel, 71–72, 137
Chambliss, Daniel, 226

Chaney, David, 60
Condorcet, Marie Jean Antoine Nicolas, 32
Cooley, Charles Horton, 47, 237
Croteau, David, 167–68

D'Alembert, Jean Le Rond, 32
Dayan, Daniel, 59–60
Dewey, John, 145
Diderot, Denis, 31
Dines, Gail, 206
Durkheim, Emile, 123

Edelman, Murray, 59
Ehrenreich, Barbara, 205–6
Eisenstein, Elizabeth L., 24
Eitzen, D. Stanley, 224
Elliott, Philip, 172, 255
Elzey, Wayne, 58
Emerson, Ralph Waldo, 145
Etzioni, Amitai, 92
Ewen, Stuart, 52–53

Fallows, James, 167
Fishman, Mark, 169–70
Foley, Douglas E., 226
Ford, John, 219
Franklin, H. Bruce, 174
Fraser, Jill Andresky, 81
Frederick the Great, 185
Freud, Sigmund, 184, 260

Gans, Herbert, 169, 210
Garfinkel, Harold, 239
Garson, Barbara, 94

Gilpin, Robert, 75
Glazer, Nathan, 165
Glyn, Jean Millis, 76
Goffman, Erving, 148, 239
Golding, Peter, 172
Gramsci, Antonio, 201, 253

Habermas, Jürgen, 26, 261–62, 272n69
Hall, Edward T., 8, 257
Hamelink, Cees J., 260
Hammett, Dashiell, 219
Havelock, Eric A., 17
Hegel, Georg Wilhelm Friedrich, 272n66
Helvetius, Claude Adrien, 32
Herodotus, 182
Hitchcock, Alfred, 218–19
Hitler, Adolf, 236
Hobbes, Thomas, 163
Hobsbawn, Eric, 58–59
Hofstede, Geert, 257
Holbach, Paul-Henri Thiry, 32
Holmes, Oliver Wendell, 38
Homans, George, 239
Horwitz, M. J., 38–39
Hoynes, William, 167–68
Hume, David, 30, 163

Iacono, Suzanne, 101–2
Iyengar, Shanto, 174

Jacobs, Jane, 148
Jacoby, Russell, 264
James, Henry, 145
Jamieson, Kathleen Hall, 127, 175–76
Jefferson, Thomas, 49, 50, 55, 145
Jewett, Robert, 205

Katz, Elihu, 59–60
Katznelson, Ira, 145
Kenner, H. J., 53–54
Kenney, Martin, 88
Kersel, John H., 270n36
Kling, Rob, 101–2
Kosicki, Gerald M., 177–78
Kuhn, Thomas S., 194n6
Kuklick, Henrika, 51
Kurtz, Lester, 48

Lasswell, Harold D., 114, 185
Lawrence, John Shelton, 205
Lazarsfeld, Paul, 210, 237
Lerner, Daniel, 185
Levine, Harry G., 173
Lewis, Charles, 180
Lichter, Linda S. and Robert S. Lichter, 227
Lindblom, Charles E., 182–83, 188
Locke, John, 27, 30, 39–40, 163
Loewen, James W., 247
Lofland, Lyn, 148
Lundberg, George, 191

Madison, James, 28, 55, 118
Madonna, 233n54
Malinowski, Bronislaw, 51
Malthus, Thomas, 39–40
Mann, Michael, 12–13
Marcuse, Herbert, 253, 260–61, 272n66
Martel, Charles, 21
Mayhew, Leon H., 128
McAllister, Matthew P., 255
McCallum, Daniel C., 37
McChesney, Robert, 133, 180
McLeod, Douglas M., 177–78
McLeod, Jack M., 177–78
Mead, George Herbert, 237
Merton, Robert K., 191
Mills, C. Wright, 72, 162, 179, 253
Miringoff, Marc and Marque-Luisa Miringoff, 79–80
Montesquieu, 25, 31
Morris-Suzuki, Tessa, 88

Newton, Isaac, 159
Nie, Norman, 92
Nietzsche, Friedrich, 184
Nixon, Richard, 190
Norris, James D., 51–52

Pareto, Vilfredo, 184, 191
Park, Robert, 137, 138
Parsons, Talcott, 161
Perkin, Harold, 162
Peters, John Durham, 238–39
Pinkerton, Allan, 45
Pollack, Andy, 267–68

Subject Index

277

About the Author

Daniel W. Rossides is professor of sociology emeritus, Bowdoin College. He has also taught at Hunter College, CUNY, and York University, Toronto. He has published books on social theory, social stratification, and the professions and disciplines, as well as articles on education for *Change* and *The Journal of Higher Education*. He is currently working on a manuscript titled *Understanding American Capitalism*.